EUROPEAN HAND

CW00351119

FREN

RAILWAYS

LOCOMOTIVES & MULTIPLE UNITS

FOURTH EDITION

The complete guide to all Locomotives
and Multiple Units of the Railways of France

David Haydock

Published by Platform 5 Publishing Ltd., 3 Wyvern House, Sark Road, Sheffield S2 4HG, England.

Printed in England by Wyndeham Gait, Castle Press, Victoria Street, Grimsby DN31 1PY.

ISBN 978 1 902336 65 7

Above: BB 7323 heads a southbound train of empty stock over the Rhône right bank freight line at St. Montan d'Ardèche on 12 June 2008.　　　　　　　　　　　　　　　　**Michael J. Collins**

Front Cover: BB 22264 in En Voyages livery arrives at Nice Ville with TER train 17441 from Marseille on 4 June 2007.　　　　　　　　　　　　　　　　　　　　　　　**Brian Denton**

Back Cover Top: Chemins de fer de Provence loco T66 with a push-pull set at Entrevaux forming a special service in connection with a steam train on 22 June 2008.　　　　　　　**Peter Fox**

Back Cover Bottom: X 73731 and a second unit of the same type form the 12.18 Perigueux–Bordeaux at Mussidan on 18 September 2007.　　　　　　　　　　　　　　　　　**Brian Denton**

CONTENTS

INTRODUCTION TO FOURTH EDITION

Welcome to the long-awaited fourth edition of French Railways, which contains full details of all locomotives and multiple units of the Société Nationale des Chemins de Fer Français (SNCF), open access railway undertakings and track maintenance companies operating in France, RATP's fleet for Paris RER lines plus other operators. Data is updated to September 2008.

The main changes since the 1999 edition are the decline in SNCF locomotive numbers in the face of expanding multiple unit and TGV fleets, plus the arrival of competing freight operators. The SNCF freight electric loco fleet has changed significantly following the introduction of Classes BB 27000 and BB 37000 whilst the diesel freight fleet is now changing due to the arrival of new Classes BB 60000 and BB 75000.

The Paris suburban fleet is currently between the end of double-deck EMU deliveries and the arrival of Bombardier's "Spacium" single-deck EMU which will replace the 1960s stainless-steel EMUs.

The fleet for regional services continues to expand, with 700 AGC multiple units currently being delivered. Units now tend to stay in the same region as they are locally financed.

The division of SNCF into activities also means that loco types tend to stay on one type of duty and do not wander across the country as far as they used to.

Since the last edition, the following types have become extinct although many have been preserved:

CC 1100, CC 6500, CC 7100, BB 8100, BB 9600, BB 9700, BB 12000, BB 20200, BB 25100, BB 62400, CC 65500, BB 67000, T 1000, T 2000, X 2720, X 2800, Z 6300, Z 7100.

The following new types have been introduced:

TGV POS, TGV Dasye, BB 27000, BB 37000, BB 60000, BB 75000, B 81500, B 82500, X 73500, X 74500, X 76500, Z 21500, Z 24500, U 25500, Z 26500, and Z 27500.

As usual, the author welcomes sightings and other fresh information, particularly on private operators and locos sold to industry for which data is more difficult to obtain.

To keep this book up to date, subscribe to **Today's Railways Europe**, the monthly magazine produced by Platform 5 which gives updates of SNCF allocations plus details of usage.

LAYOUT OF INFORMATION

For each class of vehicle general data and dimensions in metric units are provided. Vehicle lengths are lengths over buffers or couplers. The following standard abbreviations are used:

km/h	kilometres per hour
kN	kilonewtons
kW	kilowatts
m	metres
mm	millimetres
CFL	Chemins de Fer Luxembourgeois (Luxembourg Railways)
DB	Deutsche Bahn (German Railways)
EU	Eurostar
NS	Nederlandse Spoorwegen (Netherlands Railways)
RIO	Rames Inox Omnibus (suburban push-pull sets)
RRR	Rames Reversibles Régionales (regional push-pull hauled sets)
RATP	Regie Autonome des Transports Parisiens (Paris Transport Authority)
SNCB	Société Nationale des Chemins de Fer Belges (Belgian Railways)
Length	Length over couplings or buffers.
Power	One hour rating.

Builder codes see Appendix I on page 205. For explanation of codes used for accommodation in hauled coaching stock and multiple units see Appendix II on page 206.

For each vehicle the number is given in the first column. Where a vehicle has been renumbered the former number is generally shown in parentheses after the current number. Further columns show, respectively, the livery (in bold condensed type), the region (for DMUs and EMUs – in italics), any detail differences, the depot allocation and name where appropriate. Full formations are provided for DMUs and EMUs. Depot and livery codes are shown in Appendix IV on pages 207/8.

TICKETS AND PASSES

Single tickets are available from station ticket windows, automatic ticket machines and the Internet. Prices taper so that long distance prices are quite reasonable. On TGV and Corail Téoz services reservation is obligatory. A wide range of reductions is available, either by reserving in advance and travelling off peak or in connection with various promotional cards on sale for under 26s, seniors and so on. These give reductions of 40–60%, the reduction falling to 25% at peak times. In general, "off peak" is away from the morning and evening weekday peaks, Friday and Sunday evenings which are very busy, and peak holiday departures. Long distance and TER tickets must be date-stamped before boarding the train in yellow "composteurs". Most Paris suburban stations have automatic barriers for which a magnetic-strip ticket or smart card are needed.

The only pass covering the whole of France is now the Inter Rail Single Country pass, which is available for adults as well as young people, for three to eight days in a month. These cost from €189 to €299 for an adult in second class in 2008. Paris has passes known as *Paris Visite* (including reductions at tourist sites) and the cheaper *Mobilis*, both of which vary in price according to the number of zones chosen. Several regions of France have their own passes, usually only available on TER services and often restricted to the weekend and/or summer holidays. These include Alsace (*Pass Évasion*, there are also passes covering Alsace plus neighbouring German states), Corsica (*Carte Zoom*), Franche Comté (*Pass Visi'TER*), Haute Normandie (*Région Transports Été*), Lorraine (*Saar-Lor-Lux* ticket including Luxembourg and Saarland), Nord-Pas-de-Calais (*Pass Libre Accès*) and Pays de la Loire (*ForfaiTER*). Most other regions sell a card which gives 50% reduction, usually at weekends and/or holidays. Full details can be found in annual features each spring in **Today's Railways Europe**.

GETTING THERE FROM GREAT BRITAIN

By Rail

Eurostar services run daily from London St. Pancras, Ebbsfleet and Ashford to Calais Fréthun, Lille Europe, Paris Nord and Marne-la-Vallée-Chessy (for Disneyland) taking around 1h20 from London to Lille and 2h20 to the other two. At weekends in summer Eurostar runs to Avignon and in winter to Bourg St. Maurice in the Alps. There are onward connections to destinations such as Rennes, Nantes, Bordeaux, Lyon, Marseille and Strasbourg in Lille. Through fares are now available from northern Britain to Paris and from London to many points in France. Eurotunnel carries cars between Folkestone and Coquelles, near Calais.

By Sea

Ferry services carrying cars and, in most cases, foot passengers, operate from Dover to Boulogne, Calais and Dunkerque, Newhaven to Dieppe and Le Havre, Portsmouth to Cherbourg, Le Havre, Ouistreham (Caen) and St. Malo, Poole to Cherbourg, and Plymouth to Roscoff. There are no longer any trains run to connect with ferries or through rail-sea-rail fares.

By Air

There are flights from all over Britain to many French airports. Only Roissy-Charles-de-Gaulle and Orly in Paris plus Lyon St. Exupéry are rail-connected.

ACKNOWLEDGEMENTS

I would like to thank all who helped me prepare this book, especially Sylvain Assez, José Banaudo, Marc Carémantrant, Laurent Charlier, Bernard Collardey, Didier Delattre, Brian Garvin, Christopher Hespel, Thierry Leleu, Sylvain Meillasson, Patrick Petit, Maurice Testu and Jean-Pierre Vergez.

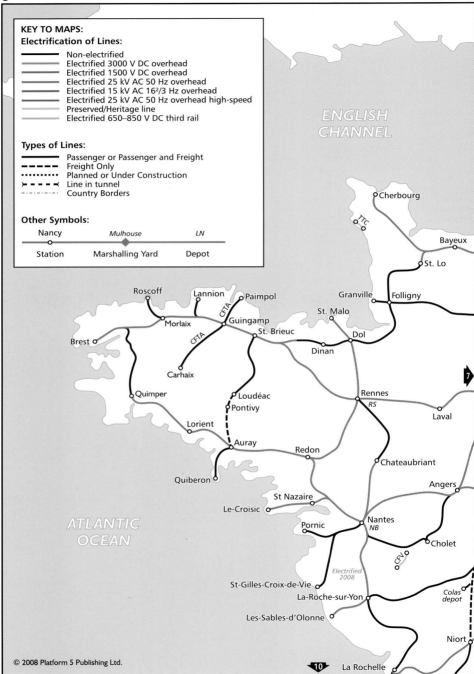

KEY TO MAPS:
Electrification of Lines:

- Non-electrified
- Electrified 3000 V DC overhead
- Electrified 1500 V DC overhead
- Electrified 25 kV AC 50 Hz overhead
- Electrified 15 kV AC 16²/3 Hz overhead
- Electrified 25 kV AC 50 Hz overhead high-speed
- Preserved/Heritage line
- Electrified 650–850 V DC third rail

Types of Lines:

- Passenger or Passenger and Freight
- Freight Only
- Planned or Under Construction
- Line in tunnel
- Country Borders

Other Symbols:

Nancy — Station · Mulhouse — Marshalling Yard · LN — Depot

© 2008 Platform 5 Publishing Ltd.

© 2008 Platform 5 Publishing Ltd.

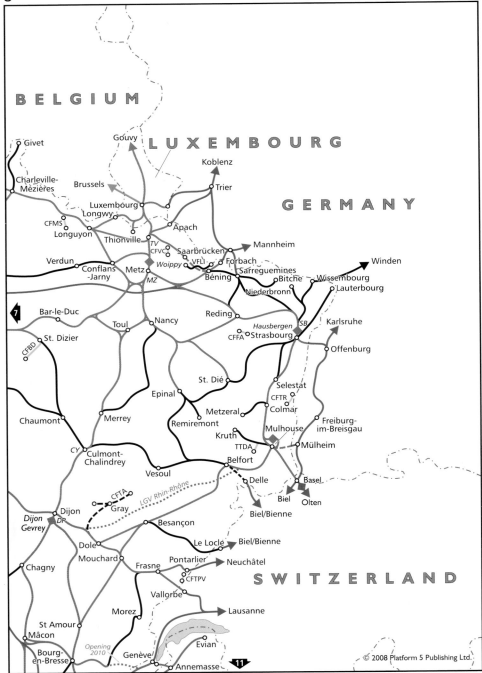

BELGIUM

Givet

Gouvy

LUXEMBOURG

Koblenz

Charleville-Mézières

Brussels

Luxembourg

Longwy

Trier

GERMANY

CFMS

Longuyon

Thionville

Apach

TV

CFVC

Saarbrücken

Mannheim

Winden

Verdun

Conflans-Jarny

Metz

Woippy

VFLI

Forbach

Sarreguemines

Wissembourg

MZ

Béning

Bitche

Lauterbourg

Bar-le-Duc

Toul

Nancy

Reding

Niederbronn

Hausbergen

SB

Karlsruhe

7

CFBD

St. Dizier

CFFA

Strasbourg

Offenburg

St. Dié

Selestat

Epinal

CFTR

Colmar

Chaumont

Merrey

Remiremont

Metzeral

Freiburg-im-Breisgau

Kruth

Mulhouse

Mülheim

CY

Culmont-Chalindrey

TTDA

Belfort

Vesoul

Delle

Basel

CFTA

LGV Rhin-Rhône

Biel

Olten

Dijon

Gray

Biel/Bienne

Dijon

DP

Gevrey

Besançon

Chagny

Dole

Le Locle

Biel/Bienne

Mouchard

Pontarlier

Neuchâtel

Frasne

CFTPV

SWITZERLAND

Vallorbe

St Amour

Morez

Lausanne

Mâcon

Bourg-en-Bresse

Opening 2010

Genève

Evian

11

Annemasse

© 2008 Platform 5 Publishing Ltd.

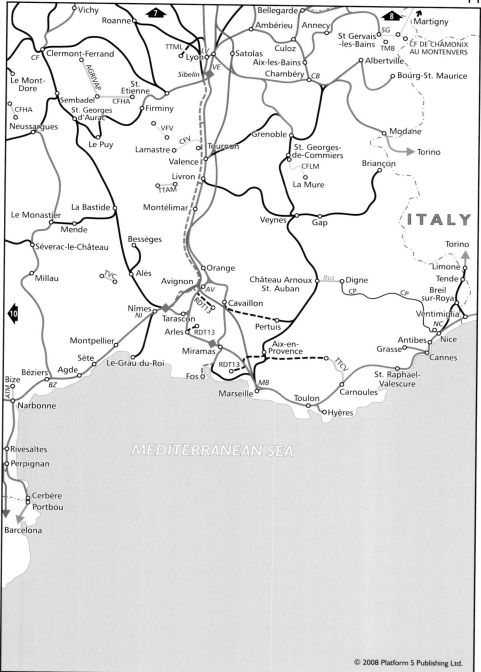

© 2008 Platform 5 Publishing Ltd.

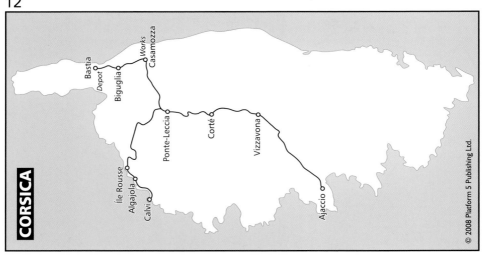

CORSICA

Bastia
Depot
Biguglia
Works
Casamozza
Ponte-Leccia
Corté
Vizzavona
Ile Rousse
Algajola
Calvi
Ajaccio

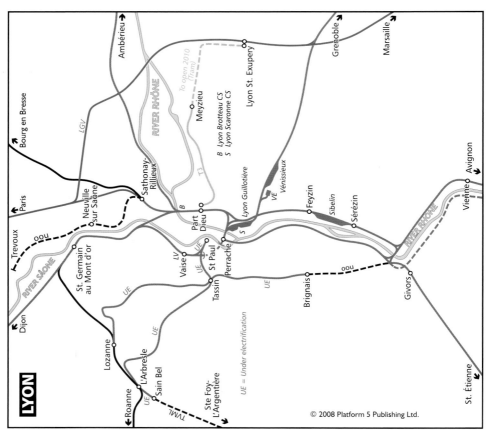

LYON

Ambérieu
To open 2010 (Tram)
RIVER RHÔNE
Meyzieu
Lyon St. Exupery
B Lyon Brotteau CS
S Lyon Scaronne CS
Grenoble
Marseille
Bourg en Bresse
LGV
T3
Vénissieux
Lyon Guillotière
VE
Feyzin
Paris
Neuville sur Saône
Sathonay-Rillieux
B
Part Dieu
S
Sibelin
Sérézin
Trevoux
oou
St. Germain au Mont d'or
RIVER SAÔNE
LV
Vaise
St Paul
Perrache
UE
UE
Avignon
Vienne
RIVER RHÔNE
Dijon
UE
Tassin
Brignais
oou
Givors
UE
Lozanne
UE
L'Arbresle
Sain Bel
UE
Ste Foy-L'Argentière
TVMI
Roanne
UE = Under electrification
St. Étienne

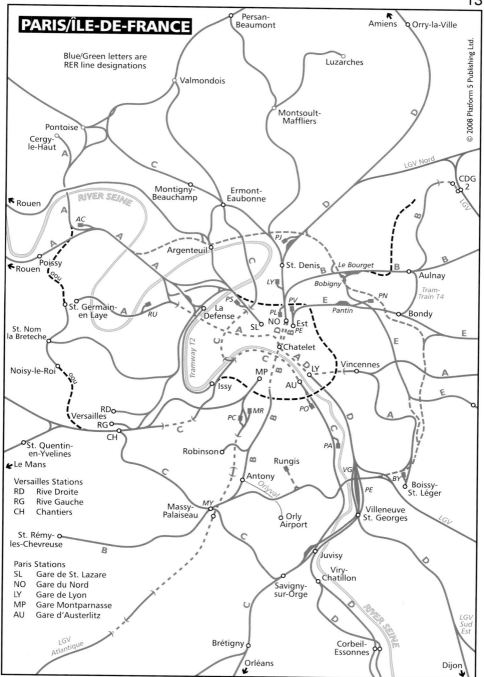

13

PARIS/ÎLE-DE-FRANCE

Blue/Green letters are
RER line designations

© 2008 Platform 5 Publishing Ltd.

Persan-Beaumont

Amiens   Orry-la-Ville

Luzarches

Valmondois

Montsoult-Maffliers

Pontoise

Cergy-le-Haut

LGV Nord

Montigny-Beauchamp

Ermont-Eaubonne

CDG 2

LGV

RIVER SEINE

Rouen

AC

PJ

Argenteuil

St. Denis   Le Bourget   B   Aulnay

Rouen

Poissy

LY   Bobigny   Tram-Train T4

St. Germain-en Laye

PS   PV   PN

RU   La Defense   PL   E   Pantin   Bondy

St. Nom la Breteche

SL   NO   Est

PE

Chatelet

Noisy-le-Roi

MP   LY   Vincennes

Issy   AU

RD   MR   PO

Versailles   PC

RG

CH

St. Quentin-en-Yvelines

Le Mans   Robinson

Rungis   PA

Versailles Stations

RD	Rive Droite
RG	Rive Gauche
CH	Chantiers

Antony   Orlyval   PE   Boissy-St. Léger

Massy-Palaiseau   MY   Orly Airport   Villeneuve St. Georges

St. Rémy-les-Chevreuse   B   Juvisy

Paris Stations

SL	Gare de St. Lazare
NO	Gare du Nord
LY	Gare de Lyon
MP	Gare Montparnasse
AU	Gare d'Austerlitz

Viry-Chatillon

Savigny-sur-Orge

RIVER SEINE

LGV Sud Est

LGV Atlantique

Brétigny   Corbeil-Essonnes   Dijon

Orléans

▲ BB 8644 heads the Béziers–Paris service (now chopped in half and usually EMU operated over this section) past Compère on 1 July 2006.   **Les Nixon**

▼ 51 years after its introduction, BB 9201 is still going strong. The loco is seen here, in Fret SNCF livery, at St. Geneviève des Bois with an Aqualys service from Paris to Tours on 20 July 2006.
                                                                                    Raimund Whynal

▲ BB 9305, in "Multiservices" livery, stands at Cerbère on 22 March 2006 with the 12.27 train to Avignon. **Keith Fender**

▼ BB 15018 passes the closed station of Mussey with EuroCity train 54 from Frankfurt to Paris (since replaced by an ICE) on 2 April 2007. **David Haydock**

▲ BB 16020 arrives at Paris Nord with the overnight train from Hamburg and Berlin on 15 March 2008. Behind the loco is the Russian coach which has come from Moskva!   **Didier Delattre**

▼ BB 16750 is seen just south of Douai with a train from Cambrai on 17 June 2008.   **David Haydock**

1. SOCIÉTÉ NATIONALE DES CHEMINS DE FER FRANÇAIS (SNCF)

THE FRENCH RAILWAY SYSTEM

SNCF (French National Railways) was formed in 1937 when several private companies were nationalised. These formed the basis of the SNCF "réseaux" or networks. They were:

1. Est (East) – former Chemin de Fer de l'Est.
2. Nord (North) – former Chemin de Fer du Nord.
3. Ouest (West) – former Chemin de Fer d'État.
4. Sud Ouest (South West) – former PO-Midi.
5. Sud Est (South East) – former Chemin de Fer Paris–Lyon–Méditerranée (PLM).

These areas remained stable for many years but réseaux 1 and 2 were then combined into a new region "Nord-Est" and 3 and 4 merged to form the "Atlantique" region.

In 1997, following EU rules, operation was split from infrastructure, the latter becoming the responsibility of Réseau Ferré de France (RFF). However, RFF subcontracts all traffic control (train planning, signalling) and all track maintenance to SNCF which therefore has its own Infrastructure fleet. SNCF has historically subcontracted much of the renewal work on track to private companies which can be found later in this book.

In 2003, the French government incorporated EU rules on open access for rail freight into national law but competition with SNCF only started in 2005 and is therefore less developed than in Germany and the Netherlands, for example. The next big date is the end of 2009 when passenger services are opened up to competition. Air France and Veolia have formed an alliance to operate high speed services but had not ordered trains in late 2008. It is expected that regional government will soon start to tender for local services and Veolia will probably be the first to respond!

DEVELOPMENTS

The great majority of trains in France are operated with electric traction and further lines are still being electrified. The main development in recent years has been the opening of new high speed lines and the consequent replacement of conventional hauled trains with TGVs. This will continue with new lines either under construction or planned. The remaining passenger locomotives are increasingly equipped for push-pull operation whilst loco-powered trains on regional services continue to be replaced with multiple units. Traffic growth on local services is leading to the increasing use of double-deck EMUs in the biggest conurbations outside Paris. In contrast, Paris will soon receive its first new single-deck EMUs for 25 years in the form of Bombardier's Spacium units.

Fret SNCF is increasingly standardising its fleet, many older classes having been replaced by Alstom Prima Classes BB 27000 and BB 37000. The same is now happening with diesels, thanks to the arrival of Classes BB 60000 and BB 75000. The Fret SNCF fleet is also shrinking because of traffic loss to competing companies. One reaction to competition has been for Fret SNCF to operate increasingly outside France. Thus the company's locos can be seen in Belgium (BB 36000 and BB 67400), Germany and Switzerland (BB 37000) and Italy (BB 36000).

SNCF PASSENGER TRAIN SERVICES

SNCF now divides its services into long distance (*TGV* and *Corail Téoz* run by *Voyages France Europe*), other *Corail* services (run by *Corail Intercités*), regional services (TER) and Paris suburban services (*Transilien*). International services are mainly operated by subsidiaries with special fare conditions and "global pricing" which often excludes normal reductions:

- Eurostar – Paris, Lille and Calais Fréthun to London.
- Thalys – Paris to Brussels, Amsterdam and Köln plus other cities in Belgium, the Netherlands and Germany.
- Alleo – Paris to Frankfurt (ICE), Stuttgart and München, plus other cities in Germany.
- Lyria – Paris and Dijon to Bern, Lausanne, Genève, Basel, Zürich and other Swiss towns.
- Artesia – overnight services Paris to Italy.
- Elipsos – overnight services to Barcelona and Madrid in Spain.

Most long-distance services are based on Paris but there is a growing network of TGV services which link the provinces.

NUMBERING SYSTEM

The SNCF numbering system for steam locomotives was based on axle grouping so that a 4–6–2 became a 231 etc. Class letters then followed the axle details and then came the running number e.g. 231 E 22. For tank locomotives an additional T followed the axle arrangement e.g. 141 TC 8. No electric locomotives were renumbered on the formation of SNCF. Most locos came from the PO-Midi system with a few others from the État and PLM. Those delivered to SNCF between 1938 and 1950 continued the PO-Midi series. However from 1950 a new system was introduced bringing the locomotives somewhat into line with the steam system, but here the axle arrangement was shown by letters so that a Bo-Bo became a BB.

Diesel locomotives were originally given a steam type number with an additional D in the number after the axle arrangement e.g. 040 DA 1 but in 1960 the whole fleet was renumbered into the present system.

SNCF traction is numbered with prefixes as shown below. In this book locomotive numbers are listed without their prefix letters, but letter prefixes are used for multiple unit power cars or shunting tractors. Multiple unit trailers are numbered as "XR" or "ZR", but these are shown without prefixes in this book for space reasons. (NB: most locomotives do not carry their prefixes).

Electric locomotives:

Electric locomotives are numbered in the following ranges:

1– 9999	DC locomotives.
10000–19999	AC locomotives.
20000–29999	Dual-voltage locomotives.
30000–39999	Triple-voltage locomotives.
40000–49999	Quadruple-voltage locomotives (none in service at present).

Examples: BB 8500, DC locomotive with BB axle arrangement; BB 17000, AC locomotive with BB axle arrangement; BB 25500 dual voltage locomotive of same type. (8500+17000=25500).

Diesel locomotives:

Diesel locomotives are numbered in the following ranges:
50000–51999   Diesel *locomoteurs* (none in service at present).
60000–79999   Diesel locomotives.
Shunting locos (*"locotracteurs"*) are prefixed Y and numbered between 2201–9999.

Multiple units:

"B" denotes a bimode (electric plus diesel) multiple unit.
"T" denotes a gas turbine unit (none in service at present).
"U" denotes a tram-train.
"X" denotes a DMU, power car numbers originally ranging between 2101 and 4999.
"Z" denotes an EMU, power car numbers originally ranging between 3711 and 9699.

Diesel and electric units owned or subsidised by local authorities or other "third parties" have numbers prefixed by "9" e.g. EMUs. Z 97381–Z 97384 belong to the local regions and are the same as Class Z 7300.

Trains à Grande Vitesse:

The first TGV power cars were numbered as 2-, 3- or 4-voltage locomotives but they also carry a set number, e.g. TGV power cars 23001/2 are set 01 and can be referred to as TGV 01.

NEW NUMBERING SYSTEM

In order to avoid confusion with the above numbering system (7301 can be a BB electric locomotive, an EMU, or a shunter), SNCF introduced a new system in the 1990s. Locomotives are numbered up to 499 in each series and 501 upwards for multiple units. For example, Class BB 75000 (75001 to 75499) are diesel locomotives while X 75500 (75501 to 75999) are DMUs. No existing stock has been renumbered.

Activity or Sector Prefixes

In 1999, SNCF introduced prefixes for locomotive numbers (not for multiple units) to designate the activity to which the unit belongs. Prefixes in 2008 are as originally designated except for the addition of "2" in the mid 2000s:

1 for Voyages France Europe – long distance passenger.
2 for Corail InterCités (CIC) – shorter distance, subsidised Corail services.
4 for Fret SNCF – freight.
5 for Train Express Régional – regional passenger.
6 for Infra – infrastructure.
8 for Île-de-France – Paris region.

Other prefixes are not used at present. These prefixes are applied in front of the series number but not to the few locos which still have cast numbers. In many cases, prefixes had still not been applied in 2008, or locos were carrying out-of-date prefix numbers – many locomotives are transferred between activities each year.

In the 1999 operation, all shunters were allocated to Fret SNCF but without application of the prefix. At the time of going to press a proper division of shunters was taking place, but full details were not available.

In both this book and the magazine **Today's Railways Europe**, we refer to a locomotive number without its prefix.

European Union standard numbering and open access companies

At the time of writing the first locomotives had just started to appear with 12-digit numbers which are now required by the EU. No SNCF locos had yet to appear with such numbers, possibly because this will affect the internal SNCF numbering system. Open access operators often have their own numbering "system" as well as using EU numbers. It seems that the new numbers are being designed to fit the French (SNCF) system. For example, all Vossloh G1206 locos are in the xx xx xx 61 700 series, thus matching SNCF's BB 61000 Vossloh G1206s. Euro Cargo Rail's Class 77 fits neatly into the list as BB 77000.

SNCF DEPOTS

The number of SNCF depots is increasing, mainly because of the desire of the 22 regions to have at least one depot within their territory. SNCF has been gradually grouping maintenance facilities and giving them new names. For example, Achères and Paris St. Lazare are grouped as Technicentre de Paris St. Lazare. We continue to show the exact place of maintenance here.

Depot allocations are usually stencilled in full on SNCF traction units. **Unofficial** depot codes are used in this book and are shown in Appendix IV on page 207. SNCF's traction and operating departments have different codes for depots ranging from one to three letters. Those used by the traction department are not widely known or used.

STABLING POINTS

Generally speaking, depots have large allocations but many locomotives and units are stabled at other places. The most important stabling points are Ambérieu, Amiens, Aulnoye, Batignolles (Paris), Belfort, Besançon, Blainville, Bourges, Brive, Cerbère, Châlons-en-Champagne, Conflans-Jarny, Creil Petit Thérain, Dole, Dunkerque Grande Synthe, Forbach, Fréthun (Calais), Grenoble, Hausbergen (Strasbourg), La Rochelle Ville, Laroche-Migennes, Le Bourget (Paris), Le Havre, Le Mans, Les Aubrais (Orléans), Lille-Fives, Lyon Mouche, Marseille St. Charles, Miramas, Modane, Mohon, Mulhouse Ville, Narbonne, Nancy, Paris Charolais, Poitiers, Portes-les-Valence, Reims, Somain, Sotteville yard (Rouen), St. Étienne, St. Jean-de-Maurienne, St. Jory (Toulouse), Sibelin, Tarbes, Tergnier, Thouars, Troyes, Vaires (Paris), Vaugirard (Paris), Vierzon and Woippy.

WORKSHOPS

The SNCF has no really large locomotive works, but has kept open many pre-nationalisation workshops. Each of these deals with specific classes for major overhauls. Rationalisation is continuing so Béziers and Épernay works are under particular threat and Le Mans has closed. Increasing amounts of work are being farmed out to depots or private companies.

Workshop	Types overhauled
Béziers	BB 80000, Z 100, Z 150, Z 200.
Bischheim (Strasbourg)	TGV Sud-Est, TGV Atlantique, TGV Dasye, TGV POS.
Épernay	BB 16500.
Hellemmes (Lille)	TGV Duplex, TGV Réseau, Thalys, Eurostar. Hellemmes also "manages" SNCF-owned Class 92 locos.
Nevers	BB 64700, BB 66000, BB 66400, BB 66700, X 200, X 240, X 2100, X 2200, X 4300, X 4500, X 4630, X 4750, X 4900, X 72500, X 73500, X 74500, X 76500, B 81500, B 82500, XR 6000, XR 6200, Y 7100, Y 7400, Y 8000, Y 8400, U 25500, Z 21500, Z 27500.
Oullins (Lyon)	BB 7200, BB 9200, BB 9300, BB 15000, BB 16000, BB 16100, BB 22200, BB 25150, BB 25200, BB 26000, BB 27000, BB 27300, BB 37000, BB 36000, Z 600, Z 800, Z 850.
Quatres Mares (Rouen)	BB 8500, BB 17000, BB 25500, BB 60000, BB 63000, BB 63400, BB 63500, BB 64800, BB 67200, BB 67300, BB 67400, A1AA1A 68000, A1AA1A 68500, CC 72000, BB 75000.
Tours	Z 5300, Z 5600, Z 6100, Z 6400, Z 7300, Z 7500, Z 8100, Z 8800, Z 9500, Z 9600, Z 11500, Z 20500, Z 20900, Z 22500, Z 23500, Z 24500, Z 26500, Z 92050.

1.1. SNCF ELECTRIC LOCOMOTIVES

The French rail network is electrified at two voltages – mainly 1500 V DC south of Paris and 25 kV AC 50 Hz north of Paris. Since the 1950s most new electrification south of Paris has been at 25 kV AC which means that SNCF has needed to develop dual-voltage motive power. All electric traction now being built is dual-voltage. All high speed lines are electrified at 25 kV AC.

Many SNCF locos have monomotor bogies whose gearing can be changed when the loco is at rest. An arrow on the bogie will be found pointing to the letter 'M' or 'V' denoting "marchandises" or "voyageurs" (freight or passenger) and this indicator is one of the items a driver must check when preparing a locomotive. In this publication, where two sets of figures are shown for maximum speed, tractive effort, power etc., the first refers to the low gear ratio and the second to the high gear ratio.

Note: All electric locomotives are livery **C** (cement grey with orange bands) unless otherwise shown.

CLASS BB 7200   B-B

This mixed traffic class is part of a large family of locomotives – Class BB 7200 is the DC version, Class BB 15000 the AC version and Class BB 22200 the dual-voltage version (7200 + 15000 = 22200). Unlike most French monomotor-bogied locomotives, Class BB 7200 has fixed gearing for freight or passenger use, certain locos being limited to 100 km/h with the remainder having the higher rating of 160 km/h or 200 km/h. BB 7411–40 also have microprocessor controls and regenerative braking. Members of the class have moved around depots in recent years but duties have not changed much apart from a decline in long distance passenger work with the arrival of TGVs. The class dominates on passenger services on the Sud-Est region and also hauls most express freight services. Less dominant on the Sud-Ouest region but common on both freight and passenger. BB 7209, 7210, 7308 and 7348 were destroyed in accidents. Locos operating TER local services with Corail stock are being equipped for push-pull operation. They carry their numbers with an "R" suffix meaning *"reversible"*.

Built: 1976–85.   **System:** 1500 V DC.
Builders: Alsthom/MTE.
Traction Motors: Two TAB 674 frame-mounted monomotors.
Continuous Rating: 4040 kW.   **Weight:** 84 tonnes.
Maximum Tractive Effort: 288 (300*†) kN.   **Length:** 17.48 m.
Wheel Diameter: 1250 mm.   **Maximum Speed:** 160 (100*†, 200§) km/h.

Fitted with cowcatchers, rheostatic brakes, electro-pneumatic brakes and driver-guard communication.

c Modified for working the 'Catalan Talgo'.
† Fitted with self-ventilated motors and multiple working for use on the Maurienne line. BB 7411–40 also have regenerative braking.
§ Fitted with *"préannonce"* cab signalling.
p Equipped for push-pull operation with Corail stock. These locos carry a letter 'R' after the number.

No.			Code	No.			Code	No.			Code	No.			Code
407201	P	*	DP	407220		*	DP	507237	E	p	DP	107254			VG
407202		*	DP	407221	P	*	DP	507238	E	p	DP	107255			VG
407203		*	DP	407222		*	DP	507239	E	p	DP	207256			VG
407204		*	DP	407223	F	*	DP	507240	E	p	DP	107257			VG
407205		*	DP	407224		*	DP	507241	E	p	DP	107258	P		VG
407206	F	*	DP	407225		*	DP	407242	F		VG	107259			MB
407207		*	DP	407226	F	*	DP	507243	E	p	DP	107260			MB
407208		*	DP	407227		*	BD	507244	E	p	DP	107261		§	VG
407211		*	DP	407228		*	BD	507245	E	p	DP	107262		§	VG
407212	F	*	DP	407229		*	BD	507246	E	p	DP	107263		§	VG
407213		*	DP	407230		*	BD	507247	E	p	DP	107264			MB
407214		*	DP	407231		*	BD	507248	E	p	DP	107265			MB
407215		*	DP	407232		*	BD	507249	E	p	DP	107266			MB
407216		*	DP	407233		*	BD	207250			VG	107267			MB
407217		*	DP	407234		*	BD	107251			VG	107268			MB
407218		*	DP	407235		*	BD	207252			VG	507269			VG
407219	F	*	DP	507236	E	p	DP	107253			VG	207270			VG

No.				No.				No.				No.			
107271			VG	407314			VG	407357		†	DP	407399			VG
207272			VG	207315			VG	407358		†	DP	407400	F		VG
207273			VG	207316			VG	407359		†	DP	407401			VG
507274			VG	407317			BD	407360		†	DP	407402	E		VG
507275			VG	207318			VG	407361		†	DP	407403			VG
507276			VG	507319			DP	407362		†	DP	407404			VG
107277			MB	507320			DP	407363		†	DP	407405			VG
507278			VG	507321			DP	407364		†	DP	407406			VG
407279			BD	507322			DP	407365		†	DP	107407			MB
407280			BD	507323			DP	407366		†	DP	107408			MB
107281			MB	207324			VG	407367		†	DP	507409	E	p	DP
107282			MB	407325			BD	407368		†	DP	507410	E	p	DP
107283			MB	407326			BD	407369		†	DP	407411	F	†	DP
107284	E		MB	407327			BD	407370		†	DP	407412		†	DP
107285			MB	407328			BD	407371		†	DP	407413		†	DP
107286			MB	407329			BD	407372		†	DP	407414		†	DP
107287			MB	407330			BD	407373		†	DP	407415		†	DP
107288			MB	407331			BD	407374		†	DP	407416		†	DP
107289			MB	407332			BD	407375		†	DP	407417		†	DP
507290	E	p	DP	407333			BD	407376		†	DP	407418		†	DP
507291	E	p	DP	407334			BD	407377		†	DP	407419		†	DP
107292	P	c	VG	407335			MB	407378		†	DP	407420		†	DP
107293		c	VG	407336			MB	407379		†	DP	407421		†	DP
107294		c	VG	407337			BD	407380		†	DP	407422		†	DP
107295		c	VG	507338			MB	407381			BD	407423		†	DP
107296		c	VG	407339			MB	407382			BD	407424		†	DP
107297		c	VG	507340			DP	407383			BD	407425		†	DP
107298		c	VG	407341			BD	407384			BD	407426		†	DP
107299		c	VG	407342			BD	407385			BD	407427		†	DP
107300			VG	407343		†	BD	407386			BD	407428		†	DP
107301			VG	407344		†	BD	407387			BD	407429		†	DP
107302			VG	407345		†	BD	407388			BD	407430		†	DP
107303			VG	407346		†	BD	407389			BD	407431		†	DP
207304			MB	407347		†	BD	407390			BD	407432		†	DP
407305			VG	407349		†	BD	207391	E		VG	407433		†	DP
407306			VG	407350		†	BD	407392			BD	407434		†	DP
407307			VG	407351		†	BD	107393			MB	407435		†	DP
407309			VG	407352		†	BD	407394			VG	407436		†	DP
407310			VG	407353		†	BD	407395			VG	407437		†	DP
407311			VG	407354		†	BD	407396	F		VG	407438		†	DP
407312			VG	407355		†	BD	407397			VG	407439		†	DP
407313			VG	407356		†	DP	407398			VG	407440		†	DP

Names:

7203	SAINT-FLOUR	7241	VILLEURBANNE
7221	SAINT-AMAND-MONTROND	7242	VIENNE
7223	LA SOUTERRAINE	7243	VILLENEUVE-SAINT-GEORGES
7232	SOUILLAC	7244	VERNOU-LA CELLE-SUR-SEINE
7236	CHAMBÉRY	7253	MONTRÉJEAU
7237	PIERRELATTE	7256	VALENTON
7238	THONON-LES-BAINS	7270	ENTRAIGUES-SUR-SORGUES
7239	SAINT-PIERRE-D'ALBIGNY	7410	FONTENAY-SOUS-BOIS
7240	SAINT-ETIENNE	7411	LAMURE-SUR-AZERGUES

CLASS BB 8500 & BB 88500 B-B

A mixed traffic loco being a DC version of Class BB 17000. Monomotor bogies with two gear ratios. Being such a large class there are detail variations between batches. BB 8501 to 8587 have smaller cabs and are unpopular with drivers so most have been withdrawn or downgraded to empty stock movements (renumbered as BB 88500). The class has lost all of its freight work and most suburban services from Paris and now mainly works push-pull TER services around Dijon, Toulouse and on Paris-Montparnasse–Le Mans. The others are employed on empty stock movements around Lyon and Paris Gare de Lyon.

Built: 1964–74.
Builder: Alsthom.
System: 1500 V DC.
Traction Motors: Two TAB 660B1 frame-mounted monomotors.
Continuous Rating: 2940 kW except 8501–36 which are 2610 kW.
Maximum Tractive Effort: 323 /197 kN.
Weight: 79 tonnes (8537–87), 80 tonnes (8588–8646), 78 tonnes (88501–36).
Length: 14.94 m (8537–87), 15.57 m (8588–8646), 14.70 m (88501–36).
Wheel Diameter: 1100 mm.   **Maximum Speed:** 100/140 km/h.

Multiple working fitted. Rheostatic braking. Push-pull fitted.

Class BB 8500.

508549	DP	508595	I	MR	508611		TL	508626	E	TL
508552	DP	508596	I	MR	508612	P	TL	408627	E	TL
508562	DP	508597	E	MR	508613	E	TL	508628	P	TL
508565	DP	508598	E	MR	508614	P	TL	508629	P	TL
508567	DP	508599		TL	508615	E	TL	508630	F	TL
508576	VE	508601	F	TL	508616		TL	508632	F	TL
108581	TL	508602	F	TL	508617	E	TL	508633		DP
508587	DP	508603	F	TL	508618	E	TL	108638		VG
508588	E	MR	508604	F	TL	508620		VE	108640		VG
508589	I	MR	508606	P	TL	508622	P	TL	108641		VG
508591	I	MR	508607	P	TL	508623	P	TL	508642		TL
508592	E	MR	508608		TL	508624	P	TL	508645		VE
508593	E	MR	508609	P	TL	508625		DP	508646	E	MR
508594	I	MR	508610	P	TL						

Names:

8601	AX-LES-THERMES		8604	CERDAGNE
8602	FOIX		8626	FLEURY-LES-AUBRAIS
8603	LANNEMEZAN		8627	SAINT-GAUDENS

Class BB 88500. Downgraded to 100 km/h for e.c.s. working and renumbered.

588501	VE	188508	VG	288517	VG	188527	VG
188504	VG	188509	VG	288519	VG	188529	VG
188505	VG	188511	VG	288523	VG	188531	VG
188506	VG	188514	VG	288526	VG	188534	VG
188507	VG						

CLASS BB 9200   Bo-Bo

This class was the first of the SNCF standard types of the late 1950s. The same styling is also found on Classes BB 9300, 16000, 25150 and 25200. Class BB 9200 was originally scattered over the DC network south of Paris, seen on both passenger and freight. All freight locos are now withdrawn and the last passenger locos are concentrated at Tours and Dijon and are used on Paris Montparnasse–Le Mans, Paris Austerlitz–Orléans–Tours and services around Dijon.

Built: 1957–64.
Builders: Schneider-Jeumont/CEM/MTE.
System: 1500 V DC.
Traction Motors: Four Alsthom GLM 931B.
Continuous Rating: 3850 kW.
Maximum Tractive Effort: 260 kN.
Weight: 82 tonnes.
Wheel Diameter: 1250 mm.
Length: 16.20 m.
Maximum Speed: 160 km/h.

BB 9263–9290 are fitted with rheostatic braking.

t   TDM push-pull fitted.

509214		TP	209240		TP	509256	P	TP	209272		TP
209217		TP	509242	F	DP	509257		TP	209273	E t	TP
509220	F	TP	509243		TP	509265	E t	TP	509282	E	DP
509222		TP	509245	F	TP	509269		DP	509284	P	DP
509231		TP	509247	P	TP	509270		DP	509290	P t	DP

CLASS BB 9300 Bo-Bo

An updated version of Class BB 9200. All are grouped at Toulouse but see widespread use on the main lines south of Tours and Limoges and on the Toulouse–Marseille route.

Built: 1967–69.
Builders: Schneider-Jeumont/MTE/CEM.
Traction Motors: Four Alsthom GLM 931B.
Continuous Rating: 3850 kW.
Maximum Tractive Effort: 260 kN.
Wheel Diameter: 1250 mm.

System: 1500 V DC.

Weight: 84 tonnes.
Length: 16.20 m.
Maximum Speed: 160 km/h.

Fitted with rheostatic braking, electro-pneumatic brakes and driver-guard communication.

509301	P	TL	509311	P	TL	109321		TL	509330		TL
509303	E	TL	509312	P	TL	509322	E	TL	509331		TL
109304	P	TL	509313	P	TL	509323		TL	209333		TL
509305	P	TL	509315	P	TL	509324		TL	509334		TL
509306	E	TL	509316	E	TL	509325	P	TL	209335	P	TL
209307	P	TL	509317	P	TL	509326	E	TL	209337		TL
509308	P	TL	509318	E	TL	509327		TL	109338	P	TL
209309		TL	509319		TL	109328		TL	509339		TL
509310		TL	109320	P	TL	209329		TL	109340		TL

Names:

109326 MONTRABÉ | 109329 CASTRES

CLASS BB 15000 B-B

The first of the 1970s generation of locomotives which includes BB 7200 and BB 22200. Until 2007, when the LGV Est opened, they worked all passenger services from Paris Est to Basel, Luxembourg and Longwy as well as from Mulhouse to Besançon. They have now lost most of this work but remain on the Paris Est to Bar-le-Duc and St. Dizier service plus other local trains. The others have moved to Achères depot from where they work Paris Nord–Amiens/Maubeuge and from Paris St. Lazare to Caen, Cherbourg, Rouen and Le Havre. Several locos were being equipped for push-pull operation in 2008 and carry an R after their numbers. 15007 became prototype 7003 later becoming 10003 and 15055 became prototype 10004, but both have since reverted to their previous identities. Several have been scrapped after accidents.

Built: 1971–78.
Builders: Alsthom/MTE.
Traction Motors: Two TAB 674 frame-mounted monomotors.
Continuous Rating: 4400 kW.
Maximum Tractive Effort: 294 kN.
Wheel Diameter: 1250 mm.
Class Specific Livery: S Pale grey with red band lined in orange. Grand Confort livery.

System: 25 kV AC.

Weight: 90 tonnes.
Length: 17.48 m.
Maximum Speed: 160 km/h.

Rheostatic braking.

p Modified for push-pull operation with Corail stock.
f Equipped with forced air ventilation for traction motors.

515001	K f	AC	GRETZ-ARMAINVILLIERS	115019	P		SB	MONTIGNY-LÈS-METZ
515002	K f	AC	LONGWY	115020	P		SB	PAU
515003	K f	AC	SARREGUEMINES	115021	P		SB	CHÂTEAU-THIERRY
515004	K f	AC	SEDAN	215022	K		AC	PANTIN
115005	K f	SB	SAINT-LOUIS	115023	P		SB	MEAUX
515007	P f	AC		515024	K		AC	LUNÉVILLE
115008	K f	SB	NANCY	115025	K		SB	TOUL
215009	K f	AC	REIMS	215026	P	p	AC	ÉPERNAY
515010	K f	AC	STRASBOURG	215027	P	p	AC	CREUTZWALD
515012	K f	AC	CHÂLONS SUR MARNE	215028	P	p	SB	VILLIERS-LE-BEL
215013	K f	AC	LONGUYON	215029	P	p	AC	AURILLAC
215014	K f	AC	THIONVILLE	215030	P	f	AC	FORBACH
115016	P	SB	CHARLEVILLE-MÉZIÈRES	215031	P	fp	AC	MOYEUVRE-GRANDE
115017	K	SB	SAINT-AVOLD	215032	P	f	AC	CHAMBLY
115018	K	SB	BONDY	215034	E	fp	AC	SÈTE

115035	P	f	SB	NOGENT-SUR-MARNE	215050	P		AC	VITRY-LE-FRANÇOIS
215036	P	f	AC	LE PERREUX-SUR-MARNE	215051	P		AC	AULNOYE-AYMÉRIES
515037	P	f	AC	LA FERTÉ-SOUS-JOUARRE	215052	P	p	AC	CAMBRAI
515038	P	f	AC	ARS SUR MOSELLE	215053	E		AC	TROUVILLE-SUR-MER
515039	P	f	AC	ROSNY-SOUS-BOIS	215054	P	p	AC	
515040	P	fp	AC	LIVRY GARGAN	215055	E		AC	
515041	P	fp	AC	SAINTE MENEHOULD	515056	E		AC	VANNES
215042	P	fp	AC	ETIVAL-CLAIREFONTAINE	515058	E		AC	ÉPINAL
215043	P	f	AC	MAIZIÈRES LES METZ	515059	P	p	AC	TOURCOING
215044	P	fp	AC	SUIPPES	515060	P	p	AC	CREIL
215045	P	fp	AC	RAON L'ÉTAPE	215061	P		AC	SARREBOURG
515046	P	fp	AC		215062	E		AC	MONTMÉDY
515047	P	fp	AC	CHELLES	515063	E		AC	VERDUN
515048	P	fp	AC	HAGUENAU	215064	E		AC	SAVERNE
515049	P	fp	AC		215065	E		AC	VAIRES-SUR-MARNE

CLASSES BB 16000 & BB 16100   Bo-Bo

Class BB 16000 is an AC version of Class BB 9200. At one time split between Paris La Chapelle and Strasbourg the delivery of Class BB 15000 allowed all Class BB 16000 to be concentrated at La Chapelle and used on Paris Nord passenger services plus Paris–Le Havre. From 1996, a number of the class started operating on the Paris St. Lazare to Cherbourg line and the whole class was reallocated to Achères. Most of the class are expected to be withdrawn in the next few years, once again replaced by Class BB 15000, this time definitively.

Built: 1958–63.
Builder: MTE.
Traction Motors: Four Jeumont TO 136-8.
Continuous Rating: 4130 kW.
System: 25 kV AC.
Maximum Tractive Effort: 309 kN.
Weight: 88 tonnes.
Wheel Diameter: 1250 mm.
Length: 16.68 m.
Maximum Speed: 160 km/h.

p Equipped for Push-pull operation with Corail stock.

216002	P		AC	216018		p	AC	216039	E	p	AC	216052	P		AC
216003	E	p	AC	216019	P		AC	216041	P		AC	216053	E	p	AC
216005	P		AC	216020	P		AC	216042	P		AC	216054	P		AC
216006	E	p	AC	216021	P		AC	216043	P		AC	216055			AC
216007	E	p	AC	216027	P	p	AC	216044		p	AC	216056	P	p	AC
216008	E	p	AC	216028			AC	216047		p	AC	216058	P		AC
216011	P		AC	216029	E		AC	216050	P	p	AC	216059	P		AC
216012	E		AC	216032	E	p	AC	216051	P		AC	216061	P		AC
216015	P		AC	216033	P		AC								

The following locos were equipped with time division multiplex equipment in 1991–94 for use with double-deck outer suburban stock on the Paris Nord–St. Quentin/Amiens and Paris St. Lazare–Rouen lines.

Class Specific Livery: S Pale grey with dark grey and orange bands.

516101	(16004)	S	PL	516107	(16048)	S	PL	516112	(16010)	S	PL
516103	(16046)	S	PL	516108	(16026)	S	PL	516113	(16030)	S	PL
516104	(16040)	S	PL	516109	(16023)	S	PL	516114	(16062)	S	PL
516105	(16014)	S	PL	516110	(16035)	S	PL	516115	(16060)	S	PL
516106	(16009)	S	PL	516111	(16016)	S	PL				

Names:

16007	MANTES-LA-JOLIE	16114	DOL-DE-BRETAGNE
16008	DRANCY		

CLASS BB 16500   B-B

The monomotor bogie originated with this class and with it the idea of providing alternative gear ratios to create true mixed traffic locomotives. 16540 became the prototype of the Class BB 25500s and was numbered BB 20004 in the 1960s. Since the class was divided between activity sectors, Fret SNCF has stopped using the class, they have been eliminated from Paris area suburban services by Class BB 17000 and many have been withdrawn. All of the remaining locos are used on push-pull TER passenger services around Lille, Reims, Metz and Strasbourg where they are gradually being replaced with cascaded Class BB 25500 or EMUs.

Built: 1958–64.　　　　　　　　　　**System:** 25 kV AC.
Builder: Alsthom.
Traction Motors: Two Alsthom TAO 646A1 frame-mounted monomotors.
Continuous Rating: 2580 kW.　　　　**Weight:** 71–74 tonnes.
Maximum Tractive Effort: 324/192 kN.　**Length:** 14.40 m.
Wheel Diameter: 1100 mm.　　　　　**Maximum Speed:** 100 (90†)/140 km/h.
Non-Standard Livery: N Picardie green/grey livery for Paris–Beauvais service (now finished).

Multiple working and push-pull fitted.

516530		LE	516640		LE	516705		LE	516746		LE
516559	p	PL	516641		LE	516708		SB	516749		SB
516583	l	PL	516642		LE	516709		TV	516750		LE
216588		PL	516643		TV	516710		LE	516751		LE
516592	N	PL	516644		LE	516711		LE	516753		EP
516594		LE	516645		LE	516712		SB	516754		TV
516597		LE	516650		TV	516713		TV	516757		LE
516601		PL	516651		LE	516715		TV	516758		EP
516602		LE	516652		LE	516726		TV	516759		LE
516603		LE	516655		LE	516729		LE	516760		LE
516614		LE	516656		LE	216732		PL	516761		LE
516615	F	EP	516659		TV	516735		LE	516762		TV
516616		LE	516661		TV	516736		SB	516766		LE
516617		LE	516663		SB	516738		TV	516770		TV
516618		LE	516665		LE	516739		LE	516771		LE
516628		EP	516667		SB	516740		TV	516772		LE
516630		LE	516671		SB	516741		LE	516773		LE
516631		LE	516672		SB	216742		PL	516775		LE
516632		TV	516677		LE	516744		LE	516786		LE
516637		LE	516678		LE	516745		LE	516790		TV
516639		TV									

CLASS BB 17000　　　　　　　　　　　　　　　　　B-B

Similar in outline to Class BB 16500, this class is now entirely used on push-pull suburban trains from Paris Nord, Est and St. Lazare. Their replacement out of St. Lazare by Class BB 27300 is leading to movements to PL and withdrawals.

Built: 1965–68.　　　　　　　　　　**System:** 25 kV AC.
Builder: Alsthom.
Traction Motors: Two Alsthom TAB 660B1 frame-mounted monomotors.
Continuous Rating: 2940 kW.　　　　**Weight:** 78 tonnes.
Maximum Tractive Effort: 323/197 kN.
Length: 14.70 m (17001–17037), 14.94 m (17038–17105).
Wheel Diameter: 1100 mm.　　　　　**Maximum Speed:** 90/140 km/h.

Multiple working and push-pull fitted.

817001	I	AC	817019	I	AC	817036	I	AC	817053	E	PL
817002	I	AC	817020	E	AC	817037	I	AC	817054	I	PL
817003	E	AC	817021	I	AC	517038	I	AC	817055	I	PL
817004	I	AC	817022	I	AC	817039	I	PL	817056	E	AC
517006	I	AC	817023	E	AC	817040	I	AC	517057	I	AC
517007	I	AC	817024	I	AC	817041	I	AC	817058	I	AC
817008	E	PL	817025	I	AC	817042	E	AC	817059	I	PL
817009	I	AC	817026	I	AC	517043	E	AC	817060	I	PL
817010	I	AC	817027	I	AC	817044	I	AC	817061	E	AC
817011	E	AC	817028	I	AC	817045	I	AC	817062	I	PL
817012	I	AC	817029		AC	817046	I	PL	817063	I	PL
817013	I	AC	817030	I	AC	817047	I	PL	817064	I	PL
517014	I	AC	817031	I	AC	817048	I	AC	217065	I	PL
817015	I	AC	817032	I	AC	817049	E	AC	817066	I	PL
817016	I	AC	517033	I	AC	817050	I	AC	817067	I	PL
817017	I	AC	517034	I	AC	817051	I	PL	817068	I	PL
817018	E	AC	817035	I	AC	817052	I	PL	817069	I	PL

817070	E	PL	817079	I	AC	817088	I	PL	817096	I	PL
817071	I	PL	817080	E	AC	817089	I	PL	817097	I	PL
817072	I	PL	817081	I	PL	817090	E	PL	817098	I	PL
817073	I	PL	817082	I	PL	817091	I	PL	817100	E	PL
817074	I	PL	817083	E	PL	817092	E	PL	517102	I	AC
817075	I	PV	817084	I	PL	817093	E	PL	217103	I	PL
817076	I	PL	817085	E	PL	817094	I	PL	817104	I	PL
817077	I	PL	817086	E	PL	817095	E	PL	817105	I	PL
817078	I	AC	817087	I	PL						

Names:

17011	COLOMBES
17042	CHAUMONT-EN-VEXIN
17051	CORMEILLES-EN-PARISIS

CLASS BB 22200   B-B

This dual-voltage version of Classes BB 7200 and BB 15000 started off working in the Marseille. The class now works passenger and freight throughout almost the whole of France. Nine of the class were modified for operation in the Channel Tunnel – 22379/80, 22399–22405, but have now gone back to "normal" service, although 22379/80/99 are equipped for testing high-speed lines and have cable plugs on the front ends. The other locos equipped with TVM 430 are used on postal trains at 200 km/h over the LGV Sud-Est. Like BB 7200 and BB 15000 some locos are currently being fitted with time division multiplex equipment for use in push-pull mode and have numbers with an R suffix. Several locos were withdrawn after accidents.

Built: 1976–1986.
Builders: Alsthom/MTE.
Traction Motors: Two Alsthom TAB 674 frame-mounted monomotors.
Continuous Rating: 4360 kW.
Maximum Tractive Effort: 294 kN.
Wheel Diameter: 1250 mm.
Systems: 1500 V DC/25 kV AC.
Weight: 90 tonnes.
Length: 17.48 m.
Maximum Speed: 160 (200 t) km/h.

Fitted with rheostatic braking, electro-pneumatic brakes, cowcatchers and driver-guard communication.

p   Equipped for push-pull operation with Corail stock. These locos carry a letter 'R' after the number.
t   200 km/h locos equipped with TVM430 cab signalling for working parcels trains over high speed lines.

422201		VG		422229		LE	
422202		VG	OYONNAX	422230		LE	
422203		VG		422231		LE	
422204		VG		422232		LE	
422205		VG		422233		LE	
422206		VG		422234		VG	
422207		VG		422235		LE	
122208		MB		422236		LE	
522209		CB		422237		LE	
422210		VG		422238		LE	
422211		VG		122239		MB	LONS LE SAUNIER
422212	F	VG		422240		LE	
422213		VG		422241		LE	
522214	E	CB	DOLE	422242		LE	
422215		VG		422243		LE	
422216		VG	LAGNY-SUR-MARNE	422244		LE	
422217		LE		422245		LE	
422218		VG	FOURMIES	422246		LE	
422219		VG	ALBERTVILLE	422247		LE	
422221		VG		422248		LE	
422222		VG		422249		LE	VELAUX
422223		VG		422250		LE	
422224		VG		422251		LE	
422225		VG		422252		LE	
422226		LE		422254		LE	
422227		LE		422255		LE	
422228		LE		422256		LE	ROGNAC

Num			Code	Ville
422257			LE	
422258			LE	
422259			LE	
422260			LE	
422261			VG	
422262			LE	
422263			LE	
522264	E	p	CB	
422265			LE	
522266	E	p	CB	
422267			LE	LA CIOTAT
422268			LE	
522269	E	p	CB	
422270			LE	
422271			LE	
422272			LE	
422273			VG	
422274			LE	
422275	F		VG	
422276			LE	DIJON
422277			LE	IS-SUR TILLE
422278			LE	
122280			MB	HAZEBROUCK
422281			LE	
422282			VG	
422284			LE	GEVREY-CHAMBERTIN
422285			LE	CHANTILLY
422286			LE	BÉTHUNE
422287			LE	SAINT-JEAN-DE-MAURIENNE
422288			LE	LOUHANS
422289			LE	
422290			LE	
422291			LE	LA FERTÉ-ALAIS
422292			LE	
422293			LE	
122294			MB	
422295			LE	
422296			LE	
422297			VG	
422298	F		LE	
422299			LE	
422300			LE	CHALON-SUR-SAÔNE
422301			VG	VILLENEUVE-D'ASCQ
422302			LE	RIVE-DE-GIER
422303			LE	CROIX
422304	P		LE	
422305			LE	ST-RAMBERT-D'ALBON
422306			VG	
522307	E	p	CB	LE TEIL
522308	E	p	MB	GISORS
522309	E	p	CB	
522310	E	p	MB	
522311			MB	PIERREFITTE
522312			MB	ANTIBES JUAN-LES-PINS
522313	E	p	CB	DIGNE-LES-BAINS
522314	E	p	CB	TAIN-L'HERMITAGE
522315	E	p	CB	MIRAMAS
522316	E	p	CB	LOMME
122317			TP	LA-TOUR-DU-PIN
122318			MB	CARPENTRAS
122319			MB	SORGUES-SUR OUVÈZE
122320			MB	ISTRES
122321			MB	BELLEVILE
122322			MB	BOLLÈNE

Num			Code	Ville
122323			MB	CAGNES-SUR-MER
122324			MB	LANNION
122325			MB	CHAMPIGNY-SUR-MARNE
122326			MB	
122327			MB	
122328			MB	
122329			MB	QUIMPER
122330			MB	
122331			MB	
122332			MB	
122333			MB	
122334			MB	
122335			MB	
122337			MB	
222338			MB	
122339			MB	
122340			MB	CAVAILLON
122341			MB	
122342			MB	CARNOULES
222343			MB	
122344			MB	
122345			MB	
222346			TP	AUBAGNE
122347	P		TP	
222348			TP	SAINT-MARTIN-DE-CRAU
122349			TP	
522350	E	p	CB	
222351			MB	VALOGNES
222352			TP	SABLÉ-SUR-SARTHE
122353			CB	PLAISIR
122354			CB	ANCENIS
122355			CB	SÈVRES
522356	E	p	CB	LORIENT
522357			MB	
522358			TP	
522359	E	p	CB	
522360	E	p	CB	
522361	E	p	CB	
522362			CB	
522363			TP	
522364			TP	
422365	F		LE	
422366			LE	MALAKOFF
422367			LE	5ÈME REGIMENT DU GÉNIE
422368			LE	
422369	F		LE	
422370			VG	THOUARS
422371			LE	LADOIX-SERRIGNY
422372			LE	MAURIAC
422373			LE	AULNAY-SOUS-BOIS
422374			LE	NOYON
422375			LE	MÉRICOURT
422376			LE	DOUAI
422377			LE	ROUBAIX
622378	t		VG	LE QUESNOY
622379	t		VG	
622380	t		VG	
422381			LE	LE BOURGET
422382			LE	CLERMONT DE L'OISE
422383			LE	BULLY-LES-MINES
422384			LE	SAINT-ANDRÉ-LÈS-LILLE
422385			LE	LONGUEAU
422386	t		VG	BAILLEUL
422387	P		LE	LIÉVIN

422388		LE	SOMAIN	522397		CB	PAGNY-SUR-MEUSE
422389		LE	COMINES	522398		CB	COUDERKERQUE-BRANCHE
422390		LE	LESQUIN	622399	t	VG	MORMANT
522391	E p	CB	HIRSON	522400		CB	MONTIGNY-EN-OSTREVENT
522392		CB	CHARLES TELLIER	422401	t	VG	MOULINS
			PÈRE DU FROID	522402	E p	MB	SAINT-DIÉ-DES-VOSGES
522393		MB	PONT-À-VENDIN	622403	t	VG	NEUVES-MAISONS
522394	E p	CB	JOINVILLE-LE-PONT	522404	E p	MB	LES PAVILLONS-SOUS-BOIS
522395	E p	CB	NEUILLY-PLAISANCE	422405	t	VG	VILLIERS-SUR-MARNE
522396		CB	BAIE-DE-SOMME				

CLASS BB 25150 — Bo-Bo

Similar to Class BB 25100 (now all withdrawn) from which it was developed, an early dual-voltage design with the same body as Class BB 16000. The last few Chambéry locos work local passenger trains over Alpine lines. The class originally had three sub-series but all remaining locos are from the most recent batch with a large bodyside grille. BB 25180, 25183, 25184, 25194 and 25195 were converted to Class BB 25200.

Built: 1976–77.
Builder: MTE.
Traction Motors: Four Jeumont TO 136-8.
Continuous Rating: 3400 kW (1500 V)/4130 kW (25 kV).
Weight: 89 tonnes.
Maximum Tractive Effort: 367 kN.
Wheel Diameter: 1250 mm.
Systems: 1500 V DC/25 kV AC.
Length: 16.73 m.
Maximum Speed: 130 km/h.

Fitted with rheostatic braking. 25186–95 are fitted with snowploughs.

525176	F	CB		525182	F	CB		525188		CB		525192		CB
525179	F	CB		525186		CB		525190		CB		525193		CB

CLASS BB 25200 — Bo-Bo

A faster version of Class BB 25150, being a dual-voltage version of Classes BB 9200 and BB 16000. Most of the class were downgraded to freight work in the 1990s and operated from Rennes depot. Fret SNCF has now withdrawn all of its locos and many have been sold to Romanian operators. Remaining locos are used on fast TER services in the Alps, all but one being equipped for push-pull operation with Corail stock. 25201/2 were renumbered 25252/3 to keep t.d.m.-equipped locos in the same batch. BB 25254 to 25259 were converted from 25184, 25194, 25195, 25225, 25180 and 25183 respectively. Classes BB 25150 and BB 25200 are expected to be replaced by Class BB 22200 in the near future.

Built: 1965–67/1974*.
Builder: MTE.
Traction Motors: Four Jeumont TO 136-8.
Continuous Rating: 3400 kW (1500 V)/4130 kW (25 kV).
Weight: 85 (89*) tonnes.
Maximum Tractive Effort: 304 kN.
Wheel Diameter: 1250 mm.
Systems: 1500 V DC/25 kV AC.
Length: 16.20 (16.68*) m.
Maximum Speed: 130 (160 p) km/h.
Non-Standard Livery: N Preserved by the SNCF in original blue livery.

p Equipped for push-pull operation with Corail stock. These locos carry a letter 'R' after the number.

525213	F		CB		525240	P	p	VE		525250	P	p*	VE		525256	E	p*	VE
525236	N	p	VE		525241	E	p	VE		525251	P	p*	VE		525257	E	p	VE
525237	P	p	VE		525244	E	p	VE		525252	E	p	VE		525258	E	p*	VE
525238	E	p	VE		525246	P	p	VE		525254	E	p*	VE		525259	E	p*	VE
525239	P	p	VE		525249	P	p*	VE		525255	E	p*	VE					

Names:

525250	VITRÉ	525252	LE MANS
525251	VERSAILLES		

CLASS BB 25500 B-B

A dual-voltage version of Classes BB 8500 and BB 17000 and built in three batches with detail variations in styling and cabs. Like the latter, early locos had small cabs and were unpopular with drivers and so were withdrawn quickly, some being sold to Romania. The class lost all freight duties in 2006. Most now work push-pull TER trains around Marseille, Lyon, Dijon, Rennes and, since 2007, Strasbourg. A number are expected to move to Lens to replace Class BB 16500.

Built: 1964–76. **Systems:** 1500 V DC/25 kV AC.
Builder: Alsthom.
Traction Motors: Two Alsthom TAB 660B1 frame-mounted monomotors.
Continuous Rating: 2940 kW. **Maximum Tractive Effort:** 330/197 kN.
Wheel Diameter: 1100 mm. **Maximum Speed:** 100/140 km/h.
Weight: 80 tonnes (25546–55), 77 tonnes (25556–85), 81 tonnes (25588–25694).
Length: 14.94 m (25565–85), 15.57 m (25588–25694).

Rheostatic braking. Multiple working and push-pull fitted.
e Fitted with snowploughs.

525546	P	VE	825609	E	MR	525638		DP	525666			VE
525547	P	VE	825610	I	MR	525639		DP	525667			MB
525549	P	RS	825611	I	MR	525640		DP	525668			MB
525550	P	VE	525612	E	SB	525641		DP	525669			MB
525553	P	VE	525613	I	SB	525642		MB	525670			VE
525554	P	RS	525614		MB	525643		RS	525671		e	RS
525555	P	VE	525615	F	RS	525644		MB	525673	F	e	DP
425556		AC	525616		SB	525645		MB	525674		e	RS
525574		RS	525617	P	MB	525646		MB	525675		e	VE
525585	P	VE	525618		MB	525647		VE	525677		e	MB
525588		SB	525619		MB	525648		MB	525678			MB
525590		DP	525620		VE	525649		VE	525679			VE
525591		SB	525621		MB	525650		RS	525680			VE
525592		MB	525622		VE	525651		MB	525681			VE
525594		VE	525623		VE	525652		MB	525682			DP
525595	P	VE	525624		VE	525653		DP	525683			DP
525596	I	SB	525625		RS	525654		VE	525684			DP
525597	I	VE	525626		VE	525655		RS	525685			DP
525598	I	MR	525627		VE	525656		VE	525686			DP
525599	I	VE	525628		VE	525657		VE	525687			DP
525600	I	VE	525629		VE	525658		MB	525688			DP
525601	I	VE	525630	P	VE	525659		MB	525689			RS
525602	I	MR	525631		LE	525660		VE	525690			RS
525603	E	SB	525633		MB	525661		MB	525691			RS
525605	E	MR	525634		DP	525662		VE	525692			RS
525606	I	SB	525635		MB	525663		VE	525693			RS
525607	E	SB	525636		VE	525664		VE	525694		e	RS
825608	E	MR	525637		RS	525665	e	MB				

CLASS BB 26000 B-B

These dual-voltage locomotives feature synchronous motors and are known as "Sybics" (**Sy**nchronous-**bi**courant). The original order for 264 locos was cut by 30 which were replaced by 30 Class BB 36000. Following the division between passenger and freight activities, their zones of operation have changed considerably. Passenger locos, often operating at 200 km/h, can still be found on Paris–Cherbourg, Paris–Limoges–Toulouse (some now allocated to Toulouse), and Nancy–Strasbourg–Mulhouse–Basel lines. The latter are now allocated to Strasbourg and operate in push-pull mode at 200 km/h by specially-equipped 26140 to 26153 which carry an "R" suffix. Freight locos now work mainly south of Paris, whereas they dominated in the north in the past. Locos from 26188 onwards have a third, central headlight. Many names have been transferred from Class CC 6500 locos after their withdrawal.

Built: 1988–98. **Systems:** 1500 V DC/25 kV AC.
Builder: Alsthom.
Traction Motors: Two Jeumont-Schneider STS 105-37-8 frame-mounted three-phase synchronous monomotors.

Continuous Rating: 5600 kW. **Weight:** 91 tonnes.
Maximum Tractive Effort: 320 kN. **Length:** 17.48 m.
Wheel Diameter: 1250 mm. **Maximum Speed:** 200 km/h.
Class Specific Livery: S Two-tone grey with orange front ends.
Non-Standard Livery: N Alsace Region livery.

m equipped with MEMOR for operation in Luxembourg.
p Equipped for push-pull operation with Corail stock. These locos carry a letter 'R' after the number.

526001	S	VG	GIEN		126054	S	TL	JARNY
526002	S	VG	SOUFFELWEYERSHEIM		126055	S	TL	
526003	S	VG	FONTVIEILLE		126056	S	TL	
126004	S	VG	CERNAY		126057	S	TL	
126005	E	VG	NEMOURS/ST PIERRE-		126058	S	VG	
			LES-NEMOURS		126059	S	VG	
526006	S	VG	MUSÉE FRANÇAIS DU		126060	S	VG	
			CHEMIN DE FER		426061	S	VG	
226007	S	VG	BÉNING-LÈS-SAINT-AVOLD		426062	S	VG	
226008	E	VG			426063	S	VG	
226009	S	VG	LONGVIC-EN-BOURGOGNE		426064	S	VG	
226010	S	VG	VALLORBE		426065	S	VG	
226011	S	VG	LE PIENNOIS		426066	S	VG	
226012	S	VG	HAGONDANGE		426067	S	VG	
226013	S	VG	MIRAMAS		426068	S	VG	
226014	P	VG	DOLE		426069	S	VG	
226015	S	VG	FLORANGE		126070	N	TL	
226016	S	VG	CAUSSADE TARN ET GARONNE		126071	S	TL	
226017	S	VG			126072	S	TL	ISSOUDUN
226018	S	VG			126073	S	DP	
126019	S	VG			126074	S	DP	
126020	S	VG	MENTON		126075	S	DP	
126021	S	VG			426076	S	VG	
126022	S	VG			426077	S	VG	
126023	S	VG			426078	S	VG	
126024	S	VG			426079	S	VG	
126025	S	VG			426080	S	VG	
126026	S	VG			426081	S	VG	
126027	S	VG			426082	S	VG	
126028	S	VG	NARBONNE		426083	S	VG	
226029	S	VG			426085	S	VG	
226030	S	VG			426086	F	VG	COGNAC
226031	S	VG			426087	S	VG	ARCACHON
226032	S	VG			426088	S	VG	REMIREMONT
226033	S	VG	LAVAL		426089	S	VG	
226034	S	VG			426090	S	VG	AIX-LES-BAINS
226035	S	VG			426091	S	VG	
126036	S	VG			426092	S	VG	
126037	S	VG			426093	S	VG	
126038	S	VG			426094	S	VG	
126039	S	VG	LIMOGES		426095	S	VG	
126040	S	VG			426096	F	VG	
126041	S	TL	MÉZIDON-CANON		426097	S	VG	
126042	S	TL			426098	S	AV	VIERZON
126043	S	TL	EMERAINVILLE		426099	S	AV	
126044	S	TL	PONTAULT-COMBAULT		426100	S	VG	POMPEY
126045	S	TL			426101	S	AV	
126046	S	TL	SELESTAT		426102	S	AV	
126047	S	TL	JARVILLE		426103	S	AV	
126048	P	TL			426104	S	AV	
126049	S	TL			426105	S	AV	
126050	S	TL			426106	S	AV	
126051	S	TL			426107	S	AV	
126052	S	TL	SAINT DIZIER		426108	S	AV	IVRY-SUR-SEINE
126053	S	TL			426109	S	AV	

426110	S		AV		426172	S	AV	
426111	S		AV		426173	S	AV	
426112	S		AV		426174	S	AV	
426113	S		AV	BEAUTIRAN	426175	S	AV	
426114	S		AV		426176	S	AV	
426115	S		AV		426177	S	AV	
426116	S		AV	RUFFEC	426178	S	AV	
426117	S		AV		426179	S	AV	
426118	S		AV		426180	S	AV	
426119	S		AV		426181	S	AV	
426120	S		AV		426182	S	AV	JEUMONT
426121	S		AV	COMPIÈGNE/	426183	S	AV	
				Margny-les-Compiègne	426184	F	AV	BOURGOGNE
426122	S		AV		426185	S	AV	
426123	S		AV		426186	S	AV	
426124	S		AV		426187	S	AV	
426125	S		AV	CHOISY-LE-ROI	426188	S	AV	
426126	S		AV		426189	S	AV	
426127	S		AV		426190	S	AV	SAINT CHAMOND
426128	S		AV	AMBOISE	426191	S	AV	GAGNY
426129	S		AV		426192	S	AV	
426130	S		AV		426193	S	AV	
426131	S		AV		426194	S	AV	
426132	S		AV	CARCASSONNE	426195	S	AV	
426133	S		AV		426196	S	AV	BREST
426134	S		AV		426197	S	AV	CHÂTEAUROUX
426135	S		AV		426198	S	AV	SAINTES
426136	S		AV	OULLINS	426199	S	AV	SAINT PIERRE DES CORPS
426137	S		AV		426200	S	AV	
126138	S		DP		426201	S	AV	RIORGES
126139	S		DP		426202	S	AV	
526140	S	p	SB		426203	S	AV	ANGOULÊME
526141	S	p	SB	LIBOURNE	426204	S	AV	
526142	S	p	SB		426205	S	AV	
526143	S	p	SB		426206	S	AV	CASTELNAUDARY
526144	S	p	SB		426207	S	AV	SALON-DE-PROVENCE
526145	S	p	SB		426208	S	AV	PAMIERS
526146	S	p	SB		426209	S	AV	SAINTE-FOY-LA-GRANDE
526147	S	p	SB		426210	S	AV	VITRY-SUR-SEINE
526148	S	p	SB		426211	S	AV	
526149	S	p	SB	ORLEANS	426212	S	AV	
526150	S	p	SB		426213	S	AV	
526151	S	p	SB		426214	S	AV	
526152	S	p	SB		426215	S	AV	
526153	S	p	SB		426216	S	AV	
126154	S		DP		426217	S	AV	
126155	S		DP		426218	S	AV	
126156	S		DP		426219	S	AV	
126157	S		DP		426220	S	AV	
126158	S		DP		426221	S	AV	MONTAUBAN
126159	S		DP		426222	S	AV	
126160	P		DP		426223	S	AV	
126161	S	m	DP		426224	S	AV	CHÂTELLERAULT
126162	S	m	DP		426225	S	AV	
126163	E	m	DP		426226	S	AV	
126164	E	m	DP		426227	P	AV	
126165	S	m	DP		426228	S	AV	
126166	S	m	DP		426229	S	AV	
126167	S	m	DP		426230	S	AV	AGEN
126168	S	m	DP		426231	S	AV	
426169	S		AV		426232	S	AV	NANTES
426170	S		AV		426233	S	AV	
426171	S		AV		426234	S	AV	

CLASS BB 27000 Bo-Bo

These are Alstom Prima electric locomotives, being dual-voltage whilst BB 37000 are the tri-voltage version. Class BB 27000 work freight over the whole of north and east France plus the corridor through Dijon to Lyon and to Rouen and Caen in the west. They are now increasingly appearing south of Paris. Equipped for operation in multiple, with a small number of such duties on trains such as Dunkerque–Lorraine iron ore traffic.

Built: 2001–2005.
Builder: Alstom.
Continuous Rating: 4200 kW.
Maximum Tractive Effort: 320 kN.
Wheel Diameter:

Systems: 1500 V DC/25 kV AC.

Weight: 90 tonnes.
Length: 19.72 m.
Maximum Speed: 140 km/h.

427001	F	TV	427046	F	TV	427091	F	LE	427136	F	LE
427002	F	TV	427047	F	TV	427092	F	LE	427137	F	LE
427003	F	TV	427048	F	TV	427093	F	LE	427138	F	LE
427004	F	TV	427049	F	TV	427094	F	LE	427139	F	LE
427005	F	TV	427050	F	TV	427095	F	LE	427140	F	LE
427006	F	TV	427051	F	TV	427096	F	LE	427141	F	LE
427007	F	TV	427052	F	TV	427097	F	LE	427142	F	LE
427008	F	TV	427053	F	TV	427098	F	LE	427143	F	LE
427009	F	TV	427054	F	TV	427099	F	LE	427144	F	LE
427010	F	TV	427055	F	TV	427100	F	LE	427145	F	LE
427011	F	TV	427056	F	TV	427101	F	LE	427146	F	LE
427012	F	TV	427057	F	TV	427102	F	LE	427147	F	LE
427013	F	TV	427058	F	TV	427103	F	LE	427148	F	LE
427014	F	TV	427059	F	TV	427104	F	LE	427149	F	LE
427015	F	TV	427060	F	TV	427105	F	LE	427150	F	LE
427016	F	TV	427061	F	TV	427106	F	LE	427151	F	LE
427017	F	TV	427062	F	TV	427107	F	LE	427152	F	LE
427018	F	TV	427063	F	LE	427108	F	LE	427153	F	LE
427019	F	TV	427064	F	LE	427109	F	LE	427154	F	LE
427020	F	TV	427065	F	LE	427110	F	LE	427155	F	LE
427021	F	TV	427066	F	LE	427111	F	LE	427156	F	LE
427022	F	TV	427067	F	LE	427112	F	LE	427157	F	LE
427023	F	TV	427068	F	LE	427113	F	LE	427158	F	LE
427024	F	TV	427069	F	LE	427114	F	LE	427159	F	LE
427025	F	TV	427070	F	LE	427115	F	LE	427160	F	LE
427026	F	TV	427071	F	LE	427116	F	LE	427161	F	LE
427027	F	TV	427072	F	LE	427117	F	LE	427162	F	LE
427028	F	TV	427073	F	LE	427118	F	LE	427163	F	LE
427029	F	TV	427074	F	LE	427119	F	LE	427164	F	LE
427030	F	TV	427075	F	LE	427120	F	LE	427165	F	LE
427031	F	TV	427076	F	LE	427121	F	LE	427166	F	LE
427032	F	TV	427077	F	LE	427122	F	LE	427167	F	LE
427033	F	TV	427078	F	LE	427123	F	LE	427168	F	LE
427034	F	TV	427079	F	LE	427124	F	LE	427169	F	LE
427035	F	TV	427080	F	LE	427125	F	LE	427170	F	LE
427036	F	TV	427081	F	LE	427126	F	LE	427171	F	LE
427037	F	TV	427082	F	LE	427127	F	LE	427172	F	LE
427038	F	TV	427083	F	LE	427128	F	LE	427173	F	LE
427039	F	TV	427084	F	LE	427129	F	LE	427174	F	LE
427040	F	TV	427085	F	LE	427130	F	LE	427175	F	LE
427041	F	TV	427086	F	LE	427131	F	LE	427176	F	LE
427042	F	TV	427087	F	LE	427132	F	LE	427177	F	LE
427043	F	TV	427088	F	LE	427133	F	LE	427178	F	LE
427044	F	TV	427089	F	LE	427134	F	LE	427179	F	LE
427045	F	TV	427090	F	LE	427135	F	LE	427180	F	LE

Names:

27001	Port Autonome de Marseille		27062	MÉRICOURT

CLASS BB 27300 Bo-Bo

This is a version of Class BB 27000 equipped to power push-pull trains of double-deck stock in the Paris region. The first batch of 22 locos are allocated to Montrouge for services from Paris Montparnasse to Dreux and Mantes-la-Jolie where they replaced Class BB 25500. The remainder will go to Achères for services from Paris St. Lazare to Mantes-la-Jolie where they are replacing Class BB 17000. Trains at St Lazare are having to be shortened by one coach as nobody noticed that a BB 27300 was almost five metres longer than a BB 17000 and could not fit between buffer stops and starting signals! The initial order was for 60 locos but an extra four were added in 2008. Apart from the livery, the main visible differences compared with BB 27000 are the line of six cable sockets on the right of the front end. Not equipped for multiple operation.

Details as Class BB 27000, except:
Built : 2006–2008.

827301	S	MR	827317	S	MR	827333	S	AC	827349	S	AC
827302	S	MR	827318	S	MR	827334	S	AC	827350	S	AC
827303	S	MR	827319	S	MR	827335	S	AC	827351	S	AC
827304	S	MR	827320	S	MR	827336	S	AC	827352	S	AC
827305	S	MR	827321	S	MR	827337	S	AC	827353	S	AC
827306	S	MR	827322	S	MR	827338	S	AC	827354	S	AC
827307	S	MR	827323	S	AC	827339	S	AC	827355	S	AC
827308	S	MR	827324	S	AC	827340	S	AC	827356	S	AC
827309	S	MR	827325	S	AC	827341	S	AC	827357	S	
827310	S	MR	827326	S	AC	827342	S	AC	827358	S	
827311	S	MR	827327	S	AC	827343	S	AC	827359	S	
827312	S	MR	827328	S	AC	827344	S	AC	827360	S	
827313	S	MR	827329	S	AC	827345	S	AC	827361	S	
827314	S	MR	827330	S	AC	827346	S	AC	827362	S	
827315	S	MR	827331	S	AC	827347	S	AC	827363	S	
827316	S	MR	827332	S	AC	827348	S	AC	827364	S	

CLASS BB 36000   Bo-Bo

After ordering 264 Class BB 26000 "Sybic" locos from GEC Alsthom, SNCF decided to ask for a change to the contract and the last 30 locos (plus 30 more ordered after) were built as completely different three-voltage locos, with asynchronous motors driving each axle. In order to accommodate two traction motors per bogie, the locos are slightly longer than Sybics. The class is nicknamed "Astride" by SNCF, the previous named "Asytrit" having been dropped.

Originally designed as a "universal" locomotive, the class only operates freight services. Locos were originally expected to operate through from Belgium to Italy but they are now split into two batches. The first 30, in red and grey livery, work from Somain and Aulnoye in the Lille area into Belgium, reaching Antwerpen daily. The second 30 locos, in green and grey and now all numbered in the BB 36300 series, work from Dijon into Italy. Of the latter, 12 locos are also equipped to work the Modalohr service between Aiton and Torino, two locos heading the trains with a Corail coach sandwiched between them! The locos working in Italy now carry the numbers E.436 031 to E.436 060 with the suffix MF, for Monferail, the name of the company which holds SNCF's operating licence. Locos now reach Alessandria and Domodossola in Italy.

Built: 1996–2002
Builder: GEC-Alsthom.
Traction Motors: 4 FXA 4559 three-phase asynchronous.
Continuous rating: 5600 kW.
Maximum Tractive Effort: 320 kN.
Continuous Tractive Effort: 250 kN.
Wheel Diameter: 1250 mm.
Class Specific Livery: S Grey with red front ends and roof band and dark grey side band.

Systems: 1500 V DC/3000 V DC/25 kV AC.

Weight: 89 tonnes.
Length: 19.11 m.

Maximum Speed: 140 km/h.

Regenerative and rheostatic braking. BB 36300 can operate in multiple.

36000 Series. Equipped to operate in Belgium.

436001	S	DP	436009	S	DP	436017	S	DP	436024	S	DP
436002	S	DP	436010	S	DP	436018	S	DP	436025	S	DP
436003	S	DP	436011	S	DP	436019	S	DP	436026	S	DP
436004	S	DP	436012	S	DP	436020	S	DP	436027	S	DP
436005	S	DP	436013	S	DP	436021	S	DP	436028	S	DP
436006	S	DP	436014	S	DP	436022	S	DP	436029	S	DP
436007	S	DP	436015	S	DP	436023	S	DP	436030	S	DP
436008	S	DP	436016	S	DP						

Names:

36003	MAUBEUGE/RATINGEN	36012	YUTZ
36005	HIRSON/CHARLEROI	36013	BONNENCONTRE
36006	VILLE DE CHAMPIGNEULLES	36029	LONGWY
36008	BLAINVILLE-DAMELEVIÈRES		

36300 Series. Equipped to operate in Italy. Fitted for multiple working.

Notes:

36331 to 36338 and 36351 to 36360 are hired to Fret SNCF's Italian subsidiary SFI.
36339 and 36348 are now owned by Trenitalia.
m Equipped for Modalohr service.

436331	F		DP	436339	F	m	DP	436347	F	m	DP	436354	F	DP
436332	F		DP	436340	F	m	DP	436348	F	m	DP	436355	F	DP
436333	F		DP	436341	F	m	DP	436349	F	m	DP	436356	F	DP
436334	F		DP	436342	F	m	DP	436350	F	m	DP	436357	F	DP
436335	F		DP	436343	F	m	DP	436351	F		DP	436358	F	DP
436336	F		DP	436344	F	m	DP	436352	F		DP	436359	F	DP
436337	F		DP	436345	F	m	DP	436353	F		DP	436360	F	DP
436338	F		DP	436346	F	m	DP							

Names:

36331   BONS EN CHABLAIS/CASTIONE DELLA PRESOLANA
36342   ST ÉTIENNE-ANDRÉZIEU–1RE LIGNE DE CHEMIN DE FER D'EUROPE CONTINENTALE 1827–2002

CLASS BB 37000   Bo-Bo

This is a tri-voltage version of Class BB 27000 with the addition of 15 kV AC equipment for use in Germany and Switzerland. Apart from electrical equipment and an extra pantograph, the locos are identical to their dual-voltage sisters. BB 37021 to 37040 are equipped for operation in Germany and haul freight between the Woippy/Metz area and Köln Gremberg. BB 37051 to 37060 are equipped to operate within Switzerland and work freight from Mulhouse to Zürich and Buchs SG on the border with Austria. The other members of the class can only operate through to Basel in Switzerland and are mainly employed shuttling freight between Luxembourg and Basel via Metz, Strasbourg and Mulhouse within the Sibelit partnership involving Belgian, Luxembourg and Swiss Railways. BB 37007 was severely damaged in a head-on crash on the border with Luxembourg on 11 October 2006 and was expected to be withdrawn but may now be rebuilt.

Details as BB 27000 except:

Built: 2004–2006.   **Systems:** 1500 V DC/15 kV AC/25 kV AC.

437001	F	TV	437016	F	TV	437031	F	TV	437046	F	TV
437002	F	TV	437017	F	TV	437032	F	TV	437047	F	TV
437003	F	TV	437018	F	TV	437033	F	TV	437048	F	TV
437004	F	TV	437019	F	TV	437034	F	TV	437049	F	TV
437005	F	TV	437020	F	TV	437035	F	TV	437050	F	TV
437006	F	TV	437021	F	TV	437036	F	TV	437051	F	TV
437007	F	TV	437022	F	TV	437037	F	TV	437052	F	TV
437008	F	TV	437023	F	TV	437038	F	TV	437053	F	TV
437009	F	TV	437024	F	TV	437039	F	TV	437054	F	TV
437010	F	TV	437025	F	TV	437040	F	TV	437055	F	TV
437011	F	TV	437026	F	TV	437041	F	TV	437056	F	TV
437012	F	TV	437027	F	TV	437042	F	TV	437057	F	TV
437013	F	TV	437028	F	TV	437043	F	TV	437058	F	TV
437014	F	TV	437029	F	TV	437044	F	TV	437059	F	TV
437015	F	TV	437030	F	TV	437045	F	TV	437060	F	TV

Name: BB 37039 CUSTINES/BÖBINGEN

CLASS BB 80000   Bo-Bo

These are a modified version of Class BB 8100 converted for empty coaching stock movements from Masséna to Paris Austerlitz. Class BB 8100 was a post-War development of Class BB 300 (ordered by the PO-Midi railway pre-War) which was also exported to other countries, such as the Netherlands (Class 1100). Modifications are restricted to a reduction in maximum speed, removal of multiple operation cables and equipment with radio. In the case of locos converted from two locos, the new loco is a combination of the body of one and the bogies of the other. Conversions stopped after 12 locos of 27 originally programmed. Instead, Class BB 8500 were downgraded for this work.

BB 8120, 8216 and 8216 are still at Avignon and occasionally used to scrape ice of the overhead wires.

Built: 1947–55.   **System:** 1500 V DC.
Modified: 1995–98 by SNCF Béziers works.
Builder-Mechanical Parts: Alsthom/Schneider-Jeumont/CGC.
Builder-Electrical Parts: Alsthom/Siemens/Jeumont/Oerlikon.
Traction Motors: Four Alsthom M1 TC.
Continuous Rating: 2100 kW.   **Weight:** 92 tonnes.
Maximum Tractive Effort: 152 kN.   **Length:** 12.93 m.
Wheel Diameter: 1400 mm.   **Maximum Speed:** 100 km/h.

280004	(8175)	VG	180007	(8121)	VG	280010	(8188)	VG
180005	(8139)	VG	180009	(8162)	VG	180012	(8193)	VG

1.2. SNCF DIESEL LOCOMOTIVES

Note: All diesel locomotives are livery **D** (blue and grey with white lining) unless otherwise shown

CLASS BB 60000   Bo-Bo

Fret SNCF has ordered 160 of these low powered locomotives in order to replace Class BB 63500, and to a lesser extent BB 66000, on trip freights and heavy shunting. The first locos went into service in the Rouen, Le Havre and Caen areas before appearing in the Paris region. One problem with the class is the higher weight than Class BB 63500 given the poor state of many branch lines. The design is based on Alstom's Class 311.1 for RENFE and Class Am 841 for SBB but there are many differences between these and the SNCF locos, particularly the MTU engine replaced by a Caterpiller and a redesigned cab. The order for the locos went to Alstom's Valencia, Spain factory, but the company sold this plant shortly after to Vossloh.

Built: 2006–.
Builder: Alstom/Vossloh Espagna. Works numbers 2301 to 2460.
Engine: Caterpillar CAT 3508B of 1000 kW (CAT 3508C of 1000 kW to be used in later locos).
Transmission: Electric. Four Type 6FRA 3055A three–phase asynchronous traction motors.
Heating: None.   **Weight:** 76 tonnes.
Maximum Tractive Effort: 170 kN.   **Length:** 15.05 m.
Wheel Diameter: **Maximum Speed:** 100 km/h.
Multiple Working: Within class.

460001	F			460041	F	SO		460081	F		460121	F
460002	F			460042	F	SO		460082	F		460122	F
460003	F			460043	F	SO		460083	F		460123	F
460004	F	SO		460044	F	SO		460084	F		460124	F
460005	F	SO		460045	F	SO		460085	F		460125	F
460006	F	SO		460046	F	SO		460086	F		460126	F
460007	F	SO		460047	F	SO		460087	F		460127	F
460008	F	SO		460048	F	SO		460088	F		460128	F
460009	F	SO		460049	F	SO		460089	F		460129	F
460010	F	SO		460050	F	SO		460090	F		460130	F
460011	F	SO		460051	F	SO		460091	F		460131	F
460012	F	SO		460052	F	SO		460092	F		460132	F
460013	F	SO		460053	F	SO		460093	F		460133	F
460014	F	SO		460054	F	SO		460094	F		460134	F
460015	F	SO		460055	F	SO		460095	F		460135	F
460016	F	SO		460056	F	SO		460096	F		460136	F
460017	F	SO		460057	F	SO		460097	F		460137	F
460018	F	SO		460058	F	SO		460098	F		460138	F
460019	F	SO		460059	F	SO		460099	F		460139	F
460020	F	SO		460060	F	SO		460100	F		460140	F
460021	F	SO		460061	F	SO		460101	F		460141	F
460022	F	SO		460062	F	SO		460102	F		460142	F
460023	F	SO		460063	F	SO		460103	F		460143	F
460024	F	SO		460064	F	SO		460104	F		460144	F
460025	F	SO		460065	F	SO		460105	F		460145	F
460026	F	SO		460066	F	SO		460106	F		460146	F
460027	F	SO		460067	F			460107	F		460147	F
460028	F	SO		460068	F			460108	F		460148	F
460029	F	SO		460069	F	SO		460109	F		460149	F
460030	F	SO		460070	F	SO		460110	F		460150	F
460031	F	SO		460071	F	SO		460111	F		460151	F
460032	F	SO		460072	F			460112	F		460152	F
460033	F	SO		460073	F	SO		460113	F		460153	F
460034	F	SO		460074	F	SO		460114	F		460154	F
460035	F	SO		460075	F	SO		460115	F		460155	F
460036	F	SO		460076	F	SO		460116	F		460156	F
460037	F	SO		460077	F	SO		460117	F		460157	F
460038	F	SO		460078	F			460118	F		460158	F
460039	F	SO		460079	F	SO		460119	F		460159	F
460040	F	SO		460080	F			460120	F		460160	F

CLASS BB 61000 — B-B

Faced with a shortage of diesel locomotives in 2000, Fret SNCF hired 23 Vossloh G1206 locos from Angel Trains Cargo and numbered them as Class BB 61000. As the locos are equipped to operate in Germany, they were allocated to Strasbourg and put to work on local trip freights plus cross-border freights to Ludwigshafen and Saarbrücken. The lease finishes at the end of 2008. In late 2007, VFLI started to use some of the class from Corbehem to Le Havre, Béning to Dillingen in Germany, then Dunkerque to Lens and Chauny. VFLI has taken over further locos of this batch and will hire more G1206 locos from Angel Trains.

Builder: Vossloh, Kiel.
Built: 2001–2003.
Engine: Caterpillar 3512 B DI-TA of 1500 kW.
Transmission: Hydraulic. Voith L5r4 zU2.   **Wheel Diameter:** 1000 mm.
Maximum Tractive Effort: 254 kN.   **Length over Buffers:** 14.70 m.
Weight: 87.3 tonnes.   **Maximum Speed:** 100 km/h.
Works numbers: 1001118, 121, 122, 124, 126, 128, 143, 144, 372, 376 and 377 respectively.

461001	F	SB	461004	F	SB	461007	F	SB	461012	F	SB
461002	F	SB	461005	F	SB	461008	F	SB	461013	F	SB
461003	F	SB	461006	F	SB	461011	F	SB			

CLASS BB 63000 — Bo-Bo

Classes BB 63000, BB 63400 and BB 63500 are all virtually identical from the outside and once formed a family of over 800 locomotives. These low-powered locomotives are found on station pilot, freight trips and general shunting duties and appear all over France. Following loss of freight traffic and replacement by Class Y 8000 shunters, Class BB 63000 are now almost all withdrawn. Several have been sold into industrial use, preserved or transferred to VFLI which has rebuilt some locos. A number have been converted to Class BB 64800.

Built: 1953–64.   **Builder:** Brissonneau & Lotz.
Engine: Sulzer 6LDA22C (440 kW) (63074–108), Sulzer 6LDA22D (535 kW) (63131–193), Sulzer 6LDA22E (550 kW) (63196–250).
Transmission: Electric. Four B&L 453-29 traction motors.
Heating: None.   **Weight:** 64–69 tonnes.
Maximum Tractive Effort: 167 kN.   **Length:** 14.68 m.
Wheel Diameter: 1050 mm.   **Maximum Speed:** 90 km/h.

*   Based at Modane for Frejus tunnel rescue train.

163095	J	NC	663160	J	*	CB	163181	J	NC	163248	V	NC
163136	J	NC	263165	J	VG	263240	V	VG			

CLASSES BB 63400 & BB 63500 — Bo-Bo

These two classes are identical but Class BB 63400 are numbered separately as they were financed by the Eurofima organisation. The class is a more powerful version of Class BB 63000 but with many detail variations within the class, the most important being the batches which can work in multiple. A number of the class were converted into Class BB 64700. Locos in poor condition are now being withdrawn as Class BB 60000 are delivered. Some are being transferred to VFLI and rebuilt.

Built: 1956–71.   **Builder:** Brissonneau & Lotz.
Engine: SACM MGO V12SH (605 kW).
Transmission: Electric. Four B&L 453-29 traction motors.
Heating: None.   **Weight:** 64–68 tonnes.
Maximum Tractive Effort: 167 kN.   **Length:** 14.68 m.
Wheel Diameter: 1050 mm.   **Maximum Speed:** 90 km/h.
Non-Standard livery: N Yellow for Infra department.

m   Multiple working fitted.
e   E.t.h. fitted.
c   Equipped with cab signalling for maintenance work on TGV Atlantique line.

Class BB 63400.

663401	J	LN	663404	V	DP	163406	J	NB	463408	J	VE
463402	J	VG	163405	J	NB	663407	J	LN	663409	V	LN

463410 **J** SO	463413 **J** TP	463416 **J** VG	663423 **V** VG
663411 **V** AC	463415 **J** VG	663418 **V** VG	

Class BB 63500.

463501 **J** VE	663609 **J** BD	463723 **J** m SO	463828 **J** m MZ
463502 **J** LE	463610 **J** VE	463724 **J** m TP	463829 **J** m LE
663503 **J** AC	463613 **J** AV	463727 **J** m LE	463830 **J** m VE
663505 **J** DP	463614 **J** SO	463728 **J** m SB	463831 **J** m VE
663508 **J** LE	663617 **N** MZ	463730 **J** m LE	463832 **J** m TP
663510 **J** VG	663619 **J** MZ	463731 **J** m SO	463833 **J** m MZ
663517 **J** MZ	663620 **J** VE	463732 **J** m SO	663835 **J** m DP
663518 **V** TP	663623 **J** TP	463733 **J** m TP	463836 **J** m DP
663519 **J** DP	463624 **J** VE	463736 **J** m SO	463837 **J** m SO
463521 **J** LE	463629 **J** VE	463737 **J** m BD	463838 **F** m TP
463522 **J** LE	463630 **J** VG	663738 **J** m BD	463839 **J** m TP
663523 **J** VE	663631 **J** LN	463740 **J** m SB	663840 **J** m MZ
463525 **J** LE	663632 **V** LN	463741 **J** m LE	463841 **J** m LE
663526 **V** SO	663634 **V** VE	463744 **J** m VE	463842 **J** m TP
663528 **J** MZ	663636 **V** AC	663746 **J** m LN	663843 **J** m MZ
463529 **J** MZ	663641 **J** VE	463748 **J** m SO	663844 **J** m MZ
663530 **J** SO	463642 **J** LE	463750 **J** m LE	663845 **J** m DP
163532 **J** AC	663643 **V** MZ	463754 **J** SO	663846 **V** m DP
663536 **J** TP	663645 **V** DP	663755 **V** VE	663847 **J** m MZ
463538 **F** DP	663647 **J** BD	463756 **J** SB	663849 **J** m MZ
663542 **V** VG	663650 **J** SO	663757 **V** TP	663850 **J** m MZ
163544 **J** MB	663652 **V** AC	663758 **J** AV	463851 **J** m DP
463550 **F** VE	663654 **J** BD	663759 **J** VE	463853 **J** m TP
663552 **V** BD	463655 **J** NV	663760 **V** AC	463855 **J** m TP
463553 **J** AC	163660 **J** VG	663762 **J** TP	663856 **J** m AC
463554 **J** VG	663663 **J** VG	663765 **J** AC	663857 **J** m AC
663558 **V** TP	463665 **V** SO	663766 **J** LN	463861 **J** m VE
663561 **J** TP	663668 **J** LN	663767 **V** AC	463862 **J** m SO
663562 **J** BD	663670 **V** MZ	663768 **J** BD	463864 **V** m SO
663563 **J** SO	463671 **J** BD	663773 **J** LN	663865 **J** m VE
663564 **V** DP	663673 **J** LN	663777 **V** MZ	463866 **J** m AC
663565 **J** AV	663674 **V** TP	663779 **J** AV	463869 **J** m TP
663567 **J** AC	663675 **J** VE	163780 **J** NC	463871 **J** m LE
663568 **J** RS	663676 **J** VG	163781 **J** MZ	463873 **J** m LE
463569 **J** VG	663679 **J** AC	663784 **J** VE	463874 **J** m LE
463571 **J** SO	463680 **J** BD	163785 **J** AC	463875 **J** m LE
663572 **J** AC	463682 **V** SO	663786 **V** BD	463876 **J** m LE
663574 **J** TP	463683 **J** BD	463787 **J** AV	463877 **J** m LE
663576 **V** LN	463684 **J** LE	663788 **V** AV	463878 **J** m LE
463577 **V** LE	463685 **J** LE	463789 **F** VE	463879 **J** m BD
163579 **V** VG	663686 **V** VG	163790 **J** VE	463880 **J** m VE
463581 **J** VG	663687 **J** TP	663792 **J** AC	463881 **J** m BD
463582 **J** TL	463689 **J** VE	663794 **J** AC	463882 **F** m MZ
463585 **J** MZ	463692 **J** AC	163798 **J** AC	463884 **J** m BD
463586 **J** BD	463693 **J** VE	663799 **J** AC	663893 **V** VG
663587 **J** SB	663695 **J** MZ	663800 **V** LN	463895 **J** BD
463590 **J** TP	463696 **J** NV	663802 **V** AC	463897 **J** RS
463591 **J** RS	463697 **J** VE	663803 **V** AC	463898 **J** BD
663592 **J** MZ	663698 **J** BD	663804 **J** AC	463899 **J** LE
663593 **V** VG	463699 **J** AV	663808 **V** SO	663900 **V** BD
663594 **V** BD	663704 **J** SB	663809 **J** AC	663901 **V** e AV
663596 **J** MZ	663707 **V** LN	463812 **J** m MZ	663902 **V** e PV
663597 **J** TP	663708 **V** VE	463813 **J** m BD	163905 **V** VG
463599 **J** VE	463709 **J** VG	663815 **V** m AC	663906 **J** e VG
463602 **J** TP	663710 **J** LE	463816 **J** m MZ	463907 **J** AC
663604 **J** TP	663717 **J** DP	663817 **V** m BD	163912 **E** VG
463605 **J** BD	463718 **J** SB	463820 **V** m VE	163913 **J** VG
663606 **V** BD	663719 **V** LN	663821 **V** m VE	463915 **J** VG
463607 **J** SB	663720 **J** BD	463823 **J** m BD	463917 **J** BD
463608 **J** AV	463721 **J** m TP	463826 **V** m MZ	463919 **J** TP

663922	V		VE	463968	J		AC	464008	J	m	MZ	464044	J		VG
463923	J		RS	463970	J		MZ	464009	J	m	AV	464045	J		TP
163925	J		MZ	463971	J		VE	464010	J	m	AC	164046	V		VG
163926	J		AC	163972	V		MB	464011	J	m	TP	464047	F		RS
163928	E		VG	463973	J		SB	464012	J	m	MZ	664048	V		RS
463929	J		RS	463975	V		AC	464013	J	m	SO	464049	V		BD
463930	J		MZ	663977	J		MZ	464014	J	m	SO	664050	J		MZ
463931	J		MZ	663979	J	c	AC	464015	J	m	SO	164055	J		VG
463932	J		AC	463981	F	m	BD	464016	J	m	SO	646056	V		AC
463933	J		SO	463982	J	m	BD	464017	J	m	AC	464057	J		MZ
463935	J		RS	663985	J	m	VE	464018	J	m	SO	164060	E		VG
463938	J		AC	463986	J	m	BD	464019	J	m	AC	164061	J		SB
663939	J		TP	663988	J	m	DP	464020	J	m	SO	164062	J		SB
463940	J		MB	663989	J	m	VE	464021	F		MZ	164063	J		VG
463942	J		DP	663992	J	m	VE	164023	J		VG	464064	J		MZ
163947	J		BD	463993	J	m	BD	664024	V		VE	464065	J		SB
163948	J		BD	663994	J	m	VE	164025	J		NC	464066	J		TP
163950	E		VG	463995	J	m	MZ	664029	J		AV	164068	E		NC
463951	V		DP	463996	J	m	SO	464030	V		MZ	664069	J		LN
463952	J		LE	463997	J	m	AC	464031	J		AV	664070	J		AV
463954	J		VG	463998	J	m	AC	664032	V		TP	664071	J		AV
663955	V		BD	464000	J	m	AC	464033	J		MZ	464072	J		AV
663957	V		BD	464001	J	m	BD	464035	J		VE	464073	J		SO
463960	J		AC	464002	J	m	MZ	664037	V		AC	664075	J		AV
163962	V		VG	464003	F	m	SO	664038	J		SO	164076	J		PV
663964	J		BD	464004	J	m	DP	463039	J		LE	264077	J		VG
663965	J	c	AC	464005	J	m	BD	464040	J		MZ	264079	J		VG
463966	J		SB	464006	J	m	AC	464041	J		AV	164080	J		VG
463967	J		RS	464007	J	m	DP	164043	J		BD				

CLASSES BB 64700 & TBB 64800   Bo-Bo + Bo-Bo

With freight train weights rising the SNCF required shunters of greater tractive effort and decided to go back to a system previously used with Class C 61000, where motored "trucks" (Class TC 61100) were coupled to them. Class BB 63500 locos were converted into "master" units by Nevers works. Sotteville Quatre Mares works converted Class BB 63000s into the new "trucks" (known as "slugs" in the USA, with no engine but with traction motors assisting tractive effort). The cab has been removed as it is unnecessary while the main frame has been shortened and the two motor bogies are much closer. The overall length of the Class BB 64700 remains the same as its predessor but the Class TBB 64800 measures only 11.39 m. As there are no fuel tanks and no diesel engine in the "truck" a large deadweight has been added to give good adhesion. Locos are used in yards at Miramas (AV), Sibelin (VE), Woippy (MZ), Villeneuve (AC) and Sotteville (SO). In late 2007, loco and truck pairs started to be refurbished, BB 64700 receiving a new MTU engine plus computerised control and monitoring.

Details as 2 x BB 63500 except:

Maximum Tractive Effort: 300 kN.
Length: 14.68 m. + 11.39 m.
Weight: 63 + 63 tonnes.
Maximum Speed: 80 km/h.

m BB 64700 modernised with MTU 8V4000 R41 engine of 650 kW.

Class 64700 Locomotives.

464701	(63920)	F	m	AV	464709	(63946)	J		MZ	464716	(63963)	J		AC
464702	(63976)	J		VE	464710	(63910)	J		AC	464717	(63937)	J		AC
464703	(63889)	F	m	VE	464711	(63974)	J		AC	464718	(63908)	J		AV
464704	(63959)	J		AV	464712	(63886)	J		VE	464719	(63892)	F	m	AC
464705	(63909)	J		AV	464713	(63945)	F	m	SO	464720	(63949)	J		MZ
464706	(63644)	J		MZ	464714	(63904)	J		MZ	464721	(63888)	J		LE
464707	(63980)	J		MZ	464715	(63918)	F	m	VE	464722	(63916)	J		AC
464708	(63887)	F	m	AC										

Class 64800 "Trucks".

464801	(63024)	**F** m	AV		464808	(63070)	**F** m	AC		464814	(63030)	**J**	MZ
464802	(63057)	**J**	VE		464809	(63051)	**J**	MZ		464815	(63063)	**F** m	VE
464803	(63043)	**F** m	VE		464810	(63089)	**J**	AC		464816	(63025)	**J**	AC
464804	(63080)	**J**	AV		464811	(63022)	**J**	AC		464817	(63047)	**J**	AC
464805	(63001)	**J**	AV		464812	(63075)	**J**	VE		464818	(63034)	**J**	AV
464806	(63014)	**J**	MZ		464813	(63086)	**F** m	SO		464819	(63093)	**F** m	AC
464807	(63059)	**J**	MZ										

CLASSES BB 66000 & BB 69000   Bo-Bo

A mixed traffic locomotive once found on passenger trains but with the introduction of electric heating they are now restricted to freight and permanent way trains. Some were rebuilt as Class BB 66600 (some now with VFLI and private track maintenance firms) and 34 others as Class BB 66700.

The class was built in three sub series – BB 66001 to 66040, BB 66041 to 66190 and BB 66191 to 66318 with minor differences. BB 66001 to 66079 were delivered as 040 DG 1 to 79. The first batch has slightly different bogies. The oldest locos are now being withdrawn, replaced by new Class BB 60000. From 2005 to 2008, 65 of the last sub-series, to be retained in the medium term by Fret SNCF, were refurbished, re-engined and renumbered in the 69000 series, retaining the original last three digits. SNCF's Infrastructure activity started to re-engine its locos in spring 2008. Infra locos remain in the original blue livery **D** but with Infra marked on the cab sides.

Built: 1959–68.
Builders: CAFL/CEM/Alsthom/Fives-Lille.
Engine: 66000: SACM MGO V16BSHR (1030 kW); 69000 MTU 12V4000R41 (1040 kW).
Transmission: Electric. Four Alsthom TA648A1 traction motors.
Heating: None.   **Weight:** 66/67 tonnes.
Maximum Tractive Effort: 167 kN.   **Length:** 14.90 m.
Wheel Diameter: 1100 mm.   **Maximum Speed:** 120 km/h.

Multiple working fitted. Some have snowploughs.

666001		AV	466060		AV	466127		BD	469203	F	SO
666002		BD	666061		LN	466129		TP	466204		AV
666003		LN	666062		NV	466130		TP	466205		LN
666004		NV	666067		AV	466131		BD	469206	F	SO
666014		NV	666073		TP	466140		TP	466207	F	TP
666016		BD	666075		BD	466145		TP	469208	F	AV
666018		NV	466077		BD	466151		TP	469209	F	SO
666019		TP	666078		TP	666160		LN	466211		TP
666020		NV	666079		TP	666164		TP	469212	F	BD
666022		AV	466082		NV	666165		AV	469213	F	SO
666023		AV	466083		BD	666169		TP	466214		LN
666024		AV	666084		BD	666170		BD	469215	F	TP
666025		LN	466085		BD	666171		AV	469216	F	SO
666026		BD	466086		LN	666175		LN	469217	F	AV
666027		NV	466090		TP	466183		TP	466218	F	LN
666028		AV	666091		NV	466184		SO	469219	F	AV
666029		NV	666095		LN	666185		TP	466220		LN
666032		BD	466099		TP	466187		TP	469221	F	AV
666033		BD	466103	F	TP	466188		BD	469222	F	AV
666036		BD	466105		TP	466189		TP	466223		TP
666037		LN	666107		LN	466190	F	TP	469224	F	AV
666038		BD	466109	F	BD	666191		TP	469225	F	SO
466041		TP	666110		NV	466192	F	LN	466226		SO
666042		NV	466111		BD	469193	F	SO	466227		LN
666043		LV	666113		LN	466194		SO	469228	F	AV
466047		BD	666114		NV	469195	F	AV	466229		SO
666049		TP	466115	F	BD	466196		LN	469230	F	SO
466051		BD	666116		LN	466197	F	LN	466231		SO
466052		BD	666118		LN	469198	F	AV	466232		LN
466054		TP	466121		BD	469199	F	SO	469233	F	AV
466055		TP	466124		TP	466200	F	LN	469234	F	SO
666057		TP	466125		BD	466201		TP	469235	F	SO
666059		TP	466126		LN	466202		LN	469236	F	AV

469237	F	SO	469259	F	SO	469279	F	AV	466299		SO
466238		SO	466260		TP	469280	F	SO	466300		SO
469239	F	BD	466261		LN	469281	F	AV	469301	F	BD
469240	F	SO	469262	F	AV	466282		SO	469302	F	SO
469241	F	SO	466263		SO	466283		TL	466303		SO
469242	F	AV	466264		SO	466284		SO	466304	F	BD
469243	F	AV	469265	F	SO	469285	F	SO	466305		BD
469244	F	SO	469266	F	SO	669286		CY	469306	F	AV
469245	F	SO	469267	F	AV	469287	F	SO	469307	F	SO
469246	F	BD	466268	F	TP	666288		CY	466308	F	BD
469248	F	AV	466269	F	LN	466289		BD	466309		SO
466249	F	LN	466270		LN	466290		SO	469310	F	SO
469250	F	AV	469271	F	SO	466291		SO	469311	F	SO
469251	F	AV	469272	F	SO	669292		CY	469312	F	SO
466252		SO	466273		TP	469293	F	TP	466313		SO
466253		TP	469274		CY	466294		TP	469314	F	AV
466254		TP	469275	F	SO	466295		TP	466315		BD
466255	F	SO	466276		TP	466296		SO	469316	F	SO
469256	F	AV	469277	F	AV	466297		SO	469317	F	BD
469257	F	AV	466278		SO	466298		BD	469318	F	SO
469258	F	SO									

Name: 66207 LE GRAND PRESSIGNY

CLASSES BB 66400 & BB 69400   Bo-Bo

This class is a development of Class BB 66000 and incorporates three-phase transmission. All are fitted with electric train heating and many are push-pull fitted. This feature is still used for passenger trains around Lille, Creil, Clermont-Ferrand and Nancy. Apart from this, most locos are now used on freight. Despite being allocated to Chalindrey, they range over a wide area of northern and eastern France. From 2004, locos operating for Fret SNCF started to be refurbished, re-engined and renumbered in the BB 69400 series, retaining the original last three digits. 75 locos were dealt with from 2004 to 2008.

Built: 1968–71.
Builders: CAFL/CEM/Alsthom/Fives-Lille.
Engine: SACM MGO V16BSHR (1030 kW).
Engine: 66400: SACM MGO V16BSHR (1030 kW); 69400 MTU 12V4000R41 (1040 kW).
Transmission: Electric. Four Alsthom TA648H2 three phase traction motors.
Heating: Electric.   **Weight:** 64 tonnes.
Maximum Tractive Effort: 167 kN.   **Length:** 14.97 m.
Wheel Diameter: 1100 mm.   **Maximum Speed:** 120 km/h.

Multiple working and e.t.h. fitted.

p Push-pull fitted.
* Fitted with particle filters.

466401	F		CY	469420	F	*	CY	469439	F		CY	469458	F			CY
466402			CY	466421			CY	469440	F		CY	566459		p		LN
469403	F		CY	469422	F		CY	469441	F		CY	566460		p		CY
466404	F		CY	469423	F		CY	566442		p	CY	469461	F			CY
466405			CY	469424	F		CY	469443	F		CY	566462		p		LN
469406	F		CY	469425	F		CY	469444	F		CY	566463		p		CY
466407	F		CY	469426	F		CY	566445		p	CY	469464	F	p		CY
466408	F		CY	466427			CY	469446	F		CY	466465				CY
469409	F		CY	469428	F		CY	469447	F		CY	469466	F			CY
469410	F		CY	469429	F	p	CY	469448	F		CY	566467	F	p		LN
566411		p	CY	469430	F		CY	466449		p	CY	566468	F	p		LN
469412	F	*	CY	469431	F		CY	566450		p	CY	469470	F	p		CY
469413	F		CY	469432	F	*	CY	469451	F	p	CY	466471		p		CY
469414	F		CY	469433	F		CY	469452	F	p	CY	469472	F			CY
469415	F		CY	469434	F		CY	466453		p	CY	469473		p		CY
469416	F		CY	466435	F	p	CY	469454	F	p	CY	469474	F	p		CY
466417	F		CY	469436	F		CY	566455		p	LN	469475	F	p		CY
469418	F		CY	469437	F		CY	466456			CY	469476	F			CY
466419	F	*	CY	469438	F		CY	466457			CY	469477	F			CY

469478	F	CY	469486	F	CY	469493	F	CY	466500	F p	CY
466479	F	CY	469487	F	CY	469494	F	CY	566501	F p	LN
469480	F	CY	469488	F	CY	469495	F	CY	466502	p	CY
469481	F	CY	469489	F	CY	469496	F p	CY	466503	p	CY
469482	F	CY	469490	F	CY	466497	p	CY	466504	F p	CY
469483	F	CY	469491	F	CY	469498	F p	CY	469505	F	CY
469484	F	CY	469492	F	CY	469499	F	CY	469506	F p	CY
469485	F p	CY									

CLASS BB 66700 — Bo-Bo

These are locos converted from Class BB 66000. The increasing weight of freight trains led to the need for more powerful shunting locomotives. These locomotives were regeared at Nevers works and the weight increased slightly. Following the first batch BB 66701 to 66724, a further ten were converted in 2003–2004. The locos hump shunt and haul freight at Dijon Gevrey (DP), Dunkerque (LE), Mulhouse Nord (SB), Hourcade (BD), Villeneuve (VG) and Sibelin (VE) yards.

Converted from BB 66000: 1985–91, 2003–2004.

Built: 1985–91.
Builders: CAFL/CEM/Alsthom/Fives-Lille.
Engine: SACM MGO V16BSHR (1030 kW).
Transmission: Electric. Four Alsthom TA648A1 traction motors.
Heating: None. **Weight:** 71 tonnes.
Maximum Tractive Effort: 220 kN. **Length:** 14.89 m.
Wheel Diameter: 1100 mm. **Maximum Speed:** 90 km/h.

466701	(66146)	J	VE	466713	(66139)	F	LE	466724	(66087)	F	LE
466702	(66080)	J	SB	466714	(66143)	F	LE	466725	(66179)	F	LE
466703	(66166)	J	VE	466715	(66081)	J	LE	466726	(66141)	F	LE
466704	(66174)	J	LE	466716	(66177)	F	LE	466727	(66154)	F	LE
466705	(66152)	J	DP	466717	(66149)	F	VG	466728	(66123)	F	VE
466706	(66172)	J	SB	466718	(66173)	F	LE	466729	(66119)	F	LE
466707	(66176)	J	SB	466719	(66076)	J	BD	466730	(66155)	F	SB
466708	(66178)	J	SB	466720	(66074)	J	BD	466731	(66181)	F	LE
466710	(66134)	F	VE	466721	(66136)	J	BD	466732	(66152)	F	LE
466711	(66158)	F	DP	466722	(66138)	J	VG	466733	(66133)	F	LE
466712	(66144)	F	VG	466723	(66137)	J	DP	466734	(66180)	F	LE

CLASS BB 67200 — B-B

With the opening of the LGV Sud Est high speed line it was realised that locomotives would be required to operate over the line on ballast trains and in emergencies. The LGV does not have conventional signalling and thus 30 Class BB 67000 were modified and fitted with cab signalling and train–signal box radio. With the construction of the LGV Atlantique, LGV Nord, LGV Méditerranée and LGV Est, a further 50 locos were converted. The class are based in pairs at strategic points near high speed lines across the country. Some are equipped with couplers to rescue TGVs.

Converted from BB 67000: 1980–2007.

Built: 1963–68.
Builders: Brissonneau and Lotz/MTE.
Engine: SEMT 16PA4 (1470 kW).
Transmission: Electric. Two SW 9209 monomotors.
Heating: None. **Weight:** 80 tonnes.
Maximum Tractive Effort: 304 kN. **Length:** 17.09 m.
Wheel Diameter: 1150 mm. **Maximum Speed:** 90 km/h.
Non-Standard livery: N Yellow for Infra department.

Snowploughs fitted. Fitted with TVM300 (TVM430*) cab signalling.

667201	(67006)	NV	667208	(67008)		NV	667215	(67102)	*	AV
667202	(67011)	NV	667209	(67118)		AV	667216	(67121)	*	AV
667203	(67040)	NV	667210	(67120)	N*	LN	667217	(67117)	*	AV
667204	(67034)	NV	667211	(67108)	*	AV	667218	(67112)	s	NV
667205	(67037)	NV	667212	(67122)	*	AV	667219	(67091)	s	NV
667206	(67030)	NV	667213	(67115)	*	LN	667220	(67114)	s	NV
667207	(67021)	AV	667214	(67123)	*	AV	667221	(67081)	s	NV

667222	(67078)	s	NV	667242	(67045)	s	TP	667262	(67023)	*	NV
667223	(67082)	s	NV	667243	(67047)	s	TP	667263	(67090)	*	NV
667224	(67103)	s*	AV	667244	(67061)		TP	667264	(67087)	*	NV
667225	(67029)	*	AV	667245	(67058)		TP	667265	(67089)	*	AV
667226	(67028)	*	AV	667246	(67050)		NV	667266	(67070)	*	NV
667227	(67007)		NV	667247	(67074)	*	LN	667267	(67019)	*	NV
667228	(67039)		NV	667248	(67071)	*	LN	667268	(67084)	*	AV
667229	(67004)		NV	667249	(67069)	*	LN	667269	(67003)	*	NV
667230	(67018)		NV	667250	(67080)	*	NV	667270	(67055)	*	NV
667231	(67048)		TP	667251	(67086)	*	NV	667271	(67097)	*	LN
667232	(67043)		TP	667252	(67076)	*	LN	667272	(67012)	*	LN
667233	(67046)		TP	667253	(67079)	*	LN	667273	(67035)	*	LN
667234	(67051)		TP	667254	(67088)	*	LN	667274	(67062)	*	LN
667235	(67041)		TP	667255	(67077)	*	LN	667275	(67013)	*	LN
667236	(67042)		TP	667256	(67085)	*	LN	667276	(67009)	*	LN
667237	(67054)		TP	667257	(67001)	*	AV	667277	(67060)	*	LN
667238	(67057)		TP	667258	(67016)	*	NV	667278	(67014)	*	LN
667239	(67052)	s	TP	667259	(67032)	*	AV	667279	(67017)	*	LN
667240	(67056)	s	TP	667260	(67065)	*	NV	667280	(67068)	*	LN
667241	(67059)		TP	667261	(67073)	*	NV				

CLASS BB 67300   B-B

A mixed traffic locomotive with some fitted for working push-pull trains. Class BB 67000 (now all withdrawn or converted) loco BB 67036 was modified to provide e.t.h. as BB 67291 and became the prototype for Class BB 67300. The production series featured other improvements such as three-phase transmission. Later, rather than build more new locomotives, 20 Class BB 67000 were converted and the old numbers of these are shown below. CB locos work mainly around the Alps, both on passenger and freight, especially between Chambéry and Valence, LN locos work push-pull around Lille and whilst TP locos work passenger on Tours–Caen. Overhauls stopped in 2005 and withdrawals of Fret SNCF locos started in 2008.

Built: 1967–69.
Builders: Brissonneau and Lotz/MTE.
Engine: SEMT 16PA4 (1764 kW).
Transmission: Electric. Two SW 9209 monomotors.
Heating: Electric.   **Weight:** 80 tonnes.
Maximum Tractive Effort: 202 kN.   **Length:** 17.09 m.
Wheel Diameter: 1150 mm.   **Maximum Speed:** 140 km/h.
Non-Standard livery: N As **P** but blue instead of red.

Multiple working fitted within class and with BB 67400. Odd examples have snowploughs.

p push-pull fitted.

567301			CB	467319			CB	467337			CB	567355			RS
567302	P	p	CB	567320	P	p	RS	567338	P		CB	567356		p	LN
567303		p	CB	467321			CB	467339			TP	567357			CB
567304		p	RS	467322	P	p	LN	567341		p	CB	167358			CB
567305		p	CB	567324	F		LN	567343	P	p	CB	567359	P		CB
567306		p	CB	567326	P	p	LN	567344	P	p	CB	167360			CB
467307			CB	467327			CB	567345		p	CB	567361	P		CB
467308			CB	467329			CB	567346			CB	467362			TP
467309			CB	167330	P		CB	567347			CB	567363			CB
467312			CB	467331			CB	567348	P	p	LN	567364			CB
467313			CB	467332			CB	567349	P	p	RS	167365	P		CB
467315	F		LN	467333			CB	467350	F		CB	167367			CB
167316	P		CB	467334			CB	567351		p	RS	467368			TP
467317	F		LN	467335			CB	567352	P	p	RS	167369			CB
567318	P	p	LN	467336			CB	567354		p	CB	167370			CB

Locos converted from BB 67000.

567371	(67092)	P	p	TP	567375	(67116)		p	CB	567379	(67113)	P	p	CB
567372	(67107)	P	p	CB	567376	(67095)	P	p	TP	567380	(67100)	P	p	CB
567373	(67110)	N	p	TP	267377	(67104)		p	CB	567381	(67111)	P	p	CB
567374	(67109)	P	p	TP	567378	(67098)		p	CB	567382	(67101)	P	p	CB

567383	(67119)	**P** p	CB	567386	(67094)	p	CB	
567384	(67099)	**P** p	CB	567387	(67124)	**P** p	CB	
567385	(67105)	p	CB	567388	(67096)	**P** p	CB	

167389	(67093)	**P** p	CB
167390	(67291)	**P** p	CB

Name: 67344 LA BERNERIE EN RETZ

CLASS BB 67400   B-B

This class used to be the first sight at Calais Maritime for visitors from Britain in the days before Eurostar. The class represents a further development of the Class BB 67000 series. Three-phase transmission and e.t.h. fitted, they can be found virtually all over the system on freight and passenger duties. One gear ratio. The bogies are the same as on Classes BB 7200, BB 15000, BB 22200 and BB 26000 but with a shorter wheelbase. Since the last edition, locos have been regrouped at fewer depots. Locos are used on push–pull duties around Lille (LN), Toulouse (BD), Marseille (MB), Clermont-Ferrand (NV), and Strasbourg (SB). Few long distance passenger duties remain but these include Nantes–Bordeaux and Nantes–Lyon. Fret SNCF locos are concentrated on Nevers and Longueau, the latter mostly replaced by new Class BB 75000. These are moving to Nevers to replace BB 67300 and CC 72000. Other increasing activity is from the Lille area into Belgium. A plan to re-engine Strasbourg's 22 locos has been dropped. Withdrawal will begin in 2009. BB 67580 has been reserved for the SNCF historic collection and retained in its original livery.

Built: 1969–75.
Builders: Brissonneau and Lotz/MTE.
Engine: SEMT 16PA4 (1765 kW).
Transmission: Electric. Two Jeumont-Schneider CTS66.43.4 three-phase monomotors.
Heating: Electric.   **Weight:** 83 tonnes.
Maximum Tractive Effort: 285 kN.   **Length:** 17.09 m.
Wheel Diameter: 1260 mm.   **Maximum Speed:** 140 km/h.

Multiple working fitted within class and with BB 67300. Some have snowploughs.

p   Push-pull fitted.
b   Equipped with radio for operation in Belgium.

Number	F/E	P	p/pb	Depot
467401	F		p	NV
467402	F			NV
267403		P		BD
267404		P		BD
567405			p	MB
867406	E		p	LN
267407		P		BD
267408		P		BD
567409			p	SB
467410	F			NV
567411			p	SB
267412		P		BD
267413	E		p	LN
567414		P	p	LN
567415			p	LN
567416	E		p	BD
567417	F			NV
567418		P		MB
867419	E		p	LN
267420		P		LN
267421		P		TP
567422			p	SB
567423			p	LN
267424		P		BD
467425	F		p	NV
467426	F			LN
567427		P		MB
267429		P		BD
567430		P	pb	LN
167431		P		BD
167432		P		BD
567433			p	SB
567434		P	p	SB
167435		P		BD
267436		P		TP
267437				BD
167438		P	p	BD
467439	F		p	NV
467440	F			NV
267441		P		BD
267442		P		BD
267443	E			TP
467444	F		p	NV
267445		P		BD
867446				LN
267447		P		BD
467448	F		p	NV
467449	F		p	NV
567450	E		p	LN
567451	E			LN
467453	F		pb	LN
467454	F			NV
267455	E		p	TP
567456			p	LN
567457			p	MB
467458	F		p	NV
467459	F		p	NV
467460	F		p	NV
467461	F			LN
467462	F		p	NV
467463	F		p	NV
567464	E		p	SB
467465	F			NV
467466	F			NV
467467	F			NV
467468	F			NV
467469	F		p	LN
867470	E		p	LN
467471	F			LN
467472	F			NV
467473	F			NV
467474	F			NV
567475		P		NV
467476	F			LN
267477	E			TP
867478	E		p	LN
467479	F		p	NV
467480	F			NV
267481	E			TP
567482			p	MB
467483	F		pb	LN
567484			p	MB
467485	F		p	NV
467486	F		p	NV
567488			p	MB
567489			p	NV
467490	F			NV
467491				NV
467492	F			NV
567493			p	MB
467494	F		p	NV
567495			p	MB
267496			p	TP
567497			p	MB
467498			p	LN
567499			p	SB
467500	F			NV
467501	F		p	NV
467502	F		p	NV
467503	F		p	NV
467504	F		p	NV
467505	F		p	NV
467506	F		p	NV
467507	F		p	NV
467508	F			NV
467509				NV
567510			p	SB
867511			p	LN

567512		p	SB	567542	E	p	MB	567572		p	SB	567602	P	p	LN
567513		p	SB	467543	F	p	LN	567573	E	p	MB	567603		p	SB
567514		p	SB	467544	F		NV	567574	P	p	NV	567604	P	p	LN
867515		p	LN	167545	P	p	BD	567575	P	p	NV	567605		p	LN
867516		p	LN	567546	P	p	NV	567576	E	p	NV	567606	P	p	LN
567517		p	SB	567547	P	p	NV	567577	P	p	NV	867607		p	LN
567518		p	SB	567548	P	p	NV	567578	E	p	MB	567608		p	LN
567519		p	SB	267549	E	p	MB	467579	E	p	NV	567609	P	p	LN
867520		p	LN	467550			NV	567580		p	MB	567610		p	NV
567521		p	SB	467551			NV	567581	P	p	NV	567611	E	p	BD
867522		p	LN	467552			NV	167582	P	p	BD	567612		p	BD
867523		p	LN	467553			NV	467583	F	p	LN	567613	E		BD
867524		p	LN	567554	P	p	MB	467584	F	p	LN	867614	E	p	LN
467525		p	NV	567555	P	p	NV	867585	E	p	LN	567615	E	p	BD
567526		p	SB	567556		p	NV	267586	F	p	LN	567616	E	p	BD
467527			NV	567557	P	p	NV	567587		p	LN	567617	P	p	LN
467528	F	pb	LN	567558	P	p	MB	467588	F	p	NV	567618	P	p	LN
467529	F		NV	467559	F		LN	567589		p	LN	567619	P	p	LN
467530	F	pb	LN	567560	E	p	MB	567590		p	LN	567620	P	p	LN
467531	F	p	NV	267561	E	p	MB	567591		p	LN	567621		p	BD
467532	F		NV	567562	P	p	NV	467592	F	p	LN	567622		p	BD
267533		p	LN	467563	F		LN	567593		p	NV	567623		p	BD
467534	F		NV	567564	P	p	NV	467594	F	p	LN	567624		p	BD
467535	F	p	NV	567565	E	p	MB	467595	F	p	LN	567625		p	NV
467536	F		NV	567566		p	NV	567596		p	LN	567626		p	LN
467537	F	pb	LN	567567	P	p	NV	467597	F	p	LN	567627		p	NV
467538	F		NV	567568		p	MB	467598	F	p	LN	567628	E	p	NV
867539	E	p	LN	567569		p	SB	567599		p	LN	467629		p	LN
867540	E	p	LN	567570		p	LN	267600		p	LN	467631		p	NV
567541	E	p	MB	567571		p	SB	567601		p	NV	567632		p	LN

Names:

67530	ROMILLY-SUR-SEINE	67581	NEVERS
67575	DRAGUIGNAN	67620	ABBEVILLE
67580	MONTPELLIER		

CLASSES A1AA1A 68000 & A1AA1A 68500   A1A-A1A

These two classes are identical except for the different engines. Because of this there were several conversions from one to another in the past. Five Class A1A–A1A 68500 were re-engined with Sulzer engines acquired from and originally tested on British Railways Class 48 (D1702–D1706). In 1995/6, several Class A1A–A1A 68000 were converted to Class A1A–A1A 68500 due a high number of cracks in the Sulzer power units. The classes have now been withdrawn from freight services and are now used on ballast trains all over France. A1AA1A 68081 has been preserved in its original blue livery by SNCF and is used on special trains.

Built: 1963–68.
Builders: CAFL/CEM/Fives-Lille.
Engine: Sulzer 12LVA24 (1950 kW) (Class 68000), SACM AGO 12DSHR (1985 kW) (Class 68500).
Transmission: Electric. Four CEM GDTM 544 traction motors.
Heating: None.   **Weight:** 102–104 tonnes.
Maximum Tractive Effort: 298 kN.   **Length:** 17.92 m.
Wheel Diameter: 1250 mm.   **Maximum Speed:** 130 km/h.

Multiple working fitted within both classes. Some fitted with snowploughs.

Note: 68538 was previously renumbered 68501 and 68539 was previously renumbered 68508.

Class 68000.

468081	CY		

Class 68500.

668504	CY	668522		CY	668535	(68019)		CY
668506	CY	668523		CY	668536	(68004)	F	CY
668507	CY	668524		CY	668537	(68023)		CY
668512	CY	668527		CY	668538	(68005)	F	CY
668520	CY	668531	(68009)	CY	668539	(68084)	F	CY
668521	CY	668533	(68017)	CY	668540	(68039)	F	CY

CLASSES CC 72000 & CC 72100   C-C

This is SNCF's really big diesel and features monomotor bogies with gear selection. The low gear was intended for freight work but was also used when hauling passenger trains over difficult routes such as Lyon–Roanne–St.Germain des Fosses. The class is one of the best-loved by enthusiasts but is now in decline. 30 locos were re-engined with less polluting power units in 2003/4 and are all used on passenger services over the Paris Est–Troyes–Mulhouse route plus Reims–Chaumont–Dijon. Freight locos are all due to be withdrawn during 2008 due to the arrival of Class BB 75000. Final workings are around Tours, Vierzon and Clermont-Ferrand.

Built: 1967–74.
Engine: 72000: SACM AGO V16ESHR (2650 kW). 72100: SEMT Pielstick V16-PA4-V200-VC (2650 kW).
Transmission: Electric. Two Alsthom TAO 656B1 monomotors.
Heating: Electric.   **Builders:** Alsthom.
Maximum Tractive Effort: 362/189 kN.   **Weight:** 114/118 tonnes.
Wheel Diameter: 1140 mm.   **Length:** 20.19 m.
     Maximum Speed: 85/160 (85/140*)km/h.

Electro-pneumatic braking. Driver-guard communication (not *).
72084 is retained in its original livery and will be preserved by SNCF.

72000 Series. Standard Locos.

472002	F	*	NV		272049	E	NV	
472004	F	*	NV		272061		NV	
472005	F	*	NV		272064		NV	
472013	F	*	NV		272065		NV	
472016	F	*	NV		472067	F	NV	
472024	F		NV	PONT AUDEMER	472069	F	NV	
472026	F		NV	LUXEUIL-LES-BAINS	472070		NV	
472031	F		NV	FOUGEROLLES	272074	E	NV	TOULON
472032	F		NV		472081		NV	
472033	F		NV		472083	F	NV	
472035	F		NV		472084		NV	AMPLEPUIS
272042			NV		472091		NV	LURE

72100 Series. Re-engined locos.

272121	E	CY			272160	E	CY	GRAY
272130	E	CY	CHALINDREY		272163	E	CY	LA ROCHE-SUR-YON
272137	E	CY			272166	E	CY	
572138	E	CY	NANGIS		572168	E	CY	
572139	E	CY			272172	E	CY	SAINT-MALO
272140	E	CY			272175	E	CY	
272141	E	CY	CHAUMONT		572176	E	CY	
272143	E	CY	LANGRES		572177	E	CY	NOISY-LE-SEC
272145	E	CY			272178	E	CY	
272147	E	CY			272179	E	CY	
272148	E	CY	HAUTE SAÔNE		272180	E	CY	MULHOUSE
272151	E	CY			272186	E	CY	
272157	E	CY	ANNONAY		272189	E	CY	
272158	E	CY			572190	E	CY	BELFORT

CLASS BB 75000 Bo-Bo

The first new diesel locomotives for SNCF in over 30 years (BB 67632 was delivered in 1975) was a joint Alstom/Siemens design. The body, bogies and traction motors are from the Alstom Prima range and the locos thus look similar to Class BB 27000 electrics. The engine, generator and IGBT converters and are the same as in the Siemens Type ER20 Herkules design, delivered to Austrian Railways and others as Class 2016. 400 locos are on order plus 100 options. The first 200 locos will be allocated to Longueau, the rest to Avignon. At the time of writing they had already replaced most of the freight Class BB 67400 at Longueau and cover much of north-east France.

Built: 2006–.
Builders: Alstom/Siemens.
Engine: MTU 16 V 4000 R41 of 2000 kW.
Transmission: Electric. Four Alstom 6 FRA 3266E three-phase asynchronous traction motors.

Heating: Electric	**Weight:** 86 tonnes.
Maximum Tractive Effort: 250 kN.	**Length:** 20.28 m.
Wheel Diameter: 1150 mm.	**Maximum Speed:** 120 km/h.
Multiple Working: within class.	

No.			No.			No.		No.	
475001	F	LN	475047	F	LN	475093	F	475139	F
475002	F	LN	475048	F	LN	475094	F	475140	F
475003	F	LN	475049	F	LN	475095	F	475141	F
475004	F	LN	475050	F	LN	475096	F	475142	F
475005	F	LN	475051	F	LN	475097	F	475143	F
475006	F	LN	475052	F	LN	475098	F	475144	F
475007	F	LN	475053	F	LN	475099	F	475145	F
475008	F	LN	475054	F	LN	475100	F	475146	F
475009	F	LN	475055	F	LN	475101	F	475147	F
475010	F	LN	475056	F	LN	475102	F	475148	F
475011	F	LN	475057	F	LN	475103	F	475149	F
475012	F	LN	475058	F	LN	475104	F	475150	F
475013	F	LN	475059	F	LN	475105	F	475151	F
475014	F	LN	475060	F	LN	475106	F	475152	F
475015	F	LN	475061	F	LN	475107	F	475153	F
475016	F	LN	475062	F	LN	475108	F	475154	F
475017	F	LN	475063	F	LN	475109	F	475155	F
475018	F	LN	475064	F	LN	475110	F	475156	F
475019	F	LN	475065	F	LN	475111	F	475157	F
475020	F	LN	475066	F	LN	475112	F	475158	F
475021	F	LN	475067	F	LN	475113	F	475159	F
475022	F	LN	475068	F	LN	475114	F	475160	F
475023	F	LN	475069	F	LN	475115	F	475161	F
475024	F	LN	475070	F	LN	475116	F	475162	F
475025	F	AV	475071	F	LN	475117	F	475163	F
475026	F	AV	475072	F	LN	475118	F	475164	F
475027	F	LN	475073	F	LN	475119	F	475165	F
475028	F	LN	475074	F		475120	F	475166	F
475029	F	LN	475075	F	LN	475121	F	475167	F
475030	F	AV	475076	F	LN	475122	F	475168	F
475031	F	LN	475077	F	LN	475123	F	475169	F
475032	F	AV	475078	F	LN	475124	F	475170	F
475033	F	LN	475079	F	LN	475125	F	475171	F
475034	F	LN	475080	F	LN	475126	F	475172	F
475035	F	LN	475081	F	LN	475127	F	475173	F
475036	F	LN	475082	F	LN	475128	F	475174	F
475037	F	LN	475083	F	LN	475129	F	475175	F
475038	F	LN	475084	F	LN	475130	F	475176	F
475039	F	LN	475085	F	LN	475131	F	475177	F
475040	F	LN	475086	F	LN	475132	F	475178	F
475041	F	LN	475087	F	LN	475133	F	475179	F
475042	F	LN	475088	F	LN	475134	F	475180	F
475043	F	LN	475089	F	LN	475135	F	475181	F
475044	F	LN	475090	F	LN	475136	F	475182	F
475045	F	LN	475091	F		475137	F	475183	F
475046	F	LN	475092	F		475138	F	475184	F

▲ BB 17096, with VB2N double-deck stock, passes Franconville-Plessis-Bouchard with a Paris Nord–Pontoise service on 14 May 2008. **Robert Pritchard**

▼ BB 25252, in En Voyages livery, leaves Gresy-sur-Isère with the 14.10 Bourg St. Maurice–Lyon on 4 March 2007. **Robin Ralston**

▲ BB 25633 heads RIO push-pull sets forming the 15.57 Ventimiglia–Les Arcs at Beaulieu sur Mer on 1 June 2007.   **Brian Denton**

▼ BB 26170 heads a southbound freight at St. Pierre d'Albigny on 4 March 2007.   **Robin Ralston**

▲ BB 27098 with BB 26093 in tow is seen at Mézy-Moulins on the Paris–Strasbourg main line on 13 June 2008. **David Haydock**

▼ BB 27325 heads a train from Ermont-Eaubonne to Paris St. Lazare past Pont Cardinet on 9 September 2008. **David Haydock**

▲ Tri-voltage BB 36013 arrives at Somain yard with a train from Antwerpen in Belgium on 14 September 2007.   **David Haydock**

▼ Class BB 80000 are used only for empty coaching stock movements. Now almost 60 years old, BB 80007 (former BB 8121) prepares to leave Paris Austerlitz on 23 July 2006.   **Raimund Whynal**

▲ Brand new BB 60057 and 60052 stand at Sotteville depot on 25 April 2008 with Rouen cathedral in the background. **David Haydock**

▼ BB 63415 is seen hump shunting at Villeneuve St. Georges marshalling yard on 11 September 2007. **David Haydock**

▲ Newly refurbished "truck" TBB 64813 and re-engined diesel loco BB 64713 stand outside Sotteville Quatre Mares works on 24 April 2008.   **David Haydock**

▼ A colourful line-up at Sotteville depot on 25 April 2008 – re-engined BB 69301 (ex 66301) in Fret livery heads 69286 in the standard blue livery with Infra markings.   **David Haydock**

▲ BB 67230 backs an engineer's train past Trenitalia E.652.109 at Modane on 24 February 2008.
Mark Darby

▼ BB 67343 arrives at Moirans on 1 June 2007 with the 13.10 Valence–Annecy.   **Gordon Wiseman**

▲ Fret SNCF BB 67474 and 67425 head a train of mineral water out of Volvic on 16 August 2007.
Gordon Wiseman

▼ The last few Class A1AA1A 68500 are now helping out with permanent way work all over France.
A1AA1A 68540 is seen with a short p.w. train at Montigny-en-Ostrevent on 4 August 2008.
David Haydock

▲ CC 72176 passes Cheppes-la-Prairie with a Dijon–Reims service on 2 April 2007.   **David Haydock**

▼ BB 75035 and 75024 leave Somain yard on 14 September 2007 with a mixed freight to Aulnoye.
David Haydock

▲ X 2137, XR 6105 and X 2143 form the 13.27 Montreuil-sur-l'Ille to Rennes on 29 October 2004.
David Haydock

▼ X 92202, with a trailer and X 2100 railcar pass through Montastruc-la-Conseillère on the Toulouse–
St. Sulpice line on 21 August 2008.   **Thierry Leleu**

▲ "Picasso" X 3997 is still used by SNCF's infrastructure division and is seen here at Sotteville depot on 25 April 2008. **David Haydock**

▼ Rebuilt "Caravelle" XR 8754 + X 4754, in the old Haute Normandie red and white TER livery, pauses at Oissel with a Rouen–Elbeuf service on 30 June 2008. **Tim Hall**

▲ Class X 4900 are now all refurbished and mainly work from Rouen to Dieppe where X 4914/13 is seen on 25 April 2008.   **David Haydock**

▼ Unit X 72539, in TER livery with red Midi Pyrénées markings, is seen at the new Toulouse Raynal outpost of the existing depot at Matabiau on 27 March 2007.   **Thierry Leleu**

▲ SNCF railcar X 73913, finished in DB livery, arrives at Forbach with the 12.35 Saarbrücken–Metz service on 17 October 2005. **Brian Denton**

▼ Bimode AGC multiple units B 82539 and B 82547 work a Provins–Paris Est service near Verneuil l'Etang on 30 July 2008. **Raimund Whynal**

▶ Y 7583 couples up to a TGV set at Paris Sud-Est depot on 7 September 2007. In the background is TGV Postal half set 954.
David Haydock

▼ Y 8113 and a second loco of the same class pass through Nanteuil-Sâacy station with a test coach on 22 May 2007.
Philip Wormald

◀ LOCMA Y5161 is seen at Avignon depot on 10 March 2006.
Sylvain Assez

▲ Z 5327 arrives at Paris Montparnasse on 11 September 2007.   **David Haydock**

▼ EMUs Z 6165, 6130 and 6134 approach Épinay-Villetaneuse with a train from Montsoult-Maffliers to Paris Nord on 16 September 2008.   **David Haydock**

▲ Z 6482/81 is one of three of the class to be modernised for use on the St. Germain GC–Noisy-le-Roi line. It is seen at St. Nom-la-Bretèche on 17 December 2004.   **David Haydock**

▼ MI79 set Z 8147/48 plus another of the same type arrive at Drancy with an RER Line B train for St. Rémy-les-Chevreuse on 27 March 2008.   **David Haydock**

475185	F	475239	F	475293	F	475347	F
475186	F	475240	F	475294	F	475348	F
475187	F	475241	F	475295	F	475349	F
475188	F	475242	F	475296	F	475350	F
475189	F	475243	F	475297	F	475351	F
475190	F	475244	F	475298	F	475352	F
475191	F	475245	F	475299	F	475353	F
475192	F	475246	F	475300	F	475354	F
475193	F	475247	F	475301	F	475355	F
475194	F	475248	F	475302	F	475356	F
475195	F	475249	F	475303	F	475357	F
475196	F	475250	F	475304	F	475358	F
475197	F	475251	F	475305	F	475359	F
475198	F	475252	F	475306	F	475360	F
475199	F	475253	F	475307	F	475361	F
475200	F	475254	F	475308	F	475362	F
475201	F	475255	F	475309	F	475363	F
475202	F	475256	F	475310	F	475364	F
475203	F	475257	F	475311	F	475365	F
475204	F	475258	F	475312	F	475366	F
475205	F	475259	F	475313	F	475367	F
475206	F	475260	F	475314	F	475368	F
475207	F	475261	F	475315	F	475369	F
475208	F	475262	F	475316	F	475370	F
475209	F	475263	F	475317	F	475371	F
475210	F	475264	F	475318	F	475372	F
475211	F	475265	F	475319	F	475373	F
475212	F	475266	F	475320	F	475374	F
475213	F	475267	F	475321	F	475375	F
475214	F	475268	F	475322	F	475376	F
475215	F	475269	F	475323	F	475377	F
475216	F	475270	F	475324	F	475378	F
475217	F	475271	F	475325	F	475379	F
475218	F	475272	F	475326	F	475380	F
475219	F	475273	F	475327	F	475381	F
475220	F	475274	F	475328	F	475382	F
475221	F	475275	F	475329	F	475383	F
475222	F	475276	F	475330	F	475384	F
475223	F	475277	F	475331	F	475385	F
475224	F	475278	F	475332	F	475386	F
475225	F	475279	F	475333	F	475387	F
475226	F	475280	F	475334	F	475388	F
475227	F	475281	F	475335	F	475389	F
475228	F	475282	F	475336	F	475390	F
475229	F	475283	F	475337	F	475391	F
475230	F	475284	F	475338	F	475392	F
475231	F	475285	F	475339	F	475393	F
475232	F	475286	F	475340	F	475394	F
475233	F	475287	F	475341	F	475395	F
475234	F	475288	F	475342	F	475396	F
475235	F	475289	F	475343	F	475397	F
475236	F	475290	F	475344	F	475398	F
475237	F	475291	F	475345	F	475399	F
475238	F	475292	F	475346	F	475400	F

PLATFORM 5 MAIL ORDER

EK ASPEKTE 27: DB LOKS UND TRIEBWAGEN 2008
Eisenbahn Kurier

This is the complete listing of locomotives and multiple units of Germany's mail rail operator Deutsche Bahn, with depot allocations as at 1st July 2008. Also includes a brief description of developments in the DB locomotive and multiple unit fleet in the past 12 months. Well illustrated with high quality colour photographs of many locomotive classes. German text. 74 pages. **£8.95** *TR Subscriber Price* **£7.50**

MALY ATLAS LOKOMOTIV 2007
Gradis Bohemia

Fully revised and updated to 2007, this is a detailed guide to the locomotives and multiple units of Czech and Slovak railways. Includes a colour photograph, descriptions and tabulated data for every class, followed by a full fleet list of all powered vehicles in depot allocation order. Also includes a chronological history of railways and rail vehicles in Czechoslovakia, an explanation of the numbering and livery schemes, lists of railway companies, lists of preserved locomotives and maps of the rail network. Czech text. 352 pages. **£14.95** *TR Subscriber Price* **£12.95**

Special Note: Also available is the 2004 edition of this book, Czech and Slovak Locomotives, in ENGLISH language. **£13.50** *TR Subscriber Price* **£11.50**

ATLAS LOKOMOTYW 2007
Poznanski Klub

Fully revised and updated to 2007, this book contains full details of all Polish diesel and electric locomotives and multiple units. For each class, a photograph, technical details and a description are included along with details of fleet allocation at the time of publication. Also included are details of non-PKP owned locomotives and multiple units. Contains information for all classes that have been operated by PKP, including early classes where no examples survive today. Also includes a brief introduction to Polish railways. Polish text. 192 pages in colour. **£14.95** *TR Subscriber Price* **£12.95**

TASCHENLEXIKON TRIEBFAHRZEUGE DER SCHWEIZ STAND 1. JANUAR 2006
Minirex

This is an encyclopaedia of locomotives and multiple units working in Switzerland. Listed by company, each page contains a high quality picture of the vehicle and also technical information such as gauge, construction dates, top speed and other details. Also included are museum locomotives which are in working condition and artist's impressions of new vehicles due to enter service during 2007/8. German text. 512 pages. **£29.50** *TR Subscriber Price* **£26.50**

HOW TO ORDER

Telephone your order and credit/debit card details to our 24-hour sales hotline:
0114 255 8000 (UK) + 44 114-255-8000 (from overseas) or Fax: +44(0)114-255-2471.
An answerphone is attached for calls made outside of normal UK office hours.
Please state type of card, card number, issue no./date (maestro cards only), expiry date and full name & address of cardholder.
Or send your credit/debit card details, sterling cheque or British Postal order payable to Platform 5 Publishing Ltd. to:

Mail Order Department (EHF), Platform 5 Publishing Ltd.,

3 Wyvern House, Sark Road, SHEFFIELD, S2 4HG, ENGLAND

Please add postage & packing: 10% UK; 20% Europe; 30% Rest of World.

1.3. SNCF DIESEL RAILCARS & MULTIPLE UNITS

In France some services are still operated by single diesel railcars which tow trailers. At the end of the journey it is necessary to run round the trailer. However, as the trailers are through wired for multiple working, trains often run with a railcar at each end with a trailer or trailers sandwiched between them. Those railcars with a "9" prefix were built specially for regional councils. In the 1990s units were turned out in four regional liveries – **B, G, R, Y** – then a standard TER livery of metallic grey and blue became standard. The regions are now again applying their own personal touches.

All diesel railcars and nultiple units are in **X** livery unless otherwise stated.

CLASS X 1500 — 2-CAR DEPARTMENTAL UNIT

This unit is formed from two diesel power cars from ETG (Eléments à Turbine à Gaz – gas turbine/diesel multiple units) which are all now withdrawn. The unit is used to test the ERTMS European signalling system.

Built: 1970.
Builder: ANF
Engine: Saurer SDHR (330 kW).
Transmission: Mechanical.
Wheel Arrangement: B-2 + 2-B.
Non-Standard Livery: Blue with white stripes.

Weight: 44 + 44 tonnes.
Length: 22.84 + 22.84 m.
Maximum Speed: 160 km/h.

X 1501 (T 1512) + X 1502 (T 1511)   **N**   SO

CLASS X 2100 — SINGLE RAILCAR

This class helped to replace the ageing Classes X 2400 and X 3800. Toulouse units are mainly used on Toulouse–Auch, Rennes units all over Brittany while Saintes units in common with Class X 2200. Units are now being re-engined and refurbished. Used with Class XR 6000 and XR 6200 trailers.

Built: 1980–83.
Builders: ANF/Schneider.
Engine: Saurer S1DHR (440 kW) [*MAN 2842 LE 604 (478 kW)].
Transmission: Hydraulic. Voith T420r.
Type: XABD.
Weight: 44 tonnes.
Wheel Arrangement: B-2.

Accommodation: 8/48 1T [**T** 8/36 (15) 1T].
Length: 22.40 m.
Maximum Speed: 140 km/h.

Hydrodynamic braking. Multiple working with X 2200, XR 6000 and XR 6200 up to a maximum of three railcars and three trailers.
Note: X 92104 was renumbered from X 2133.

X 2101	**T**	MP		TL	X 2114	**G**	BR	*	RS	X 2127	**T**	MP	*	TL	X 2141	**G**	BR		RS
X 2102	**M**	MP	*	TL	X 2115	**G**	BR		RS	X 2128	**T**	MP		TL	X 2142	**G**	BR		RS
X 2103	**M**	MP	*	TL	X 2116	**G**	BR	*	RS	X 2129	**M**	MP		TL	X 2143	**G**	BR		RS
X 2104	**M**	MP		TL	X 2117	**G**	BR		RS	X 2130	**M**	MP	*	TL	X 2144	**G**	BR		RS
X 2105	**T**	MP		TL	X 2118	**G**	MP		TL	X 2131	**M**	MP	*	TL	X 2145	**G**	BR		RS
X 2106	**M**	AQ		SA	X 2119	**M**	MP		TL	X 2132	**M**	MP	*	TL	X 2146	**G**	BR		RS
X 2107	**M**	AQ		SA	X 2120	**M**	MP	*	TL	X 2134	**G**	BR	*	RS	X 2147	**G**	BR	*	RS
X 2108	**G**	BR		RS	X 2121	**M**	MP		TL	X 2135	**G**	BR	*	RS	X 2148	**G**	BR		RS
X 2109	**G**	BR		RS	X 2122	**M**	MP		TL	X 2136	**G**	BR		RS	X 2150	**M**	MP	*	TL
X 2110	**G**	BR		RS	X 2123	**G**	BR		RS	X 2137	**G**	BR	*	RS	X 92101	**B**	AQ		BD
X 2111	**G**	BR		RS	X 2124	**G**	BR	*	RS	X 2138	**G**	BR		TL	X 92102	**B**	AQ		BD
X 2112	**G**	BR		RS	X 2125	**M**	MP		TL	X 2139	**G**	BR	*	RS	X 92103	**B**	AQ		BD
X 2113	**G**	BR		RS	X 2126	**M**	PC		SA	X 2140	**G**	BR		RS	X 92104	**T**	MP	*	TL

Names:

X 2132   DUNIÈRES. | X 92104   CONSEIL RÉGIONAL MIDI-PYRÉNÉES

CLASS X 2200 SINGLE RAILCAR

An improved version of Class X 2100 with a modified interior. NC units work on the mountainous Nice–Cuneo line. Units are being refurbished and re-engined.

Built: 1985–88.
Builders: ANF/Schneider.
Engine: Saurer S1DHR (440 kW) [*MAN 2842 LE 604 (478 kW)].
Transmission: Hydraulic. Voith T320r.
Type: XABD.　　　　　　　　　　　　　　　**Accommodation:** 8/48 1T (§ –/56 1T).
Weight: 43 tonnes.　　　　　　　　　　　　**Length:** 22.40 m.
Wheel Arrangement: B-2.　　　　　　　　　**Maximum Speed:** 140 km/h.

Hydrodynamic braking. Multiple working with X 2100, X 2800, XR 6000 and XR 6200.

Non-Standard Liveries: N X 2203/15/17 are in advertising livery for "Train des Merveilles" Nice–Tende. X 2250 has a stainless steel body with blue upper bodyside.

```
X 2202 B MP   TL  | X 2218 T PC    SA | X 2233 T AQ * BD | X 2247 T LI  | LG
X 2203 N PA   NC  | X 2219 R PC    SA | X 2234 T AQ * BD | X 2248 T LI *| LG
X 2204 R PA   NC  | X 2220 T PC    SA | X 2235 T PC   SA | X 2249 T LI  | LG
X 2205 T LI  §*LG | X 2221 T AQ  * BD | X 2236 R AQ * BD | X 2250 N AQ * BD
X 2206 T LI  §*LG | X 2222 T AQ  * BD | X 2237 T AQ * BD | X 2251 T LI *| LG
X 2207 T LI  § LG | X 2223 T AQ    BD | X 2238 T AQ * BD | X 2252 T LI  | LG
X 2208 T LI  § LG | X 2224 T PC    SA | X 2239 T PC   SA | X 2253 T LI *| LG
X 2209 T LI  § LG | X 2225 T AQ  * BD | X 2240 T PC   SA | X 2254 T LI  | LG
X 2210 T PC    SA | X 2226 T PC    SA | X 2241 T AQ * BD | X 2255 T LI  | LG
X 2211 T LI  § LG | X 2227 T AQ  * BD | X 2242 R AQ * BD | X 2256 T LI *| LG
X 2212 T AQ    BD | X 2228 T AQ  * BD | X 2243 R PC   SA | X 2257 T LI    LG
X 2213 R PA   NC  | X 2229 T AQ    BD | X 2244 R AQ * BD | X 92201 T LI   BD
X 2215 N PA   NC  | X 2230 T PC    SA | X 2245 T AQ   BD | X 92202 B MP   MB
X 2216 R PA   NC  | X 2231 T AQ  * BD | X 2246 R PC   SA | X 92203 T AQ   BD
X 2217 N PA   NC  | X 2232 T PC    SA |                  |
```

Names:

X 2201	MERCANTOUR		X 2205	CLOYES-SUR-LE-LOIR
X 2202	PAILLON		X 2215	TURBIE
X 2203	ROYA		X 2216	VALLÉE DES MERVEILLES
X 2204	TINÉE		X 2217	VERDON

CLASS X 2400 DEPARTMENTAL RAILCAR

This class of powerful railcars have now all been withdrawn except X 2464 which is in departmental service as a signal department test car and is equipped with video cameras. The unit is currently out of use but will be restored with parts from X 2468.

Type: XABDP.　　　　　　　　　　　　　　　**Wheel Arrangement:** B-B.
Built: 1953.　　　　　　　　　　　　　　　　**Accommodation:** 12/56 1T.
Engines: Two Renault 517G of 255 kW each.　**Builder:** Decauville.
Weight: 43 tonnes.　　　　　　　　　　　　**Transmission:** Mechanical.
Maximum Speed: 120 km/h.　　　　　　　　**Length:** 27.73 m.
Non-Standard Livery: N Corail livery of two-tone grey lined in orange.

```
X 2464  N      NV |
```

CLASS X 2700　RGP　2-CAR DEPARTMENTAL UNIT

This departmental unit was formed in 1987 from two power cars of former RGP sets. The set was converted from power cars X 2707 and 2714 at Bordeaux works and is used as an ultrasonic rail tester. Numbered as X 2700, it is also known as set V4. In each power car the outer engine has been replaced by test equipment leaving the inner engine in each car.

Built: 1954–55.　　　　　　　　　　　　　**Builder:** Decauville.
Engine: One Renault 517G (250 kW) per car.　**Transmission:** Mechanical.
Weight: XABDP　　　　　　　　　　　　　　**Length:** 26.63 + 26.63 m.
Wheel Arrangement: 2-B + B-2.　　　　　　**Maximum Speed:** 120 km/h.
Non-Standard Livery: N Corail livery of two-tone grey lined in orange.

```
X 2700  N      NV |
```

CLASS X 3800 — PICASSO — SINGLE RAILCAR

These classic diesel railcars are known as "Picassos" because of the strange location of the driving cab (on the roof!) and the fact that the driver has to sit side on instead of facing the direction of travel! They were built with one cab as a means of providing a cheap unit that would help to keep branch lines open, the roof cab meaning that the driver did not have to change ends during reversals en route. The two units are in departmental use and have modified front windows for better observation. X 3896 was last seen stored at Vaires. Many have also been preserved.

Type: XBD or XABD.
Built: 1951–62.
Builders: ANF/De Dietrich/Renault/Saurer.
Engine: Renault 517G (250 kW).
Weight: 53 tonnes.
Maximum Speed: 120 km/h.

Wheel Arrangement: B-2.

Transmission: Mechanical.
Length: 27.73 m.

Non-Standard Livery: N X 3896 is in pale green lined in white, X 3997 is in Corail livery of two-tone grey lined in orange.

X 3896 **N** PV | X 3997 **N** SO |

CLASSES X 4300 + X 4500 — 2-CAR UNITS

These two-car DMUs represent the 1960s generation of DMUs. Introduced in 1963, similar units continued to be built until 1981s. Their introduction led to mass withdrawals of old units many of which dated from pre-war days. The only difference between the two classes is the engine. The trailer cars have different proportions of first and second class and power cars of either class operate with either an XR 8300 or an XR 8500 driving trailer to match seating demand. Formations now tend to be permanent. Both classes have some modernised units. The ends have been altered and are now similar to RRR push-pull sets with large and one small window. The class operate all over France on diesel lines. In 1996, the class started to receive "mini" overhauls in which bench seats were replaced by those from "Pays de la Loire" Class X 4630. The modified units are painted in regional colours without changes to cabs. With the arrival of new DMUs many have now been withdrawn. Some units have been sold to Romania.

Built: 1963–70.
Engines: Poyaud C6150SRT (X 4300), Saurer SDHR (X 4500) (330 kW).
Transmission: Mechanical. De Dietrich.
Accommodation: –/60 1T + 12/69 1T (XR 8300), 24/49 1T (XR 8500), (r –/52 1T + 20/52 1T).
Weight: 35 (X 4300), 36 (X 4500) + 23 tonnes.
Wheel Arrangement: B-2 + 2-2.
Builder: ANF.
Formation: XBD + XRABx.
Length: 21.24 + 21.24 m (r 21.74 + 21.74 m).
Maximum Speed: 120 km/h.

r Refurbished units.
*Converted for French Rail Cruises. Belongs to Voyages France Europe.

X 4370	8355	**B**	CE	r	TP	X 4551	8553	**B**	BO	r	NV	X 4601	8505	**G**	BO	m	Nv
X 4372	8348	**B**	CE	r	TP	X 4552	8334	**T**	BO	m	NV	X 4603	8323	**G**	PI		LN
X 4391	8610	**B**	CE	r	TP	X 4554	8564			*	NV	X 4605	8405	**G**	PI	m	LN
X 4407	8626	**B**	CE	r	TP	X 4556	8551	**G**	BR	r	RS	X 4606	8406	**G**	BR	r	RS
X 4440	8420	**B**	CE	r	TP	X 4560	8622		BO		NV	X 4611	8636	**G**	PI		LN
X 4441	8421	**B**	CE	r	TP	X 4568	8384	**G**	PI	m	LN	X 4615	8640	**G**	BR	r	RS
X 4510	8514		BO		NV	X 4569	8413	**G**	BO	m	NV	X 4617	8407	**G**	PI	m	LN
X 4514	8414	**BO**	BO	m	NV	X 4576	8308	**BO**	BO	m	NV	X 4618	8358	**G**	PI	m	LN
X 4528	8538		BO		NV	X 4579	8338		PI		LN	X 4619	8409	**G**	PI	m	LN
X 4533	8547		BO		NV	X 4593	8641	**B**	BO	r	NV	X 4622	8574	**G**	BO	m	NV
X 4542	8333	**G**	BR	r	RS	X 4595	8624	**G**	BO	m	NV	X 4623	8433		BO		NV
X 4547	8379	**G**	PI	m	LN	X 4599	8399	**BO**	BO	m	NV						

CLASS X 4630 — 2-CAR UNITS

A development of the preceding classes but featuring hydraulic transmission. The trailers are interchangeable with those of Classes X 4300 and X 4500. Non-refurbished units are now being withdrawn. Units in all sorts of regional liveries are now gravitating to Nevers depot.

Built: 1974–78.
Engine: Saurer SDHR (330 kW).
Builder: ANF.
Transmission: Hydraulic. Voith T420r.

Formation: XBD + XRABx.
Accommodation: –/60 1T + 24/49 1T (**W** –/52 1T + 24/48 1T)(r –/52 1T + 20/59 1T or –/52 1T + 12/60 1T).
Weight: 39 + 24 tonnes.   **Length:** 21.24 + 21.24 m.
Wheel Arrangement: B-2 + 2-2.   **Maximum Speed:** 120 km/h.
Non-Standard Livery: N X 4671 is all-over white.

X 4744 + 8744 were rebuilt from postal unit X 94630.

X 4630	8642	**BO**	*BO*	r	NV		X 4663	8660	**T**	*BO*	r	NV		X 4704	8701	**T** *RA* m LV
X 4631	8643	**B**	*PL*	r	NB		X 4664	8438	**B**	*PL*	r	NB		X 4705	8702	**T** *RA* r LV
X 4632	8644		*RA*		LV		X 4665	8662	**G**	*RA*	r	LV		X 4706	87??	**T** *RA* m LV
X 4633	8645		*RA*		LV		X 4666	8663	**G**	*PI*	r	LN		X 4707	8704	**T** *RA* m LV
X 4634	8646	**BO**	*BO*	r	NV		X 4667	8664	**G**	*RA*	r	LV		X 4708	8705	**T** *RA* m LV
X 4635	8647	**T**	*RA*	m	LV		X 4670	8556	**G**	*PL*	r	NB		X 4709	8706	**T** *RA* m LV
X 4637	8649	**G**	*CA*	r	EP		X 4671	8648	**W**	*CA*	r	EP		X 4710	8707	**T** *RA* LV
X 4638	8650	**T**	*AU*		NV		X 4672	8595	**B**	*PL*	r	NB		X 4711	8708	**G** *CA* r EP
X 4639	8651		*RA*		LV		X 4673	8670	**B**	*PL*	r	NB		X 4712	8709	*AU* NV
X 4640	8652		*RA*		LV		X 4675	8672	**G**	*PI*	r	LN		X 4714	8711	*RA* LV
X 4641	8653		*RA*		LV		X 4676	8673	**B**	*PL*	r	NB		X 4716	8713	**G** *PI* r LN
X 4642	8654	**G**	*PI*	r	LN		X 4677	8674		*RA*		LV		X 4717	8714	**T** *AU* m NV
X 4643	8655	**B**	*PL*	r	NB		X 4678	8675	**B**	*PL*	r	NB		X 4718	8715	*RA* LV
X 4644	8656		*RA*		LV		X 4679	8676	**B**	*PL*	r	NB		X 4719	8716	**G** *CA* r EP
X 4645	8434	**BO**	*BO*	r	NV		X 4682	8679	**B**	*PL*	r	NB		X 4720	8717	**G** *CA* r EP
X 4646	8435		*RA*		LV		X 4683	8680		*AU*		NV		X 4722	8719	*RA* LV
X 4647	8436	**BO**	*BO*	r	NV		X 4685	8682		*RA*		LV		X 4723	8703	**T** *RA* m LV
X 4648	8437	**G**	*PI*	r	LN		X 4687	8684		*AU*		NV		X 4724	8721	**T** *AU* m NV
X 4649	8444	**G**	*RA*	r	LV		X 4689	8686		*BO*		NV		X 4728	8725	*RA* LV
X 4651	8440	**T**	*RA*	m	LV		X 4690	8687	**B**	*PL*	r	NB		X 4729	8726	**G** *RA* r LV
X 4652	8441	**BO**	*BO*	r	NV		X 4691	8688		*RA*		LV		X 4730	8600	**T** *RA* m LV
X 4654	8443	**B**	*PL*	r	NB		X 4692	8689		*RA*		LV		X 4732	8729	**T** *RA* m LV
X 4655	8445	**BO**	*BO*	r	NV		X 4694	8691		*BO*		NV		X 4733	8730	*RA* LV
X 4657	8446	**B**	*PL*	r	NB		X 4695	8692	**T**	*RA*	m	LV		X 4736	8733	**T** *RA* m LV
X 4658	8447	**Y**	*BO*	r	NV		X 4698	8695		*RA*		LV		X 4738	8735	**T** *RA* m LV
X 4659	8448	**T**	*PI*	r	LN		X 4699	8696	**T**	*RA*	r	LV		X 4740	8737	**T** *RA* m LV
X 4660	8657	**BO**	*BO*	r	NV		X 4700	8697		*AU*		NV		X 4741	8738	**G** *PI* r LN
X 4661	8658	**BO**	*BO*	r	NV		X 4701	8698		*RA*		LV		X 4744	8744	**G** *CA* r EP
X 4662	8659		*AU*		NV		X 4703	8700	**T**	*RA*	m	LV				

CLASS X 4750   2-CAR UNITS

The last of the two-car sets to appear were this series having a more powerful engine and a higher maximum speed. Further members of the class, numbered from X 4797, were later created by combining equipment from withdrawn Class X 94750 postal DMUs and Class X 4300.

Built: 1977–78.   **Builder:** ANF.
Engine: Saurer S1DHR (440 kW).   **Transmission:** Hydraulic. Voith T420r.
Formation: XBD + XRABx.
Accommodation: –/60 1T + 24/49 1T (r –/52 1T + 20/48 1T).
Weight: 39 + 25 tonnes.   **Length:** 21.24 + 21.24 m.
Wheel Arrangement: B-2 + 2-2.   **Maximum Speed:** 140 km/h.

X 4750	8750	**B**	*CE*	r	SO		X 4767	8767	**R**	*HN*	r	SO		X 4781	8781		*BO*	NV
X 4751	8751	**B**	*BN*	r	SO		X 4768	8768	**T**	*LO*		MZ		X 4782	8782	**B** *BO* r NV
X 4752	8752	**R**	*HN*	r	SO		X 4769	8769	**T**	*LO*		MZ		X 4783	8783	**B** *FC* r MZ
X 4753	8753	**B**	*PL*	r	SO		X 4770	8770	**T**	*LO*		MZ		X 4784	8784	**B** *FC* r MZ
X 4754	8754	**R**	*HN*	r	SO		X 4771	8771	**R**	*HN*	r	SO		X 4785	8785	**Y** *LO* r MZ
X 4755	8755	**B**	*HN*	r	SO		X 4772	8772	**T**	*LO*	r	MZ		X 4786	8786	**Y** *LO* r MZ
X 4757	8757	**B**	*BN*	r	SO		X 4773	8773	**T**	*LO*		MZ		X 4787	8787	**Y** *LO* r MZ
X 4759	8759	**T**	*LO*		MZ		X 4774	8774	**B**	*BO*	r	NV		X 4797	8797	**Y** *FC* r MZ
X 4760	8760	**T**	*AU*		NV		X 4775	8775	**T**	*AU*	r	NV		X 4798	8798	**Y** *LO* r MZ
X 4761	8761	**T**	*LO*		MZ		X 4776	8776	**B**	*BN*	r	SO		X 4799	8799	**Y** *LO* r MZ
X 4762	8762	**B**	*LO*	r	MZ		X 4777	8777		*HN*		SO		X 4800	8800	**Y** *LO* r MZ
X 4763	8763		*HN*		SO		X 4778	8778	**T**	*AU*	r	NV		X 4801	8801	**Y** *LO* r MZ
X 4764	8764	**T**	*LO*		MZ		X 4779	8779	**B**	*LO*	r	MZ		X 4802	8802	**Y** *LO* r MZ
X 4765	8765	**B**	*LO*	r	MZ		X 4780	8780	**T**	*AU*		NV		X 4803	8803	**Y** *LO* r MZ
X 4766	8766	**T**	*LO*		MZ											

Former Numbers.

X 4797	(X 4338)	X 4801	(X 4399)	X 8798	(X 8504)	X 8801	(X 8613)
X 4798	(X 4306)	X 4802	(X 4315)	X 8799	(X 8324)	X 8802	(X 8311)
X 4799	(X 4339)	X 4803	(X 4318)	X 8800	(X 8521)	X 8803	(X 8349)
X 4800	(X 4321)	X 8797	(X 8536)				

CLASS X 4790   2-CAR UNITS

These units are similar to Class X 4750 but have lower density seating. They initially carried orange/grey livery and worked the Paris–Granville service but are now used on other services in the Basse-Normandie region. All have now been refurbished with the new front ends.

Built: 1980–81.
Engine: Saurer S1DHR (440 kW).
Formation: XBD + XRABx.
Weight: 40 + 25 tonnes.
Wheel Arrangement: B-2 + 2-2.

Builder: ANF.
Transmission: Hydraulic. Voith T420r.
Accommodation: –/60 1T + 24/49 1T.
Length: 21.74 + 21.74 m.
Maximum Speed: 140 km/h.

X 4790	8790	**T**	*BN*	SO	BAGNOLES-DE-L'ORNE
X 4791	8791	**T**	*BN*	SO	GRANVILLE
X 4792	8792	**T**	*BN*	SO	VILLEDIEU-LES-POÊLES
X 4793	8793	**T**	*BN*	SO	VIRE
X 4794	8794	**T**	*BN*	SO	L'AIGLE
X 4795	8795	**T**	*BN*	SO	FLERS
X 4796	8796	**T**	*BN*	SO	ARGENTAN

CLASS X 4900   3-CAR UNITS

These are 3-car versions of Class X 4630 low density units and, like Class X 4790, were intended for longer distance work. They are known as EATs (*Éléments automoteurs triples*). Originally used in the Alps, X 4901–12 have snowploughs. All are now mainly used on Rouen–Dieppe.

Built: 1975–77.
Engine: Saurer SHDR (320 kW).
Formation: XBD + XRB + XBD.
Weight: 39 + 25 + 39 tonnes.
Wheel Arrangement: B-2 + 2-2 + 2-B.

Builder: ANF.
Transmission: Hydraulic. Voith T420r.
Accommodation: –/42 1T + –/78 1T + –/42 1T.
Length: 21.24 + 20.75 + 21.24 m.
Maximum Speed: 140 km/h.

X 4901	8901	X 4902	**T**	*HN*	SO		X 4915	8908	X 4916	**T**	*HN*	SO
X 4903	8902	X 4904	**T**	*HN*	SO		X 4917	8909	X 4918	**T**	*HN*	SO
X 4905	8903	X 4906	**T**	*HN*	SO		X 4919	8910	X 4920	**T**	*HN*	SO
X 4907	8904	X 4908	**T**	*HN*	SO		X 4921	8911	X 4922	**T**	*HN*	SO
X 4909	8905	X 4910	**T**	*HN*	SO		X 4923	8912	X 4924	**T**	*HN*	SO
X 4911	8906	X 4912	**T**	*HN*	SO		X 4925	8913	X 4926	**T**	*HN*	SO
X 4913	8907	X 4914	**T**	*HN*	SO							

Names:

X 4901/2   VEYNES | X 4903/4   MANOSQUE

CLASS XR 6000   TRAILERS

Trailers constructed to work with X 2100 and X 2200.

Built: 1978–87.
Type: XRAB.
Weight: 24 tonnes.
Maximum Speed: 140 km/h.

Builder: ANF.
Accommodation: 16/60 1T.
Length: 24.04 m.

6004	**M**	*LI*	LG	6046	**R**	*PA*	MB	6072	**M** *AQ*	LG	6147	**R**	*AQ*	BD
6010	**M**	*LI*	LG	6054	**M**	*LI*	LG	6074	**M** *AQ*	LG	6148	**R**	*AQ*	BD
6014	**R**	*PA*	MB	6056	**M**	*LI*	LG	6075	**M** *AQ*	LG	6149	**R**	*AQ*	BD
6024	**R**	*PA*	MB	6058	**M**	*PC*	SA	6077	**M** *AQ*	LG	6151	**R**	*PC*	SA
6027	**M**	*PC*	SA	6061	**M**	*AQ*	BD	6086	**M** *AQ*	LG	6152	**R**	*AQ*	BD
6028	**M**	*LI*	LG	6063	**M**	*AQ*	BD	6108	**G** *BR*	RS	6153	**R**	*PC*	SA
6038	**M**	*AQ*	LG	6067	**M**	*LI*	LG	6136	**R** *PA*	MB	6154	**R**	*AQ*	BD
6040	**M**	*LI*	LG	6070	**M**	*AQ*	LG	6144	**R** *PA*	MB	6159	**A**	*AQ*	BD

| 6162 | **R** *PC* | SA | 6165 | **G** *BR* | RS | 6167 | **G** *BR* | RS | 6169 | **G** *BR* | RS |
| 6164 | **G** *BR* | RS | 6166 | **G** *BR* | RS | 6168 | **G** *BR* | RS | 6170 | **G** *BR* | RS |

CLASS XR 6200 TRAILERS

These trailers are similar to Class XR 6000, but have X 2200-style interiors.

Built: 1988–90.
Type: XRAB.
Weight: 24 tonnes.
Maximum Speed: 140 km/h.

Builders: ANF.
Accommodation: 16/60 1T.
Length: 24.04 m.

6201	**G** *BR*	RS	6227	**T** *PC*	SA	6239	**T** *PC*	SA	96209	**M** *MP*	TL
6202	**G** *BR*	RS	6228	**B** *AQ*	BD	6240	**T** *AQ*	BD	96210	**M** *MP*	TL
6205	**T** *AQ*	BD	6230	**T** *AQ*	BD	6247	**R** *PA*	NC	96212	**M** *MP*	TL
6206	**T** *PC*	SA	6231	**T** *PC*	SA	6250	**R** *PC*	SA	96213	**M** *MP*	TL
6211	**M** *FC*	DP	6232	**T** *AQ*	BD	6252	**T** *AQ*	BD	96215	**M** *MP*	TL
6213	**M** *FC*	DP	6233	**T** *PC*	SA	6254	**R** *PC*	SA	96216	**M** *MP*	TL
6219	**M** *MP*	TL	6234	**T** *AQ*	BD	6255	**R** *AQ*	BD	96218	**M** *MP*	TL
6221	**M** *MP*	TL	6236	**T** *AQ*	BD	96207	**M** *MP*	TL	96219	**M** *MP*	TL
6222	**M** *RA*	LV	6237	**R** *PC*	SA	96208	**M** *MP*	TL	96221	**M** *MP*	TL
6226	**T** *AQ*	BD	6238	**T** *AQ*	BD						

CLASS X 72500

2 OR 3-CAR UNITS

Class X 72500 was SNCF's "Automoteur TER" or XTER, a new "wonder DMU" with a profile similar to the TGV and new standards of air-conditioned comfort inside. The units have automatic couplings under their streamlined nose. Large windows are better than in the TGV. Following the initial production run of 105 sets, there were a further 12 3-car sets plus several centre cars to boost 2-car sets to 3-car.

Unfortunately, despite its good looks, the class did not conform to specification, had to be modified several times by the builder and has been very unreliable. They are now being replaced by AGC sets on several routes.

At the time of writing, Class X 72500 was mainly operating on Paris Vaugirard–Granville (3-car sets at Caen are "owned" by the Corail Intercités activity, all the rest are TER), Paris Austerlitz–Châteaudun–Vendôme–Tours, Paris Nord–Laon, Genève/Annecy–Chambéry–Grenoble–Valence, Toulouse–Rodez, Lyon–Roanne, Dijon–Nevers, Nevers–Tours, Marseille–Aix–en–Provence and Nîmes–Mende.

Built: 1997–2003.
Builder: GEC Alsthom.
Engines: Two MAN D2866 LUE 602 6-cylinder in line (300 kW) per power car.
Transmission: Hydraulic. Two Voith T211 rzz per power car.
Formation: XB (+ XRB) + XAB.
Accommodation: –/78 (+ –/78 1T) + 22/50 1T except:
Caen 3-car sets for Paris-Granville are –/67 + 28/28 1T + –/67.
Weight: 58 (+ 45) + 58 tonnes.
Length: 26.45 (+ 25.60) + 26.45 m.
Wheel Arrangement: 1A-A1 (+ 2-2) + 1A-A1.
Maximum Speed: 160 km/h.

X 72501		X 72502 **T**	*AQ*	LG		X 72537		X 72538 **T**	*MP*	TL
X 72503		X 72504 **T**	*PL*	NB		X 72539		X 72540 **T**	*MP*	TL
X 72505		X 72506 **T**	*CE*	TP		X 72541		X 72542 **T**	*AU*	TL
X 72507		X 72508 **T**	*CE*	TP		X 72543		X 72544 **T**	*CE*	TP
X 72509		X 72510 **T**	*CE*	TP		X 72545		X 72546 **T**	*AQ*	LG
X 72511		X 72512 **T**	*PL*	NB		X 72547		X 72548 **T**	*PL*	NB
X 72513		X 72514 **T**	*LI*	LG		X 72549		X 72550 **T**	*CE*	TP
X 72515		X 72516 **T**	*LI*	LG		X 72551		X 72552 **T**	*PC*	LG
X 72517		X 72518 **T**	*MP*	TL		X 72553		X 72554 **T**	*LR*	MB
X 72519		X 72520 **T**	*PL*	NB		X 72555		X 72556 **T**	*CE*	TP
X 72521		X 72522 **T**	*AQ*	LG		X 72557		X 72558 **T**	*PL*	NB
X 72523		X 72524 **T**	*PC*	LG		X 72559		X 72560 **T**	*AQ*	LG
X 72525		X 72526 **T**	*LR*	MB		X 72561		X 72562 **T**	*PL*	NB
X 72527		X 72528 **T**	*CE*	TP		X 72563		X 72564 **T**	*PL*	NB
X 72529		X 72530 **T**	*CE*	TP		X 72565	725651	X 72566 **T**	*RA*	LV
X 72531	721531	X 72532 **T**	*RA*	LV		X 72567		X 72568 **T**	*LR*	MB
X 72533		X 72534 **T**	*PA*	MB		X 72569		X 72570 **T**	*LI*	LG
X 72535		X 72536 **T**	*PL*	NB		X 72571		X 72572 **T**	*PA*	MB

X	X T	code	code
X 72573	X 72574 T	LI	LG
X 72575	X 72576 T	MP	TL
X 72577	X 72578 T	PA	MB
X 72579 721579	X 72580 T	RA	LV
X 72581 721581	X 72582 T	BO	NV
X 72583	X 72584 T	MP	TL
X 72585	X 72586 T	AQ	LG
X 72587	X 72588 T	MP	TL
X 72589 721589	X 72590 T	CI	CA
X 72591	X 72592 T	CE	TP
X 72593	X 72594 T	AQ	LG
X 72595	X 72596 T	AQ	LG
X 72597	X 72598 T	PC	LG
X 72599	X 72600 T	PL	NB
X 72601	X 72602 T	AQ	LG
X 72603 721603	X 72604 T	RA	LV
X 72605	X 72606 T	AQ	LG
X 72607 721607	X 72608 T	RA	LV
X 72609	X 72610 T	PA	MB
X 72611	X 72612 T	AQ	LG
X 72613	X 72614 T	LI	LG
X 72615 721615	X 72616 T	BO	NV
X 72617	X 72618 T	AQ	LG
X 72619 721619	X 72620 T	CI	CA
X 72621	X 72622 T	PA	MB
X 72623 721623	X 72624 T	CI	CA
X 72625	X 72626 T	PA	MB
X 72627 721627	X 72628 T	CI	CA
X 72629	X 72630 T	LI	LG
X 72631 721631	X 72632 T	CI	CA
X 72633	X 72634 T	AU	TL
X 72635 721635	X 72636 T	CI	CA
X 72637	X 72638 T	LR	MB
X 72639 721639	X 72640 T	CI	CA
X 72641 721641	X 72642 T	RA	LV
X 72643 721643	X 72644 T	CI	CA
X 72645	X 72646 T	CE	TP
X 72647 721647	X 72648 T	CI	CA
X 72649	X 72650 T	CE	TP
X 72651 721651	X 72652 T	CI	CA
X 72653	X 72654 T	MP	TL
X 72655 721655	X 72656 T	CI	CA
X 72657	X 72658 T	MP	TL
X 72659 721659	X 72660 T	CI	CA
X 72661	X 72662 T	PC	LG
X 72663 721663	X 72664 T	CI	CA
X 72665	X 72666 T	LR	MB
X 72667 721667	X 72668 T	CI	CA
X 72669	X 72670 T	CE	TP
X 72671 721671	X 72672 T	CI	CA
X 72673 721673	X 72674 T	RA	LV
X 72675	X 72676 T	PL	NB
X 72677	X 72678 T	PC	LG
X 72679 721679	X 72680 T	RA	LV
X 72681 721681	X 72682 T	RA	LV
X 72683	X 72684 T	PA	MB
X 72685	X 72686 T	AU	TL
X 72687	X 72688 T	PA	MB
X 72689 721689	X 72690 T	RA	LV
X 72691	X 72692 T	PA	MB
X 72693 721693	X 72694 T	RA	LV
X 72695 721695	X 72696 T	RA	LV
X 72697	X 72698 T	PA	MB
X 72699 721699	X 72700 T	RA	LV
X 72701	X 72702 T	AQ	LG
X 72703	X 72704 T	PA	MB
X 72705	X 72706 T	PA	MB
X 72707 721701	X 72708 T	RA	LV
X 72709 721709	X 72710 T	RA	LV
X 72711 721711	X 72712 T	BO	NV
X 72713 721713	X 72714 T	CI	CA
X 72715 721715	X 72716 T	PI	LN
X 72717 721717	X 72718 T	BO	NV
X 72719 721719	X 72720 T	CI	CA
X 72721 721721	X 72722 T	PI	LN
X 72723 721723	X 72724 T	CI	CA
X 72725 721725	X 72726 T	PI	LN
X 72727 721727	X 72728 T	CI	CA
X 72729 721729	X 72730 T	PI	LN
X 72731 721731	X 72732 T	PI	LN
X 72733 721733	X 72734 T	PI	LN

Names:

X 72533/34	ÉCRINS
X 72571/72	DÉVOLUY
X 72577/78	PELVOUX
X 72581/82	BEAUNE
X 72609/10	QUEYRAS
X 72621/22	SERRE PONÇON
X 72625/26	SAINTE-VICTOIRE
X 72683/84	MONT DAUPHIN
X 72687/88	AURÉLIEN
X 72691/92	VALLOUISE
X 72697/98	UBAYE
X 72703/04	BUËCH
X 72705/06	VALGAUDEMAR
X 72715/16	Le Plâteau Picard
X 72721/22	Le Trait Vert
X 72725/26	La Baie de Somme
X 72729/30	Les Trois Rivières
X 72731/32	Le Vermandois
X 72733/34	Le Pays d'Ancre

CLASS X 73500 & X 73900 — SINGLE UNITS

Class X 73500 was the third part of SNCF's modernisation of regional (TER) services. This is a low cost single railcar for one person operation (never implemented) on lightly-used lines, known by SNCF as the "Autorail TER" or ATER. The centre section is low floor. The initial order was unique in having been organised jointly by SNCF and German Railways (DB) which took 40 each, the DB units numbered as Class 641.

The railcars tend to work all-stations services while Class X 72500 and X 76500 operate limited-stop trains. The final number ordered were Alsace region (40, SB depot), Aquitaine (12 LG), Auvergne plus Haute Loire département (34 + 2 CF), Basse Normandie (11 CA), Bourgogne (10 NV), Bretagne

(15 RS), Centre (15 TP), Champagne-Ardenne (8 EP), Franche-Comté (20 DP), Haute Normandie (11 SO), Languedoc-Roussillon (9 TL), Limousin (15 LG), Lorraine + Saarland (5 + 2 SB), Midi Pyrénées (27 TL), Nord-Pas-de-Calais (10 LN), Pays-de-la-Loire (15 NB), Picardie (12 LN), Poitou-Charentes (8 LG) and Rhône-Alpes (50 LV).

These railcars have automatic couplings and do not operate with trailers, thus ending an SNCF tradition of shunting trailers around provincial stations at great expense. The X 73900 series are equipped to work into Germany and operate Metz–Saarbrücken, Strasbourg–Saarbrücken and Strasbourg–Offenburg. X 73813 to X 73818 were former CFL 2101 to 2106 bought in 2006/7.

Built: 1999–2004.
Builder: Alstom DDF/LHB.
Engines: 2 x MAN D2866 LUH 21 6-cylinder in-line of 258 kW per car.
Transmission: Hydraulic. Voith T211 rzz.
Type: XB or XAB.
Length: 28.90 m.
Accommodation: –/61 (18) 1T [*RA* (8/53 (18) 1T]
Maximum Speed: 140 km/h.
Weight: 48 t.
Wheel Arrangement: 1A-A1.
Non-Standard Livery: **N** DB Red.

Standard Units.

X 73501	**T**	*AL*	SB	X 73547	**T**	*AL*	SB	X 73593	**T**	*FC*	DP	X 73639	**T**	*RA*	LV
X 73502	**T**	*PL*	NB	X 73548	**T**	*HN*	SO	X 73594	**T**	*MP*	TL	X 73640	**T**	*RA*	LV
X 73503	**T**	*BO*	NV	X 73549	**T**	*AL*	SB	X 73595	**T**	*PI*	LN	X 73641	**T**	*RA*	LV
X 73504	**T**	*AL*	SB	X 73550	**T**	*AL*	SB	X 73596	**T**	*BR*	RS	X 73642	**T**	*RA*	LV
X 73505	**T**	*RA*	LV	X 73551	**T**	*AL*	SB	X 73597	**T**	*BR*	RS	X 73643	**T**	*RA*	LV
X 73506	**LR**	*LR*	TL	X 73552	**T**	*HN*	SO	X 73598	**T**	*BR*	RS	X 73644	**T**	*BN*	CA
X 73507	**T**	*CE*	TP	X 73553	**T**	*AL*	SB	X 73599	**T**	*BR*	RS	X 73645	**T**	*BN*	CA
X 73508	**T**	*CE*	TP	X 73554	**T**	*AL*	SB	X 73600	**T**	*RA*	LV	X 73646	**T**	*BN*	CA
X 73509	**T**	*CE*	TP	X 73555	**T**	*AL*	SB	X 73601	**T**	*BR*	RS	X 73647	**T**	*BN*	CA
X 73510	**T**	*CE*	TP	X 73556	**T**	*AL*	SB	X 73602	**T**	*HN*	SO	X 73648	**T**	*BN*	CA
X 73511	**T**	*CE*	TP	X 73557	**T**	*CE*	TP	X 73603	**T**	*BR*	RS	X 73649	**T**	*BN*	CA
X 73512	**T**	*AL*	SB	X 73558	**T**	*AL*	SB	X 73604	**T**	*BR*	RS	X 73650	**T**	*PL*	NB
X 73513	**T**	*PL*	NB	X 73559	**T**	*AL*	SB	X 73605	**T**	*BR*	RS	X 73651	**T**	*BN*	CA
X 73514	**T**	*PL*	NB	X 73560	**T**	*CE*	TP	X 73606	**T**	*PI*	LN	X 73652	**T**	*BN*	CA
X 73515	**T**	*AL*	SB	X 73561	**T**	*RA*	LV	X 73607	**T**	*RA*	LV	X 73653	**T**	*BN*	CA
X 73516	**T**	*AL*	SB	X 73562	**LR**	*LR*	TL	X 73608	**T**	*FC*	DP	X 73654	**T**	*BN*	CA
X 73517	**T**	*AL*	SB	X 73563	**T**	*PL*	NB	X 73609	**T**	*PI*	LN	X 73655	**T**	*PL*	NB
X 73518	**T**	*AL*	SB	X 73564	**T**	*HN*	SO	X 73610	**T**	*PI*	LN	X 73656	**T**	*PL*	NB
X 73519	**T**	*AL*	SB	X 73565	**T**	*CE*	TP	X 73611	**T**	*PI*	LN	X 73657	**T**	*PL*	NB
X 73520	**T**	*AL*	SB	X 73566	**T**	*CE*	TP	X 73612	**T**	*FC*	DP	X 73658	**T**	*CA*	EP
X 73521	**T**	*AL*	SB	X 73567	**T**	*AL*	SB	X 73613	**T**	*FC*	DP	X 73659	**T**	*CA*	EP
X 73522	**T**	*BR*	RS	X 73568	**T**	*AL*	SB	X 73614	**T**	*MP*	TL	X 73660	**T**	*CA*	EP
X 73523	**T**	*MP*	TL	X 73569	**T**	*AL*	SB	X 73615	**T**	*MP*	TL	X 73661	**T**	*CA*	EP
X 73524	**T**	*RA*	LV	X 73570	**LR**	*LR*	TL	X 73616	**T**	*RA*	LV	X 73662	**T**	*AU*	CF
X 73525	**T**	*PL*	NB	X 73571	**T**	*RA*	LV	X 73617	**T**	*RA*	LV	X 73663	**T**	*RA*	LV
X 73526	**BO**	*BO*	NV	X 73572	**T**	*AL*	SB	X 73618	**T**	*RA*	LV	X 73664	**T**	*RA*	LV
X 73527	**T**	*AL*	SB	X 73573	**T**	*AL*	SB	X 73619	**T**	*RA*	LV	X 73665	**T**	*RA*	LV
X 73528	**T**	*CE*	TP	X 73574	**T**	*BR*	RS	X 73620	**T**	*RA*	LV	X 73666	**T**	*RA*	LV
X 73529	**T**	*CE*	TP	X 73575	**T**	*BR*	RS	X 73621	**T**	*RA*	LV	X 73667	**T**	*RA*	LV
X 73530	**T**	*RA*	LV	X 73576	**T**	*MP*	TL	X 73622	**T**	*RA*	LV	X 73668	**T**	*RA*	LV
X 73531	**T**	*PL*	NB	X 73577	**LR**	*LR*	TL	X 73623	**T**	*RA*	LV	X 73669	**T**	*RA*	LV
X 73532	**T**	*PL*	NB	X 73578	**T**	*CE*	TP	X 73624	**T**	*RA*	LV	X 73670	**T**	*RA*	LV
X 73533	**T**	*HN*	SO	X 73579	**T**	*HN*	SO	X 73625	**T**	*RA*	LV	X 73671	**T**	*RA*	LV
X 73534	**T**	*HN*	SO	X 73580	**BO**	*BO*	NV	X 73626	**T**	*MP*	TL	X 73672	**T**	*RA*	LV
X 73535	**T**	*MP*	TL	X 73581	**T**	*AU*	CF	X 73627	**T**	*MP*	TL	X 73673	**T**	*RA*	LV
X 73536	**T**	*CE*	TP	X 73582	**LR**	*LR*	TL	X 73628	**T**	*AU*	CF	X 73674	**T**	*AU*	CF
X 73537	**T**	*AU*	CF	X 73583	**T**	*BR*	RS	X 73629	**T**	*AU*	CF	X 73675	**T**	*AU*	CF
X 73538	**T**	*BR*	RS	X 73584	**T**	*PL*	NB	X 73630	**T**	*BN*	CA	X 73676	**T**	*AU*	CF
X 73539	**T**	*CE*	TP	X 73585	**T**	*PL*	NB	X 73631	**T**	*MP*	TL	X 73677	**T**	*AU*	CF
X 73540	**T**	*RA*	LV	X 73586	**T**	*HN*	SO	X 73632	**T**	*MP*	TL	X 73678	**T**	*AU*	CF
X 73541	**T**	*PL*	NB	X 73587	**LR**	*LR*	TL	X 73633	**T**	*MP*	TL	X 73679	**T**	*AU*	CF
X 73542	**T**	*PL*	NB	X 73588	**T**	*BR*	RS	X 73634	**T**	*RA*	LV	X 73680	**T**	*AU*	CF
X 73543	**LR**	*LR*	TL	X 73589	**T**	*RA*	LV	X 73635	**T**	*RA*	LV	X 73681	**T**	*AU*	CF
X 73544	**T**	*AL*	SB	X 73590	**T**	*BR*	RS	X 73636	**T**	*RA*	LV	X 73682	**T**	*AU*	CF
X 73545	**T**	*CE*	TP	X 73591	**T**	*MP*	TL	X 73637	**T**	*RA*	LV	X 73683	**T**	*AU*	CF
X 73546	**T**	*AL*	SB	X 73592	**T**	*RA*	LV	X 73638	**T**	*RA*	LV	X 73684	**T**	*AU*	CF

X 73685	T	AU	CF	X 73719	T	PI	LN	X 73753	T	FC	DP	X 73786	T	LI	LG
X 73686	T	AU	CF	X 73720	T	PI	LN	X 73754	T	FC	DP	X 73787	T	LI	LG
X 73687	T	AU	CF	X 73721	T	PI	LN	X 73755	T	FC	DP	X 73788	T	LI	LG
X 73688	T	AU	CF	X 73722	T	PI	LN	X 73756	T	FC	DP	X 73789	T	LI	LG
X 73689	T	AU	CF	X 73723	T	PI	LN	X 73757	T	FC	DP	X 73790	T	LI	LG
X 73690	T	AU	CF	X 73724	T	MP	TL	X 73758	T	FC	DP	X 73791	T	HN	SO
X 73691	T	AU	CF	X 73725	T	MP	TL	X 73759	T	PI	LN	X 73792	T	HN	SO
X 73692	T	AU	CF	X 73726	T	MP	TL	X 73760	BO	BO	NV	X 73793	T	CA	EP
X 73693	T	AU	CF	X 73727	T	MP	TL	X 73761	BO	BO	NV	X 73794	T	CA	EP
X 73694	T	AU	CF	X 73728	T	AQ	LG	X 73762	T	NP	LN	X 73795	T	CA	EP
X 73695	T	AU	CF	X 73729	T	AQ	LG	X 73763	T	NP	LN	X 73796	T	PC	LG
X 73696	T	AU	CF	X 73730	T	AQ	LG	X 73764	T	NP	LN	X 73797	BO	BO	NV
X 73697	T	AU	CF	X 73731	T	AQ	LG	X 73765	T	NP	LN	X 73798	BO	BO	NV
X 73698	T	AU	CF	X 73732	T	AQ	LG	X 73766	T	NP	LN	X 73799	T	FC	DP
X 73699	T	AU	CF	X 73733	T	AQ	LG	X 73767	T	NP	LN	X 73800	T	FC	DP
X 73700	T	AU	CF	X 73734	T	MP	TL	X 73768	T	NP	LN	X 73801	T	RA	LV
X 73701	T	AU	CF	X 73735	T	MP	TL	X 73769	T	NP	LN	X 73802	T	RA	LV
X 73702	T	AU	CF	X 73736	T	MP	TL	X 73770	T	NP	LN	X 73803	LR	LR	TL
X 73703	T	hl	CF	X 73737	T	MP	TL	X 73771	T	AQ	LG	X 73804	T	CA	EP
X 73704	T	hl	CF	X 73738	T	MP	TL	X 73772	T	AQ	LG	X 73805	LR	LR	TL
X 73705	T	FC	DP	X 73739	T	MP	TL	X 73773	T	AQ	LG	X 73806	T	PC	LG
X 73706	BO	BO	NV	X 73740	T	MP	TL	X 73774	T	AQ	LG	X 73807	T	PC	LG
X 73707	BO	BO	NV	X 73741	T	MP	TL	X 73775	T	HN	SO	X 73808	T	PC	LG
X 73708	T	RA	LV	X 73742	T	MP	TL	X 73776	T	LI	LG	X 73809	T	PC	LG
X 73709	T	RA	LV	X 73743	T	MP	TL	X 73777	T	LI	LG	X 73810	T	PC	LG
X 73710	T	RA	LV	X 73744	T	FC	DP	X 73778	T	LI	LG	X 73811	T	PC	LG
X 73711	T	RA	LV	X 73745	T	FC	DP	X 73779	T	LI	LG	X 73812	T	PC	LG
X 73712	T	RA	LV	X 73746	T	FC	DP	X 73780	T	LI	LG	X 73813	T	LO	SB
X 73713	T	RA	LV	X 73747	T	FC	DP	X 73781	T	LI	LG	X 73814	T	LO	SB
X 73714	T	RA	LV	X 73748	T	PI	LN	X 73782	T	LI	LG	X 73815	T	LO	SB
X 73715	BO	BO	NV	X 73749	T	NP	LN	X 73783	T	LI	LG	X 73816	T	LO	SB
X 73716	T	AQ	LG	X 73750	T	FC	DP	X 73784	T	LI	LG	X 73817	T	LO	SB
X 73717	T	AQ	LG	X 73751	T	FC	DP	X 73785	T	LI	LG	X 73818	T	LO	SB
X 73718	T	MP	TL	X 73752	T	FC	DP								

Units equipped for working into Germany.

X 73901	T	AL	SB	X 73906	T	AL	SB	X 73911	T	LO	SB	X 73916	T	AL	SB
X 73902	T	AL	SB	X 73907	T	AL	SB	X 73912	T	LO	SB	X 73917	T	AL	SB
X 73903	T	AL	SB	X 73908	T	AL	SB	X 73913	N	LO	SB	X 73918	T	LO	SB
X 73904	T	AL	SB	X 73909	T	AL	SB	X 73914	N	SL	SB	X 73919	T	LO	SB
X 73905	T	AL	SB	X 73910	T	AL	SB	X 73915	N	SL	SB				

Names:

X 73512	ERSTEIN
X 73515	THANN
X 73520	HERRLISHEIM
X 73522	argoat/argoad
X 73526	Paray-le-Monial en Charolais Brionnais
X 73538	armor/arvor
X 73546	OBERNAI
X 73549	METZERAL
X 73551	SAVERNE
X 73553	HOCHFELDEN
X 73554	URMATT
X 73558	GUEBWILLER
X 73559	LA WANTZENAU
X 73567	REICHSHOFFEN
X 73568	SAINT AMARIN
X 73572	BOLLWILLER
X 73574	hermine/erminig
X 73575	aven/aven
X 73588	lancelot/lanselod
X 73595	le Thiérachien
X 73596	Huelgoat/ar uhelgoad
X 73597	armorique/arvorig
X 73599	Cornouiaille/kerne
X 73601	Haute Bretagne/reizh Uhel
X 73603	brocéliande/breselien
X 73604	emeraude/emrodez
X 73606	le Compiègnois
X 73609	le St Quentinois
X 73610	l'Amienois
X 73611	le Santerre
X 73719	le Laonnois
X 73720	le Cotterézien
X 73721	les Vallons d'Anizy
X 73722	le Vervinois
X 73723	le Crépynois
X 73748	le Soissonnais
X 73759	le Valois
X 73774	AGEN
X 73901	Alsace/Rheinland Pfalz
X 73902	Alsace/Saarland

X 73904	OBERMODERN-ZUTZENDORF	X 73917	DRUSENHEIM
X 73906	Alsace/Saarland		

CLASS X 76500   AGC   3 OR 4-SECTION UNITS

Class X 76500 is the diesel version of the Autorail à Grande Capacité (AGC), the electric version being Class Z 27500 and the dual-mode versions B 81500 and B 82500. Altogether, 700 of these units have been ordered since 2001. Units are the first SNCF units to be articulated and are air-conditioned and low floor except for the end sections over the bogies. The units are now used over much of France and are helping to replace the vintage EAD DMUs. A total of 161 units (all 3-car except those for Pays de la Loire) has been ordered by Alsace (22), Auvergne (22), Basse Normandie (14), Champagne-Ardenne ((23), Franche Comté (5), Haute Normandie (4), Lorraine (9), Nord-pas-de-Calais (15), PACA (8), Pays de la Loire (15 4-car sets) and Picardie (24). Two versions exist for the internal layout – "Intercités" and " Grand Confort". Regions can also specify optional equipment such as ski racks, bike racks and drink/snack machine.

The AGCs have been generally reliable, coming as a big contrast after Class X 72500. Initial teething troubles mainly concerned the doors and noise when braking. The units are used on a variety of regional services, including some longer distance links such as Rouen–Caen and Caen–Rennes.

Built: 2005–   **Builder:** Bombardier.
Engines: 2 x MAN D 2842 LE 606 of 662 kW per car.
Transmission: Electric, asynchronous traction motors.
Length: 21.00 + 15.40 m (+ 15.40 m) + 21.00 m.
Accommodation: 22/29 1T + –/51 (+ –/60) + –/58.
Maximum Speed: 160 km/h.   **Weight:** 53 + 28 + (+28) + 53 t.
Wheel Arrangement: Bo-2-2(-2)-Bo.
Non-Standard livery:
N X 76603/4 have frontal flashes and markings for the 100th AGC delivered.

X 76501	761501			X 76502	**T**	*PI*	LN	X 76571	761571		
X 76503	761503			X 76504	**T**	*BN*	CA	X 76573	761573		
X 76505	761505			X 76506	**T**	*NP*	LN	X 76575	761575		
X 76507	761507			X 76508	**T**	*HN*	CA	X 76577	761577		
X 76509	761509			X 76510	**T**	*AL*	SB	X 76579	761579		
X 76511	761511			X 76512	**T**	*AU*	NV	X 76581	761581		
X 76513	761513			X 76514	**T**	*PI*	LN	X 76583	761583		
X 76515	761515			X 76516	**T**	*NP*	LN	X 76585	761585		
X 76517	761517			X 76518	**T**	*BN*	CA	X 76587	761587		
X 76519	761519			X 76520	**T**	*AL*	SB	X 76589	761589		
X 76521	761521			X 76522	**T**	*AU*	NV	X 76591	761591		
X 76523	761523			X 76524	**T**	*PA*	MB	X 76593	761593		
X 76525	761525			X 76526	**T**	*PI*	LN	X 76595	761595		
X 76527	761527			X 76528	**T**	*BN*	CA	X 76597	761597		
X 76529	761529			X 76530	**T**	*NP*	LN	X 76599	761599		
X 76531	761531			X 76532	**T**	*HN*	CA	X 76601	761601		
X 76533	761533			X 76534	**T**	*AL*	SB	X 76603	761603		
X 76535	761535			X 76536	**T**	*AU*	NV	X 76605	761605		
X 76537	761537			X 76538	**T**	*LO*	SB	X 76607	761607		
X 76539	761539			X 76540	**T**	*PI*	LN	X 76609	761609		
X 76541	761541			X 76542	**T**	*BN*	CA	X 76611	761611		
X 76543	761543			X 76544	**T**	*PA*	MB	X 76613	761613		
X 76545	761545			X 76546	**T**	*NP*	LN	X 76615	761615		
X 76547	761547			X 76548	**T**	*AL*	SB	X 76617	761617		
X 76549	761549			X 76550	**T**	*AU*	NV	X 76619	761619		
X 76551	761551			X 76552	**T**	*LO*	SB	X 76621	761621		
X 76553	761553			X 76554	**T**	*PI*	LN	X 76623	761623		
X 76555	761555			X 76556	**T**	*BN*	CA	X 76625	761625		
X 76557	761557			X 76558	**T**	*NP*	LN	X 76627	761627		
X 76559	761559			X 76560	**T**	*AL*	SB	X 76629	761629		
X 76561	761561			X 76562	**T**	*AU*	NV	X 76631	761631		
X 76563	761563			X 76564	**T**	*LO*	SB	X 76633	761633		
X 76565	761565			X 76566	**T**	*PI*	LN	X 76635	761635		
X 76567	761567			X 76568	**T**	*BN*	CA	X 76637	761637		
X 76569	761569			X 76570	**T**	*NP*	LN	X 76639	761639		

X 76572	**T**	*AL*	SB
X 76574	**T**	*PI*	LN
X 76576	**T**	*LO*	SB
X 76578	**T**	*BN*	CA
X 76580	**T**	*NP*	LN
X 76582	**T**	*AL*	SB
X 76584	**T**	*PA*	MB
X 76586	**T**	*PI*	LN
X 76588	**T**	*BN*	CA
X 76590	**T**	*NP*	LN
X 76592	**T**	*LO*	SB
X 76594	**T**	*PA*	MB
X 76596	**T**	*PI*	LN
X 76598	**T**	*BN*	CA
X 76600	**T**	*NP*	LN
X 76602	**T**	*AL*	SB
X 76604	**N**	*PI*	LN
X 76606	**T**	*BN*	CA
X 76608	**T**	*AL*	SB
X 76610	**T**	*PI*	LN
X 76612	**T**	*BN*	CA
X 76614	**T**	*NP*	LN
X 76616	**T**	*AL*	SB
X 76618	**T**	*PI*	LN
X 76620	**T**	*BN*	CA
X 76622	**T**	*AL*	SB
X 76624	**T**	*AL*	SB
X 76626	**T**	*PA*	MB
X 76628	**T**	*PI*	LN
X 76630	**T**	*PI*	LN
X 76632	**T**	*BN*	CA
X 76634	**T**	*BN*	CA
X 76636	**T**	*AL*	SB
X 76638	**T**	*PI*	LN
X 76640	**T**	*HN*	CA

X 76641 761641	X 76642 **T** *AL* SB	X 76733 761733	X 76734 **T** *PI* LN
X 76643 761643	X 76644 **T** *AL* SB	X 76735 761735	X 76736 **T** *PI* LN
X 76645 761645	X 76646 **T** *AL* SB	X 76737 761737	X 76738 **T** *LO* MZ
X 76647 761647	X 76648 **T** *AL* SB	X 76739 761739	X 76740 **T** *LO* MZ
X 76649 761649	X 76650 **T** *AU* NV	X 76741 761741	X 76742 **T** *LO* MZ
X 76651 761651	X 76652 **T** *AL* SB	X 76743 761743	X 76744 **T** *LO* MZ
X 76653 761653	X 76654 **T** *AL* SB	X 76745 761745	X 76746
X 76655 761655	X 76656 **T** *HN* CA	X 76747 761747	X 76748
X 76657 761657	X 76658 **T** *AU* NV	X 76749 761749	X 76750
X 76659 761659	X 76660 **T** *AL* SB	X 76751 761751	X 76752
X 76661 761661	X 76662 **T** *AL* SB	X 76753 761753	X 76754
X 76663 761663	X 76664 **T** *AU* NV	X 76755 761755	X 76756
X 76665 761665	X 76666 **T** *AU* NV	X 76757 761757	X 76758
X 76667 761667	X 76668 **T** *FC* DP	X 76759 761759	X 76760
X 76669 761669	X 76670 **T** *CA* EP	X 76761 761761	X 76762
X 76671 761671	X 76672 **T** *PA* MB	X 76763 761763	X 76764
X 76673 761673	X 76674 **T** *FC* DP	X 76765 761765	X 76766
X 76675 761675	X 76676 **T** *CA* EP	X 76767 761767	X 76768
X 76677 761677	X 76678 **T** *CA* EP	X 76769 761769	X 76770
X 76679 761679	X 76680 **T** *FC* DP	X 76771 761771	X 76772
X 76681 761681	X 76682 **T** *PA* MB	X 76773 761773	X 76774
X 76683 761683	X 76684 **T** *PA* MB	X 76775 761775	X 76776
X 76685 761685	X 76686 **T** *CA* EP	X 76777 761777 762777	X 76778 **T** *PL* NB
X 76687 761687	X 76688 **T** *CA* EP	X 76779 761779 762779	X 76780 **T** *PL* NB
X 76689 761689	X 76690 **T** *CA* EP	X 76781 761781 762781	X 76782 **T** *PL* NB
X 76691 761691	X 76692 **T** *CA* EP	X 76783 761783 762783	X 76784 **T** *PL* NB
X 76693 761693	X 76694 **T** *CA* EP	X 76785 761785 762785	X 76786 **T** *PL* NB
X 76695 761695	X 76696 **T** *CA* EP	X 76787 761787 762787	X 76788 **T** *PL* NB
X 76697 761697	X 76698 **T** *CA* EP	X 76789 761789	X 76790
X 76699 761699	X 76700 **T** *CA* EP	X 76791 761791	X 76792
X 76701 761701	X 76702 **T** *CA* EP	X 76793 761793	X 76794
X 76703 761703	X 76704 **T** *CA* EP	X 76795 761795	X 76796
X 76705 761705	X 76706 **T** *CA* EP	X 76797 761797	X 76798
X 76707 761707	X 76708 **T** *CA* EP	X 76799 761799	X 76800
X 76709 761709	X 76710 **T** *NP* LN	X 76801 761801	X 76702
X 76711 761711	X 76712 **T** *NP* LN	X 76803 761803	X 76704
X 76713 761713	X 76714 **T** *FC* DP	X 76805 761805	X 76706
X 76715 761715	X 76716 **T** *FC* DP	X 76807 761807	X 76708
X 76717 761717	X 76718 **T** *NP* LN	X 76809 761809	X 76710
X 76719 761719	X 76720 **T** *NP* LN	X 76811 761811	X 76712
X 76721 761721	X 76722 **T** *NP* LN	X 76813 761813	X 76714
X 76723 761723	X 76724 **T** *AU* CF	X 76815 761815	X 76716
X 76725 761725	X 76726 **T** *AU* CF	X 76817 761817	X 76718
X 76727 761727	X 76728	X 76819 761819	X 76720
X 76729 761729	X 76730 **T** *PI* LN	X 76821 761821	X 76722
X 76731 761731	X 76732 **T** *PI* LN		

Names:

X 76501/2	Le Beauvaisis	X 76603/4	Le Clermontois
X 76513/4	L'Abbevillois	X 76615/6	HAGENAU
X 76525/6	Le Val de Nièvre	X 76617/8	Le Marquenterre
X 76537/8	MIRECOURT	X 76621/2	SESSENHEIM
X 76539/40	Le Ponthieu	X 76627/8	Le Pays du Coquelicot
X 76553/4	Le Pays de Serre	X 76629/30	Le Pays de Thelle
X 76565/6	Le Vexin	X 76641/2	VENDENHEIM
X 76581/2	ROESCHWOOG	X 76653/4	WISCHES
X 76595/6	Le Pays des Sources	X 76661/2	MUHLBACH LUTELHOUSE
X 76601/2	BISCHWILLER	X 76697/8	VILLE DE FISMES

1.4. DUAL-MODE MULTIPLE UNITS

In 2001, Bombardier won a massive contract for the AGC multiple unit, of which 700 will finally be built. One of the reasons for this succes is that the units are modular and can be produced in diesel, electric or dual mode versions, the latter being the first units of their kind in the world to be produced in large quantities. There are two dual mode versions – B 81500 which is diesel plus 1500 V DC electric, and B 82500 which is diesel plus 1500 V DC and 25 kV AC. Class B 81500 was relatively easy to produce as AGCs all have electric transmission at 1500 V DC so no transformer was needed for operation under that voltage.

CLASS B 81500   AGC   3- OR 4-SECTION UNITS

These were the first dual mode version of the AGC and were ordered by many of the regions south of Paris as they were not much more expensive than a straight AGC DMU. The dual mode facility is very useful for a service such as Bordeaux–Mont-de-Marsan where there are 109 km under the wires then 38 km non-electrified. The regions were also interested in these units because they can use electric power in stations for auxiliaries such as air conditioning, even if most of a journey is not electrified. Such an example is Poitiers–Limoges. A total of 178 Class B 81500 have been ordered by Aquitaine (27 3-section), Bourgogne (8 3-section, 22 4-section), Centre (4 3-section), Languedoc-Roussillon (4 3-section, 5 4-section), Limousin (12 3-section), Midi-Pyrénées (18 3-section), PACA (27 4-section), Poutoi-Charentes (11 3-section) and Rhône-Alpes (40 3-section).

Details as Class X 76500 except:

Built: 2005–.
Systems: 1500 V DC plus diesel.
Power rating (electric): 1300 kW.

```
B 81501 811501          B 81502 T  MP  TL    B 81573 811573 812573 B 81574 BO BO DP
B 81503 811503          B 81504 BO BO  DP    B 81575 811575        B 81576 T  RA LV
B 81505 811505          B 81506 T  RA  LV    B 81577 811577 812577 B 81578 BO BO DP
B 81507 811507          B 81508 T  MP  TL    B 81579 811579 812579 B 81580 BO BO DP
B 81509 811509          B 81510 BO BO  DP    B 81581 811581        B 81582 T  AQ BD
B 81511 811511          B 81512 LR LR  MB    B 81583 811583        B 81584 T  LI LG
B 81513 811513          B 81514 T  MP  TL    B 81585 811585        B 81586 T  LI LG
B 81515 811515          B 81516 T  CE  LV    B 81587 811587        B 81588 T  AQ BD
B 81517 811517          B 81518 T  RA  LV    B 81589 811589        B 81590 T  LI LG
B 81519 811519          B 81520 BO BO  DP    B 81591 811591        B 81592 T  AQ BD
B 81521 811521          B 81522 T  RA  LV    B 81593 811593        B 81594 T  AQ BD
B 81523 811523          B 81524 T  MP  TL    B 81595 811595        B 81596 T  LI LG
B 81525 811525          B 81526 LR LR  MB    B 81597 811597        B 81598 T  AQ BD
B 81527 811527          B 81528 BO BO  LV    B 81599 811599        B 81600 T  AQ BD
B 81529 811529          B 81530 T  RA  LV    B 81601 811601        B 81602 T  AQ BD
B 81531 811531          B 81532 T  MP  TL    B 81603 811603 812603 B 81604 T  PA MB
B 81533 811533          B 81534 LR LR  MB    B 81605 811605 812605 B 81606 T  PA MB
B 81535 811535          B 81536 BO BO  DP    B 81607 811607        B 81608 T  LI LG
B 81537 811537          B 81538 T  CE  NV    B 81609 811609        B 81610 T  LI LG
B 81539 811539          B 81540 T  RA  LV    B 81611 811611 812611 B 81612 T  PA MB
B 81541 811541          B 81542 T  MP  TL    B 81613 811613 812613 B 81614 T  PA MB
B 81543 811543          B 81544 T  RA  LV    B 81615 811615 812615 B 81616 T  PA MB
B 81545 811545          B 81546 LR LR  MB    B 81617 811617        B 81618 T  LI LG
B 81547 811547          B 81548 BO BO  DP    B 81619 811619 812619 B 81620 T  PA MB
B 81549 811549          B 81550 T  MP  TL    B 81621 811621 812621 B 81622 T  PA MB
B 81551 811551          B 81552 T  CE  NV    B 81623 811623 812623 B 81624 T  PA MB
B 81553 811553          B 81554 T  RA  LV    B 81625 811625        B 81626 T  LI LG
B 81555 811555          B 81556 T  RA  LV    B 81627 811627 812627 B 81628 T  PA MB
B 81557 811557          B 81558 BO BO  DP    B 81629 811629 812629 B 81630 T  PA MB
B 81559 811559          B 81560 T  CE  NV    B 81631 811631 812631 B 81632 T  PA MB
B 81561 811561          B 81562 T  RA  LV    B 81633 811633        B 81634 T  LI LG
B 81563 811563          B 81564 BO BO  DP    B 81635 811635 812635 B 81636 T  PA MB
B 81565 811565          B 81566 T  RA  LV    B 81637 811637 812637 B 81638 T  PA MB
B 81567 811567          B 81568 T  RA  LV    B 81639 811639 812639 B 81640 T  PA MB
B 81569 811569 812569   B 81570 BO BO  DP    B 81641 811641 812641 B 81642 T  PA MB
B 81571 811571          B 81572 T  RA  LV    B 81643 811643 812643 B 81644 T  PA MB
```

B 81645	811645	812645	B 81646 **T**	*PA*	MB	B 81753	811753	B 81754
B 81647	811647		B 81648 **T**	*LI*	LG	B 81755	811755	B 81756
B 81649	811649		B 81650 **T**	*LI*	LG	B 81757	811757	B 81758
B 81651	811651		B 81652 **T**	*LI*	LG	B 81759	811759	B 81760
B 81653	811653		B 81654 **T**	*RA*	LV	B 81761	811761	B 81762
B 81655	811655		B 81656 **T**	*RA*	LV	B 81763	811763	B 81764
B 81657	811657		B 81658 **T**	*RA*	LV	B 81765	811765	B 81766
B 81659	811659		B 81660 **T**	*RA*	LV	B 81767	811767	B 81768
B 81661	811661		B 81662 **T**	*RA*	LV	B 81769	811769	B 81770
B 81663	811663		B 81664 **T**	*RA*	LV	B 81771	811771	B 81772
B 81665	811665		B 81666 **T**	*PC*	SA	B 81773	811773	B 81774
B 81667	811667		B 81668 **T**	*RA*	LV	B 81775	811775	B 81776
B 81669	811669		B 81670 **T**	*RA*	LV	B 81777	811777	B 81778
B 81671	811671		B 81672 **T**	*PC*	SA	B 81779	811779	B 81780
B 81673	811673		B 81674 **T**	*RA*	LV	B 81781	811781	B 81782
B 81675	811675		B 81676 **T**	*PC*	SA	B 81783	811783	B 81784
B 81677	811677		B 81678 **T**	*AQ*	BD	B 81785	811785	B 81786
B 81679	811679		B 81680 **T**	*PC*	SA	B 81787	811787	B 81788
B 81681	811681		B 81682 **T**			B 81789	811789	B 81790
B 81683	811683		B 81684 **T**	*AQ*	BD	B 81791	811791	B 81792
B 81685	811685		B 81686 **T**	*AQ*	BD	B 81793	811793	B 81794
B 81687	811687		B 81688 **T**	*AQ*	BD	B 81795	811795	B 81796
B 81689	811689		B 81690 **T**			B 81797	811797	B 81798
B 81691	811691		B 81692 **T**	*RA*	LV	B 81799	811799	B 81800
B 81693	811693		B 81694 **T**	*AQ*	BD	B 81801	811801	B 81802
B 81695	811695		B 81696 **T**	*AQ*	BD	B 81803	811803	B 81804
B 81697	811697		B 81698 **T**	*AQ*	BD	B 81805	811805	B 81806
B 81699	811699		B 81700 **T**	*RA*	LV	B 81807	811807	B 81808
B 81701	811701		B 81702			B 81809	811809	B 81810
B 81703	811703		B 81704			B 81811	811811	B 81812
B 81705	811705		B 81706			B 81813	811813	B 81814
B 81707	811707		B 81708			B 81815	811815	B 81816
B 81709	811709		B 81710			B 81817	811817	B 81818
B 81711	811711		B 81712			B 81819	811819	B 81820
B 81713	811713		B 81714			B 81821	811821	B 81822
B 81715	811715		B 81716			B 81823	811823	B 81824
B 81717	811717		B 81718			B 81825	811825	B 81826
B 81719	811719		B 81720			B 81827	811827	B 81828
B 81721	811721		B 81722			B 81829	811829	B 81830
B 81723	811723		B 81724			B 81831	811831	B 81832
B 81725	811725		B 81726			B 81833	811833	B 81834
B 81727	811727		B 81728			B 81835	811835	B 81836
B 81729	811729		B 81730			B 81837	811837	B 81838
B 81731	811731		B 81732			B 81839	811839	B 81840
B 81733	811733		B 81734			B 81841	811841	B 81842
B 81735	811735		B 81736			B 81843	811843	B 81844
B 81737	811737		B 81738			B 81845	811845	B 81846
B 81739	811739		B 81740			B 81847	811847	B 81848
B 81741	811741		B 81742			B 81849	811849	B 81850
B 81743	811743		B 81744			B 81851	811851	B 81852
B 81745	811745		B 81746			B 81853	811853	B 81854
B 81747	811747		B 81748			B 81855	811855	B 81856
B 81749	811749		B 81750			B 81857	811857	B 81858
B 81751	811751		B 81752			B 81859	811859	B 81860

Names:

B 81587/88 MONT DE MARSAN
B 81611/12 CAUSSOLS
B 81613/14 VENTOUX
B 81627/28 PAYS D'AIX

B 81635/36 LUBERON
B 81639/40 ALPILLES
B 81641/42 ESTAQUE

CLASS B 82500 AGC BiBi 3- OR 4-SECTION UNITS

Class B 82500 is a world first in being the *bi-mode, bi-voltage* (thus its nickname "BiBi") version of the Autorail à Grande Capacité (AGC). The units can be used in diesel mode or under either of France's standard voltages – 1500 V DC or 25 kV AC. A total of 142 units are on order – for Alsace (7), Bourgogne (5), Bretagne (9), Champagne-Ardenne (8), Haute Normandie (7), Nord Pas de Calais (30), Picardie (16), Poitou Charentes (8), Rhône Alpes (28) and Île-de-France (greater Paris). All of these units are 4-car section as a 3-car section is not available – the fourth car has the transformer on the roof. A version without 1500 V DC is not available so all regions needing only 25 kV AC get 1500 V DC too. The use of both voltages will be restricted to areas with both. The Île-de-France units will used on the Paris Est to Provins and La Ferté-Milon routes. Although allocated to Noisy, they will receive heavier maintenance at Epernay.

Île-de-France units carry the last three digits of the first power car on the nose plus N for Noisy – 521N for B 82521 and so on.

Built : 2007–. **Builder:** Bombardier.
Systems: 1500 V DC, 25 kV AC, Diesel.
Engines: 2 x MAN D 2842 LE 606 of 662 kW each.
Transmission: Electric, asynchronous traction motors.
Power rating in electric mode: 1300 kW.
Length: 21.00 + 15.40 m. + 15.40 m.
Accommodation: 22/29 1T + –/51 + –/60 + –/58.
Maximum speed: 160 km/h. 140 km/h in diesel mode.
Weight: 165 tonnes empty. **Wheel Arrangement:** Bo-2-2-Bo.

B 82501	821501	822501	B 82502	T	CA	CY
B 82503	821503	822503	B 82504	T	CA	CY
B 82505	821505	822505	B 82506	T	CA	CY
B 82507	821507	822507	B 82508	T	CA	CY
B 82509	821509	822509	B 82510	T		
B 82511	821511	822511	B 82512	T		
B 82513	821513	822513	B 82514	T		
B 82515	821515	822515	B 82516	T		
B 82517	821517	822517	B 82518	T	PC	SA
B 82519	821519	822519	B 82520	T	PC	SA
B 82521	821521	822521	B 82522	W	IF	PN
B 82523	821523	822523	B 82524	T	PC	SA
B 82525	821525	822525	B 82526	T	PC	SA
B 82527	821527	822527	B 82528	T	PC	SA
B 82529	821529	822529	B 82530	T	PC	SA
B 82531	821531	822531	B 82532	W	IF	PN
B 82533	821533	822533	B 82534	W	IF	PN
B 82535	821535	822535	B 82536	W	IF	PN
B 82537	821537		B 82538	W	IF	PN
B 82539	821539		B 82540	W	IF	PN
B 82541	821541		B 82542	W	IF	PN
B 82543	821543		B 82544	W	IF	PN
B 82545	821545		B 82546	W	IF	PN
B 82547	821547		B 82548	W	IF	PN
B 82549	821549		B 82550	W	IF	PN
B 82551	821551		B 82552	W	IF	PN
B 82553	821553		B 82554	W	IF	PN
B 82555	821555		B 82556	W	IF	PN
B 82557	821557		B 82558	W	IF	PN
B 82559	821559		B 82560	W	IF	PN
B 82561	821561		B 82562	W	IF	PN
B 82563	821563		B 82564			
B 82565	821565		B 82566	W	IF	PN
B 82567	821567		B 82568			
B 82569	821569		B 82570			
B 82571	821571		B 82572			
B 82573	821573		B 82574			
B 82575	821575		B 82576			
B 82577	821577		B 82578			

B 82579	821579	B 82580
B 82581	821581	B 82582
B 82583	821583	B 82584
B 82585	821585	B 82586
B 82587	821587	B 82588
B 82589	821589	B 82590
B 82591	821591	B 82592
B 82593	821593	B 82594
B 82595	821595	B 82596
B 82597	821597	B 82598
B 82599	821599	B 82600
B 82601	821601	B 82602
B 82603	821603	B 82604
B 82605	821605	B 82606
B 82607	821607	B 82608
B 82609	821609	B 82610
B 82611	821611	B 82612
B 82613	821613	B 82614
B 82615	821615	B 82616
B 82617	821617	B 82618
B 82619	821619	B 82620
B 82621	821621	B 82622
B 82623	821623	B 82624
B 82625	821625	B 82626
B 82627	821627	B 82628
B 82629	821629	B 82630
B 82631	821631	B 82632
B 82633	821633	B 82634
B 82635	821635	B 82636
B 82637	821637	B 82638
B 82639	821639	B 82640
B 82641	821641	B 82642
B 82643	821643	B 82644
B 82645	821645	B 82646
B 82647	821647	B 82648
B 82649	821649	B 82650
B 82651	821651	B 82652
B 82653	821653	B 82654
B 82655	821655	B 82656

B 82657 821657	B 82658	B 82721 821721	B 82722
B 82659 821659	B 82660	B 82723 821723	B 82724
B 82661 821661	B 82662	B 82725 821725	B 82726
B 82663 821663	B 82664	B 82727 821727	B 82728
B 82665 821665	B 82666	B 82729 821729	B 82730
B 82667 821667	B 82668	B 82731 821731	B 82732
B 82669 821669	B 82670	B 82733 821733	B 82734
B 82671 821671	B 82672	B 82735 821735	B 82736
B 82673 821673	B 82674	B 82737 821737	B 82738
B 82675 821675	B 82676	B 82739 821739	B 82740
B 82677 821677	B 82678	B 82741 821741	B 82742
B 82679 821679	B 82680	B 82743 821743	B 82744
B 82681 821681	B 82682	B 82745 821745	B 82746
B 82683 821683	B 82684	B 82747 821747	B 82748
B 82685 821685	B 82686	B 82749 821749	B 82750
B 82687 821687	B 82688	B 82751 821751	B 82752
B 82689 821689	B 82690	B 82753 821753	B 82754
B 82691 821691	B 82692	B 82755 821755	B 82756
B 82693 821693	B 82694	B 82757 821757	B 82758
B 82695 821695	B 82696	B 82759 821759	B 82720
B 82697 821697	B 82698	B 82821 821821	B 82722
B 82699 821699	B 82700	B 82823 821823	B 82724
B 82701 821701	B 82702	B 82825 821825	B 82726
B 82703 821703	B 82704	B 82827 821827	B 82728
B 82705 821705	B 82706	B 82829 821829	B 82770
B 82707 821707	B 82708	B 82771 821771	B 82772
B 82709 821709	B 82710	B 82773 821773	B 82774
B 82711 821711	B 82712	B 82775 821775	B 82776
B 82713 821713	B 82714	B 82777 821777	B 82778
B 82715 821715	B 82716	B 82779 821779	B 82780
B 82717 821717	B 82718	B 82781 821781	B 82782
B 82719 821719	B 82720	B 82783 821783	B 82784

Name: B 82501/2 Troyes

1.5. SNCF SHUNTERS

)Small diesel shunters are known as "locotracteurs" in France and can be operated by station staff as well as loco drivers. Locos used as depot shunters are starting to be officially withdrawn but are retained as LOCMAs (see following section). When the SNCF fleet was divided by activity in the late 1990s, all shunters were officially allocated to Fret SNCF despite some being used for passenger or infrastructure work. In June 2008, the proper division of the fleet began but was not complete by the time this book closed for press. "f" denotes freight and "i" infrastructure.

Shunters are in **V** livery unless stated otherwise. Classes Y 8000 and 8400 are in **J** livery.

CLASS Y 7100   B

The Y 6xxx series were built after World War Two and virtually continued pre-war designs. The Y 7100 series was a completely fresh design and featured hydraulic transmission. However this form of transmission was dropped for future classes after Y 7192 had been converted to mechanical transmission and renumbered Y 7001. Used on light shunting duties. Some shunters have been sold to industrial users or to VFLI.

Built: 1958–62.
Builder: Billard (7101–7230), Decauville (7231–7310).
Engine: Poyaud 6PYT (150 kW).   **Transmission:** Hydraulic. Voith.
Weight: 32 tonnes.
Maximum Tractive Effort: 73 kN.   **Length:** 8.94 m.
Wheel Diameter: 1050 mm.   **Maximum Speed:** 54 km/h.

f   Fret sector locos
i   Infra sector locos.

No.				No.				No.				No.			
Y 7101		f	EP	Y 7149	J	f	SO	Y 7194		i	EP	Y 7237	J	i	LE
Y 7102		f	MZ (S)	Y 7150		i	AC	Y 7195		i	MZ (S)	Y 7238	J	i	LE
Y 7104	J	f	MZ (S)	Y 7151	J	f	NV	Y 7196	J	f	EP	Y 7240	J	f	LG
Y 7105		i	BZ	Y 7152	J	i	AC	Y 7197		f	LV	Y 7242	J	f	BZ (S)
Y 7106	J	f	BZ	Y 7153	J	f	TP	Y 7198		f	SO	Y 7244	J	i	AV
Y 7107	J	f	LE (S)	Y 7155		f	AC	Y 7199	J	f	AC	Y 7246	J	i	BZ
Y 7108		f	SB	Y 7156	J	f	LV	Y 7201		f	NV (S)	Y 7248		f	EP (S)
Y 7109	J	i	SO	Y 7157	J	i	BZ (S)	Y 7203	J	f	SO	Y 7250	J	f	DP (S)
Y 7110		f	AC	Y 7158		i	MZ	Y 7204		f	EP (S)	Y 7251	J	i	LN
Y 7112	J	f	MZ	Y 7159	J	f	NV	Y 7205	J	i	EP	Y 7253	J	i	LN
Y 7113	J	i	MZ	Y 7160	J	f	TP	Y 7206	J	f	AC	Y 7254	J	f	NV (S)
Y 7114	J	i	EP	Y 7161		i	LE	Y 7207	J	f	LE	Y 7255	J	f	HE
Y 7115		f	EP (S)	Y 7162	J	f	AC	Y 7208	J	i	BZ	Y 7256	J	f	NV
Y 7116	J	i	EP	Y 7163	J	f	TP	Y 7209		f	BZ (S)	Y 7257		f	TP
Y 7120		i	BZ	Y 7165		i	AC	Y 7210	J	f	BZ	Y 7258	J	i	BZ
Y 7121		i	BZ	Y 7166	J	f	DP	Y 7211		f	TP	Y 7259	J	i	AV
Y 7122	J	i	LE	Y 7167		f	LV	Y 7215		f	LV	Y 7261	J	f	AV
Y 7123		i	AC	Y 7168	J	f	TP	Y 7216	J	f	LE	Y 7262	J	i	MZ
Y 7125		f	MZ	Y 7169	J	f	HE	Y 7217	J	f	LE	Y 7263		i	EP
Y 7126	J	i	LN	Y 7170	J	f	SO	Y 7218		f	SO	Y 7264		i	MZ
Y 7127		i	MZ (S)	Y 7173		i	BZ	Y 7219	J	f	TP	Y 7266	J	f	TP
Y 7129		i	AC	Y 7175		i	BZ (S)	Y 7220	J	f	NV (S)	Y 7268		f	BZ
Y 7130	J	i	SO	Y 7176	J	f	BZ (S)	Y 7221	J	f	NV	Y 7269	J	f	AC
Y 7132		i	MZ	Y 7177	J	i	AV	Y 7222	J	f	NV	Y 7270		f	CB
Y 7133		i	MZ	Y 7178	J	f	SO	Y 7223		f	NV	Y 7271	J	f	AC
Y 7134	J	i	MZ	Y 7180	J	i	AC	Y 7224		i	MZ	Y 7274			MZ (S)
Y 7135	J	i	MZ	Y 7182		f	AV	Y 7225	J	i	LN	Y 7275	J	f	MB (S)
Y 7136	J	f	AC (S)	Y 7183		f	LG	Y 7227		f	AC	Y 7279		f	CB
Y 7138	J	f	AV	Y 7184	J	i	LE	Y 7228	J	f	AV	Y 7280		f	AC
Y 7139		i	BZ (S)	Y 7185	J	i	AC	Y 7229		i	AV	Y 7281		f	AC
Y 7141		f	CB	Y 7187	J	f	LG	Y 7230	J	f	NV	Y 7283	J	i	LE
Y 7142	J	f	AV	Y 7188	J	i	LE	Y 7231		f	EP (S)	Y 7284		f	TP
Y 7144	J	i	MZ (S)	Y 7189	J	f	AC	Y 7232		f	MZ	Y 7286		i	AC
Y 7146		i	SO	Y 7190		f	EP (S)	Y 7233	J	i	MZ (S)	Y 7287		i	AV
Y 7148		f	SB	Y 7193		i	LN	Y 7235	J	f	LV (S)	Y 7288	J	i	AV

Y 7289	J	f	LV	Y 7294	J	f	SO	Y 7299		i	LN	Y 7307	J	i	AV
Y 7290	J	f	AC	Y 7295		f	AC	Y 7304	J	f	AV	Y 7308	J	f	AC
Y 7291	J	i	AC	Y 7296	J	i	LE	Y 7305	J	i	BZ	Y 7309	J	f	DP
Y 7292		f	SO	Y 7297	J	i	LE	Y 7306	J	i	BZ	Y 7310	J	i	AC
Y 7293		f	AC	Y 7298	J	f	LN (S)							

CLASS Y 7400   B

After succesful trials the mechanical transmission applied to Y 7001 became standard and the production run lasted nearly ten years. The class is found all over the network on a variety of shunting duties.

Built: 1959 (7001)/1963–72 (others).
Builder: Billard (7001), Decauville (7401–7520), De Dietrich (7521–7625), Moyse (7626–7888).
Engine: Poyaud 6PYT (150 kW).   **Transmission:** Mechanical.
Weight: 32 tonnes.
Maximum Tractive Effort: 73 kN.
Wheel Diameter: 1050 mm.

Length: 8.94 m.
Maximum Speed: 60 km/h.

f   Fret sector locos
i   Infra sector locos.

No	J	type	code	No	J	type	code	No	J	type	code	No	J	type	code
Y 7001		i	LE	Y 7465		f	LV (S)	Y 7522		i	EP	Y 7570	J	f	TL (S)
Y 7403		f	TP (S)	Y 7466		i	AV	Y 7523	J	i	EP	Y 7571		i	AC (S)
Y 7404		i	AC	Y 7467	J	i	AC	Y 7524		i	DP	Y 7573		i	BD
Y 7406		i	LN	Y 7468		f	BD (S)	Y 7526		i	CB	Y 7574		f	BD (S)
Y 7408	J	i	TP	Y 7469	J	i	AC	Y 7527	J	i	TP	Y 7575		i	CB
Y 7410		i	DP	Y 7470		f	AC	Y 7528		i	BD	Y 7576		f	DP
Y 7411		f	AC	Y 7471		f	AC (S)	Y 7529	J	f	CB (S)	Y 7577		f	EP
Y 7412	J	f	TP (S)	Y 7472	J	i	AC	Y 7530	J	i	AC	Y 7578		i	SB
Y 7413	J	i	HE	Y 7473	J	i	AC (S)	Y 7531		i	NV	Y 7579		i	DP
Y 7415	J	f	SO	Y 7475	J	i	LE	Y 7532		i	DP	Y 7580	J	i	SB (S)
Y 7416		f	LV (S)	Y 7476		f	BD (S)	Y 7533		i	DP	Y 7581		f	AC
Y 7417		i	DP	Y 7478		f	DP	Y 7534	J	i	SB	Y 7582		f	SO (S)
Y 7418		f	DP (S)	Y 7479	J	i	BZ	Y 7536		i	DP	Y 7583	J	i	AC
Y 7419	J	i	CB	Y 7480		i	AV	Y 7537		i	AC	Y 7584		f	SO (S)
Y 7420	J	f	NV	Y 7481	J	f	AC	Y 7538	J	f	LE (S)	Y 7585		i	LN
Y 7421	J	f	DP (S)	Y 7482		i	DP	Y 7539	J	i	AC	Y 7586		i	DP
Y 7425		i	AV	Y 7483	J	i	LN	Y 7540	J	f	DP (S)	Y 7587	J	i	LE
Y 7427	J	f	BZ (S)	Y 7485	J	i	BD	Y 7541	J	i	TP	Y 7588		i	LV
Y 7428		f	AV	Y 7486		i	BD	Y 7543		f	LV (S)	Y 7590	J	i	BZ (S)
Y 7429		f	BZ (S)	Y 7487		i	NV	Y 7544		i	AV	Y 7591	J	f	CB (S)
Y 7430	J	i	NV	Y 7488	J	i	AC (S)	Y 7545		i	CB	Y 7592	J	f	BD
Y 7431	J	f	AV (S)	Y 7489		f	AV (S)	Y 7546	J	f	DP (S)	Y 7594	J	f	TP
Y 7432		f	AC	Y 7490	J	f	BZ (S)	Y 7547	J	i	AC	Y 7595	J	i	AC
Y 7434		f	DP	Y 7492	J	i	AC	Y 7548		f	SB (S)	Y 7597		i	DP
Y 7435	J	i	DP	Y 7496		i	DP	Y 7549		i	AC	Y 7598	J	i	CB
Y 7436	J	i	AC	Y 7497		i	DP	Y 7550		f	DP (S)	Y 7599		f	EP (S)
Y 7438		f	AC (S)	Y 7498	J	i	CB	Y 7552	J	i	TP	Y 7600		f	SB (S)
Y 7441		i	TP	Y 7499	J	i	AV	Y 7553	J	i	CB	Y 7601	J	f	SB (S)
Y 7443		f	HE	Y 7500		i	LE	Y 7554		i	AV	Y 7602		i	AC (S)
Y 7444		f	TP (S)	Y 7501	J	i	LN	Y 7555	J	i	AV	Y 7603	J	f	RS (S)
Y 7445	J	i	AC	Y 7502		i	DP	Y 7556	J	f	CB (S)	Y 7604	J	i	AC
Y 7447		f	DP (S)	Y 7503		i	CB	Y 7557		i	CB (S)	Y 7605	J	f	DP
Y 7449		i	NB	Y 7504		f	CB (S)	Y 7558	J	i	LE	Y 7606	J	i	LE
Y 7452	J	i	LV	Y 7507		f	LE (S)	Y 7560	J	i	AC	Y 7609	J	i	LV
Y 7453		i	LV	Y 7508	J	i	BZ	Y 7561	J	i	DP	Y 7610	J	f	LV
Y 7454		f	DP	Y 7509		f	SO	Y 7562	J	i	AC	Y 7611	J	f	DP (S)
Y 7455	J	i	AC	Y 7510	J	i	AC (S)	Y 7563	J	i	AC	Y 7612	J	f	BD
Y 7457		f	AC (S)	Y 7511	J	i	LN	Y 7564	J	f	SB	Y 7613	J	i	BD
Y 7458		i	AC	Y 7512		i	LV	Y 7565	J	f	SB	Y 7614		i	BD
Y 7459	J	i	LV	Y 7513		i	AC (S)	Y 7566			CY (S)	Y 7615	J	i	BD
Y 7462	J	i	AV	Y 7514		i	AC (S)	Y 7567		f	CY	Y 7616	J	i	AC
Y 7463		i	LV	Y 7516	J	i	AC (S)	Y 7568		i	TP	Y 7617			VG
Y 7464		i	AC (S)	Y 7517		i	AC	Y 7569	J	f	DP	Y 7618	J	i	AC (S)

Code				Code				Code				Code			
Y 7619	J	f	NV (S)	Y 7690	J	f	AC	Y 7757	J	i	BD	Y 7826	J	i	TP
Y 7620	J	i	AC	Y 7691	J	i	CB	Y 7758	J	i	AC	Y 7827	J	i	BD
Y 7621	J	i	CY	Y 7693	J	f	LV	Y 7759	J	i	AC	Y 7828	J	i	AC
Y 7622	J	i	AC (S)	Y 7694	J	f	BZ (S)	Y 7760	J	i	LV	Y 7829	J	i	TL
Y 7623		i	AC (S)	Y 7695	J	i	LV	Y 7761		i	AC (S)	Y 7830	J	i	AC (S)
Y 7624		i	SB	Y 7696	J	i	DP	Y 7762	J	i	LV	Y 7831	J	i	NV
Y 7625	J	i	BD	Y 7697	J	i	TL	Y 7763	J	f	AC (S)	Y 7832	J	i	NV
Y 7626	J	i	LG	Y 7698	J	i	LG	Y 7764	J	i	BZ	Y 7833	J	i	DP
Y 7627	J	f	DP	Y 7699	J	i	LG	Y 7765	J	i	LV	Y 7834	J	i	TL
Y 7629	J	f	AC	Y 7700	J	f	AC	Y 7766	J	i	NV	Y 7835	J	i	CY
Y 7630	J	f	AC	Y 7701	J	i	RS	Y 7767	J	f	LG	Y 7836	J	i	LE
Y 7631		i	BD	Y 7702	J	i	RS	Y 7769	J	i	AC	Y 7837	J	i	DP
Y 7633	J	i	SB	Y 7703	J	i	CY	Y 7770	J	i	CY	Y 7838	J	i	RS
Y 7634	J	f	SB	Y 7704	J	i	NV	Y 7771	J	i	NB	Y 7839	J	i	SO
Y 7635	J	f	AC	Y 7705	J	i	AV	Y 7772	J	i	LE	Y 7840	J	i	TL
Y 7636	J	i	LE	Y 7706	J	i	AC	Y 7773	J	i	DP	Y 7841	J	i	TL
Y 7637	J	i	AC	Y 7707	J	f	SB	Y 7774	J	f	LE	Y 7842	J	i	TL
Y 7638	J	f	RS (S)	Y 7708	J	i	CB	Y 7775	J	i	NB	Y 7843	J	i	AC
Y 7639	J	i	AC	Y 7709	J	f	CY (S)	Y 7776	J	i	AC	Y 7844	J	i	AC
Y 7640	J	f	NV	Y 7710	J	f	DP	Y 7777	J	f	NB (S)	Y 7845	J	f	LG
Y 7641	J	i	AC	Y 7711	J	i	TL	Y 7778	J	i	LG	Y 7846	J	i	BD
Y 7642	J	f	LV	Y 7712	J	i	AC	Y 7779	J	i	LG	Y 7847	J	i	CB
Y 7643	J	f	NV	Y 7713	J	i	AC	Y 7780	J	i	TL	Y 7848	J	f	DP
Y 7644	J	f	LV (S)	Y 7714	J	f	LE	Y 7781	J	i	NV	Y 7849	J	i	AC
Y 7646	J	f	NV	Y 7715	J	f	NB	Y 7782	J	f	DP	Y 7850	J	i	AC
Y 7648	J	i	TP	Y 7716	J	f	TP	Y 7783	J	i	CB	Y 7851	J	i	LV
Y 7651	J	f	TP	Y 7717	J	i	TP	Y 7784	J	i	AV	Y 7852	J	i	CY
Y 7652	J	f	CY	Y 7718	J	i	TL (S)	Y 7785	J	i	LV	Y 7853	J	i	EP
Y 7653	J	i	NB	Y 7719	J	i	CB	Y 7786	J	i	AV	Y 7854	J	i	AC
Y 7654	J	i	LV	Y 7720	J	i	AC	Y 7787	J	i	LG	Y 7855	J	i	SO
Y 7655	J	f	AC	Y 7721	J	i	AC	Y 7788	J	f	AC	Y 7856	J	i	BD
Y 7656	J	f	LE (S)	Y 7722	J	i	LV	Y 7790	J	f	TP	Y 7857	J	i	BD
Y 7657		i	AC	Y 7723	J	i	BZ	Y 7791	J	i	BD	Y 7858	J	i	SB
Y 7658	J	i	LE	Y 7725	J	i	LG	Y 7792	J	i	TL	Y 7859	J	i	SO
Y 7659	J	i	AC	Y 7726	J	i	LE	Y 7793	J	i	CY	Y 7860	J	i	AC
Y 7660	J	i	AC	Y 7727	J	f	TL	Y 7794	J	i	EP	Y 7861	J	f	CB
Y 7661		i	AV	Y 7728	J	i	HE	Y 7796	J	i	SB	Y 7862	J	i	LV
Y 7662		i	DP	Y 7729		f	SB (S)	Y 7797	J	i	SB	Y 7863	J	i	BD
Y 7663	J	f	DP (S)	Y 7730	J	f	CY (S)	Y 7799	J	i	AC	Y 7864	J	i	SO
Y 7664	J	f	NV	Y 7731	J	i	AC	Y 7800	J	i	LE	Y 7865	J	i	SO
Y 7665		f	TL (S)	Y 7732	J	f	DP (S)	Y 7801	J	i	DP (S)	Y 7866	J	f	NB
Y 7666	J	i	BZ (S)	Y 7733	J	i	AC	Y 7802	J	i	TL	Y 7867	J	i	NB
Y 7667		f	AV (S)	Y 7735	J	f	RS (S)	Y 7803	J	i	NB	Y 7868	J	i	AC
Y 7668	J	i	BZ	Y 7736	J	f	TL (S)	Y 7804	J	i	BZ	Y 7869	J	f	TP
Y 7669	J	i	AC	Y 7737	J	f	TL (S)	Y 7805	J	f	CB (S)	Y 7870	J	i	SO
Y 7670	J	i	AC (S)	Y 7738	J	i	TL	Y 7806	J	i	NV	Y 7871	J	i	RS
Y 7671	J	i	LV	Y 7739	J	f	AC	Y 7807	J	i	AC	Y 7872	J	f	RS (S)
Y 7672	J	i	BD	Y 7740	J	i	EP	Y 7808	J	i	AC	Y 7873	J	i	RS
Y 7673		i	NB	Y 7741	J	i	NV	Y 7809	J	i	NB	Y 7874	J	i	SB
Y 7674	J	f	AC	Y 7742	J	i	LE	Y 7810	J	i	HE	Y 7875	J	f	SB (S)
Y 7675	J	i	CY	Y 7743	J	i	AV	Y 7811	J	i	SB	Y 7876	J	f	SB
Y 7676	J	i	AC	Y 7744	J	i	TL	Y 7812	J	i	NB	Y 7877	J	i	AC
Y 7677	J	i	AC (S)	Y 7745	J	i	TP	Y 7813	J	i	NB	Y 7878	J	i	AC
Y 7678	J	i	AC	Y 7746	J	i	AC	Y 7814	J	i	RS (S)	Y 7879	J	f	BZ (S)
Y 7679	J	i	AC	Y 7747	J	i	BD	Y 7815	J	f	CY	Y 7880	J	i	RS
Y 7680	J	i	RS	Y 7748	J	f	DP (S)	Y 7816	J	i	SB	Y 7881	J	i	AC
Y 7681	J	i	NB	Y 7749	J	f	SB (S)	Y 7817	J	i	TL	Y 7882	J	i	AC
Y 7682	J	i	AC	Y 7750	J	i	SO	Y 7818	J	i	LE	Y 7883	J	f	DP (S)
Y 7683	J	i	AC	Y 7751	J	i	LV	Y 7819	J	i	LN	Y 7884	J	i	DP
Y 7685	J	f	TL (S)	Y 7752	J	i	LN	Y 7820	J	i	BZ	Y 7885	J	i	LV
Y 7686	J	i	TP	Y 7753	J	i	AC	Y 7821	J	f	SB (S)	Y 7886		i	NV
Y 7687	J	i	AC	Y 7754	J	i	RS	Y 7822	J	f	RS (S)	Y 7887		i	CB
Y 7688	J	f	NV	Y 7755	J	i	NB	Y 7823	J	f	RS (S)	Y 7888		i	LV
Y 7689	J	i	LV	Y 7756	J	f	NB (S)	Y 7824	J	i	SO				

CLASS Y 8000   B

This was the new standard hydraulic shunter in the new yellow livery. Being more powerful and with a higher speed than previous designs, locos see more main line use on trip workings and are allocated to fewer depots. Some are radio fitted for use in stations. Y 8300 was tested with remote control as a prototype for the Y 8400 series. Certain later locos were used to test Renault and Unidiesel engines, the latter being adopted for Y 8491–8550. All locos now going through works are being re-engined.

Built: 1977–90.
Builder: Moyse (8001–8090), Fauvet Girel (8091–8375).
Engine: Poyaud V12-520NS (224kW) [*Renault MIDR 06-20-45 D41, † Unidiesel UD18L6R3] (219 kW).
Transmission: Hydraulic. Voith LZr4SU2 (†Electric transmission).
Weight: 36 tonnes.
Maximum Tractive Effort: 118/62 kN.   **Length:** 10.14 m.
Wheel Diameter: 1050 mm.   **Maximum Speed:** 30/60 km/h.

r Remote control fitted. Prototype loco for Class Y 8400.
i Used in Italy.

No			No			No			No		
Y 8001	J	TP	Y 8045	J	AV	Y 8089	J	TL	Y 8133	F	AC
Y 8002	J	MZ	Y 8046	J	AC	Y 8090	J †r	LG	Y 8134	F	CY
Y 8003	J	MZ	Y 8047	J	DP	Y 8091	J	LE	Y 8135	F	AC
Y 8004	J	MZ	Y 8048	J	NB	Y 8092	J	CY	Y 8136	F	LG
Y 8005	J	AC	Y 8049	J	TL	Y 8093	J	SO	Y 8137	F	TL
Y 8006	J	MZ	Y 8050	J	BZ	Y 8094	J	AC	Y 8138	F	NV
Y 8007	J	AC	Y 8051	J	SO	Y 8095	J	AC	Y 8139	J	CB
Y 8008	J	SB	Y 8052	J	CY	Y 8096	J	AV	Y 8140	F	LV
Y 8009	J	DP	Y 8053	J	LV	Y 8097	J	NB	Y 8141	F	LV
Y 8010	J	MZ	Y 8054	J	LV	Y 8098	J	BD	Y 8142	F	LV
Y 8011	J	SB	Y 8055	J	LV	Y 8099	J	TL	Y 8143	F	RS
Y 8012	J	SO	Y 8056	J	AC	Y 8100	J	NB	Y 8144	F	SO
Y 8013	J	MZ	Y 8057	J	SO	Y 8101	J	NB	Y 8145	F	SB
Y 8014	J	SB	Y 8058	J	DP	Y 8102	J	SO	Y 8146	F	AC
Y 8015	J	CY	Y 8059	J	SO	Y 8103	J	AV	Y 8147	J	AV
Y 8016	J	BZ	Y 8060	J	TL	Y 8104	J	AV	Y 8148	F	AV
Y 8017	J	BZ	Y 8061	J	AV	Y 8105	J	BZ	Y 8149	F	AC
Y 8018	J	AV	Y 8062	J	AC	Y 8106	J	DP	Y 8150	F	AC
Y 8019	J	AV	Y 8063	J	AV	Y 8107	J	RS	Y 8151	F	SB
Y 8020	J	TP	Y 8064	J	DP	Y 8108	J	AC	Y 8152	F	MZ
Y 8021	J	BD	Y 8065	J	TL	Y 8109	J	CY	Y 8153	F	AC
Y 8022	J	DP	Y 8066	J	AC	Y 8110	J	MZ	Y 8154	F	BD
Y 8023	J	RS	Y 8067	J	BD	Y 8111	J	AV	Y 8155	F	CY
Y 8024	J	SO	Y 8068	J	AV	Y 8112	J	SB	Y 8156	F	LG
Y 8025	J	SO	Y 8069	J	AC	Y 8113	J	AC	Y 8157	F	LG
Y 8026	J	AV	Y 8070	J	LE	Y 8114	J	CB	Y 8158	F	TP
Y 8027	J	LV	Y 8071	J	SO	Y 8115	J	MZ	Y 8159	F	TP
Y 8028	J	LV	Y 8072	J	BD	Y 8116	J	SB	Y 8160	F	RS
Y 8029	J	LV	Y 8073	J	BD	Y 8117	J	AC	Y 8161	F	AC
Y 8030	J	RS	Y 8074	J	SB	Y 8118	F	MZ	Y 8162	F	SO
Y 8031	J	RS	Y 8075	J	LE	Y 8119	F	DP	Y 8163	F	BZ
Y 8032	J	NB	Y 8076	J	TP	Y 8120	F i	CB	Y 8164	F	AC
Y 8033	J	RS	Y 8077	J	AC	Y 8121	F	RS	Y 8165	F	SO
Y 8034	J	AC	Y 8078	J	AC	Y 8122	F	AC	Y 8166	F	AC
Y 8035	J	BZ	Y 8079	J	AC	Y 8123	F	MZ	Y 8167	F	TP
Y 8036	J	AC	Y 8080	J	TL	Y 8124	J	MZ	Y 8168	F	TL
Y 8037	J	AC	Y 8081	J	TP	Y 8125	F	BZ	Y 8169	F	LE
Y 8038	J	CB	Y 8082	J	LN	Y 8126	F	AC	Y 8170	F	AC
Y 8039	J	SO	Y 8083	J	SB	Y 8127	F	AC	Y 8171	F	AC
Y 8040	J	BZ	Y 8084	J	AC	Y 8128	F	AC	Y 8172	F	BZ
Y 8041	J	AC	Y 8085	J	TL	Y 8129	F	DP	Y 8173	F	AC
Y 8042	J	AV	Y 8086	J	LN	Y 8130	F	LG	Y 8174	F	AV
Y 8043	J	AV	Y 8087	J	CB	Y 8131	F	RS	Y 8175	F	SB
Y 8044	J	BZ	Y 8088	J	LE	Y 8132	F	TP	Y 8176	F	S B

Y 8177	F		NV	Y 8227	F		RS	Y 8277	J		CY
Y 8178	F		AV	Y 8228	F		AC	Y 8278	J		LE
Y 8179	F		AV	Y 8229	F		RS	Y 8279	J		LV
Y 8180	F		DP	Y 8230	F		AC	Y 8280	J		LE
Y 8181	F		AC	Y 8231	F		BZ	Y 8281	J		SO
Y 8182	F		AC	Y 8232	F		CB	Y 8282	J		CB
Y 8183	F		AC	Y 8233	F		AC	Y 8283	J		AV
Y 8184	F		SB	Y 8234	F		AC	Y 8284	J		AC
Y 8185	F		AC	Y 8235	F		MZ	Y 8285	J		NB
Y 8186	F		AC	Y 8236	F		BZ	Y 8286	J		DP
Y 8187	F		AC	Y 8237	F		AV	Y 8287	J		AV
Y 8188	F		SO	Y 8238	F		AC	Y 8288	J		AC
Y 8189	F		BD	Y 8239	F		AV	Y 8289	J		LG
Y 8190	F		TP	Y 8240	F		CB	Y 8290	J		LE
Y 8191	F		TP	Y 8241	F		AC	Y 8291	J		DP
Y 8192	F		AV	Y 8242	J		SO	Y 8292	J		LG
Y 8193	F		LG	Y 8243	F		AC	Y 8293	J		CB
Y 8194	F		TP	Y 8244	F		AC	Y 8294	J		LV
Y 8195	F		BD	Y 8245	F		RS	Y 8295	J		AV
Y 8196	F		TP	Y 8246	J		NB	Y 8296	J		TP
Y 8197	F		TL	Y 8247	F		SO	Y 8297	J		AC
Y 8198	F		LG	Y 8248	F		RS	Y 8298	J		LG
Y 8199	F		TP	Y 8249	F		RS	Y 8299	J		AC
Y 8200	F		AC	Y 8250	F		SO	Y 8300	J	†	LN
Y 8201	F		AC	Y 8251	F		RS	Y 8301	J		AV
Y 8202	F		AC	Y 8252	F		BZ	Y 8302	J		BZ
Y 8203	F		AC	Y 8253	J		SO	Y 8303	J		LV
Y 8204	F		NB	Y 8254	J		AC	Y 8304	J		BD
Y 8205	F		SO	Y 8255	F		SO	Y 8305	J		AC
Y 8206	F		LV	Y 8256	F		CB	Y 8306	J		SO
Y 8207	F		AC	Y 8257	F		DP	Y 8307	J		RS
Y 8208	F		DP	Y 8258	J		CB	Y 8308	J		AC
Y 8209	F	i	CB	Y 8259	J		BD	Y 8309	J		RS
Y 8210	F		AV	Y 8260	F	*	NV	Y 8310	J		AC
Y 8211	F		LG	Y 8261	J		LE	Y 8311	J		LG
Y 8212	F		SB	Y 8262	J		LE	Y 8312	J		TL
Y 8213	F		SB	Y 8263	J		TP	Y 8313	J		TP
Y 8214	F		SO	Y 8264	J		AC	Y 8314	J		AC
Y 8215	F		LG	Y 8265	J		TP	Y 8315	J		BD
Y 8216	F		SB	Y 8266	J		NV	Y 8316	J		TP
Y 8217	F		TP	Y 8267	J		LE	Y 8317	J		NB
Y 8218	F		BD	Y 8268	J		LE	Y 8318	J		AC
Y 8219	F		TP	Y 8269	J		TP	Y 8319	J		AC
Y 8220	F		TL	Y 8270	J		LG	Y 8320	J		TP
Y 8221	F		AC	Y 8271	J		TL	Y 8321	J		SO
Y 8222	F		LE	Y 8272	J		LG	Y 8322	J		LE
Y 8223	F		LN	Y 8273	J		AC	Y 8323	J		LE
Y 8224	F		DP	Y 8274	J		BZ	Y 8324	J		CB
Y 8225	F		BD	Y 8275	J		AC	Y 8325	J		LG
Y 8226	F		NB	Y 8276	J		NB				

Y 8326	J		AC
Y 8327	J		MZ
Y 8328	J		LN
Y 8329	J		BZ
Y 8330	J		CY
Y 8331	J		LE
Y 8332	J		CY
Y 8333	J		TP
Y 8334	J		AC
Y 8335	J		AC
Y 8336	J		BD
Y 8337	J		LN
Y 8338	J		BZ
Y 8339	J		LV
Y 8340	J		CY
Y 8341	J		CB
Y 8342	J	§	AC
Y 8343	J		TP
Y 8344	J		LV
Y 8345	J		LE
Y 8346	J		MZ
Y 8347	J		CB
Y 8348	J	*	NV
Y 8349	J	*	NV
Y 8350	J	*	NV
Y 8351	J	*	NV
Y 8352	J	*	NV
Y 8354	J	*	NV
Y 8355	J	*	NV
Y 8356	J	*	NV
Y 8357	J	*	NV
Y 8358	J		TL
Y 8359	J		TP
Y 8360	J		AC
Y 8361	J		TP
Y 8362	J		BD
Y 8363	J	†	AC
Y 8364	J		LV
Y 8365	J		LV
Y 8366	J	†	AC
Y 8367	J	†	AC
Y 8368	J		BD
Y 8369	J		LE
Y 8370	J		AC
Y 8371	J		AC
Y 8372	J		AC
Y 8373	J		AC
Y 8374	J		LE
Y 8375	J		BZ

CLASS Y 8400

B

After testing remote control on loco Y 8300, the SNCF decided to follow the DB and go for radio control on its new small shunters thus allowing the duties of driver and shunter to be combined. The loco can either be controlled from a portable radio or from the cab. Externally the locos are similar to Class Y 8000, but there is an illuminated "TELE" sign at cab roof level and there are marker lights under the buffer beams at the four corners to indicate to staff that remote control is in operation.

Built: 1990–95.
Engine: Poyaud V12-520NS (224kW) [† Unidiesel UD18L6R3 (219 kW)].
Transmission: Hydraulic. Voith LZr4SU2.
Maximum Tractive Effort: 118/62 kN.
Wheel Diameter: 1050 mm.

Builder: Arbel Fauvet Rail.

Length: 10.14 m.
Maximum Speed: 30/60 km/h.

Y 8401	J	SO	Y 8439	J	AC	Y 8477	J	LE	Y 8514	J	CB
Y 8402	J	AC	Y 8440	J	BZ	Y 8478	J	NB	Y 8515	J	NB
Y 8403	J	SO	Y 8441	J	BZ	Y 8479	J	CB	Y 8516	J	NV
Y 8404	J	AC	Y 8442	J	AV	Y 8480	J	NB	Y 8517	J	AV
Y 8405	J	TP	Y 8443	J	AV	Y 8481	J	LE	Y 8518	J	NV
Y 8406	J	MZ	Y 8444	J	BZ	Y 8482	J	DP	Y 8519	J	AV
Y 8407	J	MZ	Y 8445	J	BD	Y 8483	J	MZ	Y 8520	J	DP
Y 8408	J	CY	Y 8446	J	AV	Y 8484	J	NB	Y 8521	J	AC
Y 8409	J	SO	Y 8447	J	AC	Y 8485	J	TL	Y 8522	J	BD
Y 8410	J	MZ	Y 8448	J	DP	Y 8486	J	TL	Y 8523	J	DP
Y 8411	J	AC	Y 8449	J	CB	Y 8487	J	LV	Y 8524	J	CY
Y 8412	J	AC	Y 8450	J	BZ	Y 8488	J	NB	Y 8525	J	CY
Y 8413	J	AC	Y 8451	J	DP	Y 8489	J	CB	Y 8526	J	MZ
Y 8414	J	LE	Y 8452	J	DP	Y 8490	J	AC	Y 8527	J	AC
Y 8415	J	AC	Y 8453	J	BD	Y 8491	J	AC	Y 8528	J	NB
Y 8416	J	LE	Y 8454	J	DP	Y 8492	J	AC	Y 8529	J	MZ
Y 8417	J	MZ	Y 8455	J	LV	Y 8493	J	AC	Y 8530	J	AC
Y 8418	J	AV	Y 8456	J	LE	Y 8494	J	BD	Y 8531	J	CY
Y 8419	J	TL	Y 8457	J	DP	Y 8495	J	BD	Y 8532	J	MZ
Y 8420	J	LE	Y 8458	J	DP	Y 8496	J	TL	Y 8533	J	SB
Y 8421	J	LE	Y 8459	J	NV	Y 8497	J	LE	Y 8534	J	AC
Y 8422	J	SB	Y 8460	J	DP	Y 8498	J	MZ	Y 8535	J	LV
Y 8423	J	AC	Y 8461	J	SO	Y 8499	J	BZ	Y 8536	J	SB
Y 8424	J	AC	Y 8462	J	BD	Y 8500	J	MZ	Y 8537	J	SB
Y 8425	J	CB	Y 8463	J	AC	Y 8501	J	BD	Y 8538	J	SB
Y 8426	J	LE	Y 8464	J	CB	Y 8502	J	CB	Y 8539	J	SB
Y 8427	J	LE	Y 8465	J	NB	Y 8503	J	BD	Y 8540	J	SB (S)
Y 8428	J	LE	Y 8466	J	AV	Y 8504	J	CY	Y 8541	J	AC
Y 8429	J	AV	Y 8467	J	BD	Y 8505	J	CB	Y 8542	J	SB
Y 8430	J	BZ	Y 8468	J	CB	Y 8506	J	NB	Y 8543	J	SB
Y 8431	J	AV	Y 8469	J	NV	Y 8507	J	CB	Y 8544	J	TL
Y 8432	J	AC	Y 8470	J	LE	Y 8508	J	AC	Y 8545	J	TL
Y 8433	J	AV	Y 8471	J	NB	Y 8509	J	NB	Y 8546	J	LV
Y 8434	J	BZ	Y 8472	J	CY	Y 8510	J	CY	Y 8547	J	LV
Y 8435	J	BZ	Y 8473	J	BZ	Y 8511	J	AV	Y 8548	J	LE
Y 8436	J	NV	Y 8474	J	CB	Y 8512	J	NB	Y 8549	J	TL
Y 8437	J	DP	Y 8475	J	BD	Y 8513	J	MZ	Y 8550	J	LV
Y 8438	J	AC	Y 8476	J	AC						

LOCMAs (INTERNAL USERS)

The last of Classes Y 2200, Y 2400, Y 5100, Y 6200 and Y 6400 are now considered as "machine tools", being maintained by the depot or works concerned. A number of Class Y 7100 and Y 7400 are now also concerned. These locos are known as LOCMAs ("LOComotive de MAnoeuvres") and were originally numbered 0001 upwards. Many carry their old number or no number and have been painted in special liveries by the depots. Please note that our information on these locos is incomplete as information is not centralised. Locos are in livery **V** unless shown.

CLASS Y 2200 B

Built: 1956–60.
Engine: Poyaud 2PDT (44 kW).
Transmission: Mechanical.
Maximum Tractive Effort: kN.
Wheel Diameter: 1050 mm.

Builder: Moyse (2215–49) Decauville (2285–2330).

Weight: 16 tonnes.
Length: 5.79 m.
Maximum Speed: 14/50 km/h.

Old No.	LOCMA	Location		Old No	LOCMA	Location
Y 2215	0001	TV		Y 2301		Nice St. Roch
Y 2266	0007	NV		Y 2321		Romilly carriage works
Y 2285	0030	TV "TEF"		Y 2322	0003	Metz Sablon
Y 2298	0034	CB		Y 2330	45	NB

CLASS Y 2400 B

Built: 1962–69.
Builder: Decauville.
Transmission: Mechanical.
Maximum Tractive Effort: kN.
Wheel Diameter: 1050 mm.

Engine: Agrom 6r (45 kW).
Weight: 17 tonnes.
Length: 7.18 m.
Maximum Speed: 15/58 km/h.

Old No.	LOCMA	Location		Old No	LOCMA	Location
Y 2401		Granville		Y 2465		Les Laumes-Alésia depot
Y 2404	0084	LG		Y 2467		CB
Y 2409		St Dizier p.w. depot		Y 2474	0036	CB
Y 2410	0046	Mohon		Y 2479	0031	DP (Livery **J**)
Y 2414	0042	Ambérieu wagon works		Y 2480	0065	NV
Y 2417		AV		Y 2481		PS (S)
Y 2420	0017	Paris Masséna carriage sidings		Y 2482		Toulouse St. Jory
Y 2424	0063	Perpignon Chef de Bien		Y 2483	0122	Laroche-Migennes depot
Y 2425		BZ		Y 2484	0028	AV
Y 2426		TL		Y 2490	0064	Quimper
Y 2427		Clermont Ferrand wagon works		Y 2492		PS
Y 2439	0062	EMM Cerbère		Y 2493	0115	BD
Y 2440		St. André-le-Gaz		Y 2495	0105	Clermont Ferrand wagon works
Y 2441	0048	DP (blue livery)		Y 2499		St. Priest
Y 2444	0113	AV		Y 2500	0118	Avignon Champfleury works
Y 2447	0099	MB		Y 2502	0038	TP (two-tone blue livery)
Y 2448	0016	Marseille St. Charles Car. Wks.		Y 2506	0057	VG "LULU"
Y 2450		VE		Y 2507	0058	VG
Y 2451	0108	MB		Y 2511		EIMM Béziers
Y 2453	0126	Miramas depot		Y 2514		Vichy
Y 2456	0125	Nice St. Roch		Y 2518		Clermont Ferrand wagon works
Y 2460	0059	VG		Y 2519	57001	CB
Y 2464	0109	MB				

CLASS Y 5100 B

Built: 1960–63.
Engine: Poyaud 4PYT (81 kW).
Weight: 20 tonnes.
Wheel Diameter: 1050 mm.

Builder: De Dietrich.
Transmission: Hydromechanical.
Length: 7.18 m.
Maximum Speed: 18 km/h.

Old No.	LOCMA	Location		Old No	LOCMA	Location
Y 5103	0101	Le Mans works		Y 5119	0098	LN
Y 5104	0052	Nantes carriage works		Y 5122		AC
Y 5105	0091	MR		Y 5123	0069	BD
Y 5106	0097	PO		Y 5124	0047	LG
Y 5107	0081	Les Aubrais depot		Y 5125	0114	Les Aubrais wagon works
Y 5108	0086	TL		Y 5126	0087	TL
Y 5110		LG		Y 5129	0066	TV
Y 5111		PO		Y 5131	0041	SB
Y 5116	0076	NV		Y 5132	0032	TV
Y 5117	0112	LN		Y 5133	0085	Mohon

Old No.	LOCMA	Location		Old No.	LOCMA	Location
Y 5138	0102	Le Mans works		Y 5155	0073	PL
Y 5140	0079	Villeneuve St Georges wheel shop		Y 5159	0094	TV
Y 5142	0077	CF		Y 5161	0029	AV
Y 5143	0078	PV named MILLAU		Y 5201	0092	AC
Y 5145	71	CY		Y 5210	70	CY
Y 5146		Les Laumes Alésia		Y 5211	0061	Le Mans works
Y 5147	0055	LN		Y 5212		PS
Y 5148	93	CY		Y 5213	0067	TP
Y 5150	0104	Le Mans works		Y 5214	39	CY

CLASS Y 6200   B

Built: 1949–55.
Builders: BDR (6201–30) St. Lilloise (6231–59) Moyse (6260–97).
Engine: Poyaud 6PDT (132 kW). **Transmission:** Electric. Oerlikon.
Weight: 32 tonnes. **Length:** 8.90 m.
Wheel Diameter: 1050 mm. **Maximum Speed:** 20/60 km/h.

Old No.	LOCMA	Location		Old No.	LOCMA	Location
Y 6207	0021	Nevers Works		Y 6266	0106	MB
Y 6220		Nevers Works		Y 6281	0074	TP

CLASSES Y 6400 & 6500   B

Built: 1954–58.
Builders: BDR (6301–30), De Dietrich (6401–30, 6501–6625), Decauville (6431–6500).
Engine: Poyaud 6PDT (132 kW). **Transmission:** Electric. Oerlikon.
Weight: 32 tonnes. **Length:** 8.90 m.
Wheel Diameter: 1050 mm. **Maximum Speed:** 20/60 km/h.

Old No.	LOCMA	Location		Old No.	LOCMA	Location
Y 6429	0080	VE		Y 6591	0082	Les Aubrais wagon works
Y 6467		BZ		Y 6605		RS (S)
Y 6510		TV		Y 6612	0121	Bordeaux wagon shop
Y 6513	0051	VG		Y 6617	0083	Les Aubrais depot
Y 6520	0107	MB		Y 6621		RS
Y 6565		VG		Y 6622	0012	RS
Y 6575	0072	PL				

CLASS Y 7100   B

See page 82 for details.

Old No.	LOCMA	Location		Old No.	LOCMA	Location
Y 7103		Woippy wagon works		Y 7212	4	BD
Y 7124		Saulon PW depot		Y 7213	5	BD
Y 7140		AV		Y 7226		SO
Y 7143		Perigueux		Y 7234		DP
Y 7145		Saulon PW depot		Y 7265		SA
Y 7147		LN		Y 7282		SO
Y 7154		BD		Y 7285		LE
Y 7171		HE				

CLASS Y 7400   B

See page 83 for details.

Old No.	LOCMA	Location		Old No.	LOCMA	Location
Y 7405		Chalons Wagon Works		Y 7495	6	BD
Y 7440	40	NV		Y 7647		TL
Y 7461		Lyon Mouche		Y 7825		Perigueux
Y 7494		Ambérieu wagon works				

1.6. ELECTRIC MULTIPLE UNITS

Note: Most EMUs carry set numbers on the front ends. Where applicable, these are listed in the first column followed by the individual vehicle numbers.

CLASS Z 5300   3/4-CAR UNITS

One of the 1960s generation of EMU with stainless steel bodywork. For years worked out of Paris Austerlitz and Lyon stations on suburban trains but the development of the Paris RER services and the introduction of double-deck EMUs has seen more congregating on Paris Montparnasse and Paris Lyon services. A number have gone to TP depot and are used on the Les Aubrais –Orléans and St. Pierre-des-Corps–Tours shuttles. From Z 5367, units have headcode panels for Paris RER services. All will be replaced by the Bombardier Spacium single-deck EMU from 2011.

Built: 1965–68 (5301–5361), 1972–75 (5362–5445).
System: 1500 V DC.
Builders: Carel & Fouché/MTE/TCO.
Formation: ZBD + ZRB + ZRB + ZRABx.
Wheel Arrangement: Bo-Bo + 2-2 + 2-2 + 2-2.
Traction Motors: 4 Oerlikon EMW 510 of 245 kW.
Accommodation: –/87 1T + –/112 + –/106 1T + 44/40.
Weight: 62 + 30 + 30 + 42 tonnes.
Length: 25.925 (25.80*) + 25.85 (25.60*) + 25.85 (25.60*) + 25.925 (25.80*) m.
Maximum Speed: 130 km/h.

5301–5361 are non-gangwayed. 5362–5445 have gangways for staff use only.

302	Z 5302	25304	25303	15302	**U**	*IF*	*	VG	342	Z 5342	25384	25383	15301 **U** *IF* * VG
303	Z 5303	25306	25305	15303	**U**	*IF*	*	MR	343	Z 5343	25386	25385	15343 **U** *IF* * MR
304	Z 5304	25308	25307	15304	**U**	*IF*	*	VG	344	Z 5344	25388	25387	15344 **U** *IF* * VG
305	Z 5305	25310	25309	15305	**U**	*IF*	*	MR	345	Z 5345	25390	25389	15345 **U** *IF* * VG
306	Z 5306	25312	25311	15306	**U**	*IF*	*	VG	346	Z 5346	25392	25371	15346 **U** *IF* * VG
307	Z 5307	25314	25313	15307	**U**	*IF*	*	VG	347	Z 5347	25394	25393	15347 **U** *IF* * MR
308	Z 5308	25316	25315	15308	**U**	*IF*	*	MR	348	Z 5348	25396	25395	15348 **U** *IF* * VG
309	Z 5309	25318	25317	15309	**U**	*IF*	*	MR	349	Z 5349	25398	25397	15349 **U** *IF* * MR
310	Z 5310	25320	25319	15310	**U**	*IF*	*	VG	350	Z 5350	25400	25399	15350 **U** *IF* * MR
311	Z 5311	25322	25321	15311	**U**	*IF*	*	VG	351	Z 5351	25402	25401	15351 **U** *IF* * VG
312	Z 5312	25324	25323	15312	**U**	*IF*	*	MR	352	Z 5352	25404	25403	15352 **U** *IF* * MR
313	Z 5313	25326	25325	15313	**U**	*IF*	*	MR	353	Z 5353	25406	25405	15353 **U** *IF* * VG
314	Z 5314	25328	25327	15314	**U**	*IF*	*	VG	354	Z 5354	25408	25407	15354 **U** *IF* * MR
315	Z 5315	25330	25329	15315	**U**	*IF*	*	MR	355	Z 5355	25410	25409	15355 **U** *IF* * VG
316	Z 5316	25332	25591	15316	**U**	*IF*	*	MR	356	Z 5356	25412	25411	15356 **U** *IF* * VG
317	Z 5317	25334	25333	15317	**U**	*IF*	*	VG	358	Z 5358	25350	25349	15358 **U** *IF* * VG
318	Z 5318	25336	25335	15318	**U**	*IF*	*	MR	359	Z 5359	25592	25593	15359 **U** *IF* * VG
319	Z 5319	25338	25337	15319	**U**	*IF*	*	VG	360	Z 5360	25594	25595	15360 **U** *IF* * MR
320	Z 5320	25339	25340	15320	**U**	*IF*	*	VG	361	Z 5361	25596	25597	15361 **U** *IF* * VG
322	Z 5322	25344	25343	15322	**U**	*IF*	*	MR	362	Z 5362	25424	25423	15362 **U** *IF* VG
323	Z 5323	25345	25346	15323	**U**	*IF*	*	VG	363	Z 5363	25426	25425	15363 **U** *IF* VG
324	Z 5324	25348	25347	15324	**U**	*IF*	*	VG	364	Z 5364	25428	25427	15364 **U** *IF* VG
326	Z 5326	25352	25351	15326	**U**	*IF*	*	VG	365	Z 5365	25430	25429	15365 **U** *IF* VG
327	Z 5327	25354	25353	15327	**U**	*IF*	*	MR	366	Z 5366	25432	25331	15366 **U** *IF* VG
328	Z 5328	25356	25355	15328	**U**	*IF*	*	MR	367	Z 5367	25434	25433	15367 **U** *IF* VG
329	Z 5329	25358	25357	15329	**U**	*IF*	*	VG	368	Z 5368	25436	25435	15368 **U** *IF* VG
330	Z 5330	25360	25359	15330	**U**	*IF*	*	VG	369	Z 5369	25438	25437	15369 **U** *IF* MR
331	Z 5331	25362	25361	15331	**U**	*IF*	*	VG	370	Z 5370	25440	25439	15370 **U** *IF* VG
332	Z 5332	25364	25363	15332	**U**	*IF*	*	MR	371	Z 5371	25442	25441	15371 **U** *IF* MR
333	Z 5333	25366	25415	15333	**U**	*IF*	*	VG	372	Z 5372	25444	25443	15372 **U** *IF* MR
334	Z 5334	25368	25367	15334	**U**	*IF*	*	MR	378	Z 5378		25455	15378 **U** *CI* TP
335	Z 5335	25370	25369	15335	**U**	*IF*	*	VG	383	Z 5383		25465	15383 **U** *CI* TP
337	Z 5337	25374	25373	15337	**U**	*IF*	*	VG	395	Z 5395		25489	15395 **U** *CI* TP
338	Z 5338	25376	25375	15338	**U**	*IF*	*	VG	397	Z 5397	25494	25493	15397 **U** *CI* TP
339	Z 5339	25378	25377	15339	**U**	*IF*	*	VG	423	Z 5423		25545	15423 **U** *CI* FT
340	Z 5340	25380	25379	15340	**U**	*IF*	*	MR	425	Z 5425		25549	15425 **U** *CI* TP
341	Z 5341	25382	25381	15341	**U**	*IF*	*	VG	426	Z 5426	25552	25551	15426 **U** *IF* MR

Name: Z 5395 ISSY-LES-MOULINEAUX

CLASS Z 5600   4/6-CAR DOUBLE-DECK UNITS

These were the first double-deck EMUs to operate in France and together with dual-voltage version Class Z 8800 are generically known as Z2N sets. All were originally 4-car sets. The VG 6-car sets now operate on Paris Gare de Lyon–Laroche Migennes outer suburban services, the TR 6-car sets on the RER Line C Versailles–Paris–Versailles service and the 4-car sets operate on other RER Line C services. Trailer cars are numbered ZRB 25601–25742 and ZRAB 35601–35710. This gives one second and one composite per 4-car set plus an extra two seconds for 6-car sets. Additional cars ZRB 25801–25821 and ZRABs 35801–35821 were built for Class Z 20500. These trailers are shared with Class Z 8800 and formations are non-sequential. Trailers ZR 25901 upwards were taken from push-pull sets and added to sets 33 to 52. First class accommodation has been downgraded to second.

Built: 1983–85.   **System:** 1500 V DC.
Builders–Mechanical Parts: ANF/CIMT.
Builders–Electrical Parts: Alsthom/TCO.
Traction Motors: 4 x TCO 4 FHO 3262 of 350 kW per power car.
Formation: ZB + ZRB + ZRAB + (+ZRB + ZRB) + ZB.
Wheel Arrangement: Bo-Bo + 2-2 + 2-2 + (+ 2-2 + 2-2) + Bo-Bo.
Weight: 66 t + 41 t + 42 t (+ 41 t + 41t) + 66 t.
Length: 25.10 m + 24.28 m + 24.28 m (+ 24.28 m + 24.28 m) + 25.10 m.
Accommodation: –/118 1T + –/164 1T + –/153 1T (+ –/164 + –/164 1T) + –/118 1T.
Maximum Speed: 140 km/h.

Multiple operation within class plus with Z 8800, Z 20500 and Z 20900.

01C	Z 5601	25663	25605	35695	25732	Z 5602	I	IF	VG
02C	Z 5603	25603	25656	35666	25741	Z 5604	I	IF	VG
03C	Z 5605	25650	25623	35687	25730	Z 5606	I	IF	VG
04C	Z 5607	25665	35668	25621	25737	Z 5608	I	IF	VG
05C	Z 5609	25660	25619	35678	25739	Z 5610	I	IF	VG
06C	Z 5611	25624	25657	35697	25738	Z 5612	I	IF	VG
07C	Z 5613	25637	25729	35676	25733	Z 5614	I	IF	VG
08C	Z 5615	25669	25659	35670	25735	Z 5616	I	IF	VG
09C	Z 5617	25658	25648	35736	25736	Z 5618	I	IF	VG
10C	Z 5619	25610	25662	35677	25731	Z 5620	I	IF	VG
11C	Z 5621	25654	25661	35674	25740	Z 5622	I	IF	VG
12C	Z 5623	25625	25645	35686	25742	Z 5624	I	IF	VG
13C	Z 5625	25622	25644	35681	25651	Z 5626	I	IF	VG
14C	Z 5627	25652	25666	35667	25727	Z 5628	I	IF	VG
15C	Z 5629	25667	25647	35665	25728	Z 5630	I	IF	VG
16C	Z 5631	25649	25631	35671	25734	Z 5632	I	IF	VG
17C	Z 5633	25607	35700			Z 5634	I	IF	PA
18C	Z 5635	25678	35615			Z 5636	I	IF	PA
19C	Z 5637	25641	35628			Z 5638	I	IF	PA
20C	Z 5639	25635	35654			Z 5640	I	IF	PA
21C	Z 5641	25632	35629			Z 5642	I	IF	PA
22C	Z 5643	25612	35683			Z 5644	I	IF	PA
23C	Z 5645	25601	35696			Z 5646	I	IF	PA
24C	Z 5647	25671	35624			Z 5648	I	IF	PA
25C	Z 5649	25608	35605			Z 5650	I	IF	PA
26C	Z 5651	25683	35608			Z 5652	I	IF	PA
27C	Z 5653	25628	35619			Z 5654	I	IF	PA
28C	Z 5655	25617	35622			Z 5656	I	IF	PA
29C	Z 5657	25679	35673			Z 5658	I	IF	PA
30C	Z 5659	25620	35621			Z 5660	I	IF	PA
31C	Z 5661	25677	35690			Z 5662	I	IF	PA
32T	Z 5663	25672	35694	25936	25927	Z 5664	I	IF	TR
33T	Z 5665	25653	35626	25902	25901	Z 5666	I	IF	TR
34T	Z 5667	25634	35691	25914	25915	Z 5668	I	IF	TR
35T	Z 5669	25613	35692	25926	25921	Z 5670	I	IF	TR
36T	Z 5671	25633	35623	25916	25917	Z 5672	I	IF	TR
37T	Z 5673	25636	35679	25906	25905	Z 5674	I	IF	TR
38T	Z 5675	25609	35682	25938	25937	Z 5676	I	IF	TR

39T	Z 5677	25604	35672	25928	25931	Z 5678	I	IF	TR
40T	Z 5679	25673	35625	25920	25919	Z 5680	I	IF	TR
41T	Z 5681	25606	35680	25940	25933	Z 5682	I	IF	TR
42C	Z 5683	25615	35675			Z 5684	I	IF	PA
43T	Z 5685	25682	35688	25932	25913	Z 5686	I	IF	TR
44T	Z 5687	25704	35617	25904	25903	Z 5688	I	IF	TR
45T	Z 5689	25614	35699	25934	25939	Z 5690	I	IF	TR
46T	Z 5691	25675	35632	25912	25925	Z 5692	I	IF	TR
47T	Z 5693	25674	35689	25918	25929	Z 5694	I	IF	TR
48T	Z 5695	25670	35685	25924	25935	Z 5696	I	IF	TR
49T	Z 5697	25680	35698	25930	25909	Z 5698	I	IF	TR
50T	Z 5699	25681	35693	25908	25907	Z 5700	I	IF	TR
51T	Z 5701	25616	35627	25922	25923	Z 5702	I	IF	TR
52T	Z 5703	25684	35684	25910	25911	Z 5704	I	IF	TR

Names:

Z 5601/5602	SAVIGNY-LE-TEMPLE	Z 5697/5698	BRÉTIGNY-SUR-ORGE
Z 5633/5634	ATHIS-MONS	Z 5699/5700	ÉTAMPES
Z 5635/5636	VIROFLAY		

CLASS Z 6100   3-CAR UNITS

Like the early DC units such as Z 5300 these are built of unpainted stainless steel. They operate suburban services out of Paris Nord as far north as Compiègne. The last three digits of the running number also appear on cabsides and in cab windows as set numbers. Z 6168/9 were sold to Luxembourg where they were CFL 262/1 respectively. They, like some SNCF Z 6100, have now been sold to Romania. These units have a monomotor bogie, which is the same type as on Class BB 67400 diesel locos. All of the class will be replaced by Bombardier Spacium EMUs from 2011.

Built: 1965–71.   **System:** 25 kV AC.
Builders–Mechanical Parts: Carel & Fouché/Schneider/De Dietrich.
Builders–Electrical Parts: CEM/Siemens/Alsthom.
Formation: ZBD + ZRB + ZRABx.
Wheel Arrangement: 2-B + 2-2 + 2-2.   **Traction Motor:** 690 kW.
Accommodation: –/86 1T + –/107 1T + 36/51 1T.
Weight: 51 + 28 + 31 tonnes.
Length: 25.50 + 23.80 + 25.15 m.
Maximum Speed: 120 km/h.

S121	Z 6121	26121	16121	U	IF	PL
S123	Z 6123	26123	16123	U	IF	PL
S126	Z 6126	26126	16126	U	IF	PL
S127	Z 6127	26127	16127	U	IF	PL
S129	Z 6129	26129	16129	U	IF	PL
S130	Z 6130	26130	16130	U	IF	PL
S131	Z 6131	26131	16131	U	IF	PL
S132	Z 6132	26132	16132	U	IF	PL
S134	Z 6134	26134	16134	U	IF	PL
S135	Z 6135	26135	16135	U	IF	PL
S136	Z 6136	26136	16136	U	IF	PL
S137	Z 6137	26137	16137	U	IF	PL
S139	Z 6139	26139	16139	U	IF	PL
S140	Z 6140	26140	16140	U	IF	PL
S141	Z 6141	26141	16141	U	IF	PL
S142	Z 6142	26142	16142	U	IF	PL
S143	Z 6143	26143	16143	U	IF	PL
S144	Z 6144	26144	16144	U	IF	PL
S145	Z 6145	26145	16145	U	IF	PL
S146	Z 6146	26146	16146	U	IF	PL
S147	Z 6147	26147	16147	U	IF	PL
S148	Z 6148	26148	16148	U	IF	PL
S149	Z 6149	26149	16149	U	IF	PL
S150	Z 6150	26150	16150	U	IF	PL
S151	Z 6151	26151	16151	U	IF	PL
S152	Z 6152	26152	16152	U	IF	PL
S153	Z 6153	26179	16153	U	IF	PL
S154	Z 6154	26154	16154	U	IF	PL
S155	Z 6155	26155	16155	U	IF	PL
S156	Z 6156	26156	16156	U	IF	PL
S157	Z 6157	26157	16157	U	IF	PL
S158	Z 6158	26158	16158	U	IF	PL
S159	Z 6159	26159	16159	U	IF	PL
S160	Z 6160	26160	16160	U	IF	PL
S161	Z 6161	26161	16161	U	IF	PL
S162	Z 6162	26162	16162	U	IF	PL
S163	Z 6163	26163	16163	U	IF	PL
S164	Z 6164	26164	16164	U	IF	PL
S165	Z 6165	26165	16165	U	IF	PL
S166	Z 6166	26166	16179	U	IF	PL
S167	Z 6167	26167	16167	U	IF	PL
S170	Z 6170	26170	16170	U	IF	PL
S171	Z 6171	26171	16171	U	IF	PL
S172	Z 6172	26172	16172	U	IF	PL
S173	Z 6173	26173	16173	U	IF	PL
S175	Z 6175	26175	16175	U	IF	PL
S176	Z 6176	26176	16185	U	IF	PL
S177	Z 6177	26177	16177	U	IF	PL
S178	Z 6178	26178	16178	U	IF	PL
S180	Z 6180	26180	16180	U	IF	PL

S181	Z 6181	26181	16181	U	IF	PL	
S182	Z 6182	26182	16182	U	IF	PL	
S183	Z 6183	26183	16183	U	IF	PL	
S184	Z 6184	26184	16184	U	IF	PL	

CLASS Z 6400   4-CAR UNITS

This was the last type of EMU to feature stainless steel bodywork. Introduced for services out of Paris St. Lazare, some operated out of Paris Nord for a while. Part of the fleet has high platform steps for use on the "Group II" lines from Paris St. Lazare to Versailles and Marly, whereas the rest have steps fitted for low platforms to serve the "Group III" line to Poissy. The last three digits of the power car number appear in the cab window, so that the first unit shows 401 at one end and 402 at the other. All units have been refurbished recently. Sets Z 6479 to Z 6484 have a special interior and carry the dark blue Transilien livery. They are only used on the St. Germain GC–Noisy-le-Roi service.

Built: 1976–79.   **System:** 25 kV AC.
Builders–Mechanical Parts: Carel & Fouché/De Dietrich.
Builders–Electrical Parts: Alsthom/TCO.
Formation: ZAD + ZRB + ZRB + ZBD.
Wheel Arrangement: Bo-Bo + 2-2 + 2-2 + Bo-Bo.
Accommodation: –/74 + –/92 + –/92 + –/74.
Traction Motors: 4 x 295 kW per power car. . **Weight:** 64 + 32 + 32 + 63 tonnes.
Length: 22.70 + 22.39 + 22.39 + 22.70 m.
Maximum Speed: 120 km/h.

h Fixed steps for high platform use only.

Z 6401	26401	26402	Z 6402	I	IF		PS
Z 6403	26403	26404	Z 6404	I	IF		PS
Z 6405	26405	26406	Z 6406	I	IF		PS
Z 6407	26407	26408	Z 6408	I	IF		PS
Z 6409	26409	26410	Z 6410	I	IF		PS
Z 6411	26411	26412	Z 6412	I	IF		PS
Z 6413	26413	26414	Z 6414	I	IF		PS
Z 6415	26415	26416	Z 6416	I	IF		PS
Z 6417	26417	26418	Z 6418	I	IF		PS
Z 6419	26419	26420	Z 6420	I	IF		PS
Z 6421	26421	26422	Z 6422	I	IF		PS
Z 6423	26423	26424	Z 6424	I	IF		PS
Z 6425	26425	26426	Z 6426	I	IF		PS
Z 6427	26427	26428	Z 6428	I	IF		PS
Z 6429	26429	26430	Z 6430	I	IF		PS
Z 6431	26431	26432	Z 6432	I	IF		PS
Z 6433	26433	26434	Z 6434	I	IF		PS
Z 6435	26435	26436	Z 6436	I	IF		PS
Z 6437	26437	26438	Z 6438	I	IF		PS
Z 6439	26439	26440	Z 6440	I	IF		PS
Z 6441	26441	26442	Z 6442	I	IF	h	PS
Z 6443	26443	26444	Z 6444	I	IF	h	PS
Z 6445	26445	26446	Z 6446	I	IF	h	PS
Z 6447	26447	26448	Z 6448	I	IF	h	PS
Z 6449	26449	26450	Z 6450	I	IF	h	PS
Z 6451	26451	26452	Z 6452	I	IF	h	PS
Z 6453	26453	26454	Z 6454	I	IF	h	PS
Z 6455	26455	26456	Z 6456	I	IF	h	PS
Z 6457	26457	26458	Z 6458	I	IF	h	PS
Z 6459	26459	26460	Z 6460	I	IF	h	PS
Z 6461	26461	26462	Z 6462	I	IF	h	PS
Z 6463	26463	26464	Z 6464	I	IF	h	PS
Z 6465	26465	26466	Z 6466	I	IF	h	PS
Z 6467	26467	26468	Z 6468	I	IF	h	PS
Z 6469	26469	26470	Z 6470	I	IF	h	PS
Z 6471	26471	26472	Z 6472	I	IF	h	PS
Z 6473	26473	26474	Z 6474	I	IF	h	PS
Z 6475	26475	26476	Z 6476	I	IF	h	PS
Z 6477	26477	26478	Z 6478	I	IF	h	PS
Z 6479	26479	26480	Z 6480	H	IF	h	PS
Z 6481	26481	26482	Z 6482	H	IF	h	PS
Z 6483	26483	26484	Z 6484	H	IF	h	PS
Z 6485	26485	26486	Z 6486	I	IF	h	PS
Z 6487	26487	26488	Z 6488	I	IF	h	PS
Z 6489	26489	26490	Z 6490	I	IF	h	PS
Z 6491	26491	26492	Z 6492	I	IF	h	PS
Z 6493	26493	26494	Z 6494	I	IF	h	PS
Z 6495	26495	26496	Z 6496	I	IF	h	PS
Z 6497	26497	26498	Z 6498	I	IF	h	PS
Z 6499	26499	26500	Z 6500	I	IF	h	PS
Z 6501	26501	26502	Z 6502	I	IF	h	PS
Z 6503	26503	26504	Z 6504	I	IF	h	PS
Z 6505	26505	26506	Z 6506	I	IF	h	PS
Z 6507	26507	26508	Z 6508	I	IF	h	PS
Z 6509	26509	26510	Z 6510	I	IF	h	PS
Z 6511	26511	26512	Z 6512	I	IF	h	PS
Z 6513	26513	26514	Z 6514	I	IF	h	PS
Z 6515	26515	26516	Z 6516	I	IF	h	PS
Z 6517	26517	26518	Z 6518	I	IF	h	PS
Z 6519	26519	26520	Z 6520	I	IF	h	PS
Z 6521	26521	26522	Z 6522	I	IF	h	PS
Z 6523	26523	26524	Z 6524	I	IF	h	PS
Z 6525	26525	26526	Z 6526	I	IF		PS
Z 6527	26527	26528	Z 6528	I	IF		PS
Z 6529	26529	26530	Z 6530	I	IF		PS
Z 6531	26531	26532	Z 6532	I	IF		PS
Z 6533	26533	26534	Z 6534	I	IF		PS
Z 6535	26535	26536	Z 6536	I	IF		PS
Z 6537	26537	26538	Z 6538	I	IF		PS
Z 6539	26539	26540	Z 6540	I	IF		PS
Z 6541	26541	26542	Z 6542	I	IF		PS
Z 6543	26543	26544	Z 6544	I	IF		PS
Z 6545	26545	26546	Z 6546	I	IF		PS
Z 6547	26547	26548	Z 6548	I	IF		PS
Z 6549	26549	26550	Z 6550	I	IF		PS

Names:

Z 6447/6448	CHAVILLE	Z 6485/6486	GARCHES
Z 6449/6450	COURBEVOIE	Z 6505/6506	VAUCRESSON
Z 6457/6458	LOUVECIENNES	Z 6519/6520	LA CELLE-SAINT CLOUD
Z 6471/6472	SAINT-NOM-LA-BRETÈCHE	Z 6523/6524	MARLY-LE-ROI
Z 6475/6476	L'ÉTANG-LA-VILLE	Z 6549/6550	LA GARENNE-COLOMBES

CLASS Z 7300   Z2   2-CAR UNITS

The first of a 1980s generation of EMUs not intended for Paris suburban work and known as Type Z2 (Z1 being Z 7100) - Classes Z 7300, Z 7500, Z 9500, Z 9600 and Z 11500 which all look very similar. They are used on short and medium distance stopping trains all over the south-west of France and around Avignon. All are fitted with facing seats. They were originally turned out in dark blue and red. Z 7351/2 never existed – they were built as Z 97383/4. Local regions are financing the refurbishment of sets with new seats and cool air ventilation.

Built: 1980–85.   **System:** 1500 V DC.
Builders: Alsthom/Francorail-MTE.
Formation: ZABD + ZRBx.
Wheel Arrangement: Bo-Bo + 2-2.   **Traction Motors:** 4 x 305 kW.
Accommodation: 24/43 2T + –/84 1T (*24/43 1T + –/80 1T).
Weight: 64 + 40 tonnes.   **Length:** 25.10 + 25.10 m.
Maximum Speed: 160 km/h.

Z 7301	17301	**T**	*AQ*	*	BD	Z 7326	17326	**T**	*AQ*	*	BD	Z 7353	17353	**T**	*CE*	*	TP
Z 7302	17302	**T**	*AQ*	*	BD	Z 7327	17327	**R**	*MP*		BD	Z 7354	17354	**T**	*CE*	*	TP
Z 7303	17303	**T**	*AQ*	*	BD	Z 7328	17328	**T**	*AQ*	*	BD	Z 7355	17355	**T**	*CE*	*	TP
Z 7304	17304	**T**	*AQ*	*	BD	Z 7329	17329	**T**	*AQ*	*	BD	Z 7356	17356	**T**	*CE*	*	TP
Z 7305	17305	**B**	*MP*		BD	Z 7330	17330	**R**	*MP*		BD	Z 7357	17357	**T**	*LR*	*	NI
Z 7306	17306	**B**	*MP*		BD	Z 7331	17331	**R**	*AQ*		BD	Z 7358	17358	**T**	*CE*	*	TP
Z 7307	17307	**B**	*MP*		BD	Z 7332	17332	**R**	*MP*		BD	Z 7359	17359	**T**	*CE*	*	TP
Z 7308	17308	**B**	*PC*		BD	Z 7333	17333	**R**	*MP*		BD	Z 7360	17360	**T**	*CE*	*	TP
Z 7309	17309	**T**	*AQ*	*	BD	Z 7334	17334	**R**	*AQ*		BD	Z 7361	17361	**T**	*CE*	*	TP
Z 7310	17310	**B**	*MP*		BD	Z 7335	17335	**R**	*AQ*		BD	Z 7362	17362	**T**	*CE*	*	TP
Z 7311	17311	**T**	*AQ*	*	BD	Z 7336	17336	**T**	*AQ*	*	BD	Z 7363	17363	**T**	*CE*	*	TP
Z 7312	17312	**B**	*AQ*		BD	Z 7337	17337	**T**	*AQ*	*	BD	Z 7364	17364	**T**	*LR*	*	NI
Z 7313	17313	**B**	*AQ*		BD	Z 7338	17338	**R**	*PC*		BD	Z 7365	17365	**T**	*LR*	*	NI
Z 7314	17314	**B**	*MP*		BD	Z 7339	17339	**T**	*AQ*	*	BD	Z 7366	17366	**T**	*LR*	*	NI
Z 7315	17315	**T**	*AQ*	*	BD	Z 7340	17340	**R**	*MP*		BD	Z 7367	17367	**T**	*LR*	*	NI
Z 7316	17316	**T**	*AQ*	*	BD	Z 7341	17341	**T**	*AQ*	*	BD	Z 7368	17368	**T**	*LR*	*	NI
Z 7317	17317	**R**	*MP*		BD	Z 7342	17342	**T**	*AQ*	*	BD	Z 7369	17369	**T**	*LR*	*	NI
Z 7318	17318	**R**	*PC*		BD	Z 7343	17343	**R**	*MP*		BD	Z 7370	17370	**T**	*LR*	*	NI
Z 7319	17319	**Z**	*AQ*	*	BD	Z 7344	17344	**T**	*AQ*	*	BD	Z 7371	17371	**T**	*LR*	*	NI
Z 7320	17320	**T**	*AQ*	*	BD	Z 7345	17345	**T**	*AQ*	*	BD	Z 7372	17372	**T**	*LR*	*	NI
Z 7321	17321	**R**	*MP*		BD	Z 7346	17346	**T**	*AQ*	*	BD	Z 7373	17373	**T**	*CE*	*	TP
Z 7322	17322	**T**	*AQ*	*	BD	Z 7347	17347	**T**	*CE*	*	TP	Z 97381	917381	**B**	*MP*		BD
Z 7323	17323	**T**	*AQ*	*	BD	Z 7348	17348	**T**	*CE*	*	TP	Z 97382	917382	**B**	*MP*		BD
Z 7324	17324	**R**	*MP*		BD	Z 7349	17349	**T**	*CE*	*	TP	Z 97383	917383	**T**	*LR*	*	NI
Z 7325	17325	**T**	*AQ*	*	BD	Z 7350	17350	**T**	*CE*	*	TP	Z 97384	917384	**T**	*LR*	*	NI

Names:

Z 7314	SOULAC-SUR-MER	Z 97381	MIDI-PYRENÉES
Z 7321	LESPARRE-MEDOC	Z 97382	MIDI-PYRENÉES
Z 7339	PESSAC	Z 97383	LANGUEDOC-ROUSSILLON
Z 7346	MARMANDE	Z 97384	LANGUEDOC-ROUSSILLON
Z 7370	MONTEUX		

CLASS Z 7500   Z2   2-CAR UNITS

This class is similar to Class Z 7300 but has more first class and unidirectional seating. Mainly used around Lyon and Avignon. Being refurbished like Class Z7300.

Built: 1982–83.   **System:** 1500 V DC.
Builders: Alsthom/Francorail-MTE.   **Formation:** ZABD + ZRBx.
Wheel Arrangement: Bo-Bo + 2-2.   **Traction Motors:** 4 x 305 kW.
Accommodation: 32/35 2T + –/84 1T. (*32/35 1T + –/80 1T).

Weight: 64 + 40 tonnes.
Maximum Speed: 160 km/h.
Length: 25.10 + 25.10 m.

Z 7501	17501	B	*RA*		VE	Z 7506	17506	B	*RA*		VE	Z 7511	17511	B	*RA*		VE
Z 7502	17502	B	*RA*		VE	Z 7507	17507	B	*RA*		VE	Z 7512	17512	T	*RA*		VE
Z 7503	17503	B	*RA*		VE	Z 7508	17508	T	*LR*	*	NI	Z 7513	17513	T	*RA*	*	VE
Z 7504	17504	T	*LR*	*	NI	Z 7509	17509	B	*RA*		VE	Z 7514	17514	T	*LR*	*	NI
Z 7505	17505	B	*RA*		VE	Z 7510	17510	T	*RA*		VE	Z 7515	17515	B	*RA*		VE

Names:

Z 7502 CHÂTEAUNEUF DU PAPE
Z 7513 BARBENTANE

Z 7515 ORANGE

CLASS Z 8100   MI 79/MI 84   4-CAR UNITS

This Paris area suburban stock is known as MI 79 (Matériel Interconnection 1979) stock and broke away from tradition by not using stainless steel bodywork. The units are made from aluminium alloy extrusions and have adjustable steps as the platforms on RER Line B are at different levels on the RATP and SNCF parts of the line. They are dual-voltage units for working over RER Line B which incorporates SNCF lines to Roissy and Mitry Claye.

From Z 8341 sets are known as MI 84 and are owned by Paris transport authority RATP for use on RER Line A. Ownership can be seen just behind the cabs where RER SNCF or RER RATP is marked. MI 84 has fewer seats than MI 79 to give more standing space in door wells. Although administratively allocated to Paris La Chapelle, all maintenance of SNCF sets is done at RATP's Massy depot. Refurbishment of the class is to begin in 2008.

Built: 1980–84.
Systems: 1500 V DC/25 kV AC.
Builders–Mechanical Parts: Alsthom/Franco-Belge, ANF.
Builders–Electrical Parts: Alsthom/TCO.
Formation: ZBD + ZRB + ZRAB + ZBD.
Wheel Arrangement: Bo-Bo + 2-2 + 2-2 + Bo-Bo.
Traction Motors: 4 x 350 kW per power car.
Accommodation: –/72 (24) + –/72 (24) + –/84 (32) + –/84 (28).
Weight: 56 + 48 + 48 + 56 tonnes.
Length: 26.08 + 26.00 + 26.00 + 26.08 m.
Maximum Speed: 140 km/h.

MI79 sets.

Z 8101	28101	28102	Z 8102	I	*IF*	MY	Z 8155	28155	28156	Z 8156	I	*IF*	PL
Z 8103	28103	28104	Z 8104	I	*IF*	PL	Z 8157	28157	28158	Z 8158	I	*IF*	PL
Z 8105	28105	28106	Z 8106	I	*IF*	MY	Z 8159	28159	28160	Z 8160	I	*IF*	PL
Z 8107	28107	28108	Z 8108	I	*IF*	MY	Z 8161	28161	28162	Z 8162	I	*IF*	MY
Z 8109	28109	28110	Z 8110	I	*IF*	MY	Z 8163	28163	28164	Z 8164	I	*IF*	PL
Z 8111	28111	28112	Z 8112	I	*IF*	MY	Z 8165	28165	28166	Z 8166	I	*IF*	PL
Z 8113	28113	28114	Z 8114	I	*IF*	MY	Z 8167	28167	28168	Z 8168	I	*IF*	PL
Z 8115	28115	28116	Z 8116	I	*IF*	MY	Z 8169	28169	28170	Z 8170	I	*IF*	MY
Z 8117	28117	28118	Z 8118	I	*IF*	MY	Z 8171	28171	28172	Z 8172	I	*IF*	PL
Z 8119	28119	28120	Z 8120	I	*IF*	MY	Z 8173	28173	28174	Z 8174	I	*IF*	PL
Z 8121	28121	28122	Z 8122	I	*IF*	PL	Z 8175	28175	28176	Z 8176	I	*IF*	PL
Z 8123	28123	28124	Z 8124	I	*IF*	MY	Z 8177	28177	28178	Z 8178	I	*IF*	MY
Z 8125	28125	28126	Z 8126	I	*IF*	PL	Z 8179	28179	28180	Z 8180	I	*IF*	PL
Z 8127	28127	28128	Z 8128	I	*IF*	PL	Z 8181	28181	28182	Z 8182	I	*IF*	PL
Z 8129	28129	28130	Z 8130	I	*IF*	MY	Z 8183	28183	28184	Z 8184	I	*IF*	PL
Z 8131	28131	28132	Z 8132	I	*IF*	PL	Z 8185	28185	28186	Z 8186	I	*IF*	PL
Z 8133	28133	28134	Z 8134	I	*IF*	PL	Z 8187	28187	28188	Z 8188	I	*IF*	MY
Z 8135	28135	28136	Z 8136	I	*IF*	PL	Z 8189	28189	28190	Z 8190	I	*IF*	PL
Z 8137	28137	28138	Z 8138	I	*IF*	MY	Z 8191	28191	28192	Z 8192	I	*IF*	PL
Z 8139	28139	28140	Z 8140	I	*IF*	PL	Z 8193	28193	28194	Z 8194	I	*IF*	MY
Z 8141	28141	28142	Z 8142	I	*IF*	PL	Z 8195	28195	28196	Z 8196	I	*IF*	MY
Z 8143	28143	28144	Z 8144	I	*IF*	PL	Z 8197	28197	28198	Z 8198	I	*IF*	PL
Z 8145	28145	28146	Z 8146	I	*IF*	MY	Z 8199	28199	28200	Z 8200	I	*IF*	PL
Z 8147	28147	28148	Z 8148	I	*IF*	PL	Z 8201	28201	28202	Z 8202	I	*IF*	MY
Z 8149	28149	28150	Z 8150	I	*IF*	PL	Z 8203	28203	28204	Z 8204	I	*IF*	MY
Z 8151	28151	28152	Z 8152	I	*IF*	PL	Z 8205	28205	28206	Z 8206	I	*IF*	PL
Z 8153	28153	28154	Z 8154	I	*IF*	MY	Z 8207	28207	28208	Z 8208	I	*IF*	PL

Z 8209	28209	28210	Z 8210	I	IF	MY	Z 8275	28275	28276	Z 8276	I	IF	MY
Z 8211	28211	28212	Z 8212	I	IF	MY	Z 8277	28277	28278	Z 8278	I	IF	MY
Z 8213	28213	28214	Z 8214	I	IF	PL	Z 8279	28279	28280	Z 8280	I	IF	MY
Z 8215	28215	28216	Z 8216	I	IF	PL	Z 8281	28281	28282	Z 8282	I	IF	MY
Z 8217	28217	28218	Z 8218	I	IF	MY	Z 8283	28283	28284	Z 8284	I	IF	MY
Z 8219	28219	28220	Z 8220	I	IF	MY	Z 8285	28285	28286	Z 8286	I	IF	MY
Z 8221	28221	28222	Z 8222	I	IF	PL	Z 8287	28287	28288	Z 8288	I	IF	MY
Z 8223	28223	28224	Z 8224	I	IF	PL	Z 8289	28289	28290	Z 8290	I	IF	MY
Z 8225	28225	28226	Z 8226	I	IF	MY	Z 8291	28291	28292	Z 8292	I	IF	MY
Z 8227	28227	28228	Z 8228	I	IF	MY	Z 8293	28293	28294	Z 8294	I	IF	MY
Z 8229	28229	28230	Z 8230	I	IF	PL	Z 8295	28295	28296	Z 8296	I	IF	MY
Z 8231	28231	28232	Z 8232	I	IF	PL	Z 8297	28297	28298	Z 8298	I	IF	MY
Z 8233	28233	28234	Z 8234	I	IF	MY	Z 8299	28299	28300	Z 8300	I	IF	MY
Z 8235	28235	28236	Z 8236	I	IF	MY	Z 8301	28301	28302	Z 8302	I	IF	MY
Z 8237	28237	28238	Z 8238	I	IF	PL	Z 8303	28303	28304	Z 8304	I	IF	MY
Z 8239	28239	28240	Z 8240	I	IF	PL	Z 8305	28305	28306	Z 8306	I	IF	MY
Z 8241	28241	28242	Z 8242	I	IF	MY	Z 8307	28307	28308	Z 8308	I	IF	MY
Z 8243	28243	28244	Z 8244	I	IF	PL	Z 8309	28309	28310	Z 8310	I	IF	MY
Z 8245	28245	28246	Z 8246	I	IF	PL	Z 8311	28311	28312	Z 8312	I	IF	MY
Z 8247	28247	28248	Z 8248	I	IF	PL	Z 8313	28313	28314	Z 8314	I	IF	MY
Z 8249	28249	28250	Z 8250	I	IF	PL	Z 8315	28315	28316	Z 8316	I	IF	MY
Z 8251	28251	28252	Z 8252	I	IF	PL	Z 8317	28317	28318	Z 8318	I	IF	MY
Z 8253	28253	28254	Z 8254	I	IF	PL	Z 8319	28319	28320	Z 8320	I	IF	MY
Z 8255	28255	28256	Z 8256	I	IF	PL	Z 8321	28321	28322	Z 8322	I	IF	MY
Z 8257	28257	28258	Z 8258	I	IF	PL	Z 8323	28323	28324	Z 8324	I	IF	MY
Z 8259	28259	28260	Z 8260	I	IF	PL	Z 8325	28325	28326	Z 8326	I	IF	MY
Z 8261	28261	28262	Z 8262	I	IF	PL	Z 8327	28327	28328	Z 8328	I	IF	MY
Z 8263	28263	28264	Z 8264	I	IF	PL	Z 8329	28329	28330	Z 8330	I	IF	MY
Z 8265	28265	28266	Z 8266	I	IF	MY	Z 8331	28331	28332	Z 8332	I	IF	MY
Z 8267	28267	28268	Z 8268	I	IF	MY	Z 8333	28333	28334	Z 8334	I	IF	MY
Z 8269	28269	28270	Z 8270	I	IF	MY	Z 8335	28335	28336	Z 8336	I	IF	MY
Z 8271	28271	28272	Z 8272	I	IF	MY	Z 8337	28337	28338	Z 8338	I	IF	MY
Z 8273	28273	28274	Z 8274	I	IF	MY	Z 8339	28339	28340	Z 8340	I	IF	MY

Names:

Z 8121/8122	EPINAY-SUR-SEINE		Z 8263/8264	PERSAN
Z 8257/8258	RAISMES		Z 8291/8292	BOURG LA REINE
Z 8261/8262	MITRY-MORY			

MI84 sets.

Z 8341	28341	28342	Z 8342	I	IF	BY	Z 8389	28389	28390	Z 8390	I	IF	BY
Z 8343	28343	28344	Z 8344	I	IF	BY	Z 8391	28391	28392	Z 8392	I	IF	BY
Z 8345	28345	28346	Z 8346	I	IF	BY	Z 8393	28393	28394	Z 8394	I	IF	BY
Z 8347	28347	28348	Z 8348	I	IF	BY	Z 8395	28395	28396	Z 8396	I	IF	BY
Z 8349	28349	28350	Z 8350	I	IF	BY	Z 8397	28397	28398	Z 8398	I	IF	BY
Z 8351	28351	28352	Z 8352	I	IF	BY	Z 8399	28399	28400	Z 8400	I	IF	BY
Z 8353	28353	28354	Z 8354	I	IF	BY	Z 8401	28401	28402	Z 8402	I	IF	BY
Z 8355	28355	28356	Z 8356	I	IF	BY	Z 8403	28403	28404	Z 8404	I	IF	BY
Z 8357	28357	28358	Z 8358	I	IF	BY	Z 8405	28405	28406	Z 8406	I	IF	BY
Z 8359	28359	28360	Z 8360	I	IF	BY	Z 8407	28407	28408	Z 8408	I	IF	BY
Z 8361	28361	28362	Z 8362	I	IF	BY	Z 8409	28409	28410	Z 8410	I	IF	BY
Z 8363	28363	28364	Z 8364	I	IF	BY	Z 8411	28411	28412	Z 8412	I	IF	BY
Z 8365	28365	28366	Z 8366	I	IF	BY	Z 8413	28413	28414	Z 8414	I	IF	BY
Z 8367	28367	28368	Z 8368	I	IF	BY	Z 8415	28415	28416	Z 8416	I	IF	BY
Z 8369	28369	28370	Z 8370	I	IF	BY	Z 8417	28417	28418	Z 8418	I	IF	BY
Z 8371	28371	28372	Z 8372	I	IF	BY	Z 8419	28419	28420	Z 8420	I	IF	BY
Z 8373	28373	28374	Z 8374	I	IF	BY	Z 8421	28421	28422	Z 8422	I	IF	BY
Z 8375	28375	28376	Z 8376	I	IF	BY	Z 8423	28423	28424	Z 8424	I	IF	BY
Z 8377	28377	28378	Z 8378	I	IF	BY	Z 8425	28425	28426	Z 8426	I	IF	BY
Z 8379	28379	28380	Z 8380	I	IF	BY	Z 8427	28427	28428	Z 8428	I	IF	BY
Z 8381	28381	28382	Z 8382	I	IF	BY	Z 8429	28429	28430	Z 8430	I	IF	BY
Z 8383	28383	28384	Z 8384	I	IF	BY	Z 8431	28431	28432	Z 8432	I	IF	BY
Z 8385	28385	28386	Z 8386	I	IF	BY	Z 8433	28433	28434	Z 8434	I	IF	BY
Z 8387	28387	28388	Z 8388	I	IF	BY	Z 8435	28435	28436	Z 8436	I	IF	BY

Z 8437	28437	28438	Z 8438	I	IF	BY
Z 8439	28439	28440	Z 8440	I	IF	BY
Z 8441	28441	28442	Z 8442	I	IF	BY
Z 8443	28443	28444	Z 8444	I	IF	BY
Z 8445	28445	28446	Z 8446	I	IF	BY
Z 8447	28447	28448	Z 8448	I	IF	BY
Z 8449	28449	28450	Z 8450	I	IF	BY
Z 8451	28451	28452	Z 8452	I	IF	BY
Z 8453	28453	28454	Z 8454	I	IF	BY
Z 8455	28455	28456	Z 8456	I	IF	BY
Z 8457	28457	28458	Z 8458	I	IF	BY
Z 8459	28459	28460	Z 8460	I	IF	BY
Z 8461	28461	28462	Z 8462	I	IF	BY

Z 8463	28463	28464	Z 8464	I	IF	BY
Z 8465	28465	28466	Z 8466	I	IF	BY
Z 8467	28467	28468	Z 8468	I	IF	BY
Z 8469	28469	28470	Z 8470	I	IF	BY
Z 8471	28471	28472	Z 8472	I	IF	BY
Z 8473	28473	28474	Z 8474	I	IF	BY
Z 8475	28475	28476	Z 8476	I	IF	BY
Z 8477	28477	28478	Z 8478	I	IF	BY
Z 8479	28479	28480	Z 8480	I	IF	BY
Z 8481	28481	28482	Z 8482	I	IF	BY
Z 8483	28483	28484	Z 8484	I	IF	BY
Z 8485	28485	28486	Z 8486	I	IF	BY

Names:

Z 8341/8342	BOISSY ST. LEGER
Z 8413/8414	POISSY

Z 8441	INTERLAKEN	I
Z 8459/8460	SUCY-EN-BRIE	

CLASS Z 8800   4-CAR DOUBLE-DECK UNITS

A dual-voltage version of Class Z 5600 used on RER Line C, particularly on the branch to Pontoise. The trailer cars are common with Class Z 5600.

Built: 1986–88.   **Systems:** 1500 V DC/25 kV AC.
Builders–Mechanical Parts: ANF/CIMT.
Builders–Electrical Parts: Alsthom/TCO.
Formation: ZB + ZRB + ZRAB + ZB.
Wheel Arrangement: Bo-Bo + 2-2 + 2-2 + Bo-Bo.
Traction Motors: 4 x Alsthom TCO 4 FHO of 350 kW per power car.
Accommodation: –/107 + –/168 1T + 70/82 + –/107.
Weight: 69 t + 41 t + 42 t + 69 t.
Length: 25.10 m + 24.28 m + 24.28 m + 25.10 m.
Maximum Speed: 140 km/h.

01B	Z 8801	25686	35631	Z 8802	I	IF	TR		30B	Z 8859	25709	35647	Z 8860	I	IF	PA
02B	Z 8803	25687	35662	Z 8804	I	IF	TR		31B	Z 8861	25706	35656	Z 8862	I	IF	PA
03B	Z 8805	25688	35618	Z 8806	I	IF	TR		32B	Z 8863	25708	35644	Z 8864	I	IF	PA
04B	Z 8807	25685	35658	Z 8808	I	IF	TR		33B	Z 8865	25707	35640	Z 8866	I	IF	PA
05B	Z 8809	25611	35607	Z 8810	I	IF	TR		34B	Z 8867	25618	35710	Z 8868	I	IF	PA
06B	Z 8811	25689	35659	Z 8812	I	IF	TR		35B	Z 8869	25710	35642	Z 8870	I	IF	PA
07B	Z 8813	25690	35660	Z 8814	I	IF	TR		36B	Z 8871	25626	35704	Z 8872	I	IF	PA
08B	Z 8815	25602	35650	Z 8816	I	IF	TR		37B	Z 8873	25711	35604	Z 8874	I	IF	PA
09B	Z 8817	25691	35612	Z 8818	I	IF	TR		38B	Z 8875	25725	35652	Z 8876	I	IF	PA
10B	Z 8819	25640	35664	Z 8820	I	IF	TR		39B	Z 8877	25639	35701	Z 8878	I	IF	PA
11B	Z 8821	25676	35653	Z 8822	I	IF	TR		40B	Z 8879	25664	35614	Z 8880	I	IF	PA
12B	Z 8823	25668	35611	Z 8824	I	IF	TR		41B	Z 8881	25713	35646	Z 8882	I	IF	PA
13B	Z 8825	25643	35707	Z 8826	I	IF	TR		42B	Z 8883	25724	35634	Z 8884	I	IF	PA
14B	Z 8827	25698	35630	Z 8828	I	IF	TR		43B	Z 8885	25714	35637	Z 8886	I	IF	PA
15B	Z 8829	25712	35649	Z 8830	I	IF	TR		44B	Z 8887	25716	35603	Z 8888	I	IF	PA
16B	Z 8831	25692	35639	Z 8832	I	IF	TR		45B	Z 8889	25715	35609	Z 8890	I	IF	PA
17B	Z 8833	25700	35651	Z 8834	I	IF	PA		46B	Z 8891	25630	35706	Z 8892	I	IF	PA
18B	Z 8835	25694	35645	Z 8836	I	IF	PA		47B	Z 8893	25695	35633	Z 8894	I	IF	PA
19B	Z 8837	25693	35657	Z 8838	I	IF	PA		48B	Z 8895	25718	35648	Z 8896	I	IF	PA
20B	Z 8839	25719	35606	Z 8840	I	IF	PA		49B	Z 8897	25717	35635	Z 8898	I	IF	PA
21B	Z 8841	25703	35638	Z 8842	I	IF	PA		50B	Z 8899	25642	35702	Z 8900	I	IF	PA
22B	Z 8843	25697	35663	Z 8844	I	IF	PA		51B	Z 8901	25629	35703	Z 8902	I	IF	PA
23B	Z 8845	25699	35613	Z 8846	I	IF	PA		52B	Z 8903	25720	35655	Z 8904	I	IF	PA
24B	Z 8847	25705	35610	Z 8848	I	IF	PA		53B	Z 8905	25627	35705	Z 8906	I	IF	PA
25B	Z 8849	25696	35601	Z 8850	I	IF	PA		54B	Z 8907	25722	35620	Z 8908	I	IF	PA
26B	Z 8851	25701	35636	Z 8852	I	IF	PA		55B	Z 8909	25723	35643	Z 8910	I	IF	PA
27B	Z 8853	25721	35602	Z 8854	I	IF	PA		56B	Z 8911	25638	35708	Z 8912	I	IF	PA
28B	Z 8855	25702	35641	Z 8856	I	IF	PA		57B	Z 8913	25655	35709	Z 8914	I	IF	PA
29B	Z 8857	25646	35616	Z 8858	I	IF	PA		58B	Z 8915	25726	35661	Z 8916	I	IF	PA

Names:

Z 8801/8802	SAINT GRATIEN	Z 8809/8810	ERMONT-EAUBONNE
Z 8803/8804	FRANCONVILLE	Z 8811/8812	GENNEVILLIERS
Z 8805/8806	GROSLAY	Z 8813/8814	LE PLESSIS BOUCHARD
Z 8807/8808	SANNOIS		

CLASS Z 9500   Z2   2-CAR UNITS

This is a dual-voltage version of Class Z 7500 and has unidirectional seating. Used mainly in the Jura, east of Dijon and in the Alps, east of Lyon. Being refurbished.

Built: 1982–83.
Builders: Alsthom/Francorail-MTE.
Formation: ZABD + ZRBx.
Traction Motors: 4 x 305 kW.
Accommodation: 32/35 2T + –/84 1T (*32/35 1T + –/80 1T).
Weight: 66 + 50 tonnes.
Maximum Speed: 160 km/h.

Systems: 1500 V DC/25 kV AC.

Wheel Arrangement: Bo-Bo + 2-2.

Length: 25.10 + 25.10 m.

Z 9501	19501	**B**	*RA*		VE	Z 9508	19508	**T**	*FC*	*	DP	Z 9515	19515	**T**	*BO*	*	DP
Z 9502	19502	**T**	*RA*	*	VE	Z 9509	19509	**B**	*RA*		VE	Z 9516	19516	**T**	*BO*	*	DP
Z 9503	19503	**B**	*RA*		VE	Z 9510	19510	**Z**	*FC*		DP	Z 9517	19517	**Z**	*BO*		DP
Z 9504	19504	**B**	*RA*		VE	Z 9511	19511	**B**	*RA*		VE	Z 9518	19518	**R**	*BO*		DP
Z 9505	19505	**R**	*FC*		DP	Z 9512	19512	**B**	*RA*		VE	Z 99581	919581	**B**	*FC*		DP
Z 9506	19506	**R**	*RA*		VE	Z 9513	19513	**B**	*FC*		DP	Z 99582	919582	**B**	*FC*		DP
Z 9507	19507	**T**	*RA*	*	VE	Z 9514	19514	**R**	*RA*		VE						

Names:

Z 9502	ARLES	Z 99581	FRANCHE-COMTÉ
Z 9513	AMBÉRIEU-EN-BUGEY	Z 99582	FRANCHE-COMTÉ
Z 9517	SAINT-PRIEST		

CLASS Z 9600   Z2   2-CAR UNITS

This is the dual-voltage version of Class Z 7300 and is used to the west of Le Mans, east of Dijon and in the Alps. Units in livery **T** have been refurbished but there are slight differences in seat type and some do not have air conditioning.

Built: 1984–87.
Builders: Alsthom/Francorail-MTE.
Formation: ZABD + ZRBx.
Wheel Arrangement: Bo-Bo + 2-2.
Accommodation: 24/43 2T + –/84 1T. (*24/43 1T + –/80 1T).
Weight: 66 + 50 tonnes.
Maximum Speed: 160 km/h.

Traction Motors: 4 x 305 kW.

Length: 25.10 + 25.10 m.

Z 9601	19601	**T**	*PL*	*	RS	Z 9613	19613	**T**	*PL*	*	RS	Z 9625	19625	**T**	*PL*	*	RS
Z 9602	19602	**T**	*CE*	*	RS	Z 9614	19614	**Z**	*RA*		VE	Z 9626	19626	**T**	*PL*	*	RS
Z 9603	19603	**T**	*BR*	*	RS	Z 9615	19615	**BO**	*RA*		VE	Z 9627	19627	**T**	*PL*	*	RS
Z 9604	19604	**T**	*BR*	*	RS	Z 9616	19616	**BO**	*FC*	*	DP	Z 9628	19628	**T**	*BR*	*	RS
Z 9605	19605	**T**	*BR*	*	RS	Z 9617	19617	**Z**	*RA*		VE	Z 9629	19629	**T**	*PL*	*	RS
Z 9606	19606	**T**	*BR*	*	RS	Z 9618	19618	**T**	*FC*	*	DP	Z 9630	19630	**T**	*PL*	*	RS
Z 9607	19607	**T**	*CE*	*	RS	Z 9619	19619	**T**	*RA*		VE	Z 9631	19631	**Z**	*FC*		DP
Z 9608	19608	**T**	*PL*	*	RS	Z 9620	19620	**Z**	*RA*		VE	Z 9632	19632	**Z**	*FC*		DP
Z 9609	19609	**T**	*PL*	*	RS	Z 9621	19621	**T**	*PL*	*	RS	Z 9633	19633	**Z**	*BO*		DP
Z 9610	19610	**T**	*PL*	*	RS	Z 9622	19622	**T**	*PL*	*	RS	Z 9634	19634	**T**	*RA*	*	VE
Z 9611	19611	**T**	*PL*	*	RS	Z 9623	19623	**T**	*PL*	*	RS	Z 9635	19635	**Z**	*RA*		VE
Z 9612	19612	**T**	*PL*	*	RS	Z 9624	19624	**T**	*PL*	*	RS	Z 9636	19636	**Z**	*RA*		VE

Names:

Z 9605	SOTTEVILLE-LES-ROUEN	Z 9620	RUMILLY
Z 9617	FIRMINY	Z 9633	RIVES

Z 9635 has three names: These are: CHÊNE BOURG, CHÊNE BOURGERIES and THÔNEX!
Z 9607–13/21–7/29/30 are all named 'LES PAYS DE LA LOIRE'.

CLASS Z 11500   Z2   2-CAR UNITS

An AC-only version of Class Z 7300 for use around Metz and Strasbourg. Luxembourg Railways (CFL) have 22 Class 2000 units developed from this design. Sets no longer work to Luxembourg.

Built: 1986–67.
Builders: Alsthom/Francorail-MTE.
Wheel Arrangement: Bo-Bo + 2-2.
Accommodation: 24/43 2T + –/80 1T.
Weight: 66 + 50 tonnes.
Maximum Speed: 160 km/h.

System: 25 kV AC.
Formation: ZABD + ZRBx.
Traction Motors: 4 x 305 kW.

Length: 25.10 + 25.10 m.

Z 11501	111501	**T**	*CA*	TV	Z 11509	111509	**T**	*LO*	TV	Z 11516	111516	**T**	*LO*	TV

Z 11501 111501 **T** *CA* TV   Z 11509 111509 **T** *LO* TV   Z 11516 111516 **T** *LO* TV
Z 11502 111502 **T** *LO* TV   Z 11510 111510 **T** *LO* TV   Z 11517 111517 **T** *AL* TV
Z 11503 111503 **T** *LO* TV   Z 11511 111511 **T** *LO* TV   Z 11518 111518 **T** *LO* TV
Z 11504 111504 **T** *LO* TV   Z 11512 111512 **T** *LO* TV   Z 11519 111519 **T** *LO* TV
Z 11505 111505 **T** *AL* TV   Z 11513 111513 **T** *LO* TV   Z 11520 111520 **T** *LO* TV
Z 11506 111506 **T** *LO* TV   Z 11514 111514 **T** *LO* TV   Z 11521 111521 **T** *LO* TV
Z 11507 111507 **T** *CA* TV   Z 11515 111515 **T** *AL* TV   Z 11522 111522 **T** *LO* TV
Z 11508 111508 **T** *AL* TV

Names:

Z 11501 SCHILTIGHEIM
Z 11508 REMILLY
Z 11517 ANCY-SUR-MOSELLE

Z 11521 WOIPPY
Z 11521 LONGUYON

CLASS Z 20500   4/5-CAR DOUBLE-DECK UNITS

These units are a further development of Class Z 8800 with a modified appearance and longer trailers. They have asynchronous motors. Vitry (Les Ardoines) units are four-car and operate in multiple with Classes Z 5600 and Z 8800 on RER Line C. Villeneuve units are five-car and operate on RER Line D. Noisy sets are 4-car and work Paris Est–Meaux services. Les Joncherolles sets are divided between 5-car sets for RER Line D and a few 4-car sets which work Paris Nord services. PS sets operate St. Lazare–Nanterre Université services. In 2008, units were being refurbished and receiving the STIF dark blue livery.

Systems: 1500 V DC/25 kV AC.
Built: 1988–97.
Builders–Mechanical Parts: CIMT/ANF.
Builder–Electrical Parts: GEC Alsthom.
Traction Motors: 4 x Alsthom FHA 2870 asynchronous of 350 kW per power car.
Wheel Arrangement: Bo-Bo + 2-2 + 2-2 (+ 2-2) + Bo-Bo.
Formation: ZB + ZRB + ZRAB (+ ZRB) + ZB.
Accommodation: –/110 + –/204 1T + 80/108 1T (+ –/204 1T) + –/110.
Weight: 69 t + 43 t + 43 t (+ 44 t) + 69 t.
Length: 25.10 m + 26.40 m + 26.40 m (+ 26.40 m) + 25.10 m.
Maximum Speed: 140 km/h.

*   Power cars have GEC Alsthom's ONIX traction package incorporating IGBT technology.
†   Trailer ZR 201579 has a stainless steel body.
r   Refurbished.

01A	Z 20501	201501	202501		Z 20502	I	*IF*	PA
02A	Z 20503	201503	202503		Z 20504	I	*IF*	PA
03A	Z 20505	201505	202505		Z 20506	I	*IF*	PA
04A	Z 20507	201507	202507		Z 20508	I	*IF*	PN
05J	Z 20509	201509	202509	203549	Z 20510	I	*IF*	PJ
06A	Z 20511	201511	202511		Z 20512	I	*IF*	PA
07A	Z 20513	201513	202513		Z 20514	I	*IF*	PA
08J	Z 20515	201515	202515	203515	Z 20516	I	*IF*	PJ
09J	Z 20517	201517	202517	203507	Z 20518	I	*IF*	PJ
10J	Z 20519	201519	202519	203531	Z 20520	I	*IF*	PJ
11A	Z 20521	201521	202521		Z 20522	I	*IF*	PN
12A	Z 20523	201523	202523		Z 20524	I	*IF*	PN
13A	Z 20525	201525	202525		Z 20526	I	*IF*	PA
14A	Z 20527	201527	202527		Z 20528	I	*IF*	PA

15A	Z 20529	201529	202529		Z 20530	I	*IF*		PA
16A	Z 20531	201531	202531		Z 20532	I	*IF*		PA
17A	Z 20533	201533	202533		Z 20534	I	*IF*		PA
18J	Z 20535	201535	202535	203567	Z 20536	I	*IF*		PJ
19J	Z 20537	201537	202537	203517	Z 20538	I	*IF*		PJ
20J	Z 20539	201539	202539	203539	Z 20540	I	*IF*		PJ
21A	Z 20541	201541	202541		Z 20542	I	*IF*		PN
22A	Z 20543	201543	202543	203551	Z 20544	I	*IF*		PN
23J	Z 20545	201545	202545	203545	Z 20546	I	*IF*		PJ
24A	Z 20547	201547	202547		Z 20548	I	*IF*		PA
25A	Z 20549	201549	202549		Z 20550	I	*IF*		PA
26A	Z 20551	201551	202551		Z 20552	I	*IF*		PN
27A	Z 20553	201553	202553		Z 20554	I	*IF*		PN
28A	Z 20555	201555	202555		Z 20556	I	*IF*		PN
29A	Z 20557	201557	202557		Z 20558	I	*IF*		PA
30A	Z 20559	201559	202559		Z 20560	I	*IF*		PN
31J	Z 20561	201561	202561	203511	Z 20562	I	*IF*		PJ
32J	Z 20563	201563	202563	203541	Z 20564	I	*IF*		PJ
33A	Z 20565	201565	202565		Z 20566	I	*IF*		PA
34A	Z 20567	201567	202567		Z 20568	I	*IF*		PA
35A	Z 20569	201569	202569		Z 20570	I	*IF*		PN
36A	Z 20571	201571	202571		Z 20572	I	*IF*		PA
37A	Z 20573	201573	202573		Z 20574	I	*IF*		PA
38A	Z 20575	201575	202575		Z 20576	I	*IF*		PA
39J	Z 20577	201577	202577	203553	Z 20578	I	*IF*		PJ
40A	Z 20579	201579	202579		Z 20580	I	*IF*	†	PA
41A	Z 20581	201581	202581		Z 20582	I	*IF*		PA
42A	Z 20583	201583	202583		Z 20584	I	*IF*		PA
43P	Z 20585	25944	35808	25821	Z 20586	I	*IF*		PJ
44P	Z 20587	25820	35812	25942	Z 20588	I	*IF*		PJ
45P	Z 20589	25802	35803	25943	Z 20590	I	*IF*		PJ
46P	Z 20591	25819	35806	25945	Z 20592	I	*IF*		PJ
47P	Z 20593	25819	35810	25948	Z 20594	I	*IF*		PJ
48P	Z 20595	25806	35802	25941	Z 20596	I	*IF*		PJ
49P	Z 20597	25815	35815	25946	Z 20598	I	*IF*		PJ
50P	Z 20599	25803	35814	25947	Z 20600	I	*IF*		PJ
51P	Z 20601	25812	35805	25949	Z 20602	I	*IF*		PJ
52A	Z 20603	25816	35811		Z 20604	I	*IF*		PJ
53A	Z 20605	25801	35804		Z 20606	I	*IF*		PS
54A	Z 20607	25810	35801		Z 20608	I	*IF*		PS
55A	Z 20609	25805	35816		Z 20610	I	*IF*		PJ
56A	Z 20611	25813	35813		Z 20612	I	*IF*		PJ
57A	Z 20613	25811	35807		Z 20614	I	*IF*		PJ
58A	Z 20615	25804	35820		Z 20616	I	*IF*		PJ
59A	Z 20617	25818	35817		Z 20618	I	*IF*		PS
60A	Z 20619	25808	35818		Z 20620	I	*IF*		PS
61A	Z 20621	25807	35809		Z 20622	I	*IF*		PS
62A	Z 20623	25809	35821		Z 20624	I	*IF*		PJ
63A	Z 20625	25814	35819		Z 20626	I	*IF*		PS
64V	Z 20627	201627	202627	203627	Z 20628	I	*IF*		VG
65V	Z 20629	201629	202629	203629	Z 20630	I	*IF*		VG
66V	Z 20631	201631	202631	203631	Z 20632	I	*IF*		VG
67V	Z 20633	201633	202633	203633	Z 20634	I	*IF*		VG
68D	Z 20635	201635	202635	203635	Z 20636	**H**	*IF*	r	VG
69V	Z 20637	201637	202637	203637	Z 20638	I	*IF*		VG
70V	Z 20639	201639	202639	203639	Z 20640	I	*IF*		VG
71V	Z 20641	201641	202641	203641	Z 20642	I	*IF*		VG
72V	Z 20643	201643	202643	203643	Z 20644	I	*IF*		VG
73V	Z 20645	201645	202645	203645	Z 20646	I	*IF*		VG
74D	Z 20647	201647	202647	203647	Z 20648	**H**	*IF*	r	VG
75V	Z 20649	201649	202649	203649	Z 20650	I	*IF*		VG
76V	Z 20651	201651	202651	203651	Z 20652	I	*IF*		VG
77V	Z 20653	201653	202653	203653	Z 20654	I	*IF*		VG
78V	Z 20655	201655	202655	203655	Z 20656	I	*IF*		VG

79V	Z 20657	201657	202657	203657	Z 20658	I	*IF*		VG
80V	Z 20659	201659	202659	203659	Z 20660	I	*IF*		VG
81V	Z 20661	201661	202661	203661	Z 20662	I	*IF*		VG
82V	Z 20663	201663	202663	203663	Z 20664	I	*IF*		VG
83V	Z 20665	201665	202665	203665	Z 20666	I	*IF*		VG
84V	Z 20667	201667	202667	203667	Z 20668	I	*IF*		VG
85D	Z 20669	201669	202669	203669	Z 20670	**H**	*IF*	r	VG
86D	Z 20671	201671	202671	203671	Z 20672	**H**	*IF*	r	VG
87D	Z 20673	201673	202673	203673	Z 20674	**H**	*IF*	r	VG
88D	Z 20675	201675	202675	203675	Z 20676	**H**	*IF*	r	VG
89D	Z 20677	201677	202677	203677	Z 20678	**H**	*IF*	r	VG
90D	Z 20679	201679	202679	203679	Z 20680	**H**	*IF*	r	VG
91D	Z 20681	201681	202681	203681	Z 20682	**H**	*IF*	r	VG
92V	Z 20683	201683	202683	203683	Z 20684	I	*IF*		VG
93V	Z 20685	201685	202685	203685	Z 20686	I	*IF*		VG
94D	Z 20687	201687	202687	203687	Z 20688	**H**	*IF*	r	VG
95V	Z 20689	201689	202689	203689	Z 20690	I	*IF*		VG
96V	Z 20691	201691	202691	203691	Z 20692	I	*IF*		VG
97V	Z 20693	201693	202693	203693	Z 20694	I	*IF*		VG
98V	Z 20695	201695	202695	203695	Z 20696	I	*IF*		VG
99D	Z 20697	201697	202697	203697	Z 20698	**H**	*IF*	r	VG
100V	Z 20699	201699	202699	203699	Z 20700	I	*IF*		VG
101D	Z 20701	201701	202701	203701	Z 20702	**H**	*IF*	r	VG
102V	Z 20703	201703	202703	203703	Z 20704	I	*IF*		VG
103D	Z 20705	201705	202705	203705	Z 20706	**H**	*IF*	r	VG
104V	Z 20707	201707	202707	203707	Z 20708	I	*IF*		VG
105D	Z 20709	201709	202709	203709	Z 20710	**H**	*IF*	r	VG
106D	Z 20711	201711	202711	203711	Z 20712	**H**	*IF*	r	VG
107V	Z 20713	201713	202713	203713	Z 20714	I	*IF*		VG
108V	Z 20715	201715	202715	203715	Z 20716	I	*IF*		VG
109D	Z 20717	201717	202717	203717	Z 20718	**H**	*IF*	r	VG
110D	Z 20719	201719	202719	203719	Z 20720	**H**	*IF*	r	PJ
111J	Z 20721	201721	202721	203721	Z 20722	I	*IF*		PJ
112J	Z 20723	201723	202723	203723	Z 20724	I	*IF*		PJ
113J	Z 20725	201725	202725	203725	Z 20726	I	*IF*		PJ
114J	Z 20727	201727	202727	203727	Z 20728	I	*IF*		PJ
115J	Z 20729	201729	202729	203729	Z 20730	I	*IF*		PJ
116J	Z 20731	201731	202731	203731	Z 20732	I	*IF*		PJ
117J	Z 20733	201733	202733	203733	Z 20734	I	*IF*		PJ
118J	Z 20735	201735	202735	203735	Z 20736	I	*IF*		PJ
119J	Z 20737	201737	202737	203737	Z 20738	I	*IF*		PJ
120J	Z 20739	201739	202739	203739	Z 20740	I	*IF*		PJ
121J	Z 20741	201741	202741	203741	Z 20742	I	*IF*		PJ
122V	Z 20743	201743	202743	203743	Z 20744	I	*IF*		VG
123J	Z 20745	201745	202745	203745	Z 20746	I	*IF*		PJ
124J	Z 20747	201747	202747	203747	Z 20748	I	*IF*		PJ
125J	Z 20749	201749	202749	203749	Z 20750	I	*IF*		PJ
126J	Z 20751	201751	202751	203557	Z 20752	I	*IF*		PJ
127J	Z 20753	201753	202753	203519	Z 20754	I	*IF*		PJ
128V	Z 20755	201755	202755	203501	Z 20756	I	*IF*		VG
129J	Z 20757	201757	202757	203543	Z 20758	I	*IF*		PJ
130J	Z 20759	201759	202759	203547	Z 20760	I	*IF*		PJ
131J	Z 20761	201761	202761	203527	Z 20762	I	*IF*		PJ
132V	Z 20763	201763	202763	203559	Z 20764	I	*IF*		VG
133J	Z 20765	201765	202765	203505	Z 20766	I	*IF*		PJ
134J	Z 20767	201767	202767	203529	Z 20768	I	*IF*		PJ
135J	Z 20769	201769	202769	203523	Z 20770	I	*IF*		PJ
136J	Z 20771	201771	202771	203503	Z 20772	I	*IF*		PJ
137J	Z 20773	201773	202773	203521	Z 20774	I	*IF*		PJ
138J	Z 20775	201775	202775	203555	Z 20776	I	*IF*		PJ
139A	Z 20777	201777	202777	203569	Z 20778	I	*IF*		PN
140A	Z 20779	201779	202779	203525	Z 20780	I	*IF*		PN
141A	Z 20781	201781	202781		Z 20782	I	*IF*		PN
142A	Z 20783	201783	202783		Z 20784	I	*IF*		PN

143A	Z 20785	201785	202785		Z 20786	I	IF		PN
144A	Z 20787	201787	202787		Z 20788	I	IF		PN
145J	Z 20789	201789	202789	203535	Z 20790	I	IF		PJ
146J	Z 20791	201791	202791	203537	Z 20792	I	IF		PJ
147J	Z 20793	201793	202793	203509	Z 20794	I	IF		PJ
148J	Z 20795	201795	202795	203513	Z 20796	I	IF		PJ
149J	Z 20797	201797	202797	203533	Z 20798	I	IF		PJ
150J	Z 20799	201799	202799	203561	Z 20800	I	IF		PJ
151J	Z 20801	201801	202801	203563	Z 20802	I	IF		PJ
152A	Z 20803	201803	202803		Z 20804	I	IF		PA
153A	Z 20805	201805	202805		Z 20806	I	IF		PA
154A	Z 20807	201807	202807		Z 20808	I	IF		PA
155A	Z 20809	201809	202809		Z 20810	I	IF		PA
156A	Z 20811	201811	202811		Z 20812	I	IF		PA
157A	Z 20813	201813	202813		Z 20814	I	IF		PA
158A	Z 20815	201815	202815		Z 20816	I	IF		PA
159A	Z 20817	201817	202817		Z 20818	I	IF		PA
160A	Z 20819	201819	202819		Z 20820	I	IF		PA
161A	Z 20821	201821	202821		Z 20822	I	IF		PN
162A	Z 20823	201823	202823		Z 20824	I	IF		PN
163A	Z 20825	201825	202825		Z 20826	I	IF		PN
164A	Z 20827	201827	202827		Z 20828	I	IF		PN
165A	Z 20829	201829	202829		Z 20830	I	IF		PN
166A	Z 20831	201831	202831		Z 20832	I	IF		PN
167A	Z 20833	201833	202833		Z 20834	I	IF		PN
168A	Z 20835	201835	202835		Z 20836	I	IF		PN
169A	Z 20837	201837	202837		Z 20838	I	IF		PN
170A	Z 20839	201839	202839		Z 20840	I	IF		PA
171A	Z 20841	201841	202841		Z 20842	I	IF		PA
172A	Z 20843	201843	202843		Z 20844	I	IF		PA
173A	Z 20845	201845	202845		Z 20846	I	IF		PA
174J	Z 20847	201847	202847	203565	Z 20848	I	IF		PJ
175A	Z 20849	201849	202849		Z 20850	I	IF		PA
176A	Z 20851	201851	202851		Z 20852	I	IF		PA
177A	Z 20853	201853	202853		Z 20854	I	IF		PA
178A	Z 20855	201855	202855		Z 20856	I	IF		PA
179A	Z 20857	201857	202857		Z 20858	I	IF		PN
180A	Z 20859	201859	202859		Z 20860	I	IF		PA
181A	Z 20861	201861	202861		Z 20862	I	IF		PA
182A	Z 20863	201863	202863		Z 20864	I	IF		PA
183A	Z 20865	201865	202865		Z 20866	I	IF		PA
184A	Z 20867	201867	202867		Z 20868	I	IF		PA
185A	Z 20869	201869	202869		Z 20870	I	IF		PA
186A	Z 20871	201871	202871		Z 20872	I	IF		PA
187A	Z 20873	201873	202873		Z 20874	I	IF		PA
188J	Z 20875	201875	202875	203875	Z 20876	I	IF		PJ
189J	Z 20877	201877	202877	203877	Z 20878	I	IF		PJ
190J	Z 20879	201879	202879	203879	Z 20880	I	IF		PJ
191J	Z 20881	201881	202881	203881	Z 20882	I	IF		PJ
192J	Z 20883	201883	202883	203883	Z 20884	I	IF		PJ
193J	Z 20885	201885	202885	203885	Z 20886	I	IF		PJ
194A	Z 20887	201887	202887		Z 20888	I	IF	*	PN

Names:

Z 20513/4 VILLIERS-LE-BEL
Z 20531/2 BEAUCHAMP

Z 20871/2 SAVIGNY-SUR–ORGE

CLASS Z 20900   4-CAR DOUBLE-DECK UNITS

These units are a development of Class Z 20500 with air conditioning, proper corridir connections, more comfortable seats, arranged 2+2 rather than 3+2 and equipment to allow selective closure of coaches in the evening to increase passenger security. All units have Alstom's ONIX IGBT traction package. PA units work services on Paris RER Line C and PJ units on services out of Paris Nord.

Built: 2001–2003. **Systems:** 1500 V DC/25 kV AC 50 Hz.
Builder–Mechanical Parts: Alstom/Bombardier.
Builder–Electrical Parts: Alstom.
Wheel Arrangement: Bo-Bo + 2-2 + 2-2 (+ 2-2) + Bo-Bo.
Formation: ZB + ZRB + ZRB + ZB.
Accommodation: –/82 + –/168 1T + –/168 1T + –/82.
Weight: 74 t + 49 t + 49 t + 74 t.
Length: 25.10 m + 26.654 m + 26.654 m + 25.10 m.
Maximum Speed: 140 km/h.

Multiple operation within class and with Classes Z 5600, Z 8800 and Z 20500.

201A	Z 20901	201901	202901	Z 20902	I	IF	PJ	228A	Z 20955	201955	202955	Z 20956	I	IF	PA
202A	Z 20903	201903	202903	Z 20904	I	IF	PJ	229A	Z 20957	201957	202957	Z 20958	I	IF	PA
203A	Z 20905	201905	202905	Z 20906	I	IF	PJ	230A	Z 20959	201959	202959	Z 20960	I	IF	PJ
204A	Z 20907	201907	202907	Z 20908	I	IF	PA	231A	Z 20961	201961	202961	Z 20962	I	IF	PJ
205A	Z 20909	201909	202909	Z 20910	I	IF	PJ	232A	Z 20963	201963	202963	Z 20964	I	IF	PJ
206A	Z 20911	201911	202911	Z 20912	I	IF	PA	233A	Z 20965	201965	202965	Z 20966	I	IF	PJ
207A	Z 20913	201913	202913	Z 20914	I	IF	PJ	234A	Z 20967	201967	202967	Z 20968	I	IF	PA
208A	Z 20915	201915	202915	Z 20916	I	IF	PJ	235A	Z 20969	201969	202969	Z 20970	I	IF	PA
209A	Z 20917	201917	202917	Z 20918	I	IF	PJ	236A	Z 20971	201971	202971	Z 20972	I	IF	PA
210A	Z 20919	201919	202919	Z 20920	I	IF	PA	237A	Z 20973	201973	202973	Z 20974	I	IF	PA
211A	Z 20921	201921	202921	Z 20922	I	IF	PA	238A	Z 20975	201975	202975	Z 20976	I	IF	PA
212A	Z 20923	201923	202923	Z 20924	I	IF	PA	239A	Z 20977	201977	202977	Z 20978	I	IF	PA
213A	Z 20925	201925	202925	Z 20926	I	IF	PA	240A	Z 20979	201979	202979	Z 20980	I	IF	PA
214A	Z 20927	201927	202927	Z 20928	I	IF	PA	241A	Z 20981	201981	202981	Z 20982	**H**	IF	PA
215A	Z 20929	201929	202929	Z 20930	I	IF	PA	242A	Z 20983	201983	202983	Z 20984	**H**	IF	PA
216A	Z 20931	201931	202931	Z 20932	I	IF	PA	243A	Z 20985	201985	202985	Z 20986	**H**	IF	PA
217A	Z 20933	201933	202933	Z 20934	I	IF	PA	244A	Z 20987	201987	202987	Z 20988	**H**	IF	PA
218A	Z 20935	201935	202935	Z 20936	I	IF	PJ	245A	Z 20989	201989	202989	Z 20990	**H**	IF	PA
219A	Z 20937	201937	202937	Z 20938	I	IF	PA	246A	Z 20991	201991	202991	Z 20992	**H**	IF	PA
220A	Z 20939	201939	202939	Z 20940	I	IF	PJ	247A	Z 20993	201993	202993	Z 20994	**H**	IF	PA
221A	Z 20941	201941	202941	Z 20942	I	IF	PJ	248A	Z 20995	201995	202995	Z 20996	**H**	IF	PA
222A	Z 20943	201943	202943	Z 20944	I	IF	PA	249A	Z 20997	201997	202997	Z 20998	**H**	IF	PA
223A	Z 20945	201945	202945	Z 20946	I	IF	PA	250A	Z 20999	201999	202999	Z 21000	**H**	IF	PA
224A	Z 20947	201947	202947	Z 20948	I	IF	PA	251A	Z 21001	203901	204901	Z 21002	**H**	IF	PA
225A	Z 20949	201949	202949	Z 20950	I	IF	PA	252A	Z 21003	203903	204903	Z 21004	**H**	IF	PA
226A	Z 20951	201951	202951	Z 20952	I	IF	PA	253A	Z 21005	203905	204905	Z 21006	**H**	IF	PA
227A	Z 20953	201953	202953	Z 20954	I	IF	PA	254A	Z 21007	203907	204907	Z 21008	**H**	IF	PA

CLASS Z 21500   3-CAR UNITS

These are SNCF's first EMUs designed for 200 km/h operation on regional services. They are closely derived from Class X 72500 DMUs but have slightly more curved front ends and a low-floor centre car with access at 585 mm above the rail, built by Bombardier in Crespin. First class seating is improved, and arranged 2+1. Cab ends have been reinforced after a fatal crash with an X 72500. Units were ordered by the Centre (15), Poitou-Charentes (5) and Aquitaine (6) regions, based at TP for services from Orléans to Nantes, Bourges, Limoges, Poitiers, La Rochelle and Bordeaux, Bretagne (17) and Pays de la Loire (14), based at Rennes for Rennes to Brest, Quimper and Nantes.

Built: 2002–2004. **Systems:** 1500 V DC/25 kV AC 50 Hz.
Maximum Speed: 200 km/h.
Builder–Mechanical Parts: Alstom, Aytré & Bombardier, Crespin.
Builder–Electrical Parts: Alstom.
Power Rating: 1760 kW.
Formation: ZAB + ZRB + ZAB.
Accommodation: 18/54 1T + –/64 1T + 18/46 1T.
Weight: 180 tonnes.
Length: 26.70 + 25.60 + 26.70 m.
Maximum Speed: 200 km/h.

Z 21501	221501	Z 21502	**T**	PL	RS		Z 21509	221509	Z 21510	**T**	AQ	TP
Z 21503	221503	Z 21504	**T**	PC	TP		Z 21511	221511	Z 21512	**T**	CE	TP
Z 21505	221505	Z 21506	**T**	CE	TP		Z 21513	221513	Z 21514	**T**	CE	TP
Z 21507	221507	Z 21508	**T**	CE	TP		Z 21515	221515	Z 21516	**T**	CE	TP

Z 21517	221517	Z 21518	T	CE	TP
Z 21519	221519	Z 21520	T	CE	TP
Z 21521	221521	Z 21522	T	CE	TP
Z 21523	221523	Z 21524	T	CE	TP
Z 21525	221525	Z 21526	T	CE	TP
Z 21527	221527	Z 21528	T	CE	TP
Z 21529	221529	Z 21530	T	CE	TP
Z 21531	221531	Z 21532	T	CE	TP
Z 21533	221533	Z 21534	T	CE	TP
Z 21535	221535	Z 21536	T	BR	RS
Z 21537	221537	Z 21538	T	BR	RS
Z 21539	221539	Z 21540	T	PL	RS
Z 21541	221541	Z 21542	T	BR	RS
Z 21543	221543	Z 21544	T	PL	RS
Z 21545	221545	Z 21546	T	BR	RS
Z 21547	221547	Z 21548	T	PL	RS
Z 21549	221549	Z 21550	T	BR	RS
Z 21551	221551	Z 21552	T	BR	RS
Z 21553	221553	Z 21554	T	PL	RS
Z 21555	221555	Z 21556	T	PC	TP
Z 21557	221557	Z 21558	T	BR	RS
Z 21559	221559	Z 21560	T	PL	RS
Z 21561	221561	Z 21562	T	CE	TP
Z 21563	221563	Z 21564	T	BR	RS
Z 21565	221565	Z 21566	T	PL	RS
Z 21567	221567	Z 21568	T	AQ	TP
Z 21569	221569	Z 21570	T	BR	RS
Z 21571	221571	Z 21572	T	BR	RS
Z 21573	221573	Z 21574	T	PL	RS
Z 21575	221575	Z 21576	T	BR	RS
Z 21577	221577	Z 21578	T	PL	RS
Z 21579	221579	Z 21580	T	PL	RS
Z 21581	221581	Z 21582	T	BR	RS
Z 21583	221583	Z 21584	T	BR	RS
Z 21585	221585	Z 21586	T	PL	RS
Z 21587	221587	Z 21588	T	BR	RS
Z 21589	221589	Z 21590	T	BR	RS
Z 21591	221591	Z 21592	T	PL	RS
Z 21593	221593	Z 21594	T	BR	RS
Z 21595	221595	Z 21596	T	PL	RS
Z 21597	221597	Z 21598	T	PL	RS
Z 21599	221599	Z 21600	T	BR	RS
Z 21601	221601	Z 21602	T	PC	TP
Z 21603	221603	Z 21604	T	PC	TP
Z 21605	221605	Z 21606	T	PC	TP
Z 21607	221607	Z 21608	T	AQ	TP
Z 21609	221609	Z 21610	T	AQ	TP
Z 21611	221611	Z 21612	T	AQ	TP
Z 21613	221613	Z 21614	T	AQ	TP

Names:

Z 21509/10 Pau | Z 21607/08 Bayonne/Baiona

CLASS Z 22500   5-CAR DOUBLE-DECK UNITS

These double-deck units, though derived technically from Class Z 20500, are quite different, having been designed specifically for Paris RER services after experiments with a car inserted into an RATP set on RER line A. After this, it was decided to build the new class with three wide doors per side in order to allow fast boarding and alighting. In order to do this, electrical equipment has been spread throughout the train and the power bogies put under the second and fourth cars. It was impossible to design access to the upper decks from all three entrances so access is from the outer doors and the upper decks are closed at one end. The total effect has been to reduce seating capacity considerably although there is ample standing room. RATP has also ordered the design which it calls MI2N (Matériel Interconnection à deux Niveaux) for RER line A although these units have more axles powered. The SNCF units are all be allocated to a new depot at Noisy-le-Sec and will operate services on RER line E which will link Paris Est suburban services via a tunnel to St Lazare. This will later be extended to the western suburbs of Paris. For this, units will be shortened to four cars. 53 units are being delivered with an option for 50 more.

Built: 1996–99.   **Systems:** 1500 V DC/25 kV AC.
Builders–Mechanical Parts: CIMT/ANF.
Builder–Electrical Parts: GEC Alsthom.
Traction Motors: 4 x Alsthom FHA 2870 asynchronous of 375 kW per power car.
Formation: ZRBx + ZB + ZRB + ZAB + ZRBx.
Wheel Arrangement: 2-2 + Bo-Bo + 2-2 + Bo-Bo + 2-2.
Weight: t +   t +   t +   t (total 277 t).
Length: 22.85 m + 22.10 m + 22.10 m + 22.10 m + 22.85 m.
Accommodation: –/108 + –/110 (2) + –/116 + 51/57 + –/108.
Maximum Speed: 140 km/h.
Class specific Livery: S White with blue and red strips.

01E	221501	Z 22501	222501	Z 22502	221502	S	IF	PN
02E	221503	Z 22503	222503	Z 22504	221504	S	IF	PN
03E	221505	Z 22505	222505	Z 22506	221506	S	IF	PN
04E	221507	Z 22507	222507	Z 22508	221508	S	IF	PN
05E	221509	Z 22509	222509	Z 22510	221510	S	IF	PN
06E	221511	Z 22511	222511	Z 22512	221512	S	IF	PN
07E	221513	Z 22513	222513	Z 22514	221514	S	IF	PN
08E	221515	Z 22515	222515	Z 22516	221516	S	IF	PN

09E	221517	Z 22517	222517	Z 22518	221518	**S**	*IF*	PN
10E	221519	Z 22519	222519	Z 22520	221520	**S**	*IF*	PN
11E	221521	Z 22521	222521	Z 22522	221522	**S**	*IF*	PN
12E	221523	Z 22523	222523	Z 22524	221524	**S**	*IF*	PN
13E	221525	Z 22525	222525	Z 22526	221526	**S**	*IF*	PN
14E	221527	Z 22527	222527	Z 22528	221528	**S**	*IF*	PN
15E	221529	Z 22529	222529	Z 22530	221530	**S**	*IF*	PN
16E	221531	Z 22531	222531	Z 22532	221532	**S**	*IF*	PN
17E	221533	Z 22533	222533	Z 22534	221534	**S**	*IF*	PN
18E	221535	Z 22535	222535	Z 22536	221536	**S**	*IF*	PN
19E	221537	Z 22537	222537	Z 22538	221538	**S**	*IF*	PN
20E	221539	Z 22539	222539	Z 22540	221540	**S**	*IF*	PN
21E	221541	Z 22541	222541	Z 22542	221542	**S**	*IF*	PN
22E	221543	Z 22543	222543	Z 22544	221544	**S**	*IF*	PN
23E	221545	Z 22545	222545	Z 22546	221546	**S**	*IF*	PN
24E	221547	Z 22547	222547	Z 22548	221548	**S**	*IF*	PN
25E	221549	Z 22549	222549	Z 22550	221550	**S**	*IF*	PN
26E	221551	Z 22551	222551	Z 22552	221552	**S**	*IF*	PN
27E	221553	Z 22553	222553	Z 22554	221554	**S**	*IF*	PN
28E	221555	Z 22555	222555	Z 22556	221556	**S**	*IF*	PN
29E	221557	Z 22557	222557	Z 22558	221558	**S**	*IF*	PN
30E	221559	Z 22559	222559	Z 22560	221560	**S**	*IF*	PN
31E	221561	Z 22561	222561	Z 22562	221562	**S**	*IF*	PN
32E	221563	Z 22563	222563	Z 22564	221564	**S**	*IF*	PN
33E	221565	Z 22565	222565	Z 22566	221566	**S**	*IF*	PN
34E	221567	Z 22567	222567	Z 22568	221568	**S**	*IF*	PN
35E	221569	Z 22569	222569	Z 22570	221570	**S**	*IF*	PN
36E	221571	Z 22571	222571	Z 22572	221572	**S**	*IF*	PN
37E	221573	Z 22573	222573	Z 22574	221574	**S**	*IF*	PN
38E	221575	Z 22575	222575	Z 22576	221576	**S**	*IF*	PN
39E	221577	Z 22577	222577	Z 22578	221578	**S**	*IF*	PN
40E	221579	Z 22579	222579	Z 22580	221580	**S**	*IF*	PN
41E	221581	Z 22581	222581	Z 22582	221582	**S**	*IF*	PN
42E	221583	Z 22583	222583	Z 22584	221584	**S**	*IF*	PN
43E	221585	Z 22585	222585	Z 22586	221586	**S**	*IF*	PN
44E	221587	Z 22587	222587	Z 22588	221588	**S**	*IF*	PN
45E	221589	Z 22589	222589	Z 22590	221590	**S**	*IF*	PN
46E	221591	Z 22591	222591	Z 22592	221592	**S**	*IF*	PN
47E	221593	Z 22593	222593	Z 22594	221594	**S**	*IF*	PN
48E	221595	Z 22595	222595	Z 22596	221596	**S**	*IF*	PN
49E	221597	Z 22597	222597	Z 22598	221598	**S**	*IF*	PN
50E	221599	Z 22599	222599	Z 22600	221600	**S**	*IF*	PN
51E	221601	Z 22601	222601	Z 22602	221602	**S**	*IF*	PN
52E	221603	Z 22603	222603	Z 22604	221604	**S**	*IF*	PN
53E	221605	Z 22605	222605	Z 22606	221606	**S**	*IF*	PN

Name: Z 22599/600 VILLEMOMBLE.

CLASS Z 23500   2-CAR DOUBLE-DECK UNITS

These are two-car double-deck EMUs designed specifically for "regional" stopping services in conjunction with eight French regional councils as well as Luxembourg Railways (CFL). The new units represent a leap in quality for the passenger as they have air-conditioning, individual moquette-covered seats arranged 2+2, including in second class plus facilities for the handicapped. The units have been ordered by the Provence-Alpes-Côte d'Azur (30), Nord-Pas-de-Calais (34) and Rhône-Alpes (16) regions and were introduced at the beginning of 1998 on services such as Marseille-Toulon and Toulon-Ventimiglia plus from Lille to Maubeuge. As the cost is now low, all units are dual-voltage to allow flexibility in long-term use.

Built: 1997–2000
Builder–Mechanical Parts: CIMT/ANF
Wheel Arrangement: Bo-Bo + 2-2.
Traction Motors: 4 x Alsthom FHA 2870 asynchronous of 375 kW.
Formation: ZB + ZRABx
Accommodation: –/75 + 19/96 1T. (LI sets all second)

Systems: 1500 V DC/25 kV AC.
Builder–Electrical Parts: GEC-Alsthom.
Weight: 128.5 tonnes.

Length: 25.60 + 26.90 m.　　　　　　　　**Maximum Speed:** 140 km/h.

Note: Lille units carry set numbers on their front ends. 502B = Z 23502 etc.

Z 23501	123501	T	PA	MB	Z 23528	123528	T	PA	MB	Z 23554	123554	T	NP	LI
Z 23502	123502	T	NP	LI	Z 23529	123529	T	PA	MB	Z 23555	123555	T	NP	LI
Z 23503	123503	T	RA	VE	Z 23530	123530	T	NP	LI	Z 23556	123556	T	RA	VE
Z 23504	123504	T	PA	MB	Z 23531	123531	T	RA	VE	Z 23557	123557	T	NP	LI
Z 23505	123505	T	PA	MB	Z 23532	123532	T	PA	MB	Z 23558	123558	T	NP	LI
Z 23506	123506	T	NP	LI	Z 23533	123533	T	PA	MB	Z 23559	123559	T	NP	LI
Z 23507	123507	T	PA	MB	Z 23534	123534	T	NP	LI	Z 23560	123560	T	RA	VE
Z 23508	123508	T	PA	MB	Z 23535	123535	T	RA	VE	Z 23561	123561	T	NP	LI
Z 23509	123509	T	PA	MB	Z 23536	123536	T	PA	MB	Z 23562	123562	T	NP	LI
Z 23510	123510	T	PA	MB	Z 23537	123537	T	PA	MB	Z 23563	123563	T	NP	LI
Z 23511	123511	T	PA	MB	Z 23538	123538	T	PA	MB	Z 23564	123564	T	RA	VE
Z 23512	123512	T	RA	VE	Z 23539	123539	T	RA	VE	Z 23565	123565	T	NP	LI
Z 23513	123513	T	PA	MB	Z 23540	123540	T	PA	MB	Z 23566	123566	T	NP	LI
Z 23514	123514	T	NP	LI	Z 23541	123541	T	PA	MB	Z 23567	123567	T	RA	VE
Z 23515	123515	T	RA	VE	Z 23542	123542	T	NP	LI	Z 23568	123568	T	NP	LI
Z 23516	123516	T	PA	MB	Z 23543	123543	T	NP	LI	Z 23569	123569	T	NP	LI
Z 23517	123517	T	NP	LI	Z 23544	123544	T	PA	MB	Z 23570	123570	T	RA	VE
Z 23518	123518	T	NP	LI	Z 23545	123545	T	PA	MB	Z 23571	123571	T	NP	LI
Z 23519	123519	T	PA	MB	Z 23546	123546	T	NP	LI	Z 23572	123572	T	NP	LI
Z 23520	123520	T	PA	MB	Z 23547	123547	T	PA	MB	Z 23573	123573	T	RA	VE
Z 23521	123521	T	PA	MB	Z 23548	123548	T	RA	VE	Z 23575	123575	T	RA	VE
Z 23522	123522	T	NP	LI	Z 23549	123549	T	PA	MB	Z 23576	123576	T	NP	LI
Z 23523	123523	T	RA	VE	Z 23550	123550	T	PA	MB	Z 23577	123577	T	NP	LI
Z 23524	123524	T	PA	MB	Z 23551	123551	T	NP	LI	Z 23578	123578	T	NP	LI
Z 23525	123525	T	PA	MB	Z 23552	123552	T	NP	LI	Z 23579	123579	T	NP	LI
Z 23526	123526	T	NP	LI	Z 23553	123553	T	PA	MB	Z 23580	123580	T	NP	LI
Z 23527	123527	T	RA	VE										

Names:

Z 23501	CAMARGUE		Z 23528	CRAU
Z 23504	CAP CANAILLE		Z 23529	EN-VAU
Z 23505	EMBRIEZ		Z 23532	PORT-PIN
Z 23507	VAR		Z 23533	SAINT-CASERN
Z 23508	GAPEAU		Z 23536	PORT MIOU
Z 23509	CANJUERS		Z 23537	TANNERON
Z 23510	LOUP		Z 23538	SORMIOU
Z 23511	GARLABAN		Z 23540	MAURES
Z 23513	ARTUBY		Z 23541	CHEIRON
Z 23516	VENTOUX		Z 23544	BORRIGO
Z 23519	DURANCE		Z 23545	ESTÉREL
Z 23520	FRIOUL		Z 23547	ALPILLES
Z 23521	LADIÈRE		Z 23549	ÉTOILE
Z 23524	SAINTE-BAUME		Z 23550	JABRON
Z 23525	ARGENS		Z 23553	SUGITON
Z 23526	Aulnoye Aymeries une ville pour tous.			

CLASSES Z 24500 & Z 26500
TER2N NG 3-, 4- & 5-CAR DOUBLE-DECK UNITS

As mentioned above, Class Z 23500 could not be lengthened without affecting performance, so a consortium of Alstom and Bombardier produced a new design, the TER2N NG (Train Express Régional à Deux Niveaux Nouvelle Génération or New Generation Double Deck Regional Express Train) in which each car has one powered bogie rated at 850 kW. These units also have a higher maximum speed of 160 km/h.

The most common formation in service is 3-car Class Z 24500 of which 25 have been orderred by the Lorraine region, 46 by Nord-Pas-de-Calais, ten by Pays de la Loire and 60 by Rhône Alpes; most Class Z 26500 are 4-car sets but Picardie will take 23 5-car sets mainly for services from Paris Nord to Amiens, Compiègne and Beauvais whilst Haute Normandie has ordered 16 sets for the Paris-Rouen service. The new units were designed with lengthening in mind so it will not be a surprise if 3-car units are boosted to 4-car and so on.

There are four types of coach in these units, which between them carry all auxiliaries:

Z1 Driving open second with pantographs.
Z2 Open composite.
Z3 Open composite.
Z5 Driving open composite.

3-car sets are formed Z1 + Z3 + Z5; 4-car sets are Z1 + Z2 + Z2 + Z1 and 5-car sets are Z1 +Z2 + Z3 + Z2 + Z5. There are no 2-car sets.

Identical EMUs were built for Luxembourg Railways (CFL) and are known as Class 2200. They are used in multiple with Class Z 24500 on the Luxembourg–Metz–Nancy service.

Built: 2004–
Builders: Alstom/Bombardier.
Traction Motors: Two 425 kW per car.
Weight: 65 + 60 (+60) (+60) + 65 tonnes.
Wheel Arrangement: 2-Bo + 2-Bo (+ 2-Bo) (+ 2-Bo) + Bo-2.
Length: 27.35 + 26.40 (+ 26.40) (+ 26.40) + 27.35 m.
Accommodation: 3-car 41/298 2T; 4-car 54/378 2T; 5-car 68/502 2T.
Maximum Speed: 160 km/h.
Systems: 1500 V DC/25 kV AC 50 Hz.

Non-Standard Livery: N Z 24649/50 carries advertising livery for Alstom and Nord-Pas-de-Calais region. Z 26577/78 and Z 25679/80 carry red and white for Monaco.

Operate in multiple within class and with Z 23500.

Class Z 24500 3-Car Units.

301	Z 24501	241501	Z 24502	**T**	*RA*	VE	340	Z 24579	241579	Z 24580	**T**	*LO*	MZ
302	Z 24503	241503	Z 24504	**T**	*LO*	MZ	341	Z 24581	241581	Z 24582	**T**	*LO*	MZ
303	Z 24505	241505	Z 24506	**T**	*RA*	VE	342	Z 24583	241583	Z 24584	**T**	*RA*	VE
304	Z 24507	241507	Z 24508	**T**	*NP*	LI	343	Z 24585	241585	Z 24586	**T**	*LO*	MZ
305	Z 24509	241509	Z 24510	**T**	*NP*	LI	344	Z 24587	241587	Z 24588	**T**	*LO*	MZ
306	Z 24511	241511	Z 24512	**T**	*LO*	MZ	345	Z 24589	241589	Z 24590	**T**	*RA*	VE
307	Z 24513	241513	Z 24514	**T**	*RA*	VE	346	Z 24591	241591	Z 24592	**T**	*RA*	VE
308	Z 24515	241515	Z 24516	**T**	*NP*	LI	347	Z 24593	241593	Z 24594	**T**	*LO*	MZ
309	Z 24517	241517	Z 24518	**T**	*NP*	LI	348	Z 24595	241595	Z 24596	**T**	*RA*	VE
310	Z 24519	241519	Z 24520	**T**	*LO*	MZ	349	Z 24597	241597	Z 24598	**T**	*RA*	VE
311	Z 24521	241521	Z 24522	**T**	*NP*	LI	350	Z 24599	241599	Z 24600	**T**	*RA*	VE
312	Z 24523	241523	Z 24524	**T**	*NP*	LI	351	Z 24601	241601	Z 24602	**T**	*RA*	VE
313	Z 24525	241525	Z 24526	**T**	*LO*	MZ	352	Z 24603	241603	Z 24604	**T**	*RA*	VE
314	Z 24527	241527	Z 24528	**T**	*RA*	VE	353	Z 24605	241605	Z 24606	**T**	*RA*	VE
315	Z 24529	241529	Z 24530	**T**	*NP*	LI	354	Z 24607	241607	Z 24608	**T**	*RA*	VE
316	Z 24531	241531	Z 24532	**T**	*NP*	LI	355	Z 24609	241609	Z 24610	**T**	*RA*	VE
317	Z 24533	241533	Z 24534	**T**	*RA*	VE	356	Z 24611	241611	Z 24612	**T**	*RA*	VE
318	Z 24535	241535	Z 24536	**T**	*RA*	VE	357	Z 24613	241613	Z 24614	**T**	*RA*	VE
319	Z 24537	241537	Z 24538	**T**	*RA*	VE	358	Z 24615	241615	Z 24616	**T**	*RA*	VE
320	Z 24539	241539	Z 24540	**T**	*RA*	VE	359	Z 24617	241617	Z 24618	**T**	*RA*	VE
321	Z 24541	241541	Z 24542	**T**	*RA*	VE	360	Z 24619	241619	Z 24620	**T**	*RA*	VE
322	Z 24543	241543	Z 24544	**T**	*RA*	VE	361	Z 24621	241621	Z 24622	**T**	*RA*	VE
323	Z 24545	241545	Z 24546	**T**	*NP*	LI	362	Z 24623	241623	Z 24624	**T**	*LO*	MZ
324	Z 24547	241547	Z 24548	**T**	*LO*	MZ	363	Z 24625	241625	Z 24626	**T**	*LO*	MZ
325	Z 24549	241549	Z 24550	**T**	*NP*	LI	364	Z 24627	241627	Z 24628	**T**	*LO*	MZ
326	Z 24551	241551	Z 24552	**T**	*LO*	MZ	365	Z 24629	241629	Z 24630	**T**	*LO*	MZ
327	Z 24553	241553	Z 24554	**T**	*NP*	LI	366	Z 24631	241631	Z 24632	**T**	*RA*	VE
328	Z 24555	241555	Z 24556	**T**	*NP*	LI	367	Z 24633	241633	Z 24634	**T**	*RA*	VE
329	Z 24557	241557	Z 24558	**T**	*NP*	LI	368	Z 24635	241635	Z 24636	**T**	*RA*	VE
330	Z 24559	241559	Z 24560	**T**	*LO*	MZ	369	Z 24637	241637	Z 24638	**T**	*LO*	MZ
331	Z 24561	241561	Z 24562	**T**	*NP*	LI	370	Z 24639	241639	Z 24640	**T**	*LO*	MZ
332	Z 24563	241563	Z 24564	**T**	*NP*	LI	371	Z 24641	241641	Z 24642	**T**	*RA*	VE
333	Z 24565	241565	Z 24566	**T**	*NP*	LI	372	Z 24643	241643	Z 24644	**T**	*RA*	VE
334	Z 24567	241567	Z 24568	**T**	*NP*	LI	373	Z 24645	241645	Z 24646	**T**	*RA*	VE
335	Z 24569	241569	Z 24570	**T**	*LO*	MZ	374	Z 24647	241647	Z 24648	**T**	*NP*	LI
336	Z 24571	241571	Z 24572	**T**	*LO*	MZ	375	Z 24649	241649	Z 24650	**N**	*NP*	LI
337	Z 24573	241573	Z 24574	**T**	*RA*	VE	376	Z 24651	241651	Z 24652	**T**	*NP*	LI
338	Z 24575	241575	Z 24576	**T**	*LO*	MZ	377	Z 24653	241653	Z 24654	**T**	*NP*	LI
339	Z 24577	241577	Z 24578	**T**	*RA*	VE	378	Z 24655	241655	Z 24656	**T**	*NP*	LI

379	Z 24657	241657	Z 24658	T	NP	LI
380	Z 24659	241659	Z 24660	T	NP	LI
381	Z 24661	241661	Z 24662	T	NP	LI
382	Z 24663	241663	Z 24664	T	NP	LI
383	Z 24665	241665	Z 24666	T	NP	LI
384	Z 24667	241667	Z 24668	T	LO	MZ
385	Z 24669	241669	Z 24670	T	LO	MZ
386	Z 24671	241671	Z 24672	T	LO	MZ
387	Z 24673	241673	Z 24674	T	LO	MZ
388	Z 24675	241675	Z 24676	T	PL	NB
389	Z 24677	241677	Z 24678	T	PL	NB
390	Z 24679	241679	Z 24680	T	PL	NB
391	Z 24681	241681	Z 24682	T	PL	NB
392	Z 24683	241683	Z 24684	T	PL	NB
393	Z 24685	241685	Z 24686	T	PL	NB
394	Z 24687	241687	Z 24688	T	PL	NB
395	Z 24689	241689	Z 24680	T	PL	NB
396	Z 24691	241691	Z 24692	T	PL	NB
397	Z 24693	241693	Z 24694	T	PL	NB
398	Z 24695	241695	Z 24696	T	NP	LI
399	Z 24697	241697	Z 24698	T	RA	VE
600	Z 24699	241699	Z 24700	T	RA	VE
601	Z 24701	241701	Z 24702	T	RA	VE
602	Z 24703	241703	Z 24704	T	RA	VE
603	Z 24705	241705	Z 24706	T	RA	VE
604	Z 24707	241707	Z 24708	T	RA	VE
605	Z 24709	241709	Z 24710	T	RA	VE
606	Z 24711	241711	Z 24712	T	RA	VE
607	Z 24713	241713	Z 24714	T	RA	VE
608	Z 24715	241715	Z 24716	T	RA	VE
	Z 24717	241717	Z 24718	T		
	Z 24719	241719	Z 24720	T		

Z 24721	241721	Z 24722	T
Z 24723	241723	Z 24724	T
Z 24725	241725	Z 24726	T
Z 24727	241727	Z 24728	T
Z 24729	241729	Z 24730	T
Z 24731	241731	Z 24732	T
Z 24733	241733	Z 24734	T
Z 24735	241735	Z 24736	T
Z 24737	241737	Z 24738	T
Z 24739	241739	Z 24740	T
Z 24741	241742	Z 24742	T
Z 24743	241743	Z 24744	T
Z 24745	241745	Z 24746	T
Z 24747	241747	Z 24748	T
Z 24749	241749	Z 24750	T
Z 24741	241751	Z 24752	T
Z 24753	241753	Z 24754	T
Z 24755	241755	Z 24756	T
Z 24757	241757	Z 24758	T
Z 24759	241759	Z 24760	T
Z 24761	241761	Z 24762	T
Z 24763	241763	Z 24764	T
Z 24765	241765	Z 24766	T
Z 24767	241767	Z 24768	T
Z 24769	241769	Z 24770	T
Z 24771	241771	Z 24772	T
Z 24773	241773	Z 24774	T
Z 24775	241775	Z 24776	T
Z 24777	241777	Z 24778	T
Z 24779	241779	Z 24780	T
Z 24781	241781	Z 24782	T

Class Z 26500 4 or 5 Car Units.

401	Z 26501	262501			262502	Z 26502	T	CE	MR
502	Z 26503	262503	261503		262504	Z 26504	T	PI	LY
403	Z 26505	262505			262505	Z 26506	T	PA	MB
404	Z 26507	262507			262508	Z 26508	T	CE	MR
405	Z 26509	262509			262510	Z 26510	T	PA	MB
406	Z 26511	262511			262512	Z 26512	T	CE	MR
407	Z 26513	262513			262514	Z 26514	T	PA	MB
408	Z 26515	262515			262516	Z 26516	T	PA	MB
409	Z 26517	262517			262518	Z 26518	T	CE	MR
410	Z 26519	262519			262520	Z 26520	T	PA	MB
411	Z 26521	262521			262522	Z 26522	T	CE	MR
412	Z 26523	262523			262524	Z 26524	T	PA	MB
413	Z 26525	262525			262526	Z 26526	T	CE	MR
414	Z 26527	262527			262528	Z 26528	T	PA	MB
415	Z 26529	262529			262530	Z 26530	T	CE	MR
516	Z 26531	262531	261531		262532	Z 26532	T	PI	LY
517	Z 26533	262533	261533		262534	Z 26534	T	PI	LY
418	Z 26535	262535			262536	Z 26536	T	PA	MB
419	Z 26537	262537			262538	Z 26538	T	PA	MB
420	Z 26539	262539			262540	Z 26540	T	PA	MB
521	Z 26541	262541	261541		262542	Z 26542	T	PI	LY
522	Z 26543	262543	261543		262544	Z 26544	T	PI	LY
523	Z 26545	262545	261545		262546	Z 26546	T	PI	LY
524	Z 26547	262547	261547		262548	Z 26548	T	PI	LY
525	Z 26549	262549	261549		262550	Z 26550	T	PI	LY
426	Z 26551	262551			262552	Z 26552	T	PI	LY
427	Z 26553	262553			262554	Z 26554	T	PI	LY
428	Z 26555	262555			262556	Z 26556	T	PI	LY
429	Z 26557	262557			262558	Z 26558	T	PI	LY
430	Z 26559	262559			262560	Z 26560	T	PI	LY

431	Z 26561	262561	262562	Z 26562	T	*PI*	LY
432	Z 26563	262563	262564	Z 26564	T	*CE*	MR
433	Z 26565	262565	262566	Z 26566	T	*CE*	MR
434	Z 26567	262567	262568	Z 26568	T	*CE*	MR
435	Z 26569	262569	262570	Z 26570	T	*CE*	MR
436	Z 26571	262571	262572	Z 26572	T	*CE*	MR
437	Z 26573	262573	262574	Z 26574	T	*PI*	LY
438	Z 26575	262575	262576	Z 26576	T	*PI*	LY
439	Z 26577	262577	262578	Z 26578	N	*MO*	MB
440	Z 26579	262579	262580	Z 26580	N	*MO*	MB
	Z 26581	262581	262582	Z 26582	T		
	Z 26583	262583	262584	Z 26584	T		
	Z 26585	262585	262586	Z 26586	T		
	Z 26587	262587	262588	Z 26588	T		
	Z 26589	262589	262590	Z 26590	T		
	Z 26591	262591	262592	Z 26592	T		
	Z 26593	262593	262594	Z 26594	T		
	Z 26595	262595	262596	Z 26596	T		
	Z 26597	262597	262598	Z 26598	T		
	Z 26599	262599	262600	Z 26600	T		
	Z 26601	262601	262602	Z 26602	T		
	Z 26603	262603	262604	Z 26604	T		
	Z 26605	262605	262606	Z 26606	T		
	Z 26607	262607	262608	Z 26608	T		
	Z 26609	262609	262610	Z 26610	T		
	Z 26611	262611	262612	Z 26612	T		
	Z 26613	262613	262614	Z 26614	T		
	Z 26615	262615	262616	Z 26616	T		
	Z 26617	262617	262618	Z 26618	T		
	Z 26619	262619	262620	Z 26620	T		
	Z 26621	262621	262622	Z 26622	T		
	Z 26623	262623	262624	Z 26624	T		
	Z 26625	262625	262626	Z 26626	T		
	Z 26627	262627	262628	Z 26628	T		
	Z 26629	262629	262630	Z 26630	T		
	Z 26631	262631	262632	Z 26632	T		
	Z 26633	262633	262634	Z 26634	T		
	Z 26635	262635	262636	Z 26636	T		

Names:

Z 26505/6   ARTUBY SAINTE BAUME | Z 26577/8   MONTE CARLO

CLASS Z 27500   AGC   3-CAR or 4-CAR UNITS

This is the electric version of the AGC, the diesel version being Class X 76500 and the dual-mode versions B81500 and B 82500. 217 units are on order – six 3-car for Alsace, three 3-car for Auvergne, ten 3-car for Bourgogne, six 3-car and eight 4-car for Bretagne, ten 4-car for Centre, 13 3-car for Champagne-Ardenne, four 3-car for Franche-Comté, 37 4-car for Languedoc-Roussillon, 17 3-car and 15 4-car for Lorraine, 19 3-car for Midi-Pyrénées, nine 3-car for Basse Normandie, 23 3-car for Haute Normandie, 22 4-car for Pays de la Loire and 15 4-car for Rhône-Alpes. Given passenger growth, many of the 3-car units could well be extended in future.

Built: 2005–
Builder: Bombardier, Crespin.
Systems: 1500 V DC/25 kV AC 50 Hz.
Power rating: 1300 kW.
Length: 21.00 m + 15.40 m (+ 15.40 m) + 21.00 m.
Accommodation: 22/29 1T + –/51 (+ –/60) + –/58.
Other details as B 81500.

Z 27501	271501		Z 27502	T	*MP*	TL		Z 27509	271509		Z 27510	T	*AU*	NV
Z 27503	271503		Z 27504	T	*BN*	CA		Z 27511	271511		Z 27512	T	*HN*	SO
Z 27505	271505		Z 27506	**BO** *BO*		DP		Z 27513	271513		Z 27514	T	*BN*	CA
Z 27507	271507		Z 27508	T	*MP*	TL		Z 27515	271515		Z 27516	**BO** *BO*		DP

Z 27517	271517		Z 27518	**T**	*AU*	NV
Z 27519	271519		Z 27520	**T**	*HN*	SO
Z 27521	271521		Z 27522	**T**	*MP*	TL
Z 27523	271523		Z 27524	**T**	*BN*	CA
Z 27525	271525		Z 27526	**BO**	*BO*	DP
Z 27527	271527		Z 27528	**T**	*AU*	NV
Z 27529	271529	272529	Z 27530	**T**	*RA*	VE
Z 27531	271531	272531	Z 27532	**LR**	*LR*	NI
Z 27533	271533	272533	Z 27534	**T**	*RA*	VE
Z 27535	271535	272535	Z 27536	**LR**	*LR*	NI
Z 27537	271537	272537	Z 27538	**LY**	*LR*	NI
Z 27539	271539		Z 27540	**T**	*HN*	SO
Z 27541	271541		Z 27542	**T**	*MP*	TL
Z 27543	271543		Z 27544	**T**	*BN*	CA
Z 27545	271545		Z 27546	**BO**	*BO*	DP
Z 27547	271547		Z 27548	**T**	*MP*	TL
Z 27549	271549		Z 27550	**T**	*BN*	CA
Z 27551	271551		Z 27552	**T**	*LO*	TV
Z 27553	271553		Z 27554	**T**	*LO*	TV
Z 27555	271555		Z 27556	**T**	*LO*	TV
Z 27557	271557		Z 27558	**T**	*LO*	TV
Z 27559	271559		Z 27560	**T**	*LO*	TV
Z 27561	271561		Z 27562	**T**	*LO*	TV
Z 27563	271563		Z 27564	**T**	*LO*	TV
Z 27565	271565		Z 27566	**T**	*MP*	TL
Z 27567	271567		Z 27568	**T**	*BN*	CA
Z 27569	271569		Z 27570	**BO**	*BO*	DP
Z 27571	271571		Z 27572	**BO**	*BO*	DP
Z 27573	271573	272573	Z 27574	**T**	*RA*	VE
Z 27575	271575		Z 27576	**T**	*HN*	SO
Z 27577	271577		Z 27578	**T**	*MP*	TL
Z 27579	271579		Z 27580	**T**	*BN*	CA
Z 27581	271581		Z 27582	**BO**	*BO*	DP
Z 27583	271583		Z 27584	**T**	*MP*	TL
Z 27585	271585		Z 27586	**T**	*MP*	TL
Z 27587	271587		Z 27588	**T**	*BN*	CA
Z 27589	271589		Z 27590	**T**	*FC*	DP
Z 27591	271591	272591	Z 27592	**T**	*RA*	VE
Z 27593	271593		Z 27594	**T**	*MP*	TL
Z 27595	271595		Z 27596	**T**	*BN*	CA
Z 27597	271597		Z 27598	**T**	*FC*	DP
Z 27599	271599		Z 27600	**T**	*FC*	DP
Z 27601	271601	272601	Z 27602	**LR**	*LR*	NI
Z 27603	271603		Z 27604	**T**	*MP*	TL
Z 27605	271605	272605	Z 27606	**T**	*RA*	VE
Z 27607	271607	272607	Z 27608	**LR**	*LR*	NI
Z 27609	271609	272609	Z 27610	**LR**	*LR*	NI
Z 27611	271611		Z 27612	**T**	*HN*	SO
Z 27613	271613		Z 27614	**T**	*FC*	DP
Z 27615	271615		Z 27616	**T**	*MP*	TL
Z 27617	271617		Z 27618	**T**	*MP*	TL
Z 27619	271619	272619	Z 27620	**LR**	*LR*	NI
Z 27621	271621		Z 27622	**T**	*HN*	SO
Z 27623	271623		Z 27624	**T**	*HN*	SO
Z 27625	271625		Z 27626	**T**	*MP*	TL
Z 27627	271627		Z 27628	**T**	*MP*	TL
Z 27629	271629		Z 27630	**T**	*MP*	TL
Z 27631	271631		Z 27632	**T**	*HN*	SO
Z 27633	271633		Z 27634	**T**	*HN*	SO
Z 27635	271635		Z 27636	**T**	*HN*	SO
Z 27637	271637		Z 27638	**T**	*HN*	SO
Z 27639	271639		Z 27640	**T**	*MP*	TL
Z 27641	271641		Z 27642	**T**	*MP*	TL
Z 27643	271643		Z 27644	**T**	*MP*	TL

Z 27645	271645		Z 27646	**T**	*BR*	RS
Z 27647	271647		Z 27648	**T**	*BR*	RS
Z 27649	271649	272649	Z 27650	**LR**	*LR*	NI
Z 27651	271651		Z 27652	**T**	*HN*	SO
Z 27653	271653		Z 27654	**T**	*HN*	SO
Z 27655	271655	272655	Z 27656	**LR**	*LR*	NI
Z 27657	271657		Z 27658	**T**	*HN*	SO
Z 27659	271659		Z 27660	**T**	*HN*	SO
Z 27661	271661	272661	Z 27662	**LR**	*LR*	NI
Z 27663	271663		Z 27664	**T**	*HN*	SO
Z 27665	271665		Z 27666	**T**	*BR*	RS
Z 27667	271667		Z 27668	**T**	*HN*	SO
Z 27669	271669		Z 27670	**T**	*HN*	SO
Z 27671	271671	272671	Z 27672	**T**	*RA*	VE
Z 27673	271673		Z 27674	**T**	*HN*	SO
Z 27675	271675		Z 27676	**T**	*HN*	SO
Z 27677	271677	272677	Z 27678	**T**	*RA*	VE
Z 27679	271679		Z 27680	**T**	*BR*	RS
Z 27681	271681		Z 27682	**T**	*HN*	SO
Z 27683	271683	272683	Z 27684	**T**	*RA*	VE
Z 27685	271685	272685	Z 27686	**T**	*RA*	VE
Z 27687	271687		Z 27688	**T**	*CA*	EP
Z 27689	271689		Z 27690	**T**	*CA*	EP
Z 27691	271691	272691	Z 27692	**T**	*RA*	VE
Z 27693	271693	272693	Z 27694	**T**	*RA*	VE
Z 27695	271695		Z 27696	**T**	*BR*	RS
Z 27697	271697		Z 27698	**T**	*CA*	EP
Z 27699	271699		Z 27700	**T**	*CA*	EP
Z 27701	271701		Z 27702	**T**	*CA*	EP
Z 27703	271703		Z 27704	**T**	*CA*	EP
Z 27705	271705		Z 27706	**T**	*BR*	RS
Z 27707	271707		Z 27708	**T**	*CA*	EP
Z 27709	271709	272709	Z 27710	**T**	*PL*	NB
Z 27711	271711	272711	Z 27712	**T**	*LO*	MZ
Z 27713	271713	272713	Z 27714	**T**	*BR*	RS
Z 27715	271715	272715	Z 27716	**T**	*BR*	RS
Z 27717	271717	272717	Z 27718	**T**	*PL*	NB
Z 27719	271719	272719	Z 27720	**T**	*LO*	MZ
Z 27721	271721	272721	Z 27722	**T**	*BR*	RS
Z 27723	271723		Z 27724	**T**	*CA*	EP
Z 27725	271725		Z 27726	**T**	*CA*	EP
Z 27727	271727		Z 27728	**T**	*CA*	EP
Z 27729	271729	272729	Z 27730	**T**	*LO*	MZ
Z 27731	271731		Z 27732	**BO**	*BO*	DP
Z 27733	271733	272733	Z 27734	**T**	*LO*	MZ
Z 27735	271735		Z 27736	**BO**	*BO*	DP
Z 27737	271737		Z 27738	**BO**	*BO*	DP
Z 27739	271739	272739	Z 27740	**T**	*LO*	MZ
Z 27741	271741	272741	Z 27742	**T**	*RA*	VE
Z 27743	271743	272743	Z 27744	**LR**	*LR*	NI
Z 27745	271745	272745	Z 27746	**LR**	*LR*	NI
Z 27747	271747	272747	Z 27748	**T**	*PL*	NB
Z 27749	271749	272749	Z 27750	**T**	*LO*	MZ
Z 27751	271751	272751	Z 27752	**T**	*RA*	VE
Z 27753	271753	272753	Z 27754	**T**	*RA*	VE
Z 27755	271755	272755	Z 27756	**T**	*RA*	VE
Z 27757	271757	272757	Z 27758	**LR**	*LR*	NI
Z 27759	271759	272759	Z 27760	**LR**	*LR*	NI
Z 27761	271761	272761	Z 27762	**LR**	*LR*	NI
Z 27763	271763	272763	Z 27764	**LR**	*LR*	NI
Z 27765	271765	272765	Z 27766	**LR**	*LR*	NI
Z 27767	271767	272767	Z 27768	**T**	*PL*	NB
Z 27769	271769	272769	Z 27770	**T**	*PL*	NB
Z 27771	271771	272771	Z 27772	**T**	*PL*	NB

Z 27773	271773	272773	Z 27774	T	PL	NB
Z 27775	271775	272775	Z 27776	T	PL	NB
Z 27777	271777	272777	Z 27778	T	PL	NB
Z 27779	271779	272779	Z 27780	T	PL	NB
Z 27781	271781	272781	Z 27782	T	PL	NB
Z 27783	271783	272783	Z 27784	T	PL	NB
Z 27785	271785	272785	Z 27786	T	PL	NB
Z 27787	271787		Z 27788	T	LO	TV
Z 27789	271789		Z 27790	T	LO	TV
Z 27791	271791		Z 27792	T	LO	TV
Z 27793	271793		Z 27794	T	LO	TV
Z 27795	271795	272795	Z 27796	T	BR	RS
Z 27797	271797		Z 27798			
Z 27799	271799		Z 27800			
Z 27801	271801		Z 27802			
Z 27803	271803		Z 27804			
Z 27805	271805		Z 27806			
Z 27807	271807		Z 27808			
Z 27809	271809		Z 27810			
Z 27271	271271		Z 27812			
Z 27813	271813		Z 27814			
Z 27815	271815		Z 27816			
Z 27817	271817		Z 27818			
Z 27819	271819		Z 27820			
Z 27821	271821		Z 27822			
Z 27823	271823		Z 27824			
Z 27825	271825	272835	Z 27826	T	CE	TP
Z 27827	271827	272827	Z 27828	T	CE	TP
Z 27829	271829	272829	Z 27830	T	CE	TP
Z 27831	271831	272831	Z 27832	T	CE	TP
Z 27833	271833		Z 27834			
Z 27835	271835		Z 27836			
Z 27837	271837		Z 27838			
Z 27839	271839		Z 27840			
Z 27841	271841		Z 27842			
Z 27843	271843		Z 27844			
Z 27845	271845		Z 27846			
Z 27847	271847		Z 27848			
Z 27849	271849		Z 27850			
Z 27851	271851		Z 27852			
Z 27853	271853		Z 27854			
Z 27855	271855		Z 27856			
Z 27857	271857		Z 27858			
Z 27859	271859		Z 27860			
Z 27861	271861		Z 27862			

Z 27863	271863	Z 27864			
Z 27865	271865	Z 27866			
Z 27867	271867	Z 27868			
Z 27869	271869	Z 27870			
Z 27871	271871	Z 27872			
Z 27873	271873	Z 27874			
Z 27875	271875	Z 27876			
Z 27877	271877	Z 27878			
Z 27879	271879	Z 27880			
Z 27881	271881	Z 27882			
Z 27883	271883	Z 27884			
Z 27885	271885	Z 27886			
Z 27887	271887	Z 27888			
Z 27889	271889	Z 27890			
Z 27891	271891	Z 27892			
Z 27893	271893	Z 27894			
Z 27895	271895	Z 27896			
Z 27897	271897	Z 27898			
Z 27899	271899	Z 27900			
Z 27901	271901	Z 27902			
Z 27903	271903	Z 27904			
Z 27905	271905	Z 27906			
Z 27907	271907	Z 27908			
Z 27909	271909	Z 27910			
Z 27271	271271	Z 27912			
Z 27913	271913	Z 27914			
Z 27915	271915	Z 27916			
Z 27917	271917	Z 27918			
Z 27919	271919	Z 27920			
Z 27921	271921	Z 27922			
Z 27923	271923	Z 27924			
Z 27925	271925	Z 27926			
Z 27927	271927	Z 27928			
Z 27929	271929	Z 27930			
Z 27931	271931	Z 27932			
Z 27933	271933	Z 27934			
Z 27935	271935	Z 27936			
Z 27937	271937	Z 27938			
Z 27939	271939	272939 Z 27940	T	LO	MZ
Z 27941	271941	Z 27942			
Z 27943	271943	Z 27944			
Z 27945	271945	Z 27946			
Z 27947	271947	Z 27948			
Z 27949	271949	Z 27950			

CLASS Z 92050   4-CAR DOUBLE-DECK UNITS

These are a special version of Class Z 20500 with lower density seating, with headrests, for services in the Nord-Pas-de-Calais around Lille, whose livery they are finished in. They were the first powered rolling stock to be allocated to Lille depot which can be found south of Lille Flandres station, west of Champ de Mars yard.

Details as Class Z 20500 except:
Built: 1996 **Formation:** ZB + ZRAB + ZRB + ZB.
Weight: 69 t + 43 t + 43 t + 69 t.
Class specific Livery: S White with dark blue band plus yellow doors and front end.

Z401	Z 92051	920151	920251	Z 92052	S	NP	LI
Z402	Z 92053	920153	920253	Z 92054	S	NP	LI
Z403	Z 92055	920155	920255	Z 92056	S	NP	LI
Z404	Z 92057	920157	920257	Z 92058	S	NP	LI
Z405	Z 92059	920159	920259	Z 92060	S	NP	LI
Z406	Z 92061	920161	920261	Z 92062	S	NP	LI

TRAM-TRAINS

CLASS U 25500 5-SECTION TRAM-TRAINS

In 2006, the 8 km Aulnay-sous-Bois to Bondy line, in the north-eastern suburbs of Paris, was converted from heavy rail to tram-train operation although retaining its 25 kV AC overhead. The line is now used by no other types of train. The eventual aim is to open branches or extensions with street running. The service is operated by "Avanto" tram-train vehicles, the first stock to be supplied to SNCF by Siemens. These run from Bondy along the Paris-Strasbourg main line to reach Noisy-le-Sec depot and also stable at Pantin. Somewhat stupidly, SNCF has numbered each section but units carry small set numbers TT01 upwards in the cab window! Units can work in multiple, coupling retracting under the nose cover. All are in STIF dark blue livery. A further batch of 12 Avanto tram-trains is on order for the Mulhouse tram-train scheme and SNCF has ordered Alstom Dualis tram-trains for schemes in Lyon and Nantes.

SNCF has ordered 200 tram-trains from Alstom for use in Lyon, Nantes, Paris and Strasbourg. No numbers have yet been announced.

Built: 2005/6.
Systems: 750 V DC/25 kV AC 50 Hz.
Builder: Siemens.
Traction Motors: Four Siemens asynchronous of 130 kW each.
Weight: 59.7 tonnes.
Wheel Arrangement: Bo-2-2-Bo.
Length: 11.409 m + 4.040 m + 5.780 m + 4.040 m + 11.409 m = 36.678 m.
Accommodation: –/80 (6).
Maximum Speed: 70 km/h in service; 100 km/h running light to depot.

TT01	25501	251501	252501	253501	25502	**H**	*IF*	PN
TT02	25503	251503	252503	253503	25504	**H**	*IF*	PN
TT03	25505	251505	252505	253505	25506	**H**	*IF*	PN
TT04	25507	251507	252507	253507	25508	**H**	*IF*	PN
TT05	25509	251509	252509	253509	25510	**H**	*IF*	PN
TT06	25511	251511	252511	253511	25512	**H**	*IF*	PN
TT07	25513	251513	252513	253513	25514	**H**	*IF*	PN
TT08	25515	251515	252515	253515	25516	**H**	*IF*	PN
TT09	25517	251517	252517	253517	25518	**H**	*IF*	PN
TT10	25519	251519	252519	253519	25520	**H**	*IF*	PN
TT11	25521	251521	252521	253521	25522	**H**	*IF*	PN
TT12	25523	251523	252523	253523	25524	**H**	*IF*	PN
TT13	25525	251525	252525	253525	25526	**H**	*IF*	PN
TT14	25527	251527	252527	253527	25528	**H**	*IF*	PN
TT15	25529	251529	252529	253529	25530	**H**	*IF*	PN
TT16	25531	251531	252531	253531	25532			
TT17	25533	251533	252533	253533	25534			
TT18	25535	251535	252535	253535	25536			
TT19	25537	251537	252537	253537	25538			
TT20	25539	251539	252539	253539	25540			
TT21	25541	251541	252541	253541	25542			
TT22	25543	251543	252543	253543	25544			
TT23	25545	251545	252545	253545	25546			
TT24	25547	251547	252547	253547	25548			
TT25	25549	251549	252549	253549	25550			
TT26	25551	251551	252551	253551	25552			
TT27	25553	251553	252553	253553	25554			
TT28	25555	251555	252555	253555	25556			

1.7. TRAINS À GRAND VITESSE (TGVs)

The TGV is a modern day success story for SNCF and Alstom with more sets in service than any other high-speed train. Once the fastest service train in the world, other countries are catching up.

TGV SUD-EST   8-CAR TWO-VOLTAGE SETS

The first version of the TGV. Each TGV Sud-Est set is a 10-car EMU with 1½ power cars at each end – each set has six motor bogies – two under each outer power car and one next to the power car on the adjoining vehicles. The power cars are numbered as dual-voltage locomotives but with the prefix TGV. Each set also has a number – set 01 has power cars 23001/2 etc.

Since their introduction, various modifications have been made. All sets have received new trailer bogies with better suspension and have been refurbished internally. There are two version of refurbishment known as Renov 1 and Renov 2, the latter having coach R3 converted to second class and symmetrical seating to aid reservations. Renov 2 units have been transferred to services from Paris Nord and cross-country routes from Lille. Most sets have received TVM 430 signalling in order to operate at 300 km/h over the whole TGV network. Other sets are now restricted to 270 km/h on Paris–Dijon (Bourgogne/Franche-Comté) services. Sets 33–37/100–2 which were once first class only have been rebuilt in the normal configuration. The original orange livery has been replaced by standard silver and blue on all sets.

Normally the sets keep in formation but changes can take place following accidents, etc. Set 38 was converted into a postal set in 1995. Set 46 was damaged in an accident in late 2007 and may be withdrawn. Set 70 was partially destroyed in an accident. Set 88 was the TGV Atlantique prototype then became three-voltage set 118. Set 99 never existed. Set 101 was converted to tilting prototype P01 then back to normal again. Sets can occasionally be seen with a TGV Postal power car in extreme circumstances.

Set 16 carries a plate showing that it set a world record of 380 km/h on 26 February 1981.

Electro-pneumatic brakes. Rheostatic brakes. Multiple working. Disc brakes on trailers in addition to blocks.

TGV + TGVZRADr + TGVRAr + TGVRA + TGVRBr + 3 x TGVRB + TGVZRB + TGV.
Systems: 1500 V DC + 25 kV AC
Built: 1978–86.
Builders: Alsthom/Francorail-MTE/De Dietrich.
Axle Arrangement: Bo-Bo + Bo-2-2-2-2-2-2-2-Bo + Bo-Bo.
Traction Motors: 12 x TAB676 per set of 525 kW each.
Weight: 65 + 43 + (6 x 28) + 44 + 65 tonnes.
Maximum Speed: 300 km/h. n 270 km/h.
Accommodation:
0 + 34/– 1T + 38/– 1T + 38/– 1T + –/16 1T + –/56 2T + –/54 1T + –/56 2T + –/56 1T + 0.
Length: 22.15 + 21.845 + (6 x 18.70) + 21.845 + 22.15 m.
Cab Signalling: TVM 430. n TVM 300.

2 = Renov 2

Non-driving motors and trailer cars are numbered in the sequence as follows:
Set nnn: 123nnn/223nnn/323nnn/423nnn/523nnn/623nnn/723nnn/823nnn.

01	TGV 23001	TGV 23002	A	2	LY	CANNES
02	TGV 23003	TGV 23004	A		PE	MARSEILLE
03	TGV 23005	TGV 23006	A	2	LY	BELFORT
04	TGV 23007	TGV 23008	A	2	LY	RAMBOUILLET
05	TGV 23009	TGV 23010	A		PE	RIS-ORANGIS
06	TGV 23011	TGV 23012	A		PE	FRASNE
07	TGV 23013	TGV 23014	A	2	LY	CONFLANS-SAINTE-HONORINE
08	TGV 23015	TGV 23016	A	2	LY	ROUEN
09	TGV 23017	TGV 23018	A	2	LY	VINCENNES
10	TGV 23019	TGV 23020	A	2	LY	HAYANGE
11	TGV 23021	TGV 23022	A		PE	NÎMES
12	TGV 23023	TGV 23024	A		PE	LE HAVRE
13	TGV 23025	TGV 23026	A	2	LY	ABLON-SUR-SEINE
14	TGV 23027	TGV 23028	A	2	LY	MONTPELLIER
15	TGV 23029	TGV 23030	A		PE	PAU

16	TGV 23031	TGV 23032	**A**		PE	LYON
17	TGV 23033	TGV 23034	**A**	2	LY	TERGNIER
18	TGV 23035	TGV 23036	**A**		PE	LE CREUSOT
19	TGV 23037	TGV 23038	**A**		PE	SAINT AMAND-LES-EAUX
20	TGV 23039	TGV 23040	**A**		PE	COLMAR
21	TGV 23041	TGV 23042	**A**		PE	DIJON
22	TGV 23043	TGV 23044	**A**	2	LY	VALENCIENNES
23	TGV 23045	TGV 23046	**A**	2	LY	MONTBARD
24	TGV 23047	TGV 23048	**A**		PE	ALFORTVILLE
25	TGV 23049	TGV 23050	**A**		PE	BESANÇON
26	TGV 23051	TGV 23052	**A**		PE	SAINT ÉTIENNE
27	TGV 23053	TGV 23054	**A**		PE	MÂCON
28	TGV 23055	TGV 23056	**A**		PE	MONTÉLIMAR
29	TGV 23057	TGV 23058	**A**		PE	VILLENEUVE-SAINT-GEORGES
30	TGV 23059	TGV 23060	**A**		PE	LILLE
31	TGV 23061	TGV 23062	**A**		PE	COMBS-LA-VILLE
32	TGV 23063	TGV 23064	**A**		PE	MAISONS-ALFORT
33	TGV 23065	TGV 23066	**A**	n	PE	FÉCAMP
34	TGV 23067	TGV 23068	**A**	n	PE	DUNKERQUE
35	TGV 23069	TGV 23070	**A**	n	PE	GRENOBLE
36	TGV 23071	TGV 23072	**A**	n	PE	SEINE SAINT-DENIS
37	TGV 23073	TGV 23074	**A**	n	PE	SAINT GERMAIN-EN-LAYE
39	TGV 23077	TGV 23078	**A**	2	LY	EVIAN-LES-BAINS + THONON-LES-BAINS
40	TGV 23079	TGV 23080	**A**	2	LY	VERSAILLES
41	TGV 23081	TGV 23082	**A**		PE	VILLIERS-LE-BEL
42	TGV 23083	TGV 23084	**A**	2	LY	CHAMBÉRY
43	TGV 23085	TGV 23086	**A**		PE	AIX-LES-BAINS
44	TGV 23087	TGV 23088	**A**		PE	CLERMONT-FERRAND
45	TGV 23089	TGV 23090	**A**		PE	VALENCE
46 (U)	TGV 23091	TGV 23092	**A**		PE	CONTREXÉVILLE
47	TGV 23093	TGV 23094	**A**		PE	NANCY
48	TGV 23095	TGV 23096	**A**		PE	COMTÉ-DE-NICE
49	TGV 23097	TGV 23098	**A**		PE	RENNES
50	TGV 23099	TGV 23100	**A**		PE	BEAUVAIS
51	TGV 23101	TGV 23102	**A**		PE	GIVORS/GRIGNY-BADAN
52	TGV 23103	TGV 23104	**A**		PE	GENÈVE
53	TGV 23105	TGV 23106	**A**		PE	LE PUY-EN-VELAY
54	TGV 23107	TGV 23108	**A**		PE	CHAGNY
55	TGV 23109	TGV 23110	**A**		PE	DENAIN
56	TGV 23111	TGV 23112	**A**	2	LY	ANNECY
57	TGV 23113	TGV 23114	**A**	2	LY	BOURG-EN-BRESSE
58	TGV 23115	TGV 23116	**A**		PE	OULLINS
59	TGV 23117	TGV 23118	**A**		PE	HAUTMONT
60	TGV 23119	TGV 23120	**A**	n	PE	LANGÉAC
61	TGV 23121	TGV 23122	**A**	n	PE	FONTAINEBLEAU
62	TGV 23123	TGV 23124	**A**		PE	TOULOUSE
63	TGV 23125	TGV 23126	**A**		PE	VILLEURBANNE
64	TGV 23127	TGV 23128	**A**		PE	DOLE
65	TGV 23129	TGV 23130	**A**		PE	SÈTE
66	TGV 23131	TGV 23132	**A**		PE	AVIGNON
67	TGV 23133	TGV 23134	**A**		PE	BELLEGARDE-SUR-VALSERINE
68	TGV 23135	TGV 23136	**A**	2	LY	MODANE
69	TGV 23137	TGV 23138	**A**		PE	VICHY
71	TGV 23141	TGV 23142	**A**	2	LY	BRUNOY
72	TGV 23143	TGV 23144	**A**	2	LY	CAHORS
73	TGV 23145	TGV 23146	**A**		PE	CHARENTON-LE-PONT
74	TGV 23147	TGV 23148	**A**		PE	ARBOIS/MOUCHARD/PORT-LESNEY
75	TGV 23149	TGV 23150	**A**	2	LY	VITTEL
76	TGV 23151	TGV 23152	**A**		PE	PONTARLIER
77	TGV 23153	TGV 23154	**A**		PE	NUITS-SAINT-GEORGES
78	TGV 23155	TGV 23156	**A**	2	LY	CULOZ
79	TGV 23157	TGV 23158	**A**	2	LY	ANNEMASSE
80	TGV 23159	TGV 23160	**A**	2	LY	TOULON
81	TGV 23161	TGV 23162	**A**	2	LY	TONNERRE

82	TGV 23163	TGV 23164	A	2	LY	TRAPPES
83	TGV 23165	TGV 23166	A	2	LY	MOISSY CRAMAYEL
84	TGV 23167	TGV 23168	A	2	LY	DIEPPE
85	TGV 23169	TGV 23170	A	2	LY	BEAUNE
86	TGV 23171	TGV 23172	A	2	LY	MONTLUÇON
87	TGV 23173	TGV 23174	A	2	LY	MONTCHANIN
89	TGV 23177	TGV 23178	A	2	LY	LONS-LE-SAUNIER
90	TGV 23179	TGV 23180	A	2	LY	EPINAL
91	TGV 23181	TGV 23182	A	2	LY	MULHOUSE
92	TGV 23183	TGV 23184	A	2	LY	NOYON
93	TGV 23185	TGV 23186	A	2	LY	SENS
94	TGV 23187	TGV 23188	A	2	LY	LES ARCS EN PROVENCE
95	TGV 23189	TGV 23190	A	2	LY	SAINT RAPHAËL
96	TGV 23191	TGV 23192	A	2	LY	MONTE CARLO
97	TGV 23193	TGV 23194	A	2	LY	CORBEIL-ESSONNES
98	TGV 23195	TGV 23196	A	2	LY	ALBERTVILLE
100	TGV 23199	TGV 23200	A	n	PE	SAINT GERVAIS-LES-BAINS
101	TGV 23201	TGV 23202	A	2	LY	
102	TGV 23203	TGV 23204	A	n	PE	VIGNEUX-SUR-SEINE
Spare		TGV 23140	A		PE	MELUN

Note: Trailers 523070–823070 also exist.

TGV SUD-EST   8-CAR THREE-VOLTAGE SETS

These sets are identical to sets 01–102 except that they are additionally equipped to operate under 15 kV AC 16²/₃ Hz in Switzerland. They operate from Paris via Dijon to Lausanne and Bern and also to Brig in winter. All sets received "Renov 1" refurbishment but were not equipped with TVM 430 so are limited to 270 km/h.

The sets are managed by SNCF/SBB joint venture Lyria. As part of the deal, sets 112 and 114 became property of SBB.

Details and notes as for sets 01–102 except:

Systems: 1500 V DC + 25 kV 50 Hz + 15 kV 16.7 Hz AC
Non-standard Livery: As **A**, but with red stripe and "Lyria" branding.

110	TGV 33001	TGV 33002	N	PE	PAYS DE VAUD
111	TGV 33003	TGV 33004	N	PE	SURESNES
112	TGV 33005	TGV 33006	N	PE	LAUSANNE
113	TGV 33007	TGV 33008	N	PE	NEUCHÂTEL
114	TGV 33009	TGV 33010	N	PE	CLUSES
115	TGV 33011	TGV 33012	N	PE	ZÜRICH
116	TGV 33013	TGV 33014	N	PE	VALAIS
117	TGV 33015	TGV 33016	N	PE	BERN/BERNE
118	TGV 33017	TGV 33018	N	PE	BISCHHEIM
	(ex 23175)	(ex 23176)			

TGV DUPLEX   8-CAR DOUBLE-DECK SETS

TGV Duplex sets were designed to cope with traffic growth on the Paris–Lyon route. The result is a double-deck high-speed train, carrying 40% more passengers than a TGV-Réseau within the same weight limit and for a cost of only 24% more. Power cars were of a new generation with a central driving position and disc brakes although other details are broadly the same as TGV-Réseau.

TGV Duplex sets now operate all Paris–Lyon and most Paris–Marseille–Toulon and Montpellier trains and are increasingly used on cross-country services from the Sud-Est region. PC units operate Paris Montparnasse to Rennes and Nantes as well as cross-country. Sets operate regularly in multiple with each other and with TGV-Réseau and TGV Réseau-Duplex units. They can also run in multiple with Thalys and TGV-POS sets but this seldom occurs.

Following the completion of 89 sets, SNCF ordered a new version known as TGV DASYE (sets 701 upwards). In 2006/7, 19 TGV Réseau-Duplex sets (601 to 619) were created from new Duplex trailers and TGV Réseau power cars.

In the mid 2000s, TGV Duplex sets were allowed to operate at 320 km/h, up from 300 km/h, although this only takes place on a test section of line between Valence and Marseille.

Systems: 1500 V DC / 25 kV AC 50 Hz.
Maximum Speed: 320 km/h.
Builders–Mechanical Parts: GEC-Alsthom/De Dietrich (later Alstom)
Builder–Electrical Parts: Francorail-MTE
Built: 1995–2007
Continuous rating: 25 kV AC 8800 kW; 1500 V DC 3680 kW
Traction Motors : 8 x FM 47 synchronous of 1100 kW each.
Axle Arrangement: Bo-Bo + 2-2-2-2-2-2-2-2-2 + Bo-Bo.
Accommodation: 0 + 62/– 2T + 58/– 2T + 58/– 2T + –/16 bar + –/74 2T + –/78 2T + –/78 2T + –/90 2T + 0 (toilets are for ladies upstairs, men downstairs).
Weight: 65 + 43 + 28 + 28 + 28 + 28 + 28 + 43 + 65 tonnes.
Length: 22.15 + 21.845 + 18.7 + 18.7 + 18.7 + 18.7 + 18.7 + 18.7 + 21.845 + 22.15 m.
Cab Signalling: TVM 430.

Trailer cars are numbered in the sequence as follows:

Set *nnn:* 291*nnn*/292*nnn*/293*nnn*/294*nnn*/295*nnn*/296*nnn*/297*nnn*/298*nnn*.

201	TGV 29001	TGV 29002	A	PE	
202	TGV 29003	TGV 29004	A	PE	
203	TGV 29005	TGV 29006	A	PE	
204	TGV 29007	TGV 29008	A	PE	
205	TGV 29009	TGV 29010	A	PE	
206	TGV 29011	TGV 29012	A	PE	
207	TGV 29013	TGV 29014	A	PE	
208	TGV 29015	TGV 29016	A	PE	
209	TGV 29017	TGV 29018	A	PE	
210	TGV 29019	TGV 29020	A	PE	
211	TGV 29021	TGV 29022	A	PE	
212	TGV 29023	TGV 29024	A	PE	
213	TGV 29025	TGV 29026	A	PE	
214	TGV 29027	TGV 29028	A	PE	
215	TGV 29029	TGV 29030	A	PE	
216	TGV 29031	TGV 29032	A	PE	
217	TGV 29033	TGV 29034	A	PE	
218	TGV 29035	TGV 29036	A	PE	
219	TGV 29037	TGV 29038	A	PE	
220	TGV 29039	TGV 29040	A	PE	
221	TGV 29041	TGV 29042	A	PE	
222	TGV 29043	TGV 29044	A	PE	
223	TGV 29045	TGV 29046	A	PE	
224	TGV 29047	TGV 29048	A	PE	
225	TGV 29049	TGV 29050	A	PE	
226	TGV 29051	TGV 29052	A	PE	
227	TGV 29053	TGV 29054	A	PE	L'YONNE
228	TGV 29055	TGV 29056	A	PE	
229	TGV 29057	TGV 29058	A	PE	
230	TGV 29059	TGV 29060	A	PE	
231	TGV 29061	TGV 29062	A	PC	
232	TGV 29063	TGV 29064	A	PC	
233	TGV 29065	TGV 29066	A	PC	
234	TGV 29067	TGV 29068	A	PC	
235	TGV 29069	TGV 29070	A	PC	
236	TGV 29071	TGV 29073	A	PC	
237	TGV 29073	TGV 29074	A	PC	
238	TGV 29075	TGV 29076	A	PC	
239	TGV 29077	TGV 29078	A	PC	
240	TGV 29089	TGV 29080	A	PC	
241	TGV 29081	TGV 29082	A	PC	
242	TGV 29083	TGV 29084	A	PC	
243	TGV 29085	TGV 29086	A	PC	
244	TGV 29087	TGV 29088	A	PC	
245	TGV 29089	TGV 29090	A	PC	

246	TGV 29091	TGV 29092	**A**	PC	
247	TGV 29093	TGV 29094	**A**	PC	
248	TGV 29095	TGV 29096	**A**	PC	
249	TGV 29097	TGV 29098	**A**	PC	
250	TGV 29099	TGV 29100	**A**	PC	
251	TGV 29101	TGV 29102	**A**	PC	
252	TGV 29103	TGV 29104	**A**	PC	
253	TGV 29105	TGV 29106	**A**	PC	
254	TGV 29107	TGV 29108	**A**	PC	
255	TGV 29109	TGV 29110	**A**	PC	
256	TGV 29111	TGV 29112	**A**	PC	
257	TGV 29113	TGV 29114	**A**	PC	
258	TGV 29115	TGV 29116	**A**	PC	
259	TGV 29117	TGV 29118	**A**	PC	
260	TGV 29119	TGV 29120	**A**	PC	
261	TGV 29121	TGV 29122	**A**	PC	
262	TGV 29123	TGV 29124	**A**	PC	
263	TGV 29125	TGV 29126	**A**	PC	
264	TGV 29127	TGV 29128	**A**	PC	
265	TGV 29129	TGV 29130	**A**	PC	
266	TGV 29131	TGV 29132	**A**	PE	
267	TGV 29133	TGV 29134	**A**	PE	
268	TGV 29135	TGV 29136	**A**	PE	
269	TGV 29137	TGV 29138	**A**	PE	
270	TGV 29139	TGV 29140	**A**	PE	
271	TGV 29141	TGV 29142	**A**	PE	
272	TGV 29143	TGV 29144	**A**	PE	
273	TGV 29145	TGV 29146	**A**	PE	
274	TGV 29147	TGV 29148	**A**	PE	
275	TGV 29149	TGV 29150	**A**	PE	
276	TGV 29151	TGV 29152	**A**	PE	
277	TGV 29153	TGV 29154	**A**	PE	
278	TGV 29155	TGV 29156	**A**	PE	
279	TGV 29157	TGV 29158	**A**	PE	
280	TGV 29159	TGV 29160	**A**	PE	
281	TGV 29161	TGV 29162	**A**	PE	
282	TGV 29163	TGV 29164	**A**	PE	
283	TGV 29165	TGV 29166	**A**	PE	
284	TGV 29167	TGV 29168	**A**	PE	
285	TGV 29169	TGV 29170	**A**	PE	
286	TGV 29171	TGV 29172	**A**	PE	
287	TGV 29173	TGV 29174	**A**	PE	
288	TGV 29175	TGV 29176	**A**	PE	
289	TGV 29177	TGV 29178	**A**	PE	LONS-LE-SAUNIER

TGV ATLANTIQUE   10-CAR TWO-VOLTAGE SETS

These were the second generation of TGV, being longer, more powerful and faster than the TGV Sud-Est sets. Trailer 2 has unidirectional seating with trailers 3 and 4 having facing seating including six "club" compartments with four seats in each. Trailer 1 has a wheelchair space and suitable toilet. Trailers 2, 4 and 6 have a telephone. Trailers 8 and 9 include four family semi-compartments of four seats and trailer 9 also includes facilities for nursing mothers. Trailer 10 has a special 17-seat children's compartment at the end. Sets started to be refurbished internally in 2006. Set 325 carries a plate showing that achieved a world record of 515.3 km/h on 18 May 1990.

TGV + TGVRADr + TGVRAr + TGVRA + TGVRBr + 6 TGVRB + TGV.
Systems: 1500 V DC + 25 kV AC
Built: 1988–91.
Builders: Alsthom/Francorail-MTE/De Dietrich.
Axle Arrangement: Bo-Bo + 2-2-2-2-2-2-2-2-2-2 + Bo-Bo.
Traction Motors: 8 x Type FM47 1100 kW synchronous per set.
Accommodation: 0 + 44/– 1T + 36/– 1T + 36/– 1T + Bar + –/60 2T + –/60 2T + –/60 1T + –/56 2T + –/56 1T + –/77 2T + 0.
Weight: 444 tonnes.
Length: 22.15 + 21.845 + (8 x 18.70) + 21.845 + 22.15 m.
Maximum Speed: 300 km/h
Cab Signalling: TVM 300 (^{4} TVM 430).

r   Refurbished.

Trailer cars are numbered in the following sequence:

Set nnn: 241nnn/242nnn/243nnn/244nnn/245nnn/246nnn/247nnn/248nnn/249nnn/240nnn.

301	TGV 24001	TGV 24002	**A**	r	PC
302	TGV 24003	TGV 24004	**A**		PC
303	TGV 24005	TGV 24006	**A**		PC
304	TGV 24007	TGV 24008	**A**	r	PC	LE MANS
305	TGV 24009	TGV 24010	**A**	r	PC	SAINT BRIEUC
306	TGV 24011	TGV 24012	**A**	r	PC
307	TGV 24013	TGV 24014	**A**		PC
308	TGV 24015	TGV 24016	**A**	r	PC
309	TGV 24017	TGV 24018	**A**		PC
310	TGV 24019	TGV 24020	**A**	r	PC
311	TGV 24021	TGV 24022	**A**		PC
312	TGV 24023	TGV 24024	**A**		PC	PAYS D'AURAY
313	TGV 24025	TGV 24026	**A**		PC	VILLEBON-SUR-YVETTE
314	TGV 24027	TGV 24028	**A**		PC
315	TGV 24029	TGV 24030	**A**		PC
316	TGV 24031	TGV 24032	**A**		PC	ANGOULÊME
317	TGV 24033	TGV 24034	**A**		PC
318	TGV 24035	TGV 24036	**A**	r	PC
319	TGV 24037	TGV 24038	**A**	r	PC	MARCOUSSIS
320	TGV 24039	TGV 24040	**A**		PC
321	TGV 24041	TGV 24042	**A**	r	PC	ORTHEZ
322	TGV 24043	TGV 24044	**A**		PC	LAMBALLE Côtes d'armor
323	TGV 24045	TGV 24046	**A**		PC
324	TGV 24047	TGV 24048	**A**		PC
325	TGV 24049	TGV 24050	**A**		PC	VENDÔME
326	TGV 24051	TGV 24052	**A**		PC
327	TGV 24053	TGV 24054	**A**		PC
328	TGV 24055	TGV 24056	**A**		PC
329	TGV 24057	TGV 24058	**A**		PC	MORLAIX
330	TGV 24059	TGV 24060	**A**		PC	CHINON
331	TGV 24061	TGV 24062	**A**	r	PC
332	TGV 24063	TGV 24064	**A**		PC	LIBOURNE
333	TGV 24065	TGV 24066	**A**	r	PC	BORDEAUX
334	TGV 24067	TGV 24068	**A**	r	PC	VILLEJUST
335	TGV 24069	TGV 24070	**A**		PC
336	TGV 24071	TGV 24072	**A**		PC	TOURS
337	TGV 24073	TGV 24074	**A**		PC	SAINT-PIERRE-DES-CORPS
338	TGV 24075	TGV 24076	**A**		PC	VOUVRAY
339	TGV 24077	TGV 24078	**A**	r	PC	MONTLOUIS-SUR-LOIRE
340	TGV 24079	TGV 24080	**A**		PC	DOURDAN
341	TGV 24081	TGV 24082	**A**		PC	ANGERS
342	TGV 24083	TGV 24084	**A**	r	PC
343	TGV 24085	TGV 24086	**A**		PC	SAINT-NAZAIRE
344	TGV 24087	TGV 24088	**A**		PC	NANTES
345	TGV 24089	TGV 24090	**A**	r	PC	RÉGION CENTRE LE COEUR DE FRANCE
346	TGV 24091	TGV 24092	**A**	r	PC
347	TGV 24093	TGV 24094	**A**		PC

348	TGV 24095	TGV 24096	**A**		PC	POITIERS
349	TGV 24097	TGV 24098	**A**		PC	LA BAULE
350	TGV 24099	TGV 24100	**A**		PC	
351	TGV 24101	TGV 24102	**A**		PC	
352	TGV 24103	TGV 24104	**A**		PC	
353	TGV 24105	TGV 24106	**A**		PC	LAVAL
354	TGV 24107	TGV 24108	**A**		PC	
355	TGV 24109	TGV 24110	**A**		PC	LE CROISIC
356	TGV 24111	TGV 24112	**A**		PC	Pays de Vannes
357	TGV 24113	TGV 24114	**A**		PC	
358	TGV 24115	TGV 24116	**A**		PC	
359	TGV 24117	TGV 24118	**A**		PC	CHÂTELLERAULT
360	TGV 24119	TGV 24120	**A**		PC	
361	TGV 24121	TGV 24122	**A**		PC	ALENÇON
362	TGV 24123	TGV 24124	**A**		PC	ST. JÉAN-DE-LUZ
363	TGV 24125	TGV 24126	**A**	r	PC	
364	TGV 24127	TGV 24128	**A**		PC	BAYONNE
365	TGV 24129	TGV 24130	**A**		PC	TARBES
366	TGV 24131	TGV 24132	**A**		PC	
367	TGV 24133	TGV 24134	**A**		PC	
368	TGV 24135	TGV 24136	**A**		PC	
369	TGV 24137	TGV 24138	**A**		PC	LOURDES
370	TGV 24139	TGV 24140	**A**		PC	HENDAYE
371	TGV 24141	TGV 24142	**A**		PC	LORIENT
372	TGV 24143	TGV 24144	**A**		PC	
373	TGV 24145	TGV 24146	**A**		PC	
374	TGV 24147	TGV 24148	**A**		PC	
375	TGV 24149	TGV 24150	**A**		PC	
376	TGV 24151	TGV 24152	**A**		PC	
377	TGV 24153	TGV 24154	**A**	r	PC	
378	TGV 24155	TGV 24156	**A**		PC	
379	TGV 24157	TGV 24158	**A**		PC	
380	TGV 24159	TGV 24160	**A**	r	PC	
381	TGV 24161	TGV 24162	**A**	r	PC	
382	TGV 24163	TGV 24164	**A**	r	PC	
383	TGV 24165	TGV 24166	**A**	r	PC	
384	TGV 24167	TGV 24168	**A**	r	PC	
385	TGV 24169	TGV 24170	**A**	r	PC	CHAMBRAY-LES-TOURS
386	TGV 24171	TGV 24172	**A**	4	PC	
387	TGV 24173	TGV 24174	**A**	4	PC	
388	TGV 24175	TGV 24176	**A**	4	PC	
389	TGV 24177	TGV 24178	**A**	4	PC	LE POULIGUEN
390	TGV 24179	TGV 24180	**A**	4	PC	ANCENIS
391	TGV 24181	TGV 24182	**A**	4	PC	VILLE DE MASSY
392	TGV 24183	TGV 24184	**A**	4	PC	
393	TGV 24185	TGV 24186	**A**	4	PC	PORNICHET
394	TGV 24187	TGV 24188	**A**	4	PC	
395	TGV 24189	TGV 24190	**A**	4	PC	
396	TGV 24191	TGV 24192	**A**	4	PC	LOCHES
397	TGV 24193	TGV 24194	**A**	r 4	PC	
398	TGV 24195	TGV 24196	**A**	4	PC	LANGEAIS
399	TGV 24197	TGV 24198	**A**	4	PC	
400	TGV 24199	TGV 24200	**A**	4	PC	QUIMPER
401	TGV 24201	TGV 24202	**A**	4	PC	
402	TGV 24203	TGV 24204	**A**	4	PC	
403	TGV 24205	TGV 24206	**A**	4	PC	
404	TGV 24207	TGV 24208	**A**	4	PC	
405	TGV 24209	TGV 24210	**A**	4	PC	AYTRÉ
Spare Power Car		TGV 24211	**A**		PC	

TGV RÉSEAU (TGV-R)   8-CAR TWO-VOLTAGE SETS

TGV-Réseau is basically an eight-car version of TGV-Atlantique with very similar power cars. Trailers differ in that all have an open layout and none have the "semi-compartments" found in TGV A first class. The bar vehicle is completely transformed. Another difference is slightly lower density seating in second class as TGV R sets, as their names suggest, were designed for work over the whole TGV network, often on long distance services.

Dual-voltage units first went into service in 1993 on TGV-Nord Europe services from Paris Nord to Lille, Valenciennes, Dunkerque and Calais/Boulogne, then in 1994 on the Lille–Lyon–Marseille–Nice route, via the Jonction high-speed line avoiding Paris. From 1996, they spread to Lille–Rennes, Nantes and Bordeaux services.

For the opening of the LGV Est in 2007, all of the TGV R sets were refurbished internally and maximum speed raised to 320 km/h. During this process, some trailers were swapped around but full details are not available. Sets 501, 503 to 514 and 534 to 550, plus 527, 528 and 531, renumbered 551 to 553, remain as standard TGV R sets and now operate domestic services out of Paris Est. The remaining 19 sets donated their power cars to TGV Réseau-Duplex sets 601 to 619 and their trailers to TGV POS sets 4401 to 4419. All remaining TGV R plus TGV POS sets are allocated to the Technicentre Est Européen, otherwise known as Paris Ourcq. TGV 527, 528 and 531 were renumbered as they donated their trailers to TGV POS sets and received trailers from TGV sets 4507 to 4509 respectively.

TGV 502 was involved in a crash at Bergues on 25 September 1997 which destroyed power car 28004 and damaged trailers R7 and R8. The other trailers were used to repair Thalys PBKA set 4342.

On 26 May 2001, set 531 (the power cars of which are now in set 553) set an endurance record when it ran non-stop from Calais Fréthun to Marseille, a distance of 1067.4 km in a few seconds under 3½ hours, an average of just under 305 km/h.

Systems: 1500 V DC / 25 kV AC
Maximum Speed: 320 km/h.
Builder–Mechanical Parts: GEC-Alsthom/De Dietrich
Builder–Electrical Parts: Francorail-MTE
Built: 1992–94
Continuous Rating: 25 kV AC 8800 kW; 1500 V DC 3680 kW.
Traction Motors : 8 x FM 47 synchronous of 1100 kW each.
Axle Arrangement: Bo-Bo + 2-2-2-2-2-2-2-2-2 + Bo-Bo.
Accommodation:
0 + 42/- 1T + 39/- 1T + 39/- 1T + -/16 bar + -/56 2T + -/56 2T + - /56 1T + -/73 2T + 0
Weight: 65 + 43 + 28 + 28 + 28 + 28 + 28 + 43 + 65 tonnes
Length: 22.15 + 21.845 + 18.7 + 18.7 + 18.7 + 18.7 + 18.7 + 18.7 + 21.845 + 22.15 m.
Cab Signalling: TVM 430.

Trailer cars are numbered in the following sequence, prefixed TGVR:

Set nnn: 281nnn + 282nnn + 283nnn + 284nnn + 285nnn + 286nnn + 287nnn + 288nnn

501	TGV 28001	TGV 28002	A	PQ	
503	TGV 28005	TGV 28006	A	PQ	
504	TGV 28007	TGV 28008	A	PQ	
505	TGV 28009	TGV 28010	A	PQ	
506	TGV 28011	TGV 28013	A	PQ	
507	TGV 28013	TGV 28014	A	PQ	
508	TGV 28015	TGV 28016	A	PQ	
509	TGV 28017	TGV 28018	A	PQ	
510	TGV 28019	TGV 28020	A	PQ	
511	TGV 28021	TGV 28022	A	PQ	
512	TGV 28023	TGV 28024	A	PQ	
513	TGV 28025	TGV 28026	A	PQ	
514	TGV 28027	TGV 28028	A	PQ	LA MADELEINE
534	TGV 28067	TGV 28068	A	PQ	Ville de Dunkerque
535	TGV 28069	TGV 28070	A	PQ	
536	TGV 28071	TGV 28072	A	PQ	
537	TGV 28073	TGV 28074	A	PQ	
538	TGV 28075	TGV 28076	A	PQ	
539	TGV 28077	TGV 28078	A	PQ	

540	TGV 28079		TGV 28080		A	PQ
541	TGV 28081		TGV 28082		A	PQ
542	TGV 28083		TGV 28084		A	PQ
543	TGV 28085		TGV 28086		A	PQ
544	TGV 28087		TGV 28088		A	PQ
545	TGV 28089		TGV 28090		A	PQ
546	TGV 28091		TGV 28092		A	PQ
547	TGV 28093		TGV 28094		A	PQ
548	TGV 28095		TGV 28096		A	PQ
549	TGV 28097		TGV 28098		A	PQ
550	TGV 28099		TGV 28100		A	PQ
551	TGV 28101	(28053)	TGV 28102	(28054)	A	PQ
552	TGV 28103	(28055)	TGV 28104	(28056)	A	PQ
553	TGV 28105	(28061)	TGV 28106	(28062)	A	PQ
Spare	Power Car		TGV 28003		A	PQ

TGV RÉSEAU-DUPLEX   8-CAR DOUBLE-DECK SETS

These sets were created by combining 19 new sets of double-deck trailers, identical to those in TGV Duplex sets, with power cars from 19 TGV Réseau sets (515 to 526, 529, 530, 532 and 533 plus 4507 to 4509) which donated their trailers to TGV POS sets (see below). They are used in a common diagram, and in multiple, with TGV Duplex sets on the Sud-Est network. The power cars are little changed except for the livery, with a broader blue band to match the Duplex trailers.

In the case of sets 613 to 615, the former tri-voltage power cars are equipped to operate under 3000 V DC but the units are never used outside France.

Systems: 1500 V DC / 25 kV AC.
Maximum Speed: 320 km/h.
Builders–Mechanical Parts : Alstom.
Builder–Electrical Parts : Francorail-MTE.
Built: Power cars 1992–94; trailers 2005–2007.
Continuous Rating: 25 kV AC 8800 kW; 1500 V DC 3680 kW.
Traction Motors : 8 x FM 47 synchronous of 1100 kW each.
Axle Arrangement: Bo-Bo + 2-2-2-2-2-2-2-2-2 + Bo-Bo.
Accommodation: 0 + 62/– 2T + 58/– 2T + 58/– 2T + –/16 bar + –/74 2T + –/78 2T + –/90 2T + 0 (toilets are for ladies upstairs, gentlemen downstairs).
Weight: 65 + 43 + 28 + 28 + 28 + 28 + 43 + 65 tonnes.
Length: 22.15 + 21.845 + 18.7 + 18.7 + 18.7 + 18.7 + 18.7 + 18.7 + 21.845 + 22.15 m.
Cab Signalling: TVM 430.

Trailer cars are numbered in the following sequence, prefixed TGVR:

Set nnn = 291nnn + 292nnn + 283nnn + 294nnn + 295nnn + 296nnn + 297nnn + 298nnn

601	TGV 28601	(28029)	TGV 28602	(28030)	A	PE
602	TGV 28603	(28035)	TGV 28604	(28036)	A	PE
603	TGV 28605	(28031)	TGV 28606	(28032)	A	PE
604	TGV 28607	(28033)	TGV 28608	(28034)	A	PE
605	TGV 28609	(28037)	TGV 28610	(28038)	A	PE
606	TGV 28611	(28039)	TGV 28612	(28040)	A	PE
607	TGV 28613	(28043)	TGV 28614	(28044)	A	PE
608	TGV 28615	(28051)	TGV 28616	(28052)	A	PE
609	TGV 28617	(28063)	TGV 28618	(28064)	A	PE
610	TGV 28619	(28047)	TGV 28620	(28048)	A	PE
611	TGV 28621	(28049)	TGV 28622	(28050)	A	PE
612	TGV 28623	(28041)	TGV 28624	(28042)	A	PE
613	TGV 386025	(380013)	TGV 386026	(380014)	A	PE
614	TGV 386027	(380015)	TGV 386028	(380016)	A	PE
615	TGV 386029	(380017)	TGV 386030	(380018)	A	PE
616	TGV 28631	(28059)	TGV 28632	(28060)	A	PE
617	TGV 28633	(28057)	TGV 28634	(28058)	A	PE
618	TGV 28635	(28065)	TGV 28636	(28065)	A	PE
619	TGV 28637	(28045)	TGV 28638	(28046)	A	PE

TGV DASYE   8-CAR DOUBLE-DECK SETS

TGV DAYSE (Duplex ASYchronous, ERTMS) look identical to TGV Duplex but have new power equipment with asynchronous traction motors and ERTMS signalling. Power equipment is the same as in TGV POS power cars. The interior of trailers is slightly different from Duplex sets, with dark blue and purple moquette. Units are based at Paris Sud-Est depot and operate in the same diagram as standard TGV Duplex.

Following an initial order for 24 TGV DASYE, SNCF ordered a further 25 sets, to be delivered by 2011. These will be followed by 95 of a further new generation of double-deck sets, of which 40 are currently options. This will take the number of double-deck sets to 252 – 89 Duplex, 19 Réseau-Duplex, 49 DASYE and 95 new generation Duplex.

Systems: 1500 V DC / 25 kV AC 50 Hz.
Maximum Speed: 320 km/h.
Builder–Mechanical Parts: Alstom.
Builder-Electrical Parts: Alstom.
Built: 2007–
Continuous Rating: 25 kV AC 9280 kW; 1500 V DC 3680 kW.
Traction Motors : .
Axle Arrangement: Bo-Bo + 2-2-2-2-2-2-2-2-2 + Bo-Bo.
Accommodation: 0 + 62/– 2T + 58/– 2T + 58/– 2T + –/16 bar + –/74 2T + –/78 2T + –/78 2T + –/90 2T + 0 (toilets are for ladies upstairs, gentlemen downstairs).
Weight: 65 + 43 + 28 + 28 + 28 + 28 + 28 + 43 + 65 tonnes.
Length: 22.15 + 21.845 + 18.7 + 18.7 + 18.7 + 18.7 + 18.7 + 21.845 + 22.15 m.
Cab Signalling: TVM 430 & ETCS.

Multiple operation within class and with TGV Duplex, TGV Réseau and TGV Réseau-Duplex.

701	TGV 29701	TGV 29702	**A**	PE
702	TGV 29703	TGV 29704	**A**	PE
703	TGV 29705	TGV 29706	**A**	PE
704	TGV 29707	TGV 29708	**A**	PE
705	TGV 29709	TGV 29710	**A**	PE
706	TGV 29711	TGV 29712	**A**	PE
707	TGV 29713	TGV 29714	**A**	PE
708	TGV 29715	TGV 29716	**A**	PE
709	TGV 29717	TGV 29718	**A**	PE
710	TGV 29719	TGV 29720	**A**	PE
711	TGV 29721	TGV 29722	**A**	PE
712	TGV 29723	TGV 29724	**A**	
713	TGV 29725	TGV 29726	**A**	
714	TGV 29727	TGV 29728	**A**	
715	TGV 29729	TGV 29730	**A**	
716	TGV 29731	TGV 29732	**A**	
717	TGV 29733	TGV 29734	**A**	
718	TGV 29735	TGV 29736	**A**	
719	TGV 29737	TGV 29738	**A**	
720	TGV 29739	TGV 29740	**A**	
721	TGV 29741	TGV 29742	**A**	
722	TGV 29743	TGV 29744	**A**	
723	TGV 29745	TGV 29746	**A**	
724	TGV 29747	TGV 29748	**A**	
725	TGV 29749	TGV 29750	**A**	
726	TGV 29751	TGV 29752	**A**	
727	TGV 29753	TGV 29754	**A**	
728	TGV 29755	TGV 29756	**A**	
729	TGV 29757	TGV 29758	**A**	
730	TGV 29759	TGV 29760	**A**	
731	TGV 29761	TGV 29762	**A**	
732	TGV 29763	TGV 29764	**A**	
733	TGV 29765	TGV 29766	**A**	
734	TGV 29767	TGV 29768	**A**	
735	TGV 29769	TGV 29770	**A**	

736	TGV 29771	TGV 29772	A
737	TGV 29773	TGV 29774	A
738	TGV 29775	TGV 29776	A
739	TGV 29777	TGV 29778	A
740	TGV 29779	TGV 29780	A
741	TGV 29781	TGV 29782	A
742	TGV 29783	TGV 29784	A
743	TGV 29785	TGV 29786	A
744	TGV 29787	TGV 29788	A
745	TGV 29789	TGV 29790	A
746	TGV 29791	TGV 29792	A
747	TGV 29793	TGV 29794	A
748	TGV 29795	TGV 29796	A
749	TGV 29797	TGV 29798	A

TGV POSTAL

These sets are based on TGV Sud-Est with eight trailers, but they have no windows and are equipped as postal vans. Numbers 951 to 955 are half sets. Numbers 956/7 were converted from TGV Sud-Est set 38 and form a complete set. Postal sets operate from Charolais sorting depot next to Paris Gare de Lyon to depots at Mâcon and Cavaillon.

Class Specific Livery: Yellow with grey and white bands.

951	923001	S	PE
952	923002	S	PE
953	923003	S	PE
954	923004	S	PE
955	923005	S	PE
956	923006	S	PE
957	923007	S	PE

EUROSTAR THREE CAPITALS   9-CAR HALF-SETS

Eurostar sets work services through the Channel Tunnel from London to Paris and Brussels. The three-voltage sets (750 V DC third rail equipment was removed after opening of the London–Channel Tunnel high speed line) also work London–Bourg St. Maurice ski trains in winter and London–Avignon in summer. 3203/4 and 3225–8 are not used on Channel Tunnel services, being restricted to Paris–Lille–Tourcoing. Eurostars are based on the TGV concept, and the individual cars are numbered like TGVs. Each train consists of two 9-coach half sets back-to-back with a power car at the outer end. They normally operate in pairs 3001/2, and so on. All sets are articulated with an extra motor bogie on the coach next to the power car. Coaches are referred to by their position in the set viz. R1–R9 (and in traffic R10–R18 in the second set). Coaches R18–R10 are identical to R1–R9.

TGV + TGVZBD + 4 TGVRB + TGVRr + 2 TGVRA + TGVRAD.
Systems: 3000 V DC + 25 kV AC (v + 1500 V DC).
Built: 1992–93.
Builders: GEC-Alsthom/Brush/ANF/De Dietrich/BN/ACEC.
Axle Arrangement: Bo-Bo + Bo-2-2-2-2-2-2-2-2.
Accommodation: 0 + –/48 1T + –/58 1T + –/58 2T + –/58 1T + –/58 2T + bar/kitchen + 39/– 1T + 39/– 1T + 25/– 1T.
Length: 22.15 + 21.845 + (7 x 18.70) + 21.845 m.
Maximum Speed: 300 km/h.
Cab Signalling: TVM 430.
Class Specific Livery: S White with dark blue window band roof and yellow bodysides with Eurostar branding.
Non-standard Livery: N As above, but Eurostar branding removed.
Trailer cars are numbered in the following sequence.

Set nnnn: 37nnnn1/37nnnn2/37nnnn3/37nnnn4/37nnnn5/37nnnn6/37nnnn7/37nnnn8/37nnnn9.

Set	Owner	Power Car				Set	Owner	Power Car			
3001	EU	3730010	S		TI	3202	SNCF	3732020	S	v	LY
3002	EU	3730020	S		TI	3203	SNCF	3732030	N	v	LY
3003	EU	3730030	S		TI	3204	SNCF	3732040	N	v	LY
3004	EU	3730040	S		TI	3205	SNCF	3732050	S		LY
3005	EU	3730050	S		TI	3206	SNCF	3732060	S		LY
3006	EU	3730060	S		TI	3207	SNCF	3732070	S	v	LY
3007	EU	3730070	S		TI	3208	SNCF	3732080	S	v	LY
3008	EU	3730080	S		TI	3209	SNCF	3732090	S		LY
3009	EU	3730090	S		TI	3210	SNCF	3732100	S		LY
3010	EU	3730100	S		TI	3211	SNCF	3732110	S		LY
3011	EU	3730110	S		TI	3212	SNCF	3732120	S		LY
3012	EU	3730120	S		TI	3213	SNCF	3732130	S		LY
3013	EU	3730130	S		TI	3214	SNCF	3732140	S		LY
3014	EU	3730140	S		TI	3215	SNCF	3732150	S	v	LY
3015	EU	3730150	S		TI	3216	SNCF	3732160	S	v	LY
3016	EU	3730160	S		TI	3217	SNCF	3732170	S		LY
3017	EU	3730170	S		TI	3218	SNCF	3732180	S		LY
3018	EU	3730180	S		TI	3219	SNCF	3732190	S		LY
3019	EU	3730190	S		TI	3220	SNCF	3732200	S		LY
3020	EU	3730200	S		TI	3221	SNCF	3732210	S		LY
3021	EU	3730210	S		TI	3222	SNCF	3732220	S		LY
3022	EU	3730220	S		TI	3223	SNCF	3732230	S	v	LY
3101	SNCB	3731010	S		FF	3224	SNCF	3732240	S	v	LY
3102	SNCB	3731020	S		FF	3225	SNCF	3732250	N	v	LY
3103	SNCB	3731030	S		FF	3226	SNCF	3732260	N	v	LY
3104	SNCB	3731040	S		FF	3227	SNCF	3732270	N	v	LY
3105	SNCB	3731050	S		FF	3228	SNCF	3732280	N	v	LY
3106	SNCB	3731060	S		FF	3229	SNCF	3732290	S	v	LY
3107	SNCB	3731050	S		FF	3230	SNCF	3732300	S	v	LY
3108	SNCB	3731060	S		FF	3231	SNCF	3732310	S		LY
3201	SNCF	3732010	S	v	LY	3232	SNCF	3732320	S		LY

Spare Power Car

3999	LCR	3739990	S		TI	

Names:

3007/08 Waterloo Sunset
3013/14 LONDON 2012

3207/08 MICHEL HOLLARD
3209/10 THE DA VINCI CODE

REGIONAL EUROSTAR   7-CAR HALF-SETS

These sets are similar to the "Three Capitals" sets except that they only have seven trailers. They consist of a power car plus trailers type R1/3/2/5/6/7/9 in that order. They were designed for operation north of London (and are often known as North of London or NoL sets), but as these services have not materialised, some operated London–Leeds, on hire to GNER. Six of the sets, plus half set 3307 as a spare, were then hired in 2007 by SNCF for services from Paris Nord to Lille and Valenciennes. Half set 3308 has never turned a wheel in service and is used for static trials at London Temple Mills depot.

TGV + TGVZBD + 4 TGVRB + TGVRr + 2 TGVRA + TGVRAD.

Systems: 3000 V DC + 25 kV AC
Built: 1992–93.
Builders: GEC-Alsthom/Brush/ANF/De Dietrich/BN/ACEC.
Axle Arrangement: Bo-Bo + Bo-2-2-2-2-2-2-2.
Accommodation: 0 + –/48 1T + –/58 1T + –/58 1T + –/58 2T + bar/kitchen + 39/– 1T + 25/– 1T.
Length: 22.15 + 21.845 + (5 x 18.70) + 21.845 m.
Maximum Speed: 300 km/h.
Cab Signalling: TVM 430.
Class Specific Livery: **S** White with dark blue window band roof and yellow bodysides with Eurostar branding removed.

Trailer cars are numbered in the following sequence.

Set nnnn: 37nnnn1/37nnnn3/37nnnn2/3nnnn5/37nnnn6/37nnnn737nnnn9.

3301	EU	3733010	S	LY	3308	EU	3733080	S	TD (U)
3302	EU	3733020	S	LY	3309	EU	3733090	S	LY
3303	EU	3733030	S	LY	3310	EU	3733100	S	LY
3304	EU	3733040	S	LY	3311	EU	3733110	S	LY
3305	EU	3733050	S	LY	3312	EU	3733120	S	LY
3306	EU	3733060	S	LY	3313	EU	3733130	S	LY
3307	EU	3733070	S	LY	3314	EU	3733140	S	LY

Name: 3313/4 named "ENTENTE CORDIALE"

THALYS PBKA   8-CAR FOUR-VOLTAGE SETS

This is basically a four-voltage version of TGV-Réseau but with the new generation of power car with a central driving position as first seen with TGV Duplex. Trailer cars are exactly the same as TGV-Réseau PBA sets 4531–4540 (see below). The power car includes all equipment necessary for operation in France, Belgium, the Netherlands and Germany including German Indusi and LZB cab signalling. With all this extra equipment, it was necessary to design a lighter transformer in order to keep the power car weight to 68 tonnes because of the 17 tonne axle load limit on French high-speed lines.

These sets work Paris–Brussels–Köln/Amsterdam services. Sets can operate in multiple with TGV-Réseau sets but normally only run with each other and PBA sets. The sets belong to the four railways concerned but will be based and maintained at Paris Le Landy or Brussels Forest. Units were being refurbished internally and receiving ETCS equipment in 2008.

Systems: 1500 V DC / 25 kV AC 50 Hz / 3000 V DC / 15 kV AC 16.7Hz
Built : 1996–98
Builder-Mech. Parts: GEC-Alsthom/De Dietrich/Bombardier Eurorail
Builder-Elec. Parts: GEC-Alsthom/ACEC/Holec
Axle arrangement: Bo-Bo + 2-2-2-2-2-2-2-2 + Bo-Bo
Weight: 67 + 43 + 28 + 28 + 28 + 28 + 28 + 43 + 67 tonnes
Length: 22.15 + 21.845 + 18.7 + 18.7 + 18.7 + 18.7 + 18.7 + 18.7 + 21.845 + 22.15 m.
Accommodation:
0 + 42/– 1T + 39/– 1T + 39/– 1T + –/16 bar + –/56 2T + –/56 2T + –/56 1T + –/73 2T + 0
Continuous Rating: 25 kV 8800 kW; 3000 V DC 5120 kW ; 1500 V DC and 15 kV AC 3680 kW
Maximum Speed: 300 km/h
Cab Signalling: TVM 430.
Class-specific Livery: S Metallic grey with red front end and roof.

Trailer cars are numbered in the following sequence, prefixed TGVR:

Set nnnn: nnnn1 + nnnn2 + nnnn3 + nnnn4 + nnnn5 + nnnn6 + nnnn7 + nnnn8

Set	Owner	Power Car 1	Power Car 2	Liv	Depot
4301	SNCB	TGV 43010	TGV 43019	S	FF
4302	SNCB	TGV 43020	TGV 43029	S	FF
4303	SNCB	TGV 43030	TGV 43039	S	FF
4304	SNCB	TGV 43040	TGV 43049	S	FF
4305	SNCB	TGV 43050	TGV 43059	S	FF
4306	SNCB	TGV 43060	TGV 43069	S	FF
4307	SNCB	TGV 43070	TGV 43079	S	FF
4321	DB	TGV 43210	TGV 43219	S	FF
4322	DB	TGV 43220	TGV 43229	S	FF
4331	NS	TGV 43310	TGV 43319	S	FF
4332	NS	TGV 43320	TGV 43329	S	FF
4341	SNCF	TGV 43410	TGV 43419	S	LY
4342	SNCF	TGV 43420	TGV 43429	S	LY
4343	SNCF	TGV 43430	TGV 43439	S	LY
4344	SNCF	TGV 43440	TGV 43449	S	LY
4345	SNCF	TGV 43450	TGV 43459	S	LY
4346	SNCF	TGV 43460	TGV 43469	S	LY

TGV POS   8-CAR TRI-VOLTAGE SETS

TGV POS (curiously mixing French TGV with German POS) stands for Paris Ostfrankreich Süddeutschland, as they are designed to operate from Paris via eastern France to southern Germany, although they also operate to northern Switzerland so they ought to be called TGV POS-NOS! The 19 sets were formed from pairs of brand new tri-voltage power cars and sets of refurbished trailers from TGV Réseau sets 515 to 533 – see number in brackets. The power cars look the same as those for Thalys PBKA sets but have a completely different traction chain, based on IGBTs driving asynchronous traction motors.

These sets operate all trains from Paris Est to Stuttgart and München and from Paris Est to Basel and Zürich. The latter service is now managed by Lyria. They often operate in multiple with each other or with TGV Réseau sets between Paris and Strasbourg.

Set 4406 is owned by SBB.

Systems: 1500 V DC; 15 kV AC 16.7 Hz; 25 kV AC 50 Hz.
Built: 2005–2007.
Builder–Mechanical Parts: Alstom/De Dietrich.
Builder–Electrical Parts: Alstom.
Axle Arrangement: Bo-Bo + 2-2-2-2-2-2-2-2 + Bo-Bo.
Traction Motors:
Weight:
Maximum Speed: 320 km/h.
Length: 22.15 + 21.845 + 18.7 + 18.7 + 18.7 + 18.7 + 18.7 + 18.7 + 21.845 + 22.15 m.
Cab signalling: TVM 430 and ETCS.

Non standard livery: N On 3 April 2007, the power cars of set 4402, plus three specially-equipped Duplex trailers, reached the astonishing world record speed of 574.8 km/h on the LGV Est. Power cars still carry the special black livery from this day.

Trailer cars are numbered in the following sequence:

Set nnnn = 38nnnn1 + 38nnnn2 + 38nnnn3 + 38nnnn4 + 38nnnn5 + 38nnnn6 + 38nnnn7 + 38 nnnn8

4401	TGV 384001	TGV 384002	(515)	A	PQ	
4402	TGV 384003	TGV 384004	(530)	N	PQ	
4403	TGV 384005	TGV 384006	(516)	A	PQ	DOUAI-CITÉ DES GÉANTS
4404	TGV 384007	TGV 384008	(517)	A	PQ	
4405	TGV 384009	TGV 384010	(519)	A	PQ	
4406	TGV 384011	TGV 384012	(520)	A	PQ	BASEL
4407	TGV 384013	TGV 384014	(522)	A	PQ	
4408	TGV 384015	TGV 384016	(526)	A	PQ	CHESSY
4409	TGV 384017	TGV 384018	(532)	A	PQ	CONSEIL GENERAL DU VAL D'OISE
4410	TGV 384019	TGV 384020	(524)	A	PQ	ARNOUVILLE-LES-GONESSE
4411	TGV 384021	TGV 384022	(525)	A	PQ	
4412	TGV 384023	TGV 384024	(521)	A	PQ	TOURCOING La Créative
4413	TGV 384025	TGV 384026	(527)	A	PQ	SAINT OMER AUDOMAROIS
4414	TGV 384027	TGV 384028	(528)	A	PQ	CAMBRAI
4415	TGV 384029	TGV 384030	(529)	A	PQ	
4416	TGV 384031	TGV 384032	(518)	A	PQ	
4417	TGV 384033	TGV 384034	(523)	A	PQ	
4418	TGV 384035	TGV 384036	(531)	A	PQ	
4419	TGV 384037	TGV 384038	(533)	A	PQ	TOURNAN-EN-BRIE

TGV RÉSEAU (TGV-R)   8-CAR THREE-VOLTAGE SETS

Apart from three-voltage capabilities, these sets are identical to TGV-Réseau two-voltage sets and are designed to operate Belgium–south of France services on which they often work in multiple with Duplex sets south of Lille. Sets 4501–4506 were equipped to work into Italy and started operating Paris–Torino–Milano services from September 1996.

In 2006, set 4530 was converted for use as a high-speed test train and travels all over the TGV network on these duties. The set is no longer numbered but is known as "Iris" and carries a special silver livery with red lines. Set 4551 was formerly Thalys PBA set 4531 and was refurbished as a TGV R set in 2008. This was part of deal under which SNCF allocates capacity to Air France on Brussels–Roissy–south of France services.

Details as TGV-Réseau two-voltage sets 501–553 except:

Systems: 1500 V DC; 3000 V DC; 25 kV AC.
Maximum Speed: 300 km/h (§ 320 km/h).
Built: 1994–96

i = Equipped to operate into Italy under 3000 V DC
r = Refurbished interior

N: Non-standard livery of silver with orange and red stripes.

Trailers are numbered in the following sequence, prefixed TGVR:

Set nnnn: 38nnnn1 + 38nnnn2 + 38nnnn3 + 38nnnn4 + 38nnnn5 + 38nnnn6 + 38nnnn7 + 38nnnn8

4501	TGV 380001	TGV 380002	A	i	PE	
4502	TGV 380003	TGV 380004	A	i	PE	
4503	TGV 380005	TGV 380006	A	i	PE	
4504	TGV 380007	TGV 380008	A	i	PE	
4505	TGV 380009	TGV 380010	A	i	PE	
4506	TGV 380011	TGV 380013	A	i	PE	
4510	TGV 380019	TGV 380020	A		LY	
4511	TGV 380021	TGV 380022	A		LY	Villeneuve d'Ascq
4512	TGV 380022	TGV 380023	A		LY	
4513	TGV 380024	TGV 380025	A		LY	
4514	TGV 380027	TGV 380028	A	r	LY	
4515	TGV 380029	TGV 380030	A		LY	
4516	TGV 380031	TGV 380032	A		LY	
4517	TGV 380033	TGV 380034	A		LY	
4518	TGV 380035	TGV 380036	A		LY	
4519	TGV 380037	TGV 380038	A		LY	
4520	TGV 380039	TGV 380040	A		LY	
4521	TGV 380041	TGV 380042	A		LY	
4522	TGV 380043	TGV 380044	A		LY	
4523	TGV 380045	TGV 380046	A		LY	
4524	TGV 380047	TGV 380048	A		LY	
4525	TGV 380049	TGV 380050	A		LY	
4526	TGV 380051	TGV 380052	A		LY	
4527	TGV 380053	TGV 380054	A		LY	
4528	TGV 380055	TGV 380056	A		LY	
4529	TGV 380057	TGV 380058	A	r	LY	
"Iris"	TGV 380059	TGV 380060	N	§	LY	
4551	TGV 380061	TGV 380062	A	r	LY	
Spare Power Car		TGV 380081	A		LY	

THALYS PBA   8-CAR THREE-VOLTAGE SETS

The final ten TGV Réseau three-voltage sets – 4531 to 4540 – were equipped with a special pantograph and Dutch ATB automatic train protection in order to operate Paris–Brussels–Amsterdam Thalys services. Because of this they are known as Thalys PBA sets. These units also have a completely different "Thalys" livery and improved interiors with red moquette seats throughout. They work in multiple with each other and Thalys PBKA sets. Units were being refurbished internally and receiving ETCS equipment in 2008.

In 2007, set 4531 was transferred to SNCF for use on Brussels–south of France services.

Details as TGV sets 4501–4530.

4532	TGV 380063	TGV 380064	N	FF
4533	TGV 380065	TGV 380066	N	FF
4534	TGV 380067	TGV 380068	N	FF
4535	TGV 380069	TGV 380070	N	FF
4536	TGV 380071	TGV 380072	N	FF
4537	TGV 380073	TGV 380074	N	FF
4538	TGV 380075	TGV 380076	N	FF
4539	TGV 380077	TGV 380078	N	FF
4540	TGV 380079	TGV 380080	N	FF

▲ Z 8851/2 and a Class Z 20900 set arrive at Gennevilliers on 16 September 2008 with an RER Line C service from Montigny-Beauchamp to Pont de Rungis. **David Haydock**

▼ Z 11514, in TER livery with yellow flashes to advertise the Lorraine region, leaves Châlons-en-Champagne for Épernay on 2 April 2007. **David Haydock**

▲ Z 20921/2 and another of the class in dark blue Transilien livery, arrive at Gennevilliers station with an RER Line C train from Pontoise to Massy Palaiseau on 16 September 2008.   **David Haydock**

▼ Z 21588/87 forms a Brest–Rennes near Montfort-sur-Meu on 11 February 2008.   **David Haydock**

▲ EMUs 561B (Z 23561) and 376 (Z 24651/52) approach Landas with the 17.11 Jeumont–Lille on 18 April 2007. **David Haydock**

▼ TER2N NG EMU Z 24637/38 (set 369) is seen at Luxembourg Ville station beside the CFL version of this class, set 2203, on 13 June 2008. **Philip Wormald**

▲ Tram-train TT 15 (U 25529/30) stands at Gargan station on 25 April 2007. **David Haydock**

▼ AGC EMU Z 27619/20, in the Languedoc-Roussillon livery, arrives at Montpellier on 31 July 2008.
Raimund Whynal

▲ TGV Sud-Est sets are now used on the Nord network. Set 03 "BELFORT" passes Farbus with a Dunkerque–Paris service on 5 April 2007. **David Haydock**

▼ TGV Réseau set 4505, one of six equipped to work into Italy, is seen near St. Pierre d'Albigny with the 09.10 Milano–Paris service on 4 March 2007. **Robin Ralston**

▲ TGV Réseau-Duplex set 607 plus a second Duplex set pass St. Pierre d'Albigny with 09.10 Paris–Bourg St. Maurice on 4 March 2007.   **Robin Ralston**

▼ Eurostar set 3225/6, one of three allocated to Paris–Lille services and in an adapted livery, powers through St. Denis on 16 September 2008 with a train to Tourcoing.   **David Haydock**

▲ Thalys set 4301 forms a Brussels–Paris service near Beaumont between Lille and Paris on 10 February 2004.   **David Haydock**

▼ TGV POS set 4403 leaves the LGV Est high speed line at Vaires on 26 March 2007 after a crew training run.   **David Haydock**

▲ An RATP MS61 set with 18239 leading, recently rebuilt with new cabs, stands at Joinville le Pont with a train for St. Germain-en-Laye on 9 September 2008. **David Haydock**

▼ RATP MI2N Alteo set 1546/5 arrives at Sartrouville on RER Line A while a second set heads west towards Cergy on 16 September 2008. SNCF Class Z 22500 are almost identical to these sets. **David Haydock**

▲ The two new Stadler EMUs, Z 151 and 152 approach Mont Louis la Cabanasse on the metre gauge Cerdagne line on 28 December 2007. **Thierry Leleu**

▼ EMUs Z 802 and Z 851 (the latter owned by Swiss operator TMR) are seen on the Viaduc Sainte Marie on SNCF's spectacular metre gauge Savoie line on 5 July 2008. **Christophe Masse**

▲ Blanc Argent DMU X 74501 and a second of the class are seen at La Ferté-Imbault in July 2002.
David Haydock

▼ Two of the new AMG 800 DMUs (at the time without numbers) for the Chemins de Fer Corses are seen at Ajaccio on 24 May 2008. **Sylvain Meillasson**

▲ Chemin de Fer de La Mure loco T9 awaits departure from St. Georges de Commiers on 3 July 1999. **Keith Fender**

▼ CF de Montenvers unit 46 plus trailer 56 arrive at Chamonix on 7 June 2007. **David Haydock**

▲ VFLI loco 016 (formerly SNCF BB 66614) stands at Morcenx on 12 December 2007.
Jean-Pierre Vergez-Larrouy

▼ Veolia tri-voltage electric loco E 37506 (identical to SNCF Class BB 37000) stands at Lérouville with a train for Le Boulou on 20 June 2008.   **Laurent Charlier**

▲ Colas Rail Vossloh G1206 diesels 22 and 03 head a train of empty hoppers out of Gennevilliers yard, destined for the quarry at St. Venant, on 16 September 2008. **David Haydock**

▼ An amazing sight but becoming more familiar – Euro Cargo Rail (EWS) diesel 66022 is seen at SNCF's Sotteville depot after fuelling on 7 February 2008, in the company of Fret SNCF BB 69193 and a new Class BB 60000. **Stéphane Lenglet**

▲ ETF former DB loco 211 167 (now 182 530) stands outside ETF's Montigny-Beauchamp depot on 23 March 2005.   **David Haydock**

▼ TSO former DB loco 211 359, at the time numbered V211 0762 (now 182 575), powers a track laying train at Cuperly on the LGV Est high speed line on 7 April 2005.   **David Haydock**

▲ Still in service after 76 years, former PLM shunter, once SNCF Y 6039, shunts the Glon cereal silo at Montauban-de-Bretagne on 12 February 2008. **David Haydock**

▼ 2-2-2 no. 6 "L'AIGLE" built by Stephenson of Newcastle upon Tyne in 1846 for the Compagnie Avignon-Marseille, is seen in the Cité du Train in Mulhouse on 2 July 2008. **Les Nixon**

▲ One of five operational US-built Mikados in France, 141 R 1126, leaves Capdenac on 18 August 2006 with the return of a special to Toulouse.   **Didier Delattre**

▼ Preserved electric locos CC 7107 and BB 9004 (behind), normally at the Cité du Train, were exhibited at Kinding in Germany when their 1955 record of 331 km/h was broken by ÖBB "Taurus" 1216 050 on 2 September 2006.   **Roland Beier**

2. RÉSEAU EXPRESS RÉGIONAL RER

Régie Autonome des Transports Parisiens (RATP) is the transport operator which is in charge of running buses, three tramway routes, 14 metro lines and part of the Réseau Express Régional (RER) regional express network of suburban trains in Paris. The RER network totals five lines – A to E. Operation of the RER involves both RATP and SNCF. SNCF is entirely responsible for Lines C, D and E while the two operators share operation of Lines A and B. When opened in 1969, Line A originally ran from Boissy St. Leger to St. Germain-en-Laye and was entirely operated by RATP with Type MS61 EMUs. These still operate, most having recently received a major rebuild. Line B originally ran from Châtelet to St. Rémy-les-Chevreuse and was operated by RATP Class Z 23000 EMUs which have now disappeared. Both of these lines are electrified at 1500 V DC overhead. Line B was then joined to SNCF lines from Gare du Nord and, later, Line A gained a branch to Poissy and Cergy over SNCF lines. Both service extensions required dual-voltage EMUs for operation under 25 kV AC 50 Hz. These were MI79 (MI = *Matériel Interconnexion* or interconnection stock) and MI84 stock which is included in the SNCF section as Class Z 8100. Renewal of Line A stock has now become necessary, the answer being MI2N double-deck EMUs. We include RATP EMUs for RER services here as they are not documented in any other publication. We also include RATP's small fleet of diesels for maintenance. We do not include Metro stock as it is fully documented in the excellent Paris Metro Handbook by Brian Hardy and published by Capital Transport.

ELECTRIC LOCOMOTIVES

TYPE E.4900   Bo-Bo

A class originally numbered 4901–4907. These locos are very similar looking to the Class Z 23000 EMUs used on the Sceaux line until the 1980s. 4901 has been withdrawn. Locos 4902/3/6/7, which have been modernised, are used to haul trains of components between Rueil depot on Line A and Massy depot on Line B. 4904 shunts at Rueil and 4905 at Massy.

Built: 1935/36.
Builder: CGC.
Weight: 54 tonnes.
Maximum Speed: 80 km/h light, 60 km/h with train.
Wheel Diameter: 1100 mm.

System: 1500 V DC
Power Rating: 736 kW.
Length: 12.60 metres.

Livery: Yellow/black.

| 4902 | 4903 | 4904 | 4905 | 4906 | 4907 |

DIESEL LOCOMOTIVES

TYPE C 61000   C

These shunters are the same as SNCF Class C 61000 of which 48 were once used in the Lille, Paris and Le Havre/Rouen areas, some of them with TC 61100 "calf" units doubling power. T 101 was bought direct by RATP, and the company bought another nine from SNCF in 1973/78, numbered T 104–109 and T 130–133. Only three are now left.

Built: 1946–48 (T 101 1950).
Engine: Sulzer (375 kW).
Weight: 51 tonnes.
Wheel Diameter: 1400 mm.
Livery: Dark green/yellow.

Builder: CEM.
Transmission: Electric.
Length: 9.50 m.
Maximum Speed: 60 km/h.

| T 101 RU | T 105   (C 61025)   BY | T 132   (C 61033)   MY (S) |

TYPE Y 7400   B

These shunters are the basically the same as SNCF Class Y 7400 of which almost 500 were built. They are used for shunting at their respective depots and to form works trains.

Details as SNCF Class Y 7400 except:

Built: 1969.
Livery: Orange/brown.

Builder: Moyse.

| T 102 BY | T 103 RU |

TYPE BB 63500   Bo-Bo

These locos are similar to SNCF Class BB 63500 but were bought second-hand in 1992 from the northern French coal mines (HBNPC), which also supplied the locos used by CFTA. The locos were refurbished by Fauvet-Girel in Lille but work carried out on three batches differed. T 160–163 only received a minimal overhaul and a repaint. T 165–167 were refurbished more extensively and a received a modified cab unit. Finally, T 168–170 were modernised like the previous batch but also received a turbocharger which increased their power output. RATP is considering upgrading all locos to the same standard. All can work in multiple with one another. The locos are used for works trains on the exterior sections of RER Lines A and B.

Details as SNCF Class BB 63500 except:

Built: 1959–63.
Engine: Two Deutz BF8M of 345 kW each.
Weight: 72–80 tonnes.
Livery: Orange/brown.

Maximum Speed: 100 km/h.

Length: 14.48 m.

T 160 MY	T 162 BY	T 165 MY	T 167 MY	T 169 BY	T 170 BY
T 161 BY	T 163 MY	T 166 RU	T 168 RU		

ELECTRIC MULTIPLE UNITS

TYPE MS61   3-CAR UNITS

These units are owned by RATP and operate only on Line A from Boissy-St.-Leger to St. Germain-en-Laye in trains of up to three units. Each unit is composed of an even and odd numbered Type M15000 power car and a Type B18000 central trailer (originally composite). Formations are relatively stable, but unlike MI79 and MI84 stock, can change from time to time. The units were built in five batches, with minor differences, coded A to E. Sets in the A and B batches, 15001–15124, have a different front end design to batches C to E. Most of the A/B batch are allocated to Boissy-St- Leger (BY), the depot at the eastern end of Line A whilst the later units are allocated to Rueil Malmaison (RU) on the branch from Nanterre to St.-Germain-en-Laye. The original livery was two-tone blue but sets have had a mid-life overhaul and have been repainted in Paris red, white and blue (livery I). Units are currently receiving a major rebuild with new front ends, new interiors and a revised livery. All units are equipped with the SACEM in-cab signalling system.

Built: 1966–80.
Builder–Mechanical Parts: B&L/CIMT/ANF.
Traction Motors: Four TCO (200 kW) per power car.
Formation: Bo-Bo + 2-2 + Bo-Bo.
Accommodation: –/64 (30) + –/72 (32) + –/64 (30).
Weight: 40 + 32 + 40 tonnes.

Systems: 1500 V DC overhead.
Builder–Electrical Parts : TCO/MTE.

Maximum Speed: 100 km/h.

Length: 24.555 m + 24.110 m + 24.555 m.

r = Refurbished

15007	18001	15002	r	BY	15121	18022	15020		BY	15071	18043	15028		BY
15009	18002	15012	r	BY	15087	18023	15024		BY	15001	18044	15026	r	BY
15059	18003	15120		BY	15015	18024	15050		BY	15035	18045	15006	r	BY
15011	18004	15022	r	BY	15101	18025	15116	r	BY	15053	18046	15054	r	BY
15065	18005	15070		BY	15013	18026	15086	r	BY	15041	18047	15042	r	BY
15033	18006	15078	r	BY	15085	18027	15084	r	BY	15067	18048	15066		BY
15079	18007	15080	r	BY	15093	18028	15092	r	BY	15081	18049	15058	r	BY
15103	18008	15064	r	BY	15057	18029	15048		BY	15063	18050	15052	r	BY
15039	18009	15014		BY	15017	18030	15088	r	BY	15073	18051	15102		BY
15027	18010	15032	r	BY	15045	18031	15122	r	BY	15100	18052	15023		BY
15123	18011	15104	r	BY	15111	18032	15110	r	BY	15099	18053	15008	r	BY
15029	18012	15030	r	BY	15025	18033	15098	r	BY	15229	18054	15125		RU
15089	18013	15018		BY	15047	18034	15108	r	BY	15077	18055	15082	r	BY
15097	18014	15062		BY	15083	18035	15072	r	BY	15055	18056	15034	r	BY
15105	18015	15040	r	BY	15043	18036	15044	r	BY	15021	18057	15046	r	BY
15037	18016	15038	r	BY	15019	18037	15068	r	BY	15117	18058	15118		BY
15119	18017	15076	r	BY	15091	18039	15090		BY	15107	18059	15106		BY
15075	18018	15074	r	BY	15061	18040	15060	r	BY	15113	18060	15036	r	BY
15005	18020	15112	r	BY	15003	18041	15004	r	BY	15031	18061	15124		BY
15049	18021	15056	r	BY	15051	18042	15094		BY	15115	18062	15114	r	RU

15095	18063	15096	r	RU	15177	18085	15126		RU
15185	18064	15134	r	RU	15216	18086	15175	r	RU
15143	18065	15198		RU	15212	18088	15213		RU
15191	18066	15180		RU	15182	18089	15181	r	RU
15140	18067	15139		RU	15156	18090	15155		RU
15109	18068	15127	r	RU	15158	18091	15157		RU
15138	18069			RU	15168	18092	15167	r	RU
15170	18070	15137		RU	15162	18093	15209	r	RU
15128	18071	15147	r	RU	15164	18094	15163	r	RU
15146	18072	15145		RU	15154	18095	15153		RU
15206	18073	15207		RU	15202	18096	15203	r	RU
15196	18074	15197		RU	15010	18097	15169	r	RU
15142	18075	15141		RU	15190	18098	15189		RU
15184	18076	15183	r	RU	15136	18099	15173		RU
15176	18077	15133	r	RU	15132	18100	15193		RU
15204	18078	15205		RU	15166	18101	15165		RU
15130	18079	15199	r	RU	15172	18102	15179		RU
15187	18080	15152	r	RU	15150	18103	15129		RU
15194	18081	15195		RU	15192	18104	15161		RU
15210	18082	15211		RU	15200	18105	15201		RU
15214	18083	15215	r	RU	15186	18106	15148		RU
15178	18084	15151		RU					

15227	18107	15222		RU
15188	18108	15149	r	RU
15254	18109	15245	r	RU
15242	18110	15217		RU
15225	18111	15226	r	RU
15239	18112	15228	r	RU
15252	18113	15251	r	RU
15235	18115	15236	r	RU
15250	18116	15243		RU
15233	18117	15234		RU
15159	18118	15144	r	RU
15244	18119	15221		RU
15237	18120	15238	r	RU
15241	18121	15218		RU
15247	18122	15248	r	RU
15223	18123	15224		RU
15160	18124	15131	r	RU
15253	18125	15230		RU
15249	18126	15246		RU
15220	18127	15219	r	RU
15240	18128	15135	r	RU

TYPE MI2N   5-CAR DOUBLE-DECK UNITS

These units were designed as a common project for RATP and SNCF whose units are Class Z 22500 (see SNCF section of book). The only significant differences are that RATP units have three power cars instead of two, in order to give better acceleration on RER Line A where a two-minute frequency operates in the rush-hour, and that there is stair access to the upper level from all doors in the RATP sets. RATP nickname these units "Alteo". All trains are equipped with the SACEM computer-aided driving system.

For details see SNCF Class Z 22500 except:
Total power: 3500 kW.   **Formation:** ZRB + ZB + ZB + ZB + ZRB.
Accommodation: –/104 + –/106 + –/109 + –/109 + –/104.
Weight: 288 tonnes total.

1501	2501	3501	2502	1502	BY	1545	2545	3523	2546	1546	BY
1503	2503	3502	2504	1504	BY	1547	2547	3524	2548	1548	BY
1505	2505	3503	2506	1506	BY	1549	2549	3525	2550	1550	BY
1507	2507	3504	2508	1508	BY	1551	2551	3526	2552	1552	BY
1509	2509	3505	2510	1510	BY	1553	2553	3527	2554	1554	BY
1511	2511	3506	2512	1512	BY	1555	2555	3528	2556	1556	BY
1513	2513	3507	2514	1514	BY	1557	2557	3529	2558	1558	BY
1515	2515	3508	2516	1516	BY	1559	2559	3530	2560	1560	BY
1517	2517	3509	2518	1518	BY	1561	2561	3531	2562	1562	BY
1519	2519	3510	2520	1520	BY	1563	2563	3532	2564	1564	BY
1521	2521	3511	2522	1522	BY	1565	2565	3533	2566	1566	BY
1523	2523	3512	2524	1524	BY	1567	2567	3534	2568	1568	BY
1525	2525	3513	2526	1526	BY	1569	2569	3535	2570	1570	BY
1527	2527	3514	2528	1528	BY	1571	2571	3536	2572	1572	BY
1529	2529	3515	2530	1530	BY	1573	2573	3537	2574	1574	BY
1531	2531	3516	2532	1532	BY	1575	2575	3538	2576	1576	BY
1533	2533	3517	2534	1534	BY	1577	2577	3539	2578	1578	BY
1535	2535	3518	2536	1536	BY	1579	2579	3540	2580	1580	BY
1537	2537	3519	2538	1538	BY	1581	2581	3541	2582	1582	BY
1539	2539	3520	2540	1540	BY	1583	2583	3542	2584	1584	BY
1541	2541	3521	2542	1542	BY	1585	2585	3543	2586	1586	BY
1543	2543	3522	2544	1544	BY						

3. INDEPENDENT FREIGHT OPERATORS

3.1. COLAS-RAIL

Colas is a large multinational civil engineering company based in France. The company used its Seco-Rail subsidiary to start open access freight operation in France in January 2007, hauling stone from Colas-owned quarries to various terminals, mainly in the Paris region. Seco-Rail became Colas-Rail in 2008. Initial services were from the Thouars area (with a new depot at the nearby Saint Varent quarry) and later from Anor. This should eventually total 3 million tonnes a year. The company has purchased 26 Vossloh G1206 diesel locos for this traffic. Traffic start up was slower than expected so the company hired locos to Veolia, then Railion Deutschland! Colas-Rail said originally that it would limit itself to trains from its own quarries but in 2008 started bidding for other traffic, possibly because of an over-dimensioned fleet. Colas-Rail also works open access freight in the UK.

Colas-Rail also has a branch which competes for track maintenance contracts with SNCF. See section 4.1 for details

Workshops: Les Mureaux.
Depots: Dourges, Saint Varent, Varetz.
Operator Suffix: F-COLRA

DIESEL LOCOMOTIVES

VOSSLOH TYPE G 1206   B-B

These are based at Saint Varent and mainly work stone trains from there or Anor.

Engine: Caterpillar 3512 B DI-TA-SC of 1500 kW. **Transmission:** Hydraulic. Voith L5r4zU2
Tractive Effort: 254 kN. **Wheel Diameter:** 1000 mm.
Weight: 87.3 tonnes. **Length:** 14.70 m.
Maximum Speed: 100 km/h.

1	(5001762)	14	(5001775)
2	(5001763)	15	(5001776)
3	(5001764)	16	(5001777)
4	(5001765)	17	(5001778)
5	(5001766)	18	(5001779)
6	(5001767)	19	(5001780)
7	(5001768)	20	(5001781)
8	(5001769)	21	(5001761)	92 87 0061 703-0
9	(5001770)	22	(5001810)	92 87 0061 704-8
10	(5001771)	23	(5001811)	92 87 0061 705-5
11	(5001772)	24	(5001813)	92 87 0061 706-3
12	(5001773)	25	
13	(5001774)	26	

VOSSLOH TYPE G1000   B-B

In 2008 Colas-Rail received its first Vossloh G1000 for use on lines with poor quality track.

Built: 2008
Engine: MTU 8V 4000 R41L of 1100 kW. **Transmission:** Hydraulic. Voith L4r4.
Tractive Effort: 259 kN. **Wheel Diameter:** 100 mm.
Weight: 80 tonnes. **Length:** 14.13 m.
Maximum Speed: 100 km/h.

101 (5001625)   92 87 0001 021-0 | 102   (5001826)   92 87 0001 022-8

3.2. EURO CARGO RAIL   ECR

This subsidiary of British operator English Welsh & Scottish Railway (EWS, itself taken over by Deutsche Bahn in 2007) started operations in France in May 2006 and has expanded fast. Expansion is expected to accelerate in 2008/9 during which the fleet should double.

Depot: Alizay (near Rouen).

Locos also receive light maintenance at stabling points and in customer sidings but may return to Toton in the UK for heavy work. Some work is also carried out by Alstom in Belfort.

Crew/Stabling Points: Bourg-en-Bresse, Calais Fréthun, Champigneulles (Nancy), L'Estaque (Marseille), Toulouse St. Jory.

Livery: Pale grey.

ELECTRIC LOCOMOTIVES

CLASS 186   Bo-Bo

TRAXX MS (multi-system) locomotives on order. Version DBF for operation in France, Belgium and Germany – should also be able to operate to Basel in Switzerland. The first two locos were delivered in 2008 for approval tests. The others will be delivered once approval is gained in France. Expected to take over duties such as Calais to Basel and Cerbère plus Dunkerque to Varangéville and Tavaux. We believe they are hired from Angel Trains Cargo.

Built: 2007–
Weight: 86 tonnes.
Builder: Bombardier Transportation, Kassel.
Length over Buffers: 18.80 m.
Continuous rating: 5600 kW (4000 kW at 1500 V DC)
Systems: 1500/3000 V DC, 15/25 kV AC.
Maximum Tractive Effort: 300 kN.
Maximum Speed: 140 km/h.

UIC Numbers: 91 80 6186 161-6 D-BTK upwards.

186 161	186 165	186 169	186 172	186 175	186 178
186 162	186 166	186 170	186 173	186 176	186 179
186 163	186 167	186 171	186 174	186 177	186 180
186 164	186 168				

DIESEL LOCOMOTIVES

CLASS 66   Co-Co

These 60 locos were taken from the EWS fleet of 250 Class 66 between 2005 and 2008 with a number of modifications by Toton depot for use in France including modified wheel profiles. They now operate over the whole of France. All remain in the original EWS livery.

Built: 1998–2000 by General Motors/EMD, London, Ontario, Canada (Model JT42CWR).
Engine: General Motors 12N-710G3B-EC two stroke of 2385 kW (3200 h.p.) at 904 r.p.m.
Traction Motors: General Motors D43TR.
Maximum Tractive Effort: 409 kN (92000 lbf).
Continuous Tractive Effort: 260 kN (58390 lbf) at 15.9 m.p.h.
Wheel Diameter: 1120 mm.
Length: 21.35 m.
Weight: 127 tonnes.
Maximum Speed: 120 km/h.

Locos also carry these numbers on cabside panels prefixed 92 70 00.

66010	66045	66190	66212	66224	66239
66022	66049	66191	66214	66225	66240
66026	66052	66195	66215	66226	66241
66028	66062	66202	66216	66228	66242
66029	66064	66203	66217	66229	66243
66032	66071	66205	66218	66231	66244
66033	66072	66208	66219	66237	66245
66036	66073	66209	66220	66236	66246
66038	66123	66210	66222	66235	66247
66042	66179	66211	66223	66236	66249

CLASS 77   Co-Co

An updated version of Class 66 featuring an improved cab with air conditioning – the pod sits on top of the cab roof – plus an improved engine to the latest EU emission standards. Of the 60 locos on order, by autumn 2008, 30 locos had been delivered to Tilburg works in the Netherlands and ECR hoped they would enter service before the end of the year. They will be capable of operating not only in France but also in Belgium, the Netherlands and Germany. Details as Class 66 except:

Built: 2007–.   **Builder:** EMD. Model JT42CWRM.
Engine: EMD 12N-710G3B-T2 of 2420 kW.
Traction Motors: EMD Type D43TRC.
Weight: 129.6 tonnes.
Works numbers: 20068861-001 to 070.

UIC Numbers: 92 87 0 **077 001** F-ECR upwards.

77001	77011	77021	77031	77041	77051
77002	77012	77022	77032	77042	77052
77003	77013	77023	77033	77043	77053
77004	77014	77024	77034	77044	77054
77005	77015	77025	77035	77045	77055
77006	77016	77026	77036	77046	77056
77007	77017	77027	77037	77047	77057
77008	77018	77028	77038	77048	77058
77009	77019	77029	77039	77049	77059
77010	77020	77030	77040	77050	77060

VOSSLOH TYPE G1000   B-B

For details see page 148. ECR was obliged to hire these locos for use on lines whose track is too light to take Class 66. All on hire from Angel Trains Cargo.

ECR no.	Vossloh works no.	UIC no.	Built
FB 1487	5001487	92 87 0001 001-2	2004
FB 1602	5001602	-	2006
FB 1610	5001610	92 87 0001 002-0	2006
FB 1611	5001611	92 87 0001 003-8	2006
FB 1623	5001623	92 87 0001 011-1	2008
FB 1624	5001624	92 87 0001 012-9	2008
FB 1642	5001642	92 87 0001 004-6	2007
FB 1643	5001643	92 87 0001 005-3	2007
FB 1703	5001703	92 87 0001 006-1	2007
FB 1706	5001706	92 87 0001 007-9	2007
FB 1784	5001784	92 87 0001 008-7	2007
FB 1785	5001785	92 87 0001 009-5	2007
FB 1786	5001786	92 87 0001 010-3	2007
FB 1827	5001827	92 87 0001 013-7	2008

VOSSLOH TYPE G1206   B-B

For details, see page 148. ECR was obliged to hire these locos from Angel Trains Cargo to launch services in France. The curious numbering is because ECR based them on works numbers for locos which eventually went to Veolia instead. Finished in the early ECR livery of maroon.

FB 1544	5001628	-	2005
FB 1545	5001630	-	2005
FB 1546	5001631	-	2005
FB 1547	5001516	-	2006

VOSSLOH TYPE G2000   B-B

These ten locos have been hired by ECR from Angel Trains Cargo for work in France Belgium, and the Netherlands or France/Germany, in advance of the arrival of Class 77. In the end, approval took so long that the first only started operation into Germany in summer 2008. Due to their use in Germany, they are based at Champigneulles.

Engine: Caterpillar 3516 B HD of 2240 kW.   **Transmission:** Hydraulic. Voith L620reU2.
Maximum Tractive Effort: 282 kN.   **Wheel Diameter:** 1000 mm.
Weight: 87.3 tonnes.   **Length:** 17.40 m.
Maximum Speed: 120 km/h.

ECR no.	Works no.	UIC no.	Built	Countries
-	5001632	-	2006	D/F
-	5001633	-	2006	D/F
-	5001637	-	2007	F/B/NL
-	5001640	-	2007	F/B/NL
-	5001641	-	2007	F/B/NL
-	5001667	-	2007	DF
-	5001669	-	2007	F/B/NL
-	5001670	-	2007	F/B/NL
-	5001672	-	2007	DF
-	5001735	-	2007	DF

3.3. EUROPORTE 2

This is a subsidiary of Eurotunnel set up to operate open access freight service in France and through the Channel Tunnel to the UK.

In autumn 2008, the company started to make training runs from Calais to Dourges with CB Rail locos E 37512 and E 37514 – see Veolia.

3.4. RÉGIE DÉPARTMENTALE DES TRANSPORTS DES BOUCHES-DU-RHÔNE
RDT 13

This railway operates a number of freight-only lines between Marseille and Avignon. Locos are yellow with red stripes and labelled "RDT 13" – 13 is the number of the Bouches-du-Rhône département. The company is now expanding, taking over operation on the RFF Colombiers–Cazouls line near Béziers and gaining shunting contracts around Miramas and Fos-sur-Mer. RDT 13 also runs the "Train Touristique des Alpilles" tourist service over the Arles–Fontvieille line. The company was due to buy new locos to haul 2400 tonne trains of oil in 2008. RDT 13 hauls about 1 million tonnes a year on the La Mède branch and 20 000 tonnes on the Plan d'Orgon line.

Routes:
• Pas-des-Lanciers–Bel Air-La Mède (16 km).
• Arles–Fontvieille (10 km).
• Barbantane-Rognognas–Plan d'Orgon (23 km).

Gauge: 1435 mm.
Depots: Arles, Marignane, Châteaurenard.

CLASS 50   Bo

Shunters which can operate in multiple on heavy trains. 56 was bought second-hand from CFR La Mède and 57 from Fauvet-Girel, Arras.

Built: 1958–60; 1965*; 1966 §.
Engine: Poyaud of 207 h.p.
Weight: 33–38 tonnes.

Builder: Fauvet Girel.
Transmission: Electric. CEM.
Length:

| 51 | 53 (U) | 54 | 55 | 56* | 57§ |
| 52 | | | | | |

CLASS 300   Bo

302 was second-hand from Houillères du Bassin du Nord-Pas-de-Calais.

Built: 1958/60.
Engine: Poyaud of 300 h.p.
Weight: 35 tonnes.
Maximum Speed: 35 km/h.

Builder: Fauvet Girel.
Transmission: Electric. CEM.
Length:

| 301 | 302 |

CLASS 600   B-B

Medium-sized heavy shunters.

Built:
Engine: SACM MGO V12A (441 kW)
Weight: 83 tonnes.

Builder: Fauvet-Girel.
Transmission: Electric. CEM.
Length: 12.44 m.

| 601 (ex Métaleurop no. 6) | 603 (ex Gaz de Lacq) |
| 602 (ex HBL no. 55) | |

CLASS BB 63500   Bo-Bo

These locos are all versions of SNCF Class BB 63500. Two or three Class 1200 locos in multiple are used on heavy tank trains from La Mède refinery to Pas-des-Lanciers SNCF exchange yard. Details as SNCF Class BB 63500 except:

Built: 1956 (Class 800), 1957/8 (Class 900), 1964 (701, 1201–03), 1969 (1204).
Engine: 701   Sulzer 6LDA22E of 550 kW.
              801–803   SACM MGO V12SH of 615 kW.
              901–903   SACM MGO V12SHR of 690 kW.
              1201–1205 SACM MGO V16ASHR of 900 kW.
Weight: 80 tonnes (Class 800, 900 72 tonnes).

Length: 14.68 m. (801–803, 901–903 14.75 m.)
Wheel Diameter: 1050 mm. (801–803, 901–903 1100 m)
Maximum Speed: 701 90 km/h. 800–803, 901–903 105 km/h, 1201–1204 80 km/h.
Equipped for multiple operation.

701 (ex SNCF BB 63246, ex Aciers de l'Atlantique, Tarnos)
801 (ex HBNPC 99, ex Sollac BL 2)
802 (ex CFL 853)
803 (ex CFL 855) used for spares
901 (ex CFL 910)
902 (ex CFL 909)
903 (ex CFL 911)

1201 | 1202 | 1203 | 1204
1205 (ex Sollac Metz BL 1)

CLASS 1400   Bo-Bo

Built: 1978.
Engine: SACM AGO (1030 kW).
Weight:

Builder: Moyse.
Transmission: Electric.
Length:

1401

3.5. VEOLIA TRANSPORT

Veolia Environnement, formerly part of Vivendi, is a French utilities company specialising in water, waste treatment and transport. The transport branch was formerly known as Connex. Veolia Transport was the first open access operator in France, starting up in 2005. However, the company also has a subsidiary known as CFTA which has existed since 1888. CFTA operates passenger and freight services under contract to SNCF from Carhaix and Châtillon-sur-Seine although this work is shrinking. The company also manages the Chemins de Fer de la Provence and competes for contracts to operate minor lines with a tourist interest which it markets together as Veolia Trains Touristiques. In 2008, these were:

• Chemin de Fer de La Mure
• Chemin de Fer de La Rhune

Veolia Trains Touristiques also operates a steam service from Paimpol on the former Réseau Breton each summer. Operation of the Saujon–Tremblade line as the "Train des Mouettes" was dropped in 2006.

VEOLIA CARGO

This company runs open access freight in France and across the border in conjunction with subsidiaries in Germany and the Netherlands. Veolia Cargo France started with minor contracts in the east of France and has since expanded across a wide area. The most important expansion is in intermodal traffic where the company has formed a joint venture with shipping line CMA-CGM. Many new services are expected to be launched from the ports of Le Havre and Marseille/Fos as well as Antwerpen in the future. Veolia Cargo had nine Bombardier TRAXX (Class 186) multi-voltage locomotives on order in 2008 of which some will be used in France.

Stabling/Crew Point: Dourges, Joeuf, Toulouse, Lyon.
Livery: Pale grey with red front end and lining.

ELECTRIC LOCOMOTIVES

CLASS E 37500 Bo-Bo

These are the same tri-voltage design as Fret SNCF Class BB 37000 (see for details) and can operate in France (1500 V DC/25 kV AC) and Germany (15 kV AC). The first locos were used on regular intermodal services from Marseille via Strasbourg to Ludwigshafen, Germany and Le Havre via Dourges and Metz to Mannheim, Germany. The locos have occasionally been used on German domestic freights. Locos are maintained by Train Life Services, a subsidiary of Alstom, opposite the company's plant in Belfort.

Veolia ordered 31 locos for itself but has since changed arrangements – the company often buys stock then sells it and leases it back. The situation so far is that Veolia owns 37501 to 37507/9/11/13. 37508/10/12/14 are owned by CB Rail which has hired out the last two to Europorte 2 which will use them on a new service to/from Calais. It looks like Veolia will eventually sell all to CB Rail – we will see. Locos up to E 37518 were delivered by October 2008.

Details as SNCF Class BB 37000 except:

Built: 2007–.

CB – In CB Rail plain grey livery. May be hired out to other companies.

E37501	E37509	E37517	E37525
E37502	E37510 **CB**	E37518	E37526
E37503	E37511	E37519	E37527
E37504	E37512 **CB**	E37520	E37528
E37505	E37513	E37521	E37529
E37506	E37514 **CB**	E37522	E37530
E37507	E37515	E37523	E37531
E37508	E37516	E37524	

DIESEL LOCOMOTIVES

VOSSLOH TYPE G1000 B-B

For details, see page 148.

Veolia no.	Works no.	Built	Hired from
1595	5001595	2005	ATC
1596	5001596	2005	ATC

VOSSLOH TYPE G1206 B-B

For details see page 148. Veolia owns some locos and hires others. Many locos in the fleet are registered in Germany. We have included all the locos here which have worked in France.

No.	Works no.	Built	Hired from	UIC number
1509	5001509	2006	-	
1512	5001512	2006	-	
500 1514	5001514	2006	MRCE	
-	5001573	2004	ATC	
1650	5001650	2006	MRCE	
500 1664	5001664	2006	MRCE	
-	5001722	2007	ATC	92 87 1276 003-1 D-ATLD
1725	5001725	2007	ATC	92 87 1276 004-9 D-ATLD
-	5001728	2007	-	
1729	5001729	2007	-	92 87 0061 729-5 F-VC
1732	5001732	2008	MRCE	

VOSSLOH TYPE G2000 B-B

For details, see page 150. Equipped to operate in France, Belgium and the Netherlands. Started to be used in mid 2008 on a Vitry-le-François–Antwerpen service.

1755	5001755	2007	ATC
1756	5001756	2007	ATC

CFTA

CFTA previously stood for *Société Générale de Chemins de Fer et de Transports Automobiles* and was a light railway organisation. It is now part of the Veolia group and runs services on behalf of SNCF, although increasingly the freight locos are participating in the operation of Veolia Cargo. Since the last edition of this book, CFTA has lost work on its traditional lines around Clamecy, Sézanne, Troyes and Longueville and now only operates the following:

* Paimpol–Guingamp (36 km). Guingamp–Carhaix (53 km). These lines were formerly part of the metre-gauge Réseau Breton which was converted to standard gauge in 1967, although the section from Paimpol to Guingamp had been dual gauge since 1924. CFTA works both freight and passenger.
* Villers-les-Pots–Gray–Autet (53 km). Track maintenance only.
* Brion-sur-Ource–Châtillon-sur-Seine–Nuits-sous-Ravières (45 km). Freight.

Gauge: 1435 mm.
Depots: Carhaix, Châtillon.   **Main Works:** Gray.

CFTA has made do over the years with second hand locomotives. It took delivery of a batch of surplus diesels from the Houillères du Bassin du Nord et du Pas de Calais (HBNPC – northern France coal field) and for its lines in Brittany acquired its first newly built stock for many years in the shape of three four-wheeled diesel railcars. All locos are in blue livery with red lining. CFTA has expanded into servicing industrial branches through subsidiary Socorail and has a large fleet of shunters which we cannot document here. The two Class BB 4000 GE diesels have been preserved. Whereas in the past the following locos had stable allocations, they move around far more. The majority can be found in the ports of Dunkerque, Le Havre and Marseille. Others have been on hire to RATP and ETF.

CLASS BB 4500   BB

31 locos out of fleet of 109 were purchased from HBNPC at the beginning of the 1990s. Four were cannibalised and scrapped and four more retained for spares. The other 23 were overhauled and converted at Gray from 1990 to 1995. After initial light overhauls producing Class 4500, CFTA decided to add turbochargers, increasing power, as well as equipping locos for multiple operation. BB 4500 locos have neither. Details are generally as SNCF Class BB 63500 except:

Built: 1959–63.   **Engine:** SACM MGO A (442 kW).

BB 4501	Dunkerque	BB 4503	Gray	BB 4510	Ciments Calcia,
BB 4502	-	BB 4504	Montceau-le-Mines		Couvrot

CLASS BB 4800   Bo-Bo

As Class BB 4500 but with turbochargers, pushing up power to 615 kW. Equipped for multiple operation. Purchased from HBNPC. For details see SNCF BB 63500.

Built: 1960–63.

BB 4801	Dunkerque	BB 4807	-	BB 4813	Massy (RATP)
BB 4802	Dunkerque	BB 4808	Marseille Arenc	BB 4814	Châtillon
BB 4803	Le Havre	BB 4809	Le Havre	BB 4815	Châtillon
BB 4804	Gray	BB 4810	Châtillon	BB 4816	Châtillon
BB 4805	Gray	BB 4811	Carhaix	BB 4817	Carhaix
BB 4806	Richwiller	BB 4812	-	BB 4818	Le Havre

DIESEL MULTIPLE UNITS

CLASS X 97150   XBD

France's first one-person operated railcars for Guingamp–Carhaix and Guingamp–Paimpol. Known as type "A2E" (*Autorail à 2 essieux*). These are now out of use and SNCF Class X 73500 has taken over. CFTA has also used old SNCF railcars in the past but this has ceased.

Built: 1990.   **Builder:** Soulé.
Engine: Cummins LTA10R (210 kW).   **Transmission:** Hydraulic. Voith E15 D501U.
Accommodation: –/38 1T.
Weight: 26.5 tonnes.   **Length:** 15.57 m.
Wheel Arrangement: A-A.   **Maximum Speed.:** 90 km/h.

X 97151 (U)	X 97152 (U)	X 97153 (U)

3.6. VOIES FERRÉES LOCALES ET INDUSTRIELLES   VFLI

VFLI is a wholly-owned subsidiary of Fret SNCF founded in 1997 to manage local freight lines and industrial branches taking over the Voies Ferrées des Landes (VFL) and the MDPA potash mine network near Mulhouse.

In 2000, VFLI formed a joint venture with CFD Industrie (which at this point ceased to operate trains, now concentrating on building narrow gauge stock at the former Soulé plant in Bagnères de Bigorre). The joint venture called Voies Ferrées du Morvan (VFM) was formed to operate the 87 km Avallon–Autun line. This led to the end of British Class 20s being used there. It also resulted in the takeover of the CFD workshops at Montmirail and Noyon (formerly Desbrugères).

In 2001, VFLI took over the 210 km HBL coal mine network. The company started to refurbish and rebuild locomotives, but this led to losses and VFLI is now concentrating on operations.

During work on the LGV Est, VFLI founded subsidiary Fertis to supply traction for tracklaying work and hired Class 56 and 58 from EWS as well as using its own Class BB 62400. Fertis has now been wound up. VFLI created subsidiary Gemafer in 2003 to manage the loco fleet.

In 2006, VFLI took over operations in the Clamecy area from CFTA.

On 3 October 2007, VFLI obtained its own operating licence and safety certificate for operations on the RFF national rail network and started to operate Carling–Dillingen and Corbehem–Le Havre services. The company plans to expand main line services with further Type G1206 diesels and is to obtain electric locos. VFLI also hires Fret SNCF locos as required. VFLI is now rationalising its fleet and will sell or scrap most older locos.

Depots: Autun, Clamecy, Morcenx, Richwiller.
Works: Montmirail, Noyon, Petite Rosselle.

HOUILLÈRES DU BASSIN DE LORRAINE   HBL

HBL is the network of railways formerly serving the coal mines in the Lorraine area of north-east France. The 210 km network consists of a 50 km double track main line parallelling the electrified SNCF line from Creutzwald to Béning and Béning to Forbach, with branches serving factories. The last coal mines have now closed but the railway still moves imported coal from Creutzwald to the coking plant at Carling and returns with coke. Although there are three different loco types, all have the same power unit and can be used in multiple with each other. Livery for all locos was originally dark green.

Depots: La Houve, Carling, Merlebach, Petite Rosselle.

MINES DOMINIALES DE POTASSE D'ALSACE   MDPA

VFLI has taken over rail operations for this company which had potash mines at Richwiller, Wittelsheim and Staffelden near Mulhouse in eastern France, exchanging with SNCF at Richwiller. The mines closed in 2002.

VOIES FERRÉES DES LANDES   VFL

This railway operated freight-only branches off the SNCF Bordeaux–Dax line. Several were closed and VFL took over wagonload services around Morcenx, from Mont-de-Marsan to Roquefort and Hagetmau, on the main line to Labouheyre and shunting at Artix.

• Ychoux–Lipostey Zone Industrielle (2 km).
• Laluque–Tartas (14 km).

Depot: Morcenx.

VOIES FERRÉES DU MORVAN   VFM

In 2000, VFLI took over the Avallon–Autun line (87 km), previously operated by CFD in a deal which saw VFLI take a 65% share in the latter. CFD was what remains of a much larger operator of regional light railways. CFD acquired four British Rail Class 20 diesels in 1993 for freight services on this line. All but 2004 were withdrawn in 2002.

Depot: Autun.

BB 01–16 (HBL)   Bo-Bo

These locos are basically the same as ex NS Class 2400 which became SNCF Class 62400. BB 14–16 are equipped with remote-control equipment for use at the washing plant at Freyming, signalled by the suffix T. 12 never existed.

Built: 1955–63.
Engine: SACM MGO V 12 A (441 kW).
Weight: 70 tonnes.
Wheel Diameter: 1000 mm.

Builder: Alsthom.
Transmission: Electric.
Length: 12.518 m.
Maximum Speed: 50 km/h.

01	04	07	10	13	15 T
02	05	08	11	14 T	16 T
03	06	09			

BB 20–35 (HBL)   B-B

These locos have monomotor bogies with chain drive to the axles giving them a characteristic noise. The first two locos have a different gear ratio giving them a lower maximum speed.

Built: 1965–66.
Engine: SACM MGO V 12 A (441 kW).
Weight: 83 tonnes.
Wheel Diameter: 1000 mm.

Builder: Fauvet Girel.
Transmission: Electric. CEM.
Length: 12.44 m.
Maximum Speed: 42 km/h (* 35 km/h).

20	23	26	29	32	34
21	24	27	30	33	35
22	25	28	31		

BB 40–51 (HBL)   Bo-Bo

These locos are almost identical to SNCF Class BB 63500 and only arrived on the HBL network in 1969/70 after becoming surplus in the Nord-Pas-de-Calais area. Being renumbered as Class BB 300.

Built: 1958–60.
Engine: SACM MGO V 12 A (441 kW).
Weight: 72 tonnes (* 82 tonnes).
Wheel Diameter: 1050 mm.
m equipped for multiple working operation.

Builder: Brissonneau & Lotz.
Transmission: Electric.
Length: 14.68 m.
Maximum Speed: 50 km/h.

318 (40)	42	44 m	310 (46)	315 (48)	314 (50)
41 *	43 m	304 (45) m	47	312 (49)	51

M 70–76 (HBL)   Bo

These shunters consist of two batches with different engines – 70–72 were originally numbered 3–5 whilst 73-76 were originally 1009–1013. 73 is normally based at Merlebach shunting the wagon works and in reserve for the passenger train to Merlebach Nord. Others are based at Carling Poste 12.

Built: 1958–62.
Engine: Moyse V8B (210 kW) or Daimler-Benz OM 442LA (210 kW).
Transmission: Electric.
Weight: 35 tonnes.

Builder: Moyse.
Maximum Speed: 32 km/h.
Length: 7.28 m.

70	72	73	74	75	76
71					

81/82 (HBL)   Bo+Bo

These are double units consisting of a shunter plus cabless "mule". The locos were originally numbered Y 50 + Y 50T and Y 51 + Y 51T. Unlike the rest of the fleet, the locos are in yellow livery. They are used at the VAC and at Carling coking plant.

Built: 19 .
Engine: Berliet.

Builder: Moyse.
Transmission: Electric.

BNY 81 + BNT 81	BNY 82 + BNT 82

CLASS Y 7100   B

Ex SNCF. See page 82 for details.

Y 7172	Y 7200	Y 7214	Y 7245

CLASS Y 7400   B

Y 01 and Y 02 were purchased in 1974 from CFD, built 1967 by De Dietrich, otherwise as SNCF Class Y 7400. Other locos are ex SNCF. See page 82 for details.

088 (Y 01)	Laluque	Y 7474
089 (Y 02)	Facture	Y 7684

CLASS MJ   B

These shunters were originally delivered by CMI of Belgium to Danish Railways (DSB) but were refused and returned to the builder as they did not meet specifications. CMI worked to improve the locos, and has hired all of the locos out to Luxembourg Railways, French or Belgian industry. The two locos 601 and 602 in "various shunters" are a version of this design, with an additional, central axle.

Built: 1993–96.
Engine: Caterpillar 3408 BTA of 386 kW.
Weight: 40 tonnes.
Length over Buffers: 8.90 m.
Maximum Speed: 60 km/h.

Builder: Cockerill Mechanical Industrie (CMI).
Transmission: Hydrostatic.
Maximum Tractive Effort: 120 kN.
Wheel Diameter: 950 mm.

511	514

CLASS BB 61000/VOSSLOH G1206   B-B

Vossloh Type G1206 diesel locos owned by Angel Trains Cargo. See SNCF Class BB 61000 for details. BB 61014 to 61023 were hired by Fret SNCF and used in the Strasbourg area then taken over by VFLI in 2007/8. VFLI has now started to hire more of the type.

61014	61016	61018	61020	61022
61015	61017	61019	61021	61023

Vossloh Works no.	Built	Hired from
5001683	2008	ATC
5001814	2008	ATC
5001818	2008	ATC
5001821	2008	ATC

CLASS BB 62400   Bo-Bo

In 1990 SNCF bought 44 Class 2400 diesel locos from Netherlands Railways (NS) for tracklaying work on the LGV Nord Europe line. They were later used on the LGV Jonction Paris avoiding line then reactivated for the LGV Méditerranée in 1999. The last four digits of the number are the former NS number. A further "6" was added to the beginning of the number to signify SNCF's infrastructure activity. After 2001, VFLI took over most of the fleet and refurbished 12 locos for further use. These are in VFLI livery and were only officially struck off SNCF lists at the end of 2007. They are now used on the HBL network or hired out.

Built: 1954–57.
Engine: SACM MGO V12A SHR (625 kW).
Transmission: Electric. Four Alsthom TA637 traction motors.
Heating: None.
Maximum Tractive Effort: 161 kN.
Wheel Diameter: 1000 mm.

Builder: Alsthom.

Weight: 60 tonnes.
Length: 12.52 m.
Maximum Speed: 80 km/h.

662403	662413	662418	662429	662432	662502
662412	662414	662424	662430	662453	662513

CLASSES BB 63000 & BB 63500

Bo-Bo

Most purchased from SNCF and many still carry their old numbers. VFLI is rebuilding these plus the HBL B&L locos at Montmirail and renumbering them as Class BB 300 or BB 400.

For details see SNCF Classes BB 63000 & BB 63500.

Former No.	No. VFLI	Location
SNCF BB 63068	-	For spares, Montmirail
SNCF BB 63085	306 (048)	Freyming
SNCF BB 63140	054	-
SNCF BB 63142	-	Hayange
SNCF BB 63143	-	Volvic ("Evolys" prototype)
SNCF BB 63145	049	-
SNCF BB 63152	-	For spares, Montmirail
SNCF BB 63156	-	For spares, Montmirail
SNCF BB 63157	-	-
SNCF BB 63167	313 (056)	-
SNCF BB 63168	308 (050)	Autun
SNCF BB 63170	-	For spares, Montmirail
SNCF BB 63179	-	-
SNCF BB 63182	307 (057)	-
SNCF BB 63187	-	For spares, Montmirail
SNCF BB 63188	321 (058)	-
SNCF BB 63197	-	For spares, Montmirail
SNCF BB 63195	-	Richwiller? ex MDPA
SNCF BB 63198	305 (059)	-
SNCF BB 63205	322 (060)	-
SNCF BB 63207	-	For spares, Montmirail
SNCF BB 63209	403 (061)	Lacq
SNCF BB 63217	-	For spares, Montmirail
SNCF BB 63228	-	For spares, Montmirail
SNCF BB 63230	-	ASUEPA, Artix
SNCF BB 63231	-	-
SNCF BB 63232	-	For spares, Montmirail
SNCF BB 63233	051	-
SNCF BB 63237	063	Ugine
SNCF BB 63239	052	La Seyne
SNCF BB 63243	-	For spares, Montmirail
SNCF BB 63244	309 (064)	-
SNCF BB 63249	402 (065)	-
SNCF BB 63250	401 (066)	-
SNCF BB 63540	033	Artix
SNCF BB 63583	-	-
SNCF BB 63622	317 (034)	Freyming
SNCF BB 63664	319 (067)	
SNCF BB 63717	302 (068)	
SNCF BB 63726	-	Hayange
SNCF BB 63735	-	Hayange
SNCF BB 63745	-	-
SNCF BB 63749	-	-
SNCF BB 63795	301 (035)	Renault, Corbehem.
SNCF BB 63921	-	Laluque
SNCF BB 64028	053	Morcenx
SNCF BB 64036	-	Artix
HBNPC ?	311 (042)	Freyming
HBNPC ?	-	Port E. Herriot, Lyon.
MDPA 1	-	Richwiller
MDPA 2	-	Richwiller
MDPA 3	-	Richwiller
MDPA 4	-	For spares, Montmirail
MDPA 5	-	Richwiller
MDPA 6	-	Richwiller
MDPA 7	-	Richwiller
MDPA 8	-	Staffelden (ex HBNPC 90)

CLASS BB 66000   Bo-Bo

Purchased from SNCF. Used from Morcenx, Clamecy and Autun depots.

66013	66050	66072	66097	66122	66156
66046 (U)	66065	66092	66104	66153	66163

CLASS BB 66600   Bo-Bo

These locos were acquired from SNCF having operated from Nîmes depot for many years and finally withdrawn in 1998. Locos BB 66606, 66608, 66610 and 66611 are owned by private track maintenance companies Meccoli and Vecchietti. The latter were rebuilt from SNCF Class BB 66000 with a more powerful SEMT 12PA4 engine of 1325 kW. VFM re-engined its locos with MTU engines and originally numbered them 601 to 603. Details basically as BB 66000 except for this. They have now returned to Morcenx.

Built 1960–62. Details as SNCF Class BB 66000 except for the original SEMT 12PA4 engine, now replaced in these locos by MTU 12V 4000 R40 power units of 1500 kW.

661 (016) (BB 66614) | 602 (017) (BB 66615) | 603 (018)   (BB 66616)

CLASS BB 71000 (VFL)   BB

Purchased from SNCF in 1988/9. Both were stored in Laluque in 2008.
Built: 1965–6.   **Builder:** Fives-Lille/CFD.
Engine: Poyaud V12 (615 kW).   **Transmission:** Mechanical.
Weight: 55 tonnes.   **Length:** 11.85 m.
Wheel Diameter: 860 mm.   **Maximum Speed:** 80 km/h.

036   (71003) | 037   (71011) |

VARIOUS SHUNTERS

VFLI No.	Builder	Type	Works no.	Built	Location
023	Fauvet Girel	-	-	-	Lacq
029	Moyse	4048 Bo-Bo	-	1979	Hayange
033	Moyse	-	-	-	Rhodia, St Fons
042	SACM Graff.	-	-	-	Nexan, Chauny
074	Moyse	BNC B	40	1958	Hayange
081	Moyse	-	-	-	Montmirail (S)
082	Moyse	-	-	-	Pardies
086	Decauville	TE B	302	1969	Morcenx
-	Moyse	BNC B	5	1957	Lacq (ex SNEA)
601	CMI	C	-	-	-
602	CMI	C	-	-	-

4. PRIVATE TRACK MAINTENANCE COMPANIES

In France, three major and several minor companies share contracts for track laying and renewal. Each has its own fleet of mainly second-hand locos to haul trains. Although independent, the companies work together on large contracts. Between them, the companies own around 120 former DB Class 211 and 212 (V100) locos! The locos can be found anywhere track work is taking place in France and even in other countries where the companies win contracts.

Since the last edition of this book, Cogifer and Drouard have merged to become ETF. SECO DG became Seco-Rail, which started shunting and open access freight activities then changed its name to Colas-Rail. Several small new companies have started up, but again often work with the other companies.

Many of the former DB Class 211, 212, 215 and 216 locos were imported and overhauled by Sifel at Mitry-Mory north of Paris. The company is owned by TSO.

Locos in this section have carried several numbers. SNCF has changed its approval numbers twice and the locos are all now receiving long UIC style numbers. Many locos only have very small numbers on them so the observer has to be close up to identify them. Some companies apply larger numbers in varied styles. Many of these are the new 182 500 number but others may be a mixture. For example, former DB loco 215-089, whose UIC number is 99 87 9182 504-0, carries the number V215-504. In order to identify a former DB V100 quickly, we have listed them in numerical order at the end of this section.

4.1. COLAS-RAIL

Colas-Rail was formerly known as Seco-Rail (see also section 3.1) having developed over half a century. SECO (*Société d'Étude et de Construction d'Outillage*) was created in 1931 to build and operate a new type of fast deballasting machine. The company was purchased by Desquenne et Giral in 1975 then, after several other changes, was bought by Colas in 2000. The company has existed for many years to carry out track renewal work subcontracted by SNCF, for which it put together a fleet of mainly second-hand locomotives, most of which are ex DB Class 211 and 212. The company took over smaller track maintenance company Vecchietti, based at Varetz, near Tours, in 2006.

In 2005, the company won a contract to shunt a new intermodal terminal at Dourges, south of Lille. The locos there and with Vecchietti are not integrated into the overall fleet.

CLASS 131   B

Only used for shunting at Les Mureaux depot. 131.01 (works no. 79) was scrapped.

Built: 1967.   **Builder:** Decauville. Type TE 4401. Works nos. 80.

L 131.02

CLASS 135   B-B

This loco has chain transmission which limits its speed, so it is no long allowed on the main line. Only used to shunt at Les Mureaux depot. Similar to VFLI (ex HBL) 21–35. 135.01 and 03 have been scrapped.

Built: 1970.   **Maximum Speed:** 35 km/h
Builder: Fauvet-Girel. Type BB 2800. Works no. 1058

L135.02

CLASS 136   Bo-Bo

A loco known as "Le Teckel" (dachshund) as it has a cut-down body to allow gantry cranes to pass over it during track laying. Only used on new line construction.

Built: 1977.   **Builder:** MTE. Type 1000 NV 84. Works no. 6050-063.

99 87 9 582 501-2 (ex L136-01)

CLASS BB 63500 Bo-Bo

Details as SNCF Class BB 63500. 132.02 has been scrapped. Original numbers are not known. Desquenne et Giral acquired HBNPC Centre no. 41 in 1970, Centre 36 in 1972, and Auchel-Bruay 27 in 1974. Colas-Rail also uses this type for shunting at Dourges and Anor having acquired the last HBNPC locos from Oignies and Drocourt.

UIC No.	Built	Old SECO number	Origin
99 87 9 481 507-1	1960	132.03	
99 87 9 481 508-9	1960	132.04	
99 87 9 481 509-7	1962	132.01	
26	1961	-	Cokes de Drocourt no. 26
27	1961	-	Agglonord no. 27
40	1963	-	Agglonord no. 40
45	1961	-	Cokes de Drocourt no. 45
56	1959	-	Cokes de Drocourt no. 56

CLASS CC 65500 Co-Co

Still used on main line renewal contracts. Equipped with TVM 430 cab signalling.

Built: 1955–59.   **Builders:** CAFL/CEM.
Engine: Sulzer 12LDA28 (1470 kW).
Transmission: Electric. Six CEM GDTM 532 traction motors.
Heating: None.   **Weight:** 123 tonnes.
Maximum Tractive Effort: 359 kN.   **Length:** 19.42 m.
Wheel Diameter.: 1200 mm.   **Maximum Speed:** 80 km/h.

99 87 9 481 510-5   (138.01)   SNCF CC 65507

CLASSES 211 & 212 B-B

Colas-Rail has 37 of these locos. See end of this section for details. Seco-Rail's predecessors also had 211 154, 179 and 186 but scrapped them after removing spares.

4.2. DIJONNAISE DE VOIES FERRÉES DVF

A small company located at Chevigny-Saint-Sauveur near Dijon with just one former DB Class 211 (ex ÖBB Class 2048) loco. This can be found in the list at the end of this section.

4.3. E-GÉNIE

A small company located at St. Sulpice (Tarn) near Toulouse. The loco was formerly with TSO. In the past, the company has hired another loco and may expand.

CFD TYPE BB 1540 H B-B

A loco formerly with TSO which sold this plus sister 1512 to dealer Layritz in Germany in 1999 who sold it to the Czech Republic.

Built: 1979. Works no. 1511   **Builder**: CFD.
Power: 1540 h.p.   **Weight**: 80 tonnes.

99 87 9 182 630-3

4.4. EUROVIA TRAVAUX FERROVIAIRES
ETF

This company was formed by the merger of COGIFER, Dehé and Drouard and is now a subsidiary of Eurovia, which in turn is a subsidiary of the French construction group Vinci, having been recently sold by Vossloh Infrastructure Services.

Workshops: Montigny-Beauchamp.

CLASS BB 63500   Bo-Bo

Details basically as SNCF Class BB 63500. All formerly with COGIFER.

ETF no.	Built	UIC number	Origin
-	1962	-	HBNPC Valenciennes no. 30
52002	1959	99 87 9481 505-5	HBNPC Auchel-Bruay no. 23. CAT engine.
52027	1963	99 87 9481 504-8	HBNPC Lens no. 16
52028	1962	99 87 9481 506-3	HBNPC Lens-Lièvin-Béthune no. 27

CLASS CC 65500   Co-Co

Details as Colas-Rail Class CC 65500.

52032	1956	99 87 9481 513-9	SNCF CC 65505
52029	1956	99 87 9481 514-9	SNCF CC 65510

CLASS BB 66600   Bo-Bo

Ex SNCF locos derived from Class BB 66000. See for details.

52003	1962	99 87 9181 513-2	SNCF BB 66691, Dehé 269.
52004	1962	99 87 9181 514-0	SNCF BB 66692, Dehé 270.

CLASS 211 & 212   B-B

ETF has a fleet of 25 of these locos. For details and numbering see end of this section. The two locos at the end of the list, numbered differently are special cut-down version which cannot run independently on the main line.

VOSSLOH TYPE G 1206   B-B

These were bought new by ETF while the company also hires other locos of the type as required. See Colas-Rail for details.

Works No.	Built	UIC number
5001497	2004	99 87 9181 507-1
5001498	2004	99 87 9181 502-5
5001546	2005	99 87 9181 503-3
5001547	2005	99 87 9181 504-1

4.5. FOURCHARD ET RENARD

A small company with offices in Paris and Bar-le-Duc but no depot, with two Class 212 – see list at end of this section. The company has a subsidiary known as Société de Travaux Ferroviaires in Metz but with no rolling stock.

4.6. FRASCA

A subsidiary of TSO, the only Class 211 locomotive (see end of this section) being in TSO yellow livery.

4.7. GENIFER

Not actually a track maintenance company but a small leasing company with five Class 211/212s. See list at end of this section.

4.8. MECCOLI

One of the bigger small companies, Meccoli has its depot near St. Pierre-des-Corps yard.

CLASS BB 66600   Bo-Bo

Ex SNCF. See VFLI for details. Engine type unknown.

Meccoli No.	Built	UIC no.	Origin
"Karine"	1962	99 87 91 81 515-7	SNCF BB 66610
"Nicolas"	1962	99 87 91 81 516-5	SNCF BB 66611

CLASSES 211 & 212   B-B

The company has 11 of these locos – see list at the end of this section. Has recently acquired 212 234 and 212 289 which had yet to receive UIC numbers.

CLASS Y 6200   B

Former SNCF locomotive. Built by La Lilloise in 1949. See page 89 for technical details.

SNCF approval No.	Origin
AT2 TR 038	SNCF Y 6234

4.9. OLICHON

A subsidiary of TSO in Lorient which bought its first two Class 211 locomotives in 2008, one of which is the list at the end of this section.

4.10. PICHENOT-BOUILLÉ

A small company based at Trappes, west of Paris.

CLASS BB 66600   Bo-Bo

Ex SNCF. See VFLI for details. Engine type unknown.

Built	UIC No.	Origin
1962	99 87 9181 517-3	SNCF BB 66612

CLASS 212   B-B

The company has two of this class – see list at end of this section.

4.11. TOPRAIL

A subsidiary of TSO with one Class 211 – see list at end of this section.

4.12. TRAVAUX DU SUD EST   TSO

One of the three large companies with its workshops at Chelles, south of Vaires yard east of Paris. The company has three subsidiaries with small numbers of locos and owns the company Sifel, with workshops at Mitry-Mory and Mézy-Moulins where locomotives are overhauled, re-engined and rebuilt for TSO itself and other customers. TSO also has a dozen shunters of nine types. For space reasons these are not included.

CLASS CC 65500   Co-Co

Ex SNCF locos. See Colas-Rail for details.

UIC No.	Built	Origin
99 87 9481 512-1	1956	SNCF CC 65512
99 98 9481 511-3	1956	SNCF CC 65522

CLASS 211 & 212   B-B

TSO has a fleet of 32 of these former DB locos – see list at end of this section.

CLASS 215   B-B

A former DB locomotive.
Built: 1971 for DB.
Builder: MaK.
Engine: Caterpillar 3516 (originally MAN 12 V 956 TB).
Power: 1500 kW.
Transmission: Hydraulic. MTU K252 SU.
Maximum Tractive Effort: 245 kN.   **Weight:** 80 tonnes
Driving Wheel Diameter: 1000 mm.   **Length over Buffers:** 16.40 m.
Maximum Speed: 140 km/h

99 87 9182 504-0	1971	DB 215 089

CLASS 216   B-B

More former DB locomotives.

Built: 1969 for DB.
Builder: Henschel.
Engine: Caterpillar 3516 (originally MTU MD 16V 538 TB10).
Power: 1500 kW.
Transmission: Hydraulic. Voith L218 rs.
Maximum Tractive Effort: 245 kN.   **Weight:** 77 tonnes.
Driving Wheel Dia: 1000 mm.   **Length over Buffers:** 16.00 m.
Maximum Speed: 120 km/h.

99 87 9182 608-9	1969	DB 216 214
99 87 9182 609-7	1969	DB 216 213

VOSSLOH TYPE G1206   B-B

TSO's most recent locos. Equipped with TVM 430 cab signalling for use on high speed lines. See page 148 for details.

UIC No.	Built	Vossloh works no.
99 87 0061 707-1	2008	5001816
99 87 0061 708-9	2008	5001817

4.13. VECCHIETTI

This company is now owned by Colas-Rail but its fleet is separate for now. The depot is next to St. Pierre-des-Corps (Tours) yard.

CLASS Y 51200

An ex SNCF shunter.

UIC No.	Built	Origin	Notes
-	SNCF Y 51228		

CLASS BB 66600   Bo-Bo

Ex SNCF. See VFLI for details.

99 87 9 181 518-1	1962	SNCF BB 66608	"Boxer"
99 87 9 181 519-9	1962	SNCF BB 66606	"Isabelle"

CLASSES 211 & 212   B-B

Vecchietti has ten of these ex DB locos. See list at end of section for details.

CLASS 211 & 212   B-B

Around 80 Class 211 and 40 Class 212 have been purchased by French track maintenance companies, the most important now being ETF, Colas-Rail and TSO. These locos have been overhauled several times in France and most now have Caterpillar engines. Colas-Rail locos are being re-engined with MTU 8V 4000 units at the rate of three per year. The locos have carried several different numbers. These cannot all be indicated in the book. Readers are recommended the website www.V100.de which gives full details. Below is the complete list of V100 locos in France in order of their UIC number. Missing numbers 182 504, 564, 608, 609 are allocated to other loco types.

Built: 1958–63 Class 211; 1962–65 Class 212 for DB.
Builder: MaK/Jung/Deutz/Henschel/Krauss-Maffei/Esslingen.
Original Engine: Class 211 MTU MD 12V538 TA, MB 12V493 TZ or MB 12V652 TZ.
Class 212 MTU MB 12V652 TA or MAN V6 V 18/21 TL.
Power: Class 211 820 kW; Class 212 1005 kW.
Transmission: Hydraulic. Voith L216 rs.
Maximum Tractive Effort: 183 kN.   **Weight:** 62 tonnes.
Driving Wheel Diameter: 950 mm.   **Maximum Speed:** 100 km/h.
Length over Buffers: Class 211 12.10; Class 212 12.30 m.

C Caterpillar 3512 DITA (some CAT 3508) engine.
D Deutz engine.
M MTU 8V 4000 R41engine.
T Equipped with TVM 430.

99 87 9	DB number	Operator	Other number
182 501-6	211 192	Vecchietti	
182 502-4	212 068	Pichenot	
182 503-2	212 125	Vecchietti	
182 505-7	211 151 C	TSO	
182 506-5	211 096 C	TSO	
182 507-	211 188 C	TSO	
182 508-1	212 126	Vecchietti	
182 509-9	212 258	Vecchietti	

182 510-7	212 276	Meccoli	
182 511-5	211 272	Dijonnaise	
182 512-3	211 164 C	ETF	
182 513-1	211 157 C	ETF	
182 514-9	211 187 C	ETF	
182 515-6	211 299 C	ETF	
182 516-4	211 175 C	ETF	
182 517-4	211 361 C	ETF	
182 518-0	211 081 C	ETF	
182 519-8	211 335 C	ETF	
182 520-6	211 115 C	ETF	
182 521-4	211 246 C	ETF	
182 522-2	211 127 C	ETF	
182 523-0	211 285 C	ETF	
182 524-8	211 236 C	ETF	
182 525-5	211 136 C	ETF	
182 526-3	211 188 C	ETF	
182 527-1	211 069 C	ETF	
182 528-9	211 139 C	ETF	
182 529-7	211 193 C	ETF	
182 530-5	211 167 C	ETF	
182 531-3	211 327 C	ETF	
182 532-1	211 174 C	Frasca	
182 533-9	211 010	Genifer	
182 534-7	211 128	Meccoli	
182 535-4	211 033	Colas	133.17
182 536-2	211 185	Colas	133.10
182 537-0	211 245	Colas	133.11
182 538-8	211 144	Colas	133.06
182 539-6	211 034 M	Colas	133.18
182 540-4	211 234 M	Colas	133.05
182 541-2	211 156	Colas	133.07
182 542-0	211 152	Colas	133.08
182 543-8	211 111 M	Colas	133.03
182 544-6	211 113 M	Colas	133.13
182 545-3	211 131 M	Colas	133.16
182 546-1	211 158	Colas	133.14
182 547-9	211 137 M	Colas	133.15
182 548-7	211 114 M	Colas	133.04
182 549-5	211 238 M	Colas	133.01
182 550-3	211 055 M	Colas	133.19
182 551-1	211 058	Colas	133.20
182 552-9	211 132	Toprail	
182 553-7	211 180 C	TSO	
182 554-5	211 149 C	TSO	
182 555-2	211 147 C	TSO	
182 556-0	212 137 C	TSO	
182 557-8	211 173 C	TSO	
182 558-6	211 264 C	TSO	
182 559-4	211 322 C	TSO	
182 560-2	211 328 C	TSO	
182 561-0	211 310 C	TSO	
182 562-8	211 320 C	TSO	
182 563-6	211 183 C	TSO	
182 565-1	212 305	Genifer	
182 566-9	211 197 C	TSO	
182 567-7	211 280 C	TSO	
182 568-5	211 087 C	TSO	
182 569-3	211 090 C	TSO	
182 570-1	211 102 C	TSO	
182 571-9	211 289 D	TSO	
182 572-7	211 168 C	TSO	
182 573-5	211 221 C	TSO	
182 574-3	211 269 C	TSO	

182 575-0	211 359 C	TSO	
186 576-6	211 191 C	TSO	
182 577-6	212 173 M	Colas	133.29
182 578-4	211 128	Vecchietti	
182 579-2	211 117	Vecchietti	
182 580-0	212 219 C	ETF	
182 581-8	211 318 C	ETF	
182 582-6	212 344	Fourchard	
182 583-4	212 027	Fourchard	
182 584-2	211 329 C	TSO	
182 585-9	212 282	Genifer	
182 586-7	212 221	Genifer	
182 587-5	212 154	Meccoli	
182 588-3	212 170	Meccoli	
182 589-1	212 177	Meccoli	
182 590-9	212 266 T	Colas	133.32
182 591-7	212 380	Meccoli	
182 592-5	211 232	Meccoli	
182 593-3	212 360	Pichenot	
182 594-1	212 373	Colas	133.23
182 595-8	212 061	Colas	133.25
182 596-6	212 072	Colas	133.21
182 597-4	212 099 T	Colas	133.22
182 598-2	212 319	Colas	133.35
182 599-0	212 304	Colas	133.30
182 600-6	212 262	Meccoli	
182 601-4	212 056	Colas	133.28
182 602-2	212 214	Vecchietti	
182 603-0	212 375	Meccoli	
182 604-8	212 070	Vecchietti	
182 605-5	212 088	Vecchietti	
182 606-3	212 014 C	TSO	
182 607-1	212 117 C	TSO	
182 610-5	212 179 C	TSO	
182 611-3	211 230 C	TSO	
182 612-1	212 025	Colas	133.24
182 613-9	212 073 M	Colas	133.27
182 614-7	212 038 M	Colas	133.26
182 615-4	212 253 M T	Colas	133.36
182 616-2	212 328	Colas	133.34
182 617-0	212 292	Colas	133.31
182 618-8	212 255	Colas	133.33
182 619-6	212 037	Meccoli	
182 620-4	212 296	Meccoli	
182 621-2	211 122 C	ETF	
182 622-0	212 105	Genifer	
182 623-8	211 350	Olichon	
182 624-6	211 047 C	TSO	
384 501-2	211 106	ETF	
384 502-0	211 226	ETF	
-	212 234	Meccoli	
-	212 289	Meccoli	

5. NARROW GAUGE LINES
5.1. SNCF-OPERATED LINES

There are three metre gauge lines in France operated by the SNCF, plus the Chemins de Fer de la Corse (Corsica) which is now run by the SNCF.

5.1.1. SNCF LIGNE DE CERDAGNE (LE PETIT TRAIN JAUNE)

This line opened in sections from 1910 to 1927 by the Chemin de Fer du Midi and was electrified from the beginning. Running from Villefranche-de-Conflent to La Tour-de-Carol, a distance of 62 km, it traverses mountain scenery with extremely sharp curves and steep gradients and several spectacular bridges. The line was under threat of closure for several years and freight traffic ceased in 1974. However efforts to promote the tourist potential of the line seem to have been successful and the line is now under the authority of the Languedoc-Roussillon region. All the old stock was refurbished in 1962–8 and painted in the then current red and yellow railcar livery. Commencing in 1983 the stock underwent further refurbishment and painting in a mainly yellow livery. The depot is at Villefranche-de-Conflent, although stock is nominally allocated to Béziers where major overhauls are carried out. Maximum speed on the line is limited to 50 km/h.

System: 850 V DC third rail.
Depot: Villefranche–Vernet-les-Bains

ZBD 101–118   POWER CARS

Formerly Midi E.ABDe 2–4/6–9/11/13/15–18. Cars marked * were built as trailers but were converted to motor cars in 1912/21. They were originally Midi ABDe 14/11/13/5–8 respectively. Z 105 was formerly Z 114, replacing the previous Z 105 damaged in an accident.

Built: 1908–09.
Builder–Mechanical Parts: Carde.
Traction Motors: Four TH 540 of 66 kW each.
Weight: 30 tonnes.
Wheel Arrangement: Bo-Bo.

Builder–Electrical Parts: Thomson-Houston.
Accommodation: –/40.
Length: 14.904 (14.384*) m.
Maximum Speed: 60 km/h.

Note: Car 103 has not been refurbished and is used for storage at Villefranche-de-Conflent depot.

Z 102	Z 105 *	Z 108	Z 111 *	Z 115 *	Z 117 *
Z 103 (U)	Z 106	Z 109	Z 113 * (U)	Z 116 *	Z 118 *
Z 104	Z 107				

CLASS Z 150   2-CAR EMU

Modernisation of the line started in 2004 when Stadler delivered two new air-conditioned EMUs... with toilets! There have been several problems with the new trains, not least of which was their effect on the track. In order to avoid causing damage, they are driven gently meaning they cannot keep to the timetable! The units are of the GTW 2/6 design, the traction equipment and two motored wheelsets all being contained in a short central power unit.

Built: 2003/4.
Traction Motors: Two three-phase asynchronous of 174 kW each.
Accommodation: –/38 (5) + –/38 (5).
Weight: 41 tonnes.
Wheel Arrangement: 2-Bo-2

Builder: Stadler, Bussnang.

Length over Couplers: 32.182 m.
Maximum Speed: 80 km/h.

Z 151   Z 152

Z 201/202 — SNOW PLOUGHS

Converted by Villefranche depot from postal vans ZDy 308 and 309 in 1954. Permanently coupled back-to-back. Z 202 has a bigger snow plough and always faces towards La Tour-de-Carol.

Built: 1909
Builder–Mechanical Parts: Carde.
Traction Motors: Four TH 540 of 66 kW each.
Weight: 27 tonnes.
Wheel Arrangement: Bo-Bo.

Builder–Electrical Parts: Thomson-Houston

Length: 11.284 m. excluding snow plough.
Maximum Speed: 30 km/h.

ZR 201 | ZR 202 |

ZRB 20001–20004 — TRAILERS

These are the surviving original cars not converted to motors (ex Midi ABDe 1–4).

Built: 1908–09.
Builders: Carde.
Accommodation: –/48.
Length: 14.384 m.

Weight: 16 tonnes.
Maximum Speed: 60 km/h.

ZR 20001 | ZR 20002 | ZR 20003 | ZR 20004

ZRBD 20023, ZRB 20036–20039 — BALCONY TRAILERS

Cars obtained second-hand in 1936/37 from the CF Économiques du Nord. Formerly ABF 168 and BF 268, 269, 271 and 272. ABF 169, later Z 20024, was withdrawn.

Built: 1910–12.
Builders: Decauville Ainé.
Accommodation: –/46 1T.
Length: 13.37 m.

Weight: 15 tonnes.
Maximum Speed: 60 km/h.

ZR 20023* | ZR 20036 | ZR 20037 | ZR 20038 | ZR 20039

ZRB 20030–20034 — OPEN-TOP TRAILERS

These cars were originally roofed with curtained sides (ex Midi Cye 30–4). ZR 20033/34 were converted in 1952. The remainder were converted to flat wagons in 1957/58 then to open-top coaches in 1974.

Built: 1912.
Builders: Carde.
Accommodation: –/59.
Length: 10.50 m.

Weight: 10 tonnes.
Maximum Speed: 60 km/h.

ZR 20030 | ZR 20031 | ZR 20032 | ZR 20033 | ZR 20034

5.1.2. CHEMIN DE FER DU BLANC-ARGENT BA

This line, now owned by RFF, is operated by the Compagnie du Blanc-Argent on behalf of SNCF, which owns the rolling stock, and the Centre region. Formerly running between the towns in its title, it now operates a passenger service only between Salbris and Luçay-le-Mâle. The passenger stock has been modernised, but freight traffic ceased in 1989. Railcar X 205 also belongs to SNCF but is considered as preserved and is on loan to preservation group SABA which operates the Train Touristique du Bas Berry, from Luçay-le-Mâle southwards.

Depot/workshops: Romorantin.

DIESEL LOCOS   C

Formerly BA steam locos 25/28, built by Blanc Misseron in 1901. Owned by BA.

Rebuilt: 1953.
Engine: Willème 517-F8 (132 kW).
Weight: 17 tonnes.
Wheel Diameter: 1050 mm.

Builder: SNCF Périgueux works.
Transmission: Mechanical. Minerva.
Length: 8.45 m.
Maximum Speed: 45 km/h.

BA 13 | BA 14 (U)

RAILCARS

CLASS X 210   XBD

X 211/2 came from the PO Corrèze in 1967. All four cars were refurbished in 1983–4 and fitted with new engines, when X 213/4 were renumbered from X 223/1 respectively. Sister unit X 224 has been preserved by SABA. Trailers X 701 to 703 are out of use, with two on hire to SABA.

Built: 1950/51.
Engine: Poyaud 6L.520.S1 (132 kW).
Transmission: Hydro-mechanical. Voith DiWA D 501 U+S.
Accommodation: –/54.
Length: 18.535 m.
Wheel Arrangement: B-2.

Builder: Verney.

Weight: 21.8 tonnes.
Maximum Speed: 80 km/h.
Livery: B.

Multiple working within class and with Class X 240.

X 211 | X 212

CLASS X   240   XBD

Delivered as part of a 1980s modernisation programme.

Built: 1983.
Engine: Poyaud 6 LC 520 S2 (175 kW).
Accommodation: –/52 (2).
Length: 18.28 m.
Wheel Arrangement: B-2.

Builder: CFD Montmirail/Socofer, Tours.
Transmission: Hydraulic. Voith T211 r.
Weight: 25 tonnes.
Maximum Speed: 85 km/h.
Livery: B.

Multiple working within class and with Class X 210.

X 241 ROMORANTIN LANTHENAY | X 242 VALENÇAY

CLASS X 74500   SIX-AXLE ARTICULATED UNITS

These recent units feature an off-centre bogie so that the body sections are of different lengths. Air conditioned. Panoramic windows.

Built: 2001/2.
Engine: MAN D 2866 LUE 602 of 300 kW.
Accommodation: –/66 1T.
Weight: 45 t.
Wheel Arrangement: B-2-2.

Builder: CFD.
Transmission: Hydraulic. Voith T211 RZE SP.

Length: 10.23 m + 16.01 m
Maximum Speed: 85 km/h.

X 74501 | X 74502 | X 74503 | X 74504 | X 74505

5.1.3. SNCF "LIGNE DE SAVOIE"

This line, opened in 1901, has the steepest adhesion section of railway in the world, the 9% (1 in 11) section from Chedde to Servoz. Electrified from opening by third rail, it extends from St. Gervais-les-Bains to Vallorcine, a distance of 33 km, where a connection is made with the Swiss Martigny-Châtelard Railway.

The original stock was unusual since all vehicles were powered and multiple working fitted (including wagons!). However freight operations ceased in 1970, the remaining wagons being in departmental use until withdrawn in 1986. The stock introduced in 1958 is now largely redundant except for hauling works trains. Snow plough Z 691 was recently withdrawn as were the four Class Z 20600 trailers. The line still has Beilhack snowplough CN4.

Electrification: 850 V DC third rail, top contact.
Depot: St. Gervais-les-Bains.

CLASS Z 600   SINGLE RAILCARS (ZABD)

No longer in regular use after introduction of Classes Z 800 and Z 850. Z 604 is preserved.

Built: 1958.
Builder–Mechanical Parts: Decauville.   **Builder–Electrical Parts:** Oerlikon.
Continuous Rating: 802 kW.   **Accommodation:** 8/34.
Weight: 40.9 tonnes.   **Length:** 18.20 m.
Wheel Arrangement: Bo-Bo.   **Maximum Speed:** 60 km/h.
Livery: R except Z 604 now in original maroon and cream.

| Z 601 | Z 603 | Z 604 | Z 605 | Z 607 |

Name: Z 601 CHAMONIX-MT BLANC

CLASS Z 800   2-CAR UNITS (ZB+ZB)

These units were developed in order to allow through operation between the SNCF St. Gervais–Vallorcine line and Martigny in Switzerland via the Martigny Châtelard (MC) railway. This task is very complicated as there are sections electrified by third rail and others with overhead catenary plus rack-worked sections on the MC. The units have asynchronous-motored power bogies at each end. All are rack-fitted. There are five types of brakes – electro-pneumatic tread brakes, rheostatic and regenerative, rack and emergency electromagnetic brakes. Features for the passenger are air-conditioning and panoramic windows. MC has two identical units numbered Z 821/22 and Z 823/24 and classified BDeh 4/8. All five EMUs are maintained by SNCF at St. Gervais.

Built: 1996/97.   **Systems:** 850 V DC third rail/overhead.
Builder–Mechanical Parts: Vevey/SLM.   **Builder–Electrical Parts:** Adtranz.
Continuous Rating: 1000 kW.   **Accommodation:** –/48 + –/48.
Weight: 36 + 36 tonnes.   **Length:** 18.90 m + 18.90 m.
Rack system: Strub.   **Maximum Speed:** 70 km/h
Livery: Red and white with stars.   (23 km/h upwards, 16 km/h downwards on rack).

| Z 801 Z 802 | Z 803 Z 804 | Z 805 Z 806 |

CLASS Z 850   3-CAR UNIT

Class Z 800 were found to be a little complicated and therefore expensive. The new units to replace Class Z 600 are therefore not rack-fitted and limited to the French section. They are built to the standard Stadler SPATZ design, the outer cars having only one non-powered bogie and the centre car having two powered bogies.

Built: 2005–2008.   **Builder:** Stadler, Bussnang.
Continuous rating: 696 kW   **Accommodation:** –/22 + –/64 + –/19 1T.
Weight: 61 tonnes.   **Length:** 11.995 m + 15.556 m + 11.995 m.
Maximum Speed: 80 km/h.   **Livery:** Red and white.

| ZR 1851 Z 851 Z 1852 | ZR 1855 Z 853 ZR 1856 | ZR 1859 Z 855 Z 1860 |
| ZR 1853 Z 852 Z 1854 | ZR 1857 Z 854 ZR 1858 | ZR 1861 Z 856 Z 1862 |

Name: Z 851 Saint Gervais Mont Blanc

5.1.4. CHEMINS DE FER DE LA CORSE   CFC

The SNCF took over operation of this system on 1 January 1983 after the last of a series of concessionary companies gave up. The main line runs from Bastia to Ajaccio (157 km) with a branch from Ponte Leccia to Calvi (73 km). The central section of the main line is particularly scenic. The Corse region is now investing large sums to modernise the network, the main aim being to reduce the Bastia–Ajaccio journey time from over four to 2½ hours and double service frequency and traffic. 12 powerful new AMG 800 2-car DMUs with air conditioning are being built by CFD but have had initial teething troubles.

Depot/Workshop: Casamozza.
Depot: Bastia

DIESEL LOCOMOTIVES

114   B-2

Nicknamed the "Submarine" or "La Bête de Calvi". Now stored at Bastia.

Built: 1958 using bogies from Billard A150D No. 114 (built 1938).
Builder: Bastia depot.
Engine: 75 kW.   **Transmission:** Mechanical.

114 (U)

CLASS BB 400   B-B

A design with coupling rods on bogies built for several metre gauge railways. 404 was built as 040.003 for CFD Vivarais in 1963, went to CP in 1969 where it was numbered 53 then 403, arriving on the CFC in 1974. 405 was built new for the CFC. 406 was built as a standard gauge version of the same design (Type BB650) and does not have bogie coupling rods. The loco arrived on the CFC in 1995 and was originally numbered 001. All are used for freight.

Built: 1963, 1966, 1973.   **Builder:** CFD Montmirail.
Engine: Two Poyaud 6 PYT of 152 kW each. (406 235 kW each due to turbocharger)
Transmission: Hydro-mechanical.   **Weight:** 32 tonnes (*35 tonnes).
Length: 10.76 metres.   **Maximum Speed:** 50 km/h

404 | 405 | 406* |

DIESEL RAILCARS

CLASS X 200   RENAULT ABH   XBD

Originally a batch of eight. Seating is 2+1 except refurbished vehicles which are 2+2. Units are used on the summer-only "Tramway de la Balagne" serving the beaches from Calvi to Île Rousse. X 201 and 204 are used with driving trailers XR 113 and 526.

Built: 1949–50.   **Builder:** Renault. Type ABH 8.
Engine: Renault (195 kW).   **Transmission:** Mechanical. Renault.
Accommodation: –/28 1T, (–/40 1T r).
Wheel Arrangement: B-2.   **Maximum Speed:** 75 km/h.
Weight: 28 tonnes.   **Length:** 20.87 m.

m Fitted for working with driving trailer.
r   Refurbished.

X 201 mr | X 204 mr | X 206 r |

CLASS X 500

Departmental unit used for breakdowns. Ex CFD Tarn in 1966.

Built: 1939.   **Builder:** Billard. Type A150D6.
Engine: Deutz (75 kW).   **Length:** 13.35 m.
Wheel Arrangement: B-2.

513

CLASS AMG 800 2-CAR DMU

New, powerful DMUs (AMG means *Autorails pour voie Métrique à Grande capacité* – high capacity metre gauge DMU) – both cars powered, with air conditioning and panoramic windows which will be needed to operate Bastia–Ajaccio services in the projected 2½ hours. An order for nine units in 2003 was followed by three more in 2004.

Built: 2007/8.
Engine: One Deutz of 440 kW per power car.
Wheel Arrangement: B-2 + 2-B.
Length: 20 m + 20 m.
Weight: 35.4 + 35.4 tonnes.
Builder: CFD Bagnères.
Transmission: Hydraulic. Voith.
Accommodation: –/98 (16) 1T.
Maximum speed: 100 km/h.
Livery: Black with red doors and white front ends and roof.

801 802	805 806	809 810	813 814	817 818	821 822
803 804	807 808	811 812	815 816	819 820	823 824

CLASS X 2000 XB

Originally numbered X 1201–5. X 2001, 2002 and 2005 originally had first class accommodation.

Built: 1975/76.
Engine: Two MAN of 123 kW each.
Wheel Arrangement: B-B.
Length: 15.90 m.
Weight: 18.6 tonnes.
Builder: CFD Montmirail.
Transmission: Hydraulic.
Accommodation: –/48 1T.
Maximum Speed: 85 km/h.

X 2001	X 2002	X 2003	X 2004	X 2005

CLASS X 5000 XB

A longer and more powerful version of X 2000. Used with driving trailers XR 104 and 105, often on Bastia suburban service.

Built: 1981/82.
Engines: Two MAN of 179 kW each.
Accommodation: –/48 1T.
Weight: 27 tonnes.
Wheel Arrangement: B-B.
Builder: CFD Montmirail.
Transmission: Hydraulic.

Length: 16.50 m.
Maximum Speed: 85 km/h.

X 5001	X 5002

CLASS X 97050 & XR 9700 XBD + XRBDx

Railcar-plus-driving trailer pairs for the Bastia–Ajaccio service. Normally used in the pairings shown but can change if accidents or failures occur. X 97057 is spare and often operates alone. Multiple working fitted. Once the AMG 800 units are in service and operating reliably, these units will be refurbished with new, more powerful engines and air conditioning.

Built: 1989–92; 1997 (X 97056/7 & XR 9706).
Engine: Two SSCM Poyaud UD-18 H6 R3 of 177 kW (*Two Cummins LT.A.10R of 216 kW).
Transmission: Hydraulic. Voith T211 r.
Weight: 35.6 + 22.4 tonnes.
Wheel Arrangement: B-B + 2-2.
Builder: Soulé. (X 97056/7 & XR 9706 CFD)
Accommodation: –/44 1T + –/54 1T.
Length: 18.28 + 18.28 m.
Maximum Speed: 90 km/h.

X 97051 XR 9701	X 97054 XR 9704	X 97056 * XR 9706
X 97052 XR 9702	X 97055 XR 9705	X 97057 *
X 97053 XR 9703		

RAILCAR TRAILERS

R 104/105   DRIVING TRAILER (XRBDx)

Usually used with X 5001/2. Rebuilt from Billard Type A210D railcars X 104/5.

Built: 1935.
Rebuilt: 1977 by Garnéro.
Wheel Arrangement: 2-2.   **Accommodation:** –/44 1T.
Weight: 13 tonnes.   **Length:** 19.80 m.

R 104 | R 105 |

XR 113   DRIVING TRAILER (XRBDx)

The only survivor of a batch of six Billard Type A150D railcars (111–6), this car was re-bodied by Carde in 1966, and converted to a driving trailer to run with 204 in 1987. Works between Calvi and Île Rousse.

Rebuilt: 1987. Built 1938.
Accommodation: –/37 1T.   **Length:** 14.50 m.
Wheel Arrangement: 2-2.   **Maximum Speed:** 75 km/h.

XR 113

XR 211   TRAILER (XRBD)

Built: 1949.   **Builder:** Billard.
Accommodation: –/27.   **Length:** 11.50 m.

Ex CFD Tarn in 1966. Converted from Billard Type A80D power car. Re-bodied

XR 211

XR 242   VAN (XRD)

Built: 1938.   **Builder:** Billard.
Length: 11.50 m.

Ex PO Corrèze in 1970. Converted from Billard Type A80D power car in 1970.

XR 242

XR 526   DRIVING TRAILER (XRBDx)

Converted from Billard type A150D6. Works between Calvi and Île Rousse.

Built: 1947.   **Builder:** Billard. Type A150D6.
Length: 13.35 m.

Ex Tramways d'Ille et Vilaine (until 1952) and Réseau Breton (until 1966).

XR 526

5.2. INDEPENDENT NARROW GAUGE LINES
5.2.1. CHEMINS DE FER DE PROVENCE   CP

This is the only non-SNCF adhesion non-preserved passenger railway left in France. It runs from Nice (CP) to Digne, the last remnant of the Chemins de Fer du Sud whose network included lines from Nice to Vence, Grasse, Draguignan & Meyrargues and from Saint Raphael to Toulon via St. Tropez. The diesel service is supplemented in summer by steam from Puget-Théniers. The line is now operated by Veolia on behalf of the Provence-Alpes-Côte d'Azur region. The latter has ordered four new DMUs from CFD based on the AMG 800 for Corsica for delivery in 2009.

Gauge: 1000 mm.
Route: Nice–Digne (151 km).
Depots: Nice, Digne, Puget-Théniers (steam).
Works: Lingostière.

Liveries: The standard livery is white with a blue window band. Other liveries are as follows:
N   New livery of white with a blue window band and a yellow stripe below the window.

DIESEL LOCOMOTIVES

CLASS T60   Bo-Bo

Equipped for use in push-pull mode on Nice suburban services. Also used on works trains and snow clearing. T62 is the last of four CP locos numbered T61 to T64. T66 is former Chemins de Fer du Jura (CJ, Switzerland) Gm 4/4 508, acquired in 1999.

Built: 1951, 1950.   **Builder**: Brissonneau & Lotz.
Engine: Two Deutz of 295 kW each.
Transmission: Electric.   **Weight**: 48.5 tonnes.
Maximum Speed: 60 km/h.

T 62   T66

CLASS BB 400   B-B

Ex PO Corrèze in 1971. Dumped at Lingostière. The remains of BB 402 are also there.

Built: 1962.   **Builder**: CFD.
Engine: Two Poyaud of 152 kW each.   **Transmission**: Hydro-mechanical.
Weight: 44 tonnes.

BB 401 (U)

CLASS BB 1200   B-B

Ex FEVE 1404 in 1992. A metre gauge version of the DB V 160 design. Used for works trains.

Built: 1966.   **Builder**: Henschel.
Engine: SACM BZSHR (900 kW).   **Transmission**: Hydraulic.
Weight: 56 tonnes.   **Maximum Speed**: 25 km/h.

BB 1200

DIESEL RAILCARS

CLASS X 200   XD

Ex-Vivarais in 1969. Stored at Digne. 213 & 214 still exist on the Vivarais.

Built: 1937.   **Builder**: Billard. Type A 150 D.
Engine: Berliet (155 kW).   **Transmission**: Mechanical.
Wheel Arrangement: B-2.   **Weight**: 14.5 tonnes.

212 (U)

CLASS X 300 SERIES 1 XB

Built: 1971/72.
Engine: Two MAN of 123 kW each.
Accommodation: –/48 1T (*–/46 1T & coffee machine).
Weight: 22 tonnes.
Wheel Arrangement: 1A-A1.

Builder: CFD.
Transmission: Hydro-mechanical.

Maximum Speed: 75 km/h.

These units have flat ends.

X 301 (SY 01) **N** | X 302 (SY 02) * | X 303 (SY 03) | X 304 (SY 04)

CLASS X 300 SERIES 2 XB

Built: 1977.
Engine: Two MAN of 123 kW each.
Accommodation: –/46 1T.
Wheel Arrangement: 1A-A1.

Builder: CFD.
Transmission: Hydro-mechanical.
Weight: 23 tonnes.
Maximum Speed: 75 km/h.

These units have angled ends.

X 305   (SY 05) **N** | X 306   (SY 06) |

CLASS X 320 (ZZ) XB

The survivors of twelve cars (ZZ 1–12) built 1935-45. ZZ 21/22 were formerly ZZ 1/2. The cars were allocated new numbers in the X 320 series, but were never renumbered.

Built: 1935–42.
Engine: Poyaud (243 kW).
Accommodation: –/44 1T (§ –/56 1T).
Wheel Arrangement: B-2.

Builder: Renault. Type ABH 1 (ABH 5*).
Transmission: Mechanical.
Weight: 32 (*31) tonnes.
Maximum Speed: 60 km/h.

X 326 (ZZ 6) § (U) | X 320 (ZZ 10) **R** * | X 322 (ZZ 22) (U)

The remains of ZZ 3 and ZZ 21 are dumped at Lingostière.

X 351 & XR 1351 XBD+Bx

This two-car unit was built for the "Alpazur" service, but is now in general use. It is unreliable despite being re-engined in 1992 and cannot keep time on the Nice–Digne run because of its low power/weight ratio. In June 2008, the power car caught fire and the unit is now stored awaiting a decision on its future.

Built: 1984.
Engine: One SSCM Poyaud (365 kW).
Accommodation: –/64 1T + –/65 1T.
Wheel Arrangement: Bo-Bo + 2-2.

Builder: Soulé/Garnéro.
Transmission: Hydraulic. Voith.
Weight: 40 + 31.7 tonnes.
Maximum Speed: 75 km/h.

X 351 + XR 1351 (U)

CLASS XR 1330 TRAILERS

Built: 1937–58.
Accommodation: –/34 1T.

Builder: Billard. Type R 210.
Weight: 15 tonnes (9.1 tonnes p).

g Rebuilt with Garnéro body.
p Used as a parcels van.
r Re-bodied by Lingostière works.
v ex Vivarais 1969.

XR 1331 (RL 1) **N** g | XR 1333 (RL 3) p | XR 1337 (RL 7) **N** rv

XR 1335 (g) is out of use. The remains of trailer XR 1336 which was re-bodied by Garnéro and four-wheeled ex-CF du Tarn trailer RL 4 are dumped at Lingostière.

CLASS XR 1340 HAULED STOCK

Built: 1951–53.
Accommodation: –/52 1T.
Wheel Arrangement: 2-2.

Builder: CP Lingostière Works.
Weight: 18 tonnes.

XR 1341 (AT 1) | XR 1342 (AT 2) |XR 1343 (AT 3) |XR 1344 (AT 4)

CLASS XR 1370   HAULED STOCK

Push-pull stock used for the Nice suburban push-pull service and special trains with Class T60 locos.

Built: 1948; 1953 (X 1376)   **Builder:** SIG
Accommodation: –/56 1T (1372); –/44 (9) 1T (1376)

X 1370 (U)	Ex Appenzellerbahn.
X 1372	Ex Appenzellerbahn.
X 1376	Ex Chemins de Fer du Jura Bt 706. Converted to driving trailer.

PRESERVED STEAM LOCOMOTIVES

No.	Type	Builder	Built	Notes
E 211§	2-4-6-0T	Henschel	1923	ex CP (Portugal)
E 327*	4-6-0T	Fives-Lille	1909	ex Réseau Breton (U)

* Preserved by FACS (Fédération des Amis des Chemins de Fer Secondaires).
§ Preserved by Groupe d'Étude des Chemins de Fer de la Provence. Under repair in Italy. Should be in service in 2009.

5.2.2. CHEMIN DE FER DE CHAMONIX AU MONTENVERS

This 5.4 km rack line, opened in 1908/09, climbs into amazing mountain and glacier scenery. The line was electrified in 1954 at 11 kV AC 50 Hz. However diesel traction is used for works trains and in emergency and also for extra trains at peak periods. The line is owned by the Compagnie du Mont-Blanc which also runs the Tramway du Mont-Blanc and numerous ski lifts.

Gauge: 1000 mm.   **Rack system:** Strub
Depot: Chamonix.

DIESEL LOCOS   1-B

These locos work with articulated coaches 61–63. Loco 31 was sold to the TMB.

Built: 1972.   **Builder:** SLM.
Engine: Poyaud A12-150 Se (520 kW).
Transmission: Hydraulic.
Weight: 23.3 tonnes.
Driving Wheel Diameter: 790 mm.   **Length:** 7.50 m.
     Maximum Speed: 21 km/h.

32 |33

ELECTRIC RAILCARS

These railcars have driving cabs at the lower end only. They normally work coupled to trailers 51–56. Classified by the Swiss system as Bhe 4/4. The 1954 units have wooden seats, the others plastic seats.

Built: 1954/60*/79§.
Builder-Mechanical Parts: SLM.   **Builder-Electrical Parts:** BBC.
Power: 475 kW.   **Accommodation:** –/84 (–/81 *§).
Weight: 29.5 tonnes.   **Length:** 15.37 (15.94 *§) m.
Wheel Arrangement: Bo-Bo.   **Maximum Speed:** 20 km/h.

41 |42 |43 |44 |45 * |46 §

PRESERVED STEAM LOCOMOTIVES

Three of the eight steam locomotives used on the line before electrification still survive at Chamonix:

No.	Type	Builder	Built	Notes
6	0-4-2T	SLM	1923	plinthed at Chamonix
7	0-4-2T	SLM	1926	stored
8	0-4-2T	SLM	1927	for spares

5.2.3. CHEMIN DE FER DE LA RHUNE

This rack line is the last remnant of the once extensive Voies Ferrées Départementales du Midi metre gauge system. Running from St. Ignace to La Rhune, it has been isolated from other railways since the closure of the line to St. Ignace in 1936. The line climbs into the Pyrénées giving views of the Basque coast. Electrified since opening in 1924 at 3000 V 50 Hz three-phase, the original locos are still in use together with others from the similar closed line at Luchon. The line can be reached by bus from St. Jean de Luz. Now managed by Veolia. Former Jungfraubahn BT 24 is preserved at St. Ignace.

Gauge: 1000 mm.

4 WHEEL RACK LOCOS

Built: 1912–15.
Builder-Mechanical Parts: SLM.
Power: 240 kW.
Length: 5050 mm.

Builder-Electrical Parts: BBC.
Weight: 12 tonnes.
Maximum Speed: 8.5 km/h.

* ex Luchon–Superbagnères 1966.

| 1 | |2 | |3 * | |4 * (U) | |5 * | |6 |

5.2.4. TRAMWAY DU MONT BLANC   TMB

This 12 km rack line in the Savoy Alps was opened in 1909–14 between St. Gervais les Bains and Glacier Bionnassay, but never achieved its intended terminus closer to Mont Blanc. The line was electrified in 1957 at 11 kV AC 50 Hz. The TMB is owned by the Compagnie du Mont Blanc.

Gauge: 1000 mm.
Depot: St. Gervais
Rack system: Strub

DIESEL LOCO   1-B

Used for works trains. Acquired from CF de Chamonix au Montenvers. Details as latter except:

Built: 1967.
Engine: Poyaud A12-150 Se (485 kW).

Builder: SLM.

31

RACK RAILCARS

These cars have driving cabs at the lower end only. They normally work with a trailer coupled at the upper end. The cars do not carry any numbers, but are identifiable by their different liveries and names.

Built: 1956.
Builder-Mechanical Parts: SLM/Decauville.
One hour Rating: 475 kW.
Weight: 12 tonnes.
Wheel Arrangement: Bo-Bo.

Builder-Electrical Parts: TCO.
Accommodation: –/84.
Length: 15.37 m.
Maximum Speed: 20 km/h.

Dark red	"Jeanne"
Green	"Anne"
Dark blue	"Marie"

PRESERVED STEAM LOCOMOTIVES

Three of the six steam locomotives used on the line before electrification still survive:

No.	Type	Builder	Built	Notes
2	0-4-0T	SLM	1906	Evires
3	0-4-0T	SLM	1909	St. Gervais (stored in depot)
4	0-4-0T	SLM	1909	St. Gervais (stored in depot)

5.2.5. CHEMIN DE FER DE LA MURE   SG-LM-G

This spectacular line was built mainly to move coal from the La Mure area and originally extended from St. Georges de Commiers to Corps with several short branches. The line was supposed to further extended to Gap, thus the initials SG-LM-G. Most of the system was electrified from 1903, but closures commenced in 1936, and all passenger services ceased in 1950. The section to La Mure survived as a coal carrier. During recent years tourist trains have commenced, and this is now the sole traffic. The second generation of electric locomotives are the principle motive power, but there is an assortment of other stock from various sources. The line is now run by Veolia under contract to the Isère département.

Route: St. Georges-de-Commiers–La Mure (30.1 km)

Gauge: 1000 mm.
System: 2400 DC overhead.
Livery: Red (except T10 which is green).
Depot: St. Georges de Commiers.

ELECTRIC LOCOMOTIVES

SÉCHERON LOCOS   Bo-Bo

These locos can haul 360 tonne-trains downhill and 175 tonne-trains uphill. When delivered, they could operate under two DC systems: +1200 V/0 V/ –1200 V DC (two wires) and 0 V/2400 V DC (one wire). On the roof, four twin-arm pantographs were installed (two at each end). They were "high tech" for their time having suspended traction motors and flexible drive.

Built: 1932.
Builder-Mechanical Parts: ANF.   **Builder-Electrical Parts:** Sécheron.
Weight: 60 tonnes.   **Length:** 12 m.
Power: 690 kW (920 h.p.).   **Maximum Speed:** 40 km/h.
Braking Systems: Vacuum, rheostatic, and magnetic track.

T6	ST. GEORGES DE COMMIERS	T9
T7	LA MURE D'ISÈRE	T10
T8		

ELECTRIC RAILCARS

THOMSON-BUIRE   Bo-Bo

These electric railcars were built for the never-completed La Mure–Gap section. These were designed for passenger trains and sundries traffic. They could haul 300 tonne trains at a minimum speed of 14 km/h on a 6.5% gradient.

Built: 1913–1927
Builder-Mechanical Parts: Chantiers de La Buire.
Builder-Electrical Parts: Thomson-Houston.
Traction Motors: Four 75 kW (100 h.p.).
Weight: 42 tonnes.   **Length:** 16 m.

A1 (U)	A3 (U)	A5 (U)

Ex NStCM CLASS ABDe 4/4   Bo-Bo

These railcars were built for the Nyon–St. Cergue–Morez Railway in Switzerland as Class ABDe 4/4 where they worked until 1984. They were transferred to the CF de la Mure between 1985 and 1993. Designed for operation under 2200 V DC they were modified with new pantographs and additional resistors on the roof.

Built: 1914–18.
Builder–Mechanical Parts: SWS.   **Builder–Electrical Parts:** BBC.
Traction Motors: Four 75 kW.   **Accommodation:** –/50.
Weight: 32 tonnes.   **Length:** 16.4 m.
Braking Systems: air and electric.

1	5 (U)	10 (U)	11 (U)

Ex RhB CLASS ABDe4/4 Bo-Bo

Purchased from the Swiss Rhätische Bahn. These two electric railcars were part of the 481–8 batch used on the Chur–Arosa line until converted to 11 kV AC in 1999. They had still not been used regularly in 2007.

Built: 1957/8.
Builder–Mechanical Parts: SWS.
One Hour Rating: 500 kW.
Driving Wheel Diameter: 920 mm.
Overall Length: 17.70 m.

Builder–Electrical Parts: BBC.
Maximum Tractive Effort: 113 kN.
Weight: 43 tonnes.
Maximum Speed: 65 km/h.

Fitted with track brakes.

484   486

DIESEL LOCOMOTIVES

BRISSONNEAU & LOTZ B-B

In 1984, the Isère Department gave two diesel locos to the line which had worked on the Voies Ferrées du Dauphiné (VFD) until 1964. They had been out of use for 20 years, and were transferred to St. Georges de Commiers to serve as assisting engines (in case of major electrical problems). They can haul 300 tonne trains on the level, or 120 tonne trains on a 1 in 80 gradient. They are the last of four loco (T1–T4) build for VFD and belong to a series of ten machines built in 1950/51. Two other locos of the same type are still in service on the CP (see Section 5.2.1.).

Built: 1950/51.
Engines: Two Renault 12-cylinder of 224 kW (300 h.p.) at 1500 r.p.m.
Weight: 50 tonnes.

Builder: Brissonneau & Lotz.
Maximum Speed: 60 km/h.

Multiple working within class.

T2 (U) |T4 (S)

CLASS Tm 2/2 B

Acquired from Furrer & Frey, Switzerland in 2004.

Built: 1985.   Builder: Schöma/LSB.

100

DECAUVILLE DRAISINE

This vehicle can haul 240 tonnes on the level or 30 tonnes on a gradient of 2.7% at a maximum speed of 8 km/h. It is used by the permanent way department.

Built: 1966.
Engine: 4 cylinders.
Transmission: Mechanical. Chain drive to each axle.
Weight: 7 tonnes.
Wheel Arrangement: A-A.

Builder: Decauville.
Accommodation: –/18.
Length: 7.1 m.
Maximum Speed: 50 km/h.

Unnumbered

5.2.6. PETIT TRAIN DU LAC D'ARTOUSTE

www.train-artouste.com

This 500 mm gauge line, 2000 metres up in the Pyrenees, is owned by energy group Suez through its hydroelectric power subsidiary SHEM because the line was originally built to carry materials for the construction of a dam. SHEM owns two pieces of rolling stock, the rest being the property of the Pyrénées-Atlantiques département. The line is now actually managed by the Établissement Public des Stations d'Altitude (EPSA) which promotes mountain resorts. Today it carries tourists from Artouste and Fabrèges (cable cars carry passengers from these to points to Ossau 2000), south of Laruns, to the dam which holds back the Lac d'Artouste. A daily return bus runs on Saturdays and Sundays from Pau station to Fabrèges. Operations in the summer months, from the end of May/early June to late September/early October, are intensive.

Route: Ossau 2000–Lac d'Artouste (9.5 km)

PÉTOLAT TROLLEY   .

A trolley used to carry SHEM staff up to the dam and usually hidden away in the tunnels there. The power unit is connected to a trailer carrying six passengers. Owned by SHEM.

Built: 1923.	**Builder:** Pétolat.

WEITZ LOCOMOTIVES   .

Two locos acquired post-War to cope with increasing traffic. Now only used for works trains, including pushing a rotary snow plough. D2 was donated to the CFTT near Toulouse.

Built: 1948.	**Builder:** Weitz.
Weight: 4.5 tonnes.	**Engine:** Lombardini of 45 h.p.

D1

BILLARD LOCOMOTIVES   .

These locos were built to a design submitted by SNCF and are still in service.
* D7 belongs to the SHEM and is painted blue.

Built: 1963.	**Builder:** Billard.
Weight: 7.8 tonnes.	**Engine:** 60 h.p.

D3	D4 D5	D6 D7*	D8

WHITCOMB LOCOMOTIVES   .

These were purchased second-hand in 1967 (D9 to D12), 1969 (D13) and 1978 (D14) and had to be re-gauged from 600 mm and had their cabs reduced in size for the line's tunnels. D2 and D7 were bought in 1991, taking numbers freed by withdrawals.

Built: 1953	**Builder:** Whitcomb.
Weight: 5 tonnes.	**Engine:** 45 h.p.

D2	D9	D11	D12	D13	D14
D7	D10				

6. EX-SNCF LOCOMOTIVES IN INDUSTRIAL USE

Many SNCF locomotives have been sold to industrial concerns for further use. In some cases they still carry their SNCF numbers. The following covers all known locomotives except for those covered in other sections. The number in brackets is the French "département". Many of these locos may no longer be in service. Further news and observations are welcome.

Number	Location	Notes
BB 63140	Paper plant, Alizay (76)	
BB 63213	ZI de la Martinerie, Déols (36).	
BB 63218	Ciments Lafarge, Le Teil (07).	Green/white
BB 63220	Ciments Lafarge, La Couronne (16).	Green
BB 63242	Bocahut quarry, Fourmies (59).	Blue
BB 63245	Decoexa, Irún (Spain).	Blue
BB 71001	SLAP, Rivesaltes (11).	White/blue
BB 71006	Aproport, Mâcon (71).	
BB 71007	Péchiney, Dunkerque (77)	Blue/white/yellow
BB 71008	Cipha, Le Havre terminal pondéreux (76).	
BB 71014	Quarry, Ste. Foy-l'Argentière (69).	
BB 71015	Cellulose du Pin, Tartas (40).	
BB 71016	CDRA, St. Gaudens (31)	
BB 71018	Cipha, Le Havre? (76).	
BB 71019	Kronenbourg, Strasbourg (67).	
BB 71020	Transports Bridier, La Chapelle St Ursin (18).	
BB 71023	CDRA, St. Gaudens (31).	
BB 71026	Socorail, L'Ardoise (84)	
BB 71027	Holcim, Vaires (77).	
BB 71028	Metalinor, Dunkerque (59).	
BB 71030	CCI, Colmar (67)	
Y 2102	COPAG, St. Julien-les-Villas (10).	
Y 2104	SERAGRI, Châtel Censoir (89).	
Y 2105	Soufflet, Polisot (10).	
Y 2106	Coop Agricole de la Charente, Angoulême (16).	
Y 2108	Potain, Moulins (03).	
Y 2110	Graines Selectif Tezier, Portes-les-Valence (26).	
Y 2111	Coop Agricole du Dunois, Bailleau-le-Pin (28).	
Y 2112	Centre Commercial de Gros, Toulouse (31).	
Y 2116	Franciade, Lamotte-Beuvron (41).	Green
Y 2118	ACOR, Blanquefort (33).	
Y 2126	CAPROGA La Meunière, Ladon (45).	Blue
Y 2127	Coop Agricole de Gien (45).	
Y 2128	Coop Agricole La Dauphinoise, Port de Lyon.	
Y 2129	UCP, Châlons-en-Champagne (51).	
Y 2134	SICA SERROGRAIN, Sens (89).	
Y 2135	Coop Agricole du Dunois, Châteaudun (28).	
Y 2137	SACO, Lavaur (81).	
Y 2139	Franciade, Mondoubleau (41).	AT2 PM 029
Y 2140	Coop Agricole du Dunois, Demainville (28).	
Y 2145	Alcan, Aumale (80).	Blue.
Y 2146	Coop Agricole, Corbeille-en-Gatinais (45).	
Y 2149	Purmet, Marignene (13).	
Y 2150	DAVUM, Audincourt (25).	
Y 2205	Lafarge, La Patte (69).	
Y 2210	Papeteries du Limousin, Saillat (87).	
Y 2212	Coop Agricole du Dunois, Gommiers (28).	
Y 2217	Coop Agricole du Dunois, Janville (28).	
Y 2218	Champagne Céréales, Fère-Champenoise (51).	
Y 2223	Cornet et Fils, Lignerolles (27).	

Y 2229	Kimberley Clark, Sotteville (76).	AT1 RO 239
Y 2231	Scrap yard, Angers ZI Croix Violette (49)	
Y 2235	Coop des Pyrénées Orientales, Perpignan.	
Y 2243	SAD, Port d'Illange (57).	
Y 2244	Coop Agricole du Dunois, Vieuvicq (28).	
Y 2245	Cooperative de Verneuil, Breteuil sur Iton (27).	
Y 2253	Cie. des Bases de Lubrifiants, Port Jerome (76).	
Y 2254	Coop Agricole, Le Blanc.	
Y 2256	SCAEL, Bonneval (28).	
Y 2261	Potain, St. Nizier sous Charlieu (42).	
Y 2265	Massilly Holding, ZI Sud, Mâcon (71).	
Y 2268	Bourgeois, Besançon (25).	
Y 2272	Coop Agricole, Brienon (89).	Orange
Y 2278	DAVUM, Nancy (54)	
Y 2286	Van Leer, Grand Quevilly (76).	AT1 RO 249
Y 2293	Chavanne-Ketin, Berlaimont (59).	
Y 2307	Purmet scrap yard, Marignane (13).	
Y 2312	Cie. Française de Ferraille, Villeurbanne (69).	
Y 2314	André Recerdier, Pernes-le-Fontaines (84).	
Y 2324	UCP, Châlons-en-Champagne (51).	
Y 2325	Cornet et Fils, Orgères en Beauce (28).	
Y 2327	Coop Agricole du Dunois, Noyers sur Cher.	
Y 2329	Sleeper works, La Flèche.	
Y 2332	Silo Ligea, St. Romain sur Cher (41)	
Y 2333	Epi Centre, Jean Varenne, near Issoudun (36).	
Y 2335	Scrap yard, St Avre le Chambre (73).	
Y 2338	Ateliers d'Occitanie, Narbonne (11).	
Y 2408	Factory, St. Étienne (42).	
Y 2422	L'Hermitage (35).	AT1 RO 256
Y 2437	Carrières de Pagnac, Pagnac (87).	
Y 2442	Carrières de Pagnac, Pagnac (87).	
Y 2454	Pontigliatti scrap yard, Cluses (74).	
Y 2462	Cie. Française de Ferrailles, St. Marcel (13)	
Y 2466	Ets. Lambiotte, Prémery (58).	
Y 2472	Soc. Kaolins du Finistere, Pleyber-Christ (29).	
Y 2473	Rhône Poulenc Films, Miribel (01).	
Y 2488	Gannat (63)	
Y 2503	Soc. Nouvelle de Transports, Chambéry (73).	
Y 2508	Union Agricole, Saint Gaudens (31)	
Y 2512	C. Alpine de Recyclage, Aiton-Bourgneuf (73).	
Y 2513	SA Gaston Arnould, Vittel (88).	
Y 2516	Moulins de Savoie, Chambéry (73).	
Y 2517	Carbone Savoie, N. Dame de Briançon (73).	
Y 5113	Allevard Ressorts, Douai (59).	
Y 5120	Silo, Chantenay St. Imbert (58).	
Y 5128	Coop Agricole du Dunois, Châteaudun (28).	
Y 5149	Leclerc, Bordeaux (33).	
Y 6023	Imès France scrap yard, Culoz (01).	
Y 6039	Glon, Montauban-de-Bretagne (35)	
Y 6208	Metaux Spéciaux, Pomblières-St. Marcel (73).	
Y 6211	SCAEL, Courville sur Eure (28).	
Y 6213	Factory, St. Vit (25).	
Y 6218	SCAB, Bonneval (28).	AT2 PSO 066
Y 6227	Silo, Vitry le François (51).	
Y 6228	Rubis terminal, Mole 5, port of Dunkerque (59).	AT1 LL 776
Y 6235	Grande Minoterie Dijonnaise, Dijon (21).	
Y 6236	Sogeloc, Le Mureaux (78).	
Y 6237	Guyomar'ch, Questembert (56).	
Y 6241	Total Gaz, St. Loubes (33).	White
Y 6249	Coop. Agricole Marnaise, Nuisement (51).	

Y 6254	Norsk Hydro Azote, Le Havre (76).	AT2 RO 244
Y 6259	Minoterie l'Étincelle, Gerzat (63).	
Y 6262	SPAD, Canals near Grisolles (31).	Grey
Y 6274	Rodez Engrais, Onet-le-Château (12).	
Y 6276	Mineral water source, Le Mont Dore (63).	
Y 6277	Sucrerie de Pithiviers (45).	
Y 6278	Coop Agricole La Brie, Coulommiers (77).	
Y 6279	Toulouse Raynal (31).	
Y 6284	Soc. Breizel, Vannes (56).	
Y 6288	Champagne Céréales, ZI Pompelle, Reims (51).	
Y 6292	Dijon Céréales, Darcey (21).	
Y 6303	Total Gaz, Frontenex (73).	
Y 6308	Champagne Céréales., Fère Champenoise (51).	no. 6044
Y 6315	Providence Agricole, Gondrecourt-le-Château (55).	
Y 6316	Société CA, Thouars (79).	
Y 6318	Coop Agricole, Longuejumelles.	
Y 6321	Champagne Céréales, ZI de Pompelle, Reims (51).	
Y 6322	Champagne Céréales, Matougues (51).	Chassis only.
Y 6324	Sogemi-Fillod, St. Amour (39).	AT2 DJ 046
Y 6325	Soufflet, Polisot (10).	AT2 RS 128
Y 6330	UCOP silo, Breteuil Ville (60).	
Y 6403	Calcia, Port de Rouen (76).	AT2 RO 226
Y 6405	Champagne Céréales, Révigny.	
Y 6407	Silo, Châtel-Censoir (89).	
Y 6411	Transagra, Tracy-sur-Loire (58).	
Y 6418	UNCAC, St Jean de Losne (21).	
Y 6421	SOCOMAC, La Rochelle (17).	
Y 6422	Oullins (69).	
Y 6425	Heineken/Pelforth, Schiltigheim (67).	
Y 6427	Silo Vicois, Eauze (32).	
Y 6431	Silo, Monthois (08).	
Y 6439	Coop Agricole de la Champagne, Coligny (51).	
Y 6452	Distrilux, Gonfreville l'Orcher.	AT2 RO 201
Y 6454	FRET SNCF, Rouen (76).	
Y 6466	Iton-Seine, Bonnières-sur-Seine (78)	
Y 6473	Sablières, St. Pierre-de-Vouvray (27).	AT2 RO 225
Y 6475	Oullins (69).	
Y 6479	SICA, Port-la-Nouvelle (11).	
Y 6480	Factory, Montluçon (03).	
Y 6481	Cie. Nord du Rhône, Port de Lyon (69).	
Y 6484	UCASPORT, Rouen (76).	AT2 RO 219
Y 6485	Coop de Chemin, Chemin (39).	Orange
Y 6496	Kaisersberg, Hondouville (27).	AT2 RO 206
Y 6498	TRANSAGRI, Châteauneuf-sur-Cher (18).	
Y 6499	Lesaffre, Sucrerie de Nangis, Nangis (77).	Orange/brown.
Y 6503	Dijon Céréales, Époisses (89).	
Y 6504	Sollac, Desvres (62).	
Y 6508	Tioxide, Calais (62).	
Y 6511	Comurex, Malvezy, near Narbonne (11).	
Y 6523	Générale Sucrerie, Etrepagny.	AT2 RO 232
Y 6524	Garon Lepuix, Giromagny (90).	
Y 6526	Silos du Port de Rouen (76).	AT2 RO 210
Y 6530	Decoexa, Irún, Spain.	Blue
Y 6536	Société des Talcs de Luzenac, Luzenac (09).	
Y 6537	Oullins (69)	
Y 6542	Champagne Céréales, Coolus (51).	Green no. 6006.
Y 6543	Factory, Cosne-sur-Loire (58).	
Y 6545	Transagra, Poilly-les-Gien (45).	
Y 6546	C.F. des Pyrénées Orientales, Perpignan.	
Y 6548	Magasins Généraux de Champagne-Ardenne, Langres (52)	
Y 6552	Coop. Agricole, Breteuil-sur-Iton (27).	
Y 6554	Factory, Bergerac (24).	
Y 6572	Union Sud Alim., Villefranche-de-Rouergue (12).	

Y 6579	UCACEL, Rouen (76).	AT2 RO 213
Y 6580	B. Secula, ZI Beaune Vignolles, Beaune (21).	
Y 6582	Champagne Céréales, Dontrien (51).	Green
Y 6583	Ciments Lafarge, Boussens (31).	
Y 6584	Coop Agricole, Pithiviers (45).	
Y 6593	SCAN, Guérigny (58).	
Y 6597	Rouen area.	Yellow
Y 6598	Silo Coopagri Bretagne, Plouaget (22).	
Y 6602	St. Gobain, Châlon-sur-Saône (71).	
Y 6614	Dijon Céréales, Is-sur-Tille (21).	
Y 6618	Soufflet, Strasbourg (67)	
Y 6620	SOGEMA, Grand Couronne (76).	
Y 7021	Sigma, La Grande Paroisse (77).	
Y 7030	Ph Rey Transit Groupages, Perpignan (66).	
Y 7038	SCAEL, Marchezais-Broué (28).	Blue.
Y 7118	Cie. Normande de Manutention, Rouen docks.	
Y 7128	UCAPOR, Rouen docks.	
Y BE 14022	Silo, Coulanges-Crain (89).	
Y BE 14086	SCADEC Epi Centre, Cercy-la Tour (58).	
Y DE 2001	Ciments Lafarge, Wissous (91).	
Y 50101	Magasins Généraux, Toulouse (31).	
Y 50103	Cooperative Scara, Mailly (10).	
Y 50109	Gardi-Loire, near Montoir-de-Bretagne (44).	
Y 51122	CCI Vaucluse, ZI Avignon Courtine (84).	
Y 51129	Magasins Généraux, Toulouse (31).	
Y 51130	Coop du Mans, Le Mans (72).	
Y 51139	Coop Agricole, La Hutte (72).	
Y 51201	PCUK, Brignoud (38).	
Y 51207	La Cellulose du Rhône, Tarascon (13).	Yellow/red
Y 51209	Usine Renault, Sandouville (76).	
Y 51210	Sucrerie d'Escaudoeuvres (59). For scrap 2008.	
Y 51219	Coop Agricole des Charente, Charmant (16).	
Y 51229	Hurel, Aunay-sous-Crécy (28).	

SNCF SELF-PROPELLED SNOWPLOUGHS

The SNCF has several rotary snowploughs. Brief details of those known are as follows:

No.	Type	Built	Location
CN 1	Beilhack type HB 600	1972	Chambéry
CN 2	Beilhack type HB 600	1972	Chambéry
CN 3	Beilhack/91	1981	Dijon
CN 4	Beilhack	198?	St. Gervais les Bains. (1000 mm)
CN 5	ex BB 4119	1928	Toulouse
CN 6	ex BB 4123	1928	Toulouse
CNS	ex BB 60021		Aurillac

Note: CNS has traction motors at one end only and must be pushed by a loco. Converted 1967. Equipped for push-pull with BB 66000.

7. PRESERVED LOCOMOTIVES & RAILCARS

The current status of the motive power is indicated as follows:

M	Museum, on display (not active).		MS	Museum, stored.
MA	Museum, active.		P	Plinthed.
MR	Museum, under repair.		S	Stored.

The French use a simple system to classify steam locomotives based on the number of axles. Thus, a French 141 is a 2-8-2 and so on. Most loco numbers begin with the axle arrangement, followed by a class letter then the serial number. If the class letter is preceded by a T, this denotes a tank engine. Confusingly, this is known in French as a "locomotive tender". In this section, CF stands for Chemin de Fer.

Abbreviations for diesel/petrol locomotives and multiple units are:

de	diesel-electric		dm	diesel-mechanical
dh	diesel-hydraulic		pm	petrol-mechanical

7.1. STEAM LOCOMOTIVES

Number/name	Details	Built	Status	Location
5 "SÉZANNE"	2-2-2	1847	M	CdT. Mulhouse (CF Montereau–Troyes).
6 "L'AIGLE"	2-2-2	1846	M	CdT. Mulhouse (CF Avignon–Marseille).
33 "ST. PIERRE"	2-2-2	1843	M	CdT. Mulhouse (CF Paris–Rouen).
80 "LE CONTINENT"	4-2-0	1852	M	CdT. Mulhouse (CF Paris–Strasbourg).
Nord 701	4-2-2	1885	M	CdT. Mulhouse.
État 2029 "PARTHENAY"	2-4-0	1882	MS	CdT. Mulhouse (SNCF 120 A 36).
PO 340	2-4-2	1882	M	CdT. Mulhouse (SNCF 121 A 340).
PLM C 145	4-4-0	1902	M	CdT. Mulhouse (SNCF 220 A 85).
Nord 2.670	4-4-2	1903	M	CdT. Mulhouse (SNCF 221 A 30).
PLM 1423	0-6-0	1854	M	CdT. Mulhouse (SNCF 030 A 1).
Nord 3.486	0-6-0	1890	M	Château de St. Fargeau.
030 C 815	0-6-0	1878	MS	CdT. Mulhouse.
030 C 841	0-6-0	1883	M	Canadian Rail Museum, Delson, Canada.
030 TA 628	0-6-0T	1874	MS	CdT. Mulhouse.
030 TB 2	0-6-0T	1870	P	CdT. Mulhouse.
030 TB 130	0-6-0T	1900	MA	CFTR. Volgelsheim.
030 TB 134	0-6-0T	1900	MA	CFTR. Volgelsheim.
030 TU 13	0-6-0T	1943	P	Pont Erambourg. (USATC 6102).
030 TU 22	0-6-0T	1943	M	AJECTA. Longueville (USATC 4383).
030 TU 46	0-6-0T	1943	A	CFVP. Châteaurenard.
Midi 312 "L`ADOUR"	0-6-4T	1856	M	CdT. Mulhouse (SNCF 032 TA 312).
130 B 348	2-6-0	1862	M	AJECTA. Longueville.
130 B 439	2-6-0	1882	P	Capdenac SNCF station.
130 B 476	2-6-0	1883	M	AJECTA. Longueville.
EST 32.031	2-6-2T	1925	M	CdT. Mulhouse (SNCF 131 TB 31).
Midi 1314	4-6-0	1902	M	CdT. Mulhouse (SNCF 230 B 614).
230 B 114	4-6-0	1908	M	CdT. Mulhouse.
230 C 531	4-6-0	1905	M	Château de St. Fargeau.
230 D 9	4-6-0	1908	M	CdT. Mulhouse.
230 D 116	4-6-0	1911	M	AJECTA. Longueville.
230 G 352	4-6-0	1922	M	CFTV. St. Quentin.
230 G 353	4-6-0	1922	MR	Épernay SNCF works.
PO 4546	4-6-2	1908	M	CdT. Mulhouse (SNCF 231 A 546).
231 C 78	4-6-2	1930	MS	CMCF. Oignies (SNCF).
Nord 3.1192	4-6-2	1936	M	CdT. Mulhouse (SNCF 231 E 22).
231 E 41	4-6-2	1937	MR	St. Pierre des Corps SNCF depot.
231 G 558	4-6-2	1922	MA	PVC. Sotteville Buddicom works.
231 H 8	4-6-2	1912	MS	CdT. Mulhouse.
231 K 8	4-6-2	1912	MA	MFPN. Paris La Chapelle SNCF depot.
231 K 22	4-6-2	1914	M	SEH. Heilbronn, Germany.

231 K 82	4-6-2	1920	M	St. Étienne SNCF depot.
Nord 3.1102	4-6-4	1911	M	CdT. Mulhouse.
232 U 1	4-6-4	1949	M	CdT. Mulhouse.
PLM 4 A 51	0-8-0	1878	M	Musée du Vin. Romanèche-Thorins.
PLM 4 B 9	0-8-0	1892	M	Carnoules (SNCF 040 B 9).
Nord 4.853	0-8-0	1880	M	AJECTA. Longueville.
040 TA 137	0-8-0T	1922	M	AJECTA. Longueville.
040 TA 141	0-8-0T	1923	MR	Château de St. Fargeau.
140 A 259	2-8-0	1928	MS	CdT. Mulhouse.
140 A 908	2-8-0	1892	MS	CdT. Mulhouse.
140 C 22	2-8-0	1916	M	Château de St. Fargeau.
140 C 27	2-8-0	1916	MR	CITEV. St. Jean-du-Gard.
140 C 38	2-8-0	1919	MR	TVL. Limoges.
140 C 231	2-8-0	1916	M	AJECTA. Longueville.
140 C 287	2-8-0	1917	MR	Château de La Ferté St. Aubin.
140 C 313	2-8-0	1917	P	Reims SNCF station.
140 C 314	2-8-0	1917	MR	CFTV. St. Quentin.
140 C 344	2-8-0	1917	M	CdT. Mulhouse.
141 C 100	2-8-2	1922	M	TVT. Richelieu.
141 F 282	2-8-2	1925	M	CdT. Mulhouse.
141 R 73	2-8-2	1945	MR	Winpro. Winterthur, Switzerland.
141 R 420	2-8-2	1946	MA	Clermont Ferrand SNCF depot.
141 R 568	2-8-2	1945	MA	DLM. Winterthur, Switzerland.
141 R 840	2-8-2	1946	MA	AAATV. Les Aubrais SNCF depot.
141 R 1108	2-8-2	1946	MR	Ecomusée du Haut Pays, Breil sur Roya.
141 R 1126	2-8-2	1947	MA	Toulouse St. Jory SNCF depot.
141 R 1187	2-8-2	1947	M	CdT. Mulhouse.
141 R 1199	2-8-2	1947	MA	Nantes SNCF depot.
141 R 1207	2-8-2	1947	MR	Winpro. Winterthur, Switzerland.
141 R 1244	2-8-2	1947	MA	Club Mikado. Brugg, Switzerland
141 R 1298	2-8-2	1947	M	APPAF. Miramas.
141 R 1332	2-8-2	1947	MR	Winpro. Winterthur, Switzerland.
PO 5452	2-8-2T	1922	M	CdT. Mulhouse (SNCF 141 TA 452).
141 TB 407	2-8-2T	1913	MA	AJECTA. Longueville. AJECTA.
141 TB 424	2-8-2T	1913	MA	CFTR. Volgelsheim.
141 TC 19	2-8-2T	1922	M	AJECTA. Longueville.
141 TC 51	2-8-2T	1935	M	AAATV. Ascq SNCF station. (SNCF)
141 TD 740	2-8-2T	1931	MA	TVL. Limoges Puy Imbert.
241 A 1	4-8-2	1925	M	CdT. Mulhouse.
241 A 65	4-8-2	1931	MA	Burgdorf, Switzerland.
241 P 9	4-8-2	1947	MR	AAATV, Guîtres.
241 P 16	4-8-2	1947	M	CdT. Mulhouse.
241 P 17	4-8-2	1947	MA	Le Creusot SNCF station.
241 P 30	4-8-2	1949	MS	VVT. St. Sulpice, Switzerland.
242 AT 6	4-8-4	1949	M	CdT. Mulhouse (SNCF 242 TA 6).
150 A 65	2-10-0	1912	P	Coulonnieix-Chamiers.
150 P 13	1-10-0	1940	M	Mohon SNCF depot (CdT).

7.2. ELECTRIC LOCOMOTIVES

BB 36	Bo-Bo	1924	M	CdT. Mulhouse.
BB 327	Bo-Bo	1946	M	APPAF. Miramas.
BB 346	Bo-Bo	1948	M	APPAF. Miramas.
BB 824	Bo-Bo	1924	MR	Boissy St. Léger RATP depot.
BB 833	Bo-Bo	1924	MR	Boissy St. Léger RATP depot.
CC 1110	C-C	1948	MR	Béziers SNCF works. (SNCF)
BB 1282 (PO E.1)	Bo-Bo	1900	M	CdT. Mulhouse.
BB 1501	Bo-Bo	1922	MS	Nîmes (CdT).
BB 1632	Bo-Bo	1925	MS	Nîmes (CdT).
2CC2 3402	2Co-Co2	1929	M	APMFS. Chambéry SNCF depot.
1ABBA1 3603	1ABo-BoA1	1927	M	APMFS. Chambéry SNCF depot.
E.4002	Bo-Bo	1922	M	CdT. Mulhouse. (BB 1501 & BB 1623)
BB 4110	Bo-Bo	1929	MR	Toulouse St. Jory.
BB 4175	Bo-Bo	1932	M	Pamiers SNCF station.

Midi E 4162	Bo-Bo	1932	M	APPAF. Miramas. (SNCF BB 4177).
BB 4240	Bo-Bo	1935	M	Tarbes SNCF depot.
BB 4732	Bo-Bo	1935	M	Alstom plant, Tarbes.
BB 4734	Bo-Bo	1934	M	CFLG. Sabres.
BB 4736	Bo-Bo	1934	M	AECFM. Tarascon sur Ariège SNCF station.
BB 4769	Bo-Bo	1933	M	Mohon SNCF depot.
2D2 5516	2-Do-2	1934	M	CdT. Mulhouse.
2D2 5525	2-Do-2	1935	MA	COPEF. Montrouge SNCF depot.
CC 6503	C-C	1969	M	Bahnpark museum. Augsburg, Germany.
CC 6530	C-C	1971	M	Mohon SNCF depot. (CdT)
CC 6534	C-C	1971	M	St. Etienne?
CC 6549	C-C	1971	M	APMFS, Chambéry depot. (spares)
CC 6558	C-C	1972	MA	APMFS, Chambéry depot.
CC 6559	C-C	1972	MA	APMFS, Lyon.
CC 6565	C-C	1974	M	CdT. Mulhouse. (disguised as CC 6572)
CC 6570	C-C	1975	MA	APCC 6570. Avignon SNCF depot.
CC 6575 (BB 21001)	C-C	1969	MA	Sauvons la 6575. Nîmes SNCF depot.
CC 7002	C-C	1949	M	MdC. Ambérieu.
CC 7102	C-C	1952	MA	Dijon Perrigny SNCF depot.
CC 7106	C-C	1952	M	MdC. Ambérieu.
CC 7107	C-C	1953	M	CdT. Mulhouse.
CC 7121	C-C	1953	M	APPAF. Miramas.
CC 7140	C-C	1954	M	EHP. Breil-sur-Roya.
BB 8177	B-B	1950	M	APPAF. Miramas.
BB 8238	Bo-Bo	1954	M	EHP. Breil sur Roya.
BB 8257	C-C	1955	M	Mohon SNCF depot. (CdT)
BB 9004	Bo-Bo	1954	M	CdT. Mulhouse.
2D2 9135	2-Do-2	1951	MA	AFCL. Paris Charolais SNCF depot.
BB 9401	Bo-Bo	1959	MR	APPAF. Béziers SNCF works.
BB 9411	Bo-Bo	1960	MS	AAATV. Nîmes SNCF depot.
BB 9460	Bo-Bo	1962	MS	Montpellier Boulevard Jacques Fabre.
BB 12004	Bo-Bo	1955	P	AAATV. Ascq SNCF station.
BB 12032	Bo-Bo	1957	P	Méricourt, by roundabout.
BB 12035	Bo-Bo	1957	MS	CFTPV/Conifer. Pontarlier.
BB 12051	Bo-Bo	1958	MS	Conifer. Pontarlier.
BB 12068	Bo-Bo	1957	MA	CMCF. Oignies.
BB 12083	Bo-Bo	1957	M	MMPR. Petite Rosselle.
BB 12087	Bo-Bo	1957	P	Nouvion-sur-Meuse
BB 12114	Bo-Bo	1960	P	Supermarket car park. Conflans.
BB 12120	Bo-Bo	1960	M	CFV3V, Treignes.
BB 12125	Bo-Bo	1961	M	Mohon SNCF depot. (CdT)
CC 14018	Co-Co	1959	M	Mohon SNCF depot. (CdT)
CC 14161	Co-Co	1955	M	Leclerc supermarket. Conflans Jarny.
CC 14183	Co-Co	1956	M	MMPR. Petite Rosselle.
BB 16506	Co-Co	1958	MA	CMCF. Oignies. (Dourges)
CC 20001	Co-Co	1958	M	APMFS. Chambéry SNCF depot.
CC 40101	C-C	1964	M	Mohon SNCF depot. (CdT)
CC 40109	C-C	1970	M	CMCF. Oignies (Libercourt)
CC 40110	C-C	1970	MA	MFPN. Paris La Chapelle SNCF depot.

7.3. DIESEL LOCOMOTIVES AND SHUNTERS

BB 60032	B-Bo de	1938	M	CdT. Mulhouse. As PLM 4-DM-2.
C 61002	C de	1950	MA	TVC. St. Jean du Gard. As 030 DA 2.
C 61003	C de	1950	MA	TVC. St. Jean du Gard.
C 61035	C de	1952	MA	TVC. St Jean du Gard.
C 61041	C de	1952	MA	CFTV. St. Quentin.
C 61042	C de	1952	MA	CFDV. Mortagne-sur-Sèvre. As 030 DA 42.
TC 61112	C de	1951	MS	CFDV. Mortagne-sur-Sèvre.
A1AA1A 62001	A1A-A1A de	1946	MR	CFTPV. Pontarlier.
A1AA1A 62029	A1A-A1A de	1946	MA	CFTR. Volgelsheim.
A1AA1A 62032	A1A-A1A de	1946	MA	TVT. Richelieu.
A1AA1A 62036	A1A-A1A de	1947	MA	TVT. Richelieu.
A1AA1A 62062	A1A-A1A de	1947	MR	CFTPV. Pontarlier

A1AA1A 62073	A1A-A1A de	1947	MA	CFTPV. Pontarlier.
A1AA1A 62095	A1A-A1A de	1947	MA	CMCF. Oignies.
BB 63013	Bo-Bo de	1954	M	CdT. Mulhouse.
BB 63048	Bo-Bo de	1955	MA	TPCF. St. Paul-de-Fenouillet.
BB 63050	Bo-Bo de	1955	MA	TPCF. St. Paul-de-Fenouillet.
BB 63069	Bo-Bo de	1955	MA	TTC. Carteret.
BB 63096	Bo-Bo de	1956	MS	TPCF. St. Paul-de-Fenouillet. (Spares).
BB 63121	Bo-Bo de	1958	M	CFV3V, Mariembourg, Belgium (CFTA)
BB 63123	Bo-Bo de	1958	M	CFV3V, Mariembourg, Belgium (SBB)
BB 63138	Bo-Bo de	1958	MA	TPCF. St. Paul-de-Fenouillet.
BB 63139	Bo-Bo de	1958	MA	CFBD. Wassy.
BB 63149	Bo-Bo de	1958	M	CFV3V, Treignes, Belgium (SNCF)
BB 63226	Bo-Bo de	1963	MA	TPCF. St. Paul-de-Fenouillet. (TER livery).
BB 63595	Bo-Bo de	1958	MA	CFBD. Wassy.
BB 63661	Bo-Bo de	1958	MA	CFBD. Wassy.
BB 63852	Bo-Bo de	1964	MA	CFTVA. Arques.
BB 63924	Bo-Bo de	1965	MA	CFTHQ. Martel.
BB 64042	Bo-Bo de	1969.	MA	ACPR1126. Toulouse SNCF depot.
CC 65001	Co-Co de	1956	MS	CdT. Mulhouse.
CC 65005	Co-Co de	1956	MA	AGRIVAP. Courpière.
CC 65506	Co-Co de	1955	MA	Mohon SNCF depot. (CdT)
BB 71010	B-B dm	1965	MA	Le Bouveret, Switzerland.
BB 71017	B-B dm	1965	MA	CFTS. Saujon.
CC 80001	C-C de	-	M	Renault museum. Flins.
Y 2107	B dm	1952	MA	CFBS. St. Valéry-sur-Somme.
Y 2121	B dm	1953	MA	CMCF. Oignies. (AAMCS)
Y 2141	B dm	1953	M	ATM. Félines-Minervois.
Y 2205	B dm	1956	M	TVML. L'Arbresle.
Y 2228	B dm	1956	MA	Transvap. Connérré-Beillé.
Y 2262	B dm	1959	MA	CFVE. Pacy-sur-Eure.
Y 2291	B dm	1959	MA	Mohon SNCF depot. (CdT).
Y 2296	B dm	1959	MA	TTEPAC. Étretat.
Y 2297	B dm	1959	M	Musée des Trains Miniatures. Grasse.
Y 2402	B dm	1962	MA	CFTR. Volgelsheim.
Y 2406	B dm	1962	P	Varennes-Vauzelles, near Nevers.
Y 2423	B dm	1962	M	Ecomusée du Haut Pays. Breil-sur-Roya.
Y 2475	B dm	1965	MA	TVML. L'Arbresle.
Y 2498 "OLIVIER'	B dm	1968	MA	CFTV. St. Quentin.
Y 5130 "FABIEN"	B dm	1961	MA	CFV3V. Treignes, Belgium.
Y 5136	B dm	1961	MA	Transvap. Connerré-Beillé.
Y 5137	B dm	1961	MA	CFTHQ, St Denis près Martel.
Y 5205	B dm	1962	MA	CFTHQ, St Denis près Martel.
Y 6013	B de	1953	M	APPAF. Miramas.
Y 6022	B de	1924	P	Chemin du Canal, Remiremont.
Y 6034	B de	1932	MA	CFTVC. Vigy.
Y 6035	B de	1931	MS	CFTHF. Les Ifs.
Y 6202	B de	1949	MA	CFLG. Sabres.
Y 6233	B de	1949	M	CFLG. Sabres.
Y 6312	B de	1954	MA	Mohon SNCF depot. (CdT).
Y 6424	B de	1955	MA	AATCV. Carnoules.
Y 6482	B de	1954	MA	TTAM (Viaduc 07). Vogüé.
Y 6502	B de	1956	MA	CFV3V. Mariembourg, Belgium.
Y 6546	B de	1957	MA	CFVP. Châteaurenard.
Y 6563 "CAROLE"	B de	1957	MA	CFV3V. Mariembourg, Belgium.
Y 6574	B de	1957	MA	TVML. Sainte Foy l'Argentière.
Y 7566	B de	1965	MA	CFBD. Wassy.
Y 11251	B de	1916	MA	CFVE. Pacy sur Eure.
Y BD 12004	B dm	1932	MA	CFLG. Sabres.
Y BE 14039	B dm	1927	M	MPTUR, La Barque-Fuveau.
Y BE 15053	B dm	1936	M	APMFS? Pontcharra.
Y DE 20003	C de	1942	MA	CFVE. Pacy-sur-Eure.
Y SP 30002	B dm	1936	M	Transvap. Connerré-Beillé.
Y 50105	B dm	1943	M	CFTHF. Les Ifs.
Y 50110	B dm	1939	M	CFTHQ. St. Denis-près-Martel.

Y 51125	B dm	1954	MA	CFTHQ. St. Denis près Martel.
Y 51135	B dm	1954	MA	CFTS. Saujon.
Y 51147	B dm	1955	MA	TVT. Richelieu.
Y 51232	B dm	1955	MA	CFTPV. Les Hôpitaux Neufs.

CLASS X 3800 "PICASSO" B-2 DIESEL RAILCAR

A classic SNCF diesel railcar with a strange driving cab on the roof to make room for the engine which is where the cab should be! These cheap units kept many a branch line open and unsurprisingly are the mainstay of tourist line operation.

Built: 1951–62.   **Builder:** ANF/De Dietrich.
Engine: Renault 517G or Saurer BZDS (250 kW). **Transmission:** Mechanical.
Weight: 32 tonnes.   **Length:** 21.851 m.
Seats: –/62 (some 12/32).   **Maximum Speed:** 120 km/h.

X 3801	CFTHF. Les Ifs.	1951	S
X 3810	AATCV. Carnoules. (spares).		S
X 3814	AATY. Toucy.		
X 3817	CFTVA. Arques.		MA
X 3818	CFTT. Esternay.		MA
X 3823	CFDV. Les Épesses.		
X 3824	APPAF. Miramas.		
X 3825	Quercyrail. Cajarc.		
X 3834	AGRIVAP. Courpière.		MA
X 3835	Mézy-Moulins.		
X 3837	CFVC. Vigy.		
X 3838	CCTSA. Attigny.		
X 3846	CFHA. Riom-es-Montagne.		
X 3847	CdT. Mulhouse. (Cab only).		M
X 3850	CFTSA. Attigny.		
X 3853	CFTVA. Arques.		MA
X 3858	CFTR. Volgelsheim.		
X 3865	Viaduc 07. Montfleury.		
X 3866	CFTV. St. Quentin.		S
X 3867	CFHF. Ambert.		MA
X 3871	AATY. Toucy.		
X 3876	CFTA. Carhaix.		
X 3886	ARE. Blainville.		MA
X 3889	Viaduc 07. Vogüé.		
X 3890	CFCB. Loudéac.		
X 3897	TBFCO. Montmirail.		S
X 3898	CFTSA. Attigny.		
X 3900	CFHA. Bort-les-Orgues.		
X 3907	TTEPAC. Les Loges.		S
X 3926	TBFCO. Montmirail.		
X 3934	AGRIVAP. Ambert.		
X 3943	ARE. Blainville.		MA
X 3944	TPCF. Caudiès-de-Fenouillèdes.		MA
X 3953	TRANSVAP. Connerré-Beillé.		
X 3959	CFCL. Confolens.		
X 3968	CFHQ. Martel.		
X 3976	AATCV. Carnoules.		
X 3989	Modélistes et Amis du Rail Vivarois. Vogüé.		
X 3998	CFV3V. Mariembourg, Belgium.		
X 4001	CFHF. Riom-es-Montagne.		
X 4013	Sancerre former SNCF station. Discotheque!		
X 4028	ATM. Narbonne.		
X 4039	ABFC. Dijon Perrigny.		MA
X 4042	MMPR. Petite Rosselle.		
X 4046	CEF Nord. Denain.		S
X 4051	CFTA. Carhaix.		

7.4. GAS TURBINE POWER CAR

T 2057	B-B dh	1975	M	Mohon SNCF depot (CdT).

7.5. DIESEL RAILCARS

X 2402	B-B dm	1951	MA	CFTPV. Les Hôpitaux Neufs.
X 2403	B-B dm	1951	MA	AAATV. Nîmes SNCF depot.
X 2419	B-B dm	1952	MA	TTVL. Thoré-La Rochette.
X 2423	B-B dm	1952	MA	CFCB. Pontivy.
X 2425	B-B dm	1952	MA	CFHF. Estivareilles.
X 2426	B-B dm	1952	MA	Conifer. Vallorbe.
X 2448	B-B dm	1956	MA	CMCF. Oignies. (AAMCS).
X 2468	B-B dm	1955	MA	CFTSA. Attigny.
X 2475	B-B dm	1955	M	St. Étienne. For future mining museum.
XD 2511	B-B dm	1937	MR	Alstom factory. Reichshoffen.
X 2709 + XR 7719	B-2 + 2-2 dm	1954	MA	CFHF. Estivareilles.
X 2716 + XR 7762	B-2 + 2-2 dm	1955	MA	AATY. Toucy.
X 2719 + XR 7708	B-2 + 2-2 dm	1955	MA	CFTA. Gray. (For sale)
X 2723 + XR 7723	B-2 + 2-2 dh	1955	MA	TTEPAC. Les Loges.
X 2725 + XR 7725	B-2 + 2-2 dh	1955	MA	CFHA. Riom-es-Montagne.
X 2726 + XR 7736	B-2 + 2-2 dh	1955	MA	CFHA. Riom-es-Montagne.
X 2731 + XR 7731	B-2 + 2-2 dh	1955	MA	Viaduc 07. Vogüé.
X 2804	B-2 dh	1957	M	Ecomusée du Haut Pays. Breil-sur-Roya.
X 2807	B-2 dh	1957	MA	CFHF. Estivareilles.
X 2819	B-2 dh	1958	MA	SP X 2800. Nîmes SNCF depot.
X 2825	B-2 dh	1958	MA	CFVA. Lyon Vaise SNCF depot.
X 2844	B-2 dh	1959	MA	Amis des X2800. Limoges SNCF depot.
X 2856	B-2 dh	1960	MA	AGRIVAP. Ambert.
X 2866	B-2 dh	1960	MA	Viaduc 07. Vogüé.
X 2882	B-2 dh	1961	MS	CFTA Bretagne. Carhaix.
X 2883	B-2 dh	1961	MA	CFCL. Confolens.
X 2895	B-2 dh	1961	MA	Viaduc 07, Vogüé.
X 2903	B-2 dh	1961	MA	CFCL. Confolens.
X 2907	B-2 dh	1962	MA	Amis des X2800. Limoges SNCF depot.
X 2908	B-2 dh	1962	MA	CFHA. Bort-les-Orgues.
X 2914	B-2 dh	1962	MA	Passionnés des X2800. Langogne.
X 3601	B-2 dm	1948	MA	CFVE. Pacy-sur-Eure. (AJECTA).
X 3623	B-2 dm	1949	MS	CFTV. St. Quentin. (as ABJ 28).
X 3701	B-2 dm	1949	M	Carel & Fouché plant. Aubevoye-Gaillon.
X 3710	1A-A1 dm	1949	MS	CFTVD. Burnhaupt.
X 4203	Bo-2 de	1959	MS	AGRIVAP. Ambert.
X 4204	Bo-2 de	1959	MA	Renault museum. Flins.
X 4206	Bo-2 de	1959	MA	TVC. Anduze.
X 4208	Bo-2 de	1959	MA	AGRIVAP. Ambert.
X 4345 + XR 8327	B-2 + 2-2 dm	1965	MA	CFV3V. Mariembourg, Belgium
X 4367 + XR 8362	B-2 + 2-2 dm	1966	MA	CFV3V. Mariembourg, Belgium
X 4395 + XR 8508	B-2 + 2-2 dm	1967	MA	TTDA. Épinal SNCF depot.
X 4506 + XR 8615	B-2 + 2-2 dm	1963	MA	Viaduct 07. Montfleury.
X 4511 + XR 8515	B-2 + 2-2 dm	1964	MS	Quercyrail. St. Géry.
X 4519 + XR 8528	B-2 + 2-2 dm	1964	MS	Quercyrail. St Géry.
X 4545 + XR 8601	B-2 + 2-2 dm	1965	MA	TPCF. Caudiès-de-Fenouillèdes.
X 4554 + XR 8564	B-2 + 2-2 dm	1965	MA	French Rail Cruise. Nevers.
X 4555 + XR 8582	B-2 + 2-2 dm	1965	MS	Sotteville SNCF depot.
X 4567 + XR 8380	B-2 + 2-2 dm	1966	MA	AATCV. Besse sur Issole.
X 4573 + XR 8592	B-2 + 2-2 dm	1966	MA	TPCF. Caudiès-de-Fenouillèdes.
X 4575 + XR 8529	B-2 + 2-2 dm	1966	MA	TPCF. Caudiès-de-Fenouillèdes.
X 4590 + XR 8619	B-2 + 2-2 dm	1967	MA	AATCV. Besse sur Issole.
X 4607 + XR 8415	B-2 + 2-2 dm	1967	MA	TPCF. Caudiès-de-Fenouillèdes.
X 4620 + XR 8410	B-2 + 2-2 dm	1969	MA	Transvap. Connérré-Beillé.
X 5506	1A-2 dm	1949	MA	CFVE. Pacy sur Eure. (AJECTA)
X 5509	1A-2 dm	1950	MA	CFVE. Pacy sur Eure.
X 5815	1A-2 dm	1953	MA	Corniac sur l'Isle.

X 5822	1A-2 dm	1953	M	CFLG. Sabres. CFLG.
X 5830	1A-2 dm	1954	M	CFBD. Wassy. (no motor)
X 5845	1A-2 dm	1954	MA	RDT13. Arles.
X 5852	1A-2 dm	1954	MA	CFTVD. Cernay.
X 9152	A-A dm	-	M	APPAF. Miramas.
PO ZZEty 23859	B-2 dm	1934	M	CdT. Mulhouse (SNCF X 2211).
État ZZB2 Ef 23901	A-1 pm	1922	M	CdT. Mulhouse.
État ZZy 24091	B-2 dm	1937	M	CdT. Mulhouse (SNCF X 3421).
État ZZy 24408	1B-B1 pm	1933	M	CdT. Mulhouse (SNCF XB 1008).
XABDP 52103	Bo-Bode	1945	M	Mohon SNCF depot. (CdT).
Est ZZAB Ety 54005	1AA1-4	1936	M	CdT. Mulhouse (SNCF XM 5005).

7.6. ELECTRIC MULTIPLE UNITS

Z 1208	A1A-A1A	1914	M	CdT. Mulhouse. (État TE 1080)
Z 1567	Bo-Bo	1930	M	Mohon SNCF depot. (CdT).
Z 1572 + ZR 11551	Bo-Bo + 2-2	1930	MS	PSL for Paris transport museum.
Z 3714	Bo-Bo-Bo	1938	MS	CdT. Mulhouse.
Z 4313	Bo-Bo	1927	MS	CdT. Mulhouse.
Z 4909	Bo-Bo	1913	MS	Limoges SNCF depot. (CdT).
Z 5119	Bo-Bo	1954	MS	Les Aubrais wagon works.
Z 5137	Bo-Bo	1955	MS	Les Aubrais yard.
Z 5177	Bo-Bo	1956	MS	ASTR. Trappes.
Z 7133	Bo-Bo + 2-2	1962	MS	Vénissieux SNCF depot. (CdT)
État ZABEyf 23001	Bo-2	1902	MS	CdT. Mulhouse. (Ouest BDF 9011)
Z 23156	Bo-Bo	1938	MS	CdT. Mulhouse. (SNCF Z 4156)
Z 23221	Bo-Bo	1937	M	Maison de la RATP, Paris.
Z 23237	Bo-Bo	1937	M	Musée de Île-de-France, Sceaux.
Z 23301	Bo-Bo	1961	S	Boissy RATP depot.
Z 23312	Bo-Bo	1961	S	Les Aubrais yard.
Z 23326	Bo-Bo	1961	S	Les Aubrais yard.
Z 23328	Bo-Bo	1961	S	Les Aubrais yard.
Z 23338	Bo-Bo	1961	S	Boissy RATP depot.
Z 23342	Bo-Bo	1961	S	Les Aubrais yard.
Z 23402	Bo-Bo	1938	S	Association CITR, Brétigny.

7.7. NARROW GAUGE ELECTRIC UNITS

Z 216	Bo	1908	M	CdT. Mulhouse.
Z 450	Bo	1908	M	CdT. Mulhouse. (Snowplough).

7.8. FOREIGN LOCOMOTIVES

Rly	Number	Details	Built	Status	Location
DB	50-3661	2-10-0	1941	MR	CFTHQ. Martel.
DB	52 8163	2-10-0	1943	MS	CFTPV. Pontarlier.
DB	310 347	B dm	1934	MA	CFTPV. Les Hôpitaux Neufs.
DB	310 628	B dm	1934	MA	CFTPV. Les Hôpitaux Neufs.
DB	310 700	B dm	1935	M	CFTR. Volgelsheim.
DB	322 628	B dm	1934	M	MMCW. Petite Rosselle.
DB	323 747	B dm	1960	M	MMCW. Petite Rosselle.
FS	880-157	2-6-0T	1914	MA	CFTB. Ste Foy l'Argentière.
JZ	62-046	0-6-0T	1943	MA	CFVP. Châteaurenard. As 030 TU 46.
PKP	Ty51-83	2-10-0	1955	P	Château de St. Fargeau
PKP	Ty2-6690	2-10-0	1943	MA	CFVA. Arques.

8. MUSEUMS AND MUSEUM LINES

The number of rail museums and museum lines in France has mushroomed in recent years but this proliferation has spread resources a little thin and many have difficulty staying in service. Small outfits tend to disappear and new ones appear regularly. Many of the lines are in scenic areas with tourism potential. They range from the purely tourist/children's railway where in some cases narrow gauge diesel locomotives run disguised as steam locomotives, and garden railways, to fully-fledged preserved branch lines.

This guide concentrates on the main centres and ignores garden railways and diesels disguised as steam. There are also preservation groups which own their own or look after SNCF-owned locomotives and run them over the RFF network. The main steam locos are 231 G 558 at Sotteville, 231 K 8 at Paris La Chapelle, 141 R 420 at Clermont Ferrand, 141 R 840 at Les Aubrais, 141 R 1199 at Nantes, 141 R 1126 at Toulouse and 241 P 17 at Le Creusot.

We present operators or museums below in alphabetical order with an indication of which part of France to find them (N, S, E, W, for example – C = Centre) as well as the nearest SNCF station. "Summer" generally means the French school holidays which run almost the whole of July and August. Sunday services usually also run on public holidays. In "summer" these are 14 July and 15 August. It is difficult to keep up with operating times and dates. Readers are recommended to consult the Internet web site for more and up-to-date details at:

www.trains-fr.org/unecto/_annu/index.html.

Below CFT stands for Chemin de Fer Touristique, CF Chemin de Fer, and TT Train Touristique. Initials in brackets indicate an unofficial abbreviation for use in this book.

Amicale Amandinoise de Modélisme ferroviaire et de Chemins de Fer Secondaires   AAMCS

http://ffmf.nord.free.fr/pagesclubs/aamcs/aamcs.htm

An association with a 2.5 km 600 mm track along the river Scarpe from a point near St. Amand-les-Eaux (N) station run as the Train Touristique de la Vallée de la Scarpe. A branch of the association is specialising in preservation of postal vehicles. Attempts by AAMCS to run standard gauge trains locally seem to have been stillborn and stock is being sold.

600 mm gauge: 2 steam, 8 diesel.

Association des Autorails Touristique de l'Yonne   AATY

www.lafrancevuedurail.fr/aaty

Villers St. Benoît–Toucy–Etangs de Moutiers (C). 27 km. Stock: Toucy. Nearest SNCF: Joigny. Tourist line in the Yonne département between Paris and Dijon. Also known as TT du Pays de Puisaye-Forterre (TTPF). Runs daily afternoons May–September plus mornings in July and August.

2 diesel railcars, 2 diesel.

Autorails de Bourgogne–Franche-Comté   ABFC

http://x4039.free.fr/

Association operating tours over SNCF network from Dijon with Picasso railcar X 4039.

1 diesel railcar.

Train Touristique Livradois–Forez   AGRIVAP

http://pagesperso-orange.fr/..agrivap/

Courpière–Ambert–Sembadel (C). 85 km. Stock: Ambert. Nearest SNCF: Pont-de-Dore.
One of the longest tourist lines in France in a very wild and beautiful area, with potential to expand further – from Sembadel to Darsac SNCF station to the south. AGRIVAP stands for Musée de la Machine Agricole et à Vapeur, a museum of agricultural and steam machinery at Ambert. Diesel loco CC 65005 is used for "short line" feeder freights to SNCF at Courpière. Operates diesel train Ambert to Sembadel most days in July and August. Trips to Courpière are rare. Steam operates Ambert–Olliergues Saturdays mid-July to late August. AGRIVAP now has three "Panoramique" railcars of which two are operational.

1 steam, 1 diesel, 6 diesel railcars.

Association des Jeunes pour l'Exploitation et la Conservation des Trains d'Autrefois   AJECTA

www.ajecta.org

Longueville (C).

AJECTA has taken over the old SNCF roundhouse here for use as a museum and workshop. The biggest collection of steam in France outside the Mulhouse museum. Open to public Saturday and Sunday in July and August. Operational steam to Provins over the weekend of "Historic Monuments" in mid-September. Other specials throughout the year, particularly with 141 TB 424. AJECTA acquired 230 D 116 from the Nene Valley Railway in England in 2008.

12 steam, 5 diesel, 2 diesel railcars.

Association pour la Préservation du Matériel Ferroviaire Savoyarde   APMFS

http://www.apmfs.fr/

A recently-formed association devoted to preserving trains connected with the Savoie area and based at Chambéry SNCF depot (SE) which has a listed roundhouse. The depot can only be visited by appointment through SNCF or the Chambéry tourism office in summer.
3 electric, 1 diesel.

Association Provençale de Préservation et d'Animation Ferroviaire   APPAF

An association with locos and DMUs in the old repair shop by Miramas station (SE) and at Arles.
5 electric, 1 diesel, 3 diesel railcar.

Rail Evasion   ARE

http://railevasion.free.fr/

An association running preserved Picasso diesel railcars over the SNCF network from Nancy.
2 diesel railcars.

Autorail Touristique du Minervois   ATM

http://monsite.orange.fr/autorailduminervois/

Narbonne (Rue Paul Vieu)–Bize-Minervois (S). 20 km. Nearest SNCF: Narbonne (500 metres). The service was stopped in 2007 during reconstruction of river bridges.
1 diesel, 3 diesel railcars.

Château de St. Fargeau   •

www.chateau-de-saint-fargeau.com

A private collection of five steam locomotives exposed in the open air at a castle at St. Fargeau (C) close to the AATY line. Two of the locos are the unique survivors of their classes.
5 steam.

Cité du Train   CdT

www.citedutrain.com

Nearest SNCF: Mulhouse.

Formerly the Musée National du Chemin de Fer, this is France's national rail museum, situated in Mulhouse (E), near the Swiss and German borders, and close to Basel. A superb collection of railwayana, including around 50 locomotives. Open daily except 25/26 December and 1 January. Mohon depot near Charleville-Mézières (N), which has a listed timber-framed roundhouse, is now being used to house surplus items although visits are only possible by appointment and on special occasions.

35 steam, 3 diesel, 7 electric, 9 EMUs, 6 DMUs.

Cercle d'Études Ferroviaire Nord

CEF Nord

http://cefnord.free.fr/maj/index.htm

Nearest SNCF: Denain.

Association with museum housed in a depot of the old HBNPC coal mines network. Visits possible Saturday to Monday by appointment only. The group hopes to re-launch the TT du Hainault, using a DMU over the local mining network.

5 steam, 8 diesel.

CF de la Baie de Somme

CFBS

www.chemin-fer-baie-somme.asso.fr

Le Crotoy–Noyelles-sur-Mer, Noyelles–St. Valéry-sur-Somme–Cayeux-sur-Mer (N). 27 km. 1000 mm gauge. Nearest SNCF: Noyelles.

One of the best-established preserved narrow gauge operations in France is only a short distance from the Channel ports and Tunnel. Steam operates daily May to September and at weekends or better mid March to end October. Steam festival in April every three years.

9 steam, 5 diesel, 5 diesel railcars.

CF des Côtes-du-Nord

CFCdN

http://musee.cheminot.free.fr/

A museum dedicated to the Côtes-du-Nord metre gauge system, by the sea at Boutdeville near St. Brieuc. A project exists to build a line from there to Yffeniac.

1 steam, 3 diesel, 2 diesel railcars.

CF Charente-Limousine

CFCL

www.velorail16.com

Roumazières-Loubert–Confolens (C). 17 km. Nearest SNCF: Roumazières-Loubert.
Initially a vélorail set-up with ambitions to launch a train service in late 2008 or 2009.

I diesel shunter, 4 diesel railcars.

CF Forestier d'Abreschwiller

(CFFA)

http://train-abreschviller.fr

Abreschwiller–Grand Soldat (E). 6 km 700 mm gauge. Nearest SNCF: Sarrebourg (bus).

This is a forest railway dating back to 1884 which closed in 1966. The beauty of the line was realised and a tourist service began in 1968. Operates daily on Sundays afternoons April to September, plus Saturday afternoons and Sunday mornings May to August and weekday afternoons in July and August.

4 steam, 1 diesel.

CF de Haute Auvergne

CFHA

http://traincezallier.free.fr/

Bort-les-Orgues–Lugarde-Marchastel (C). 16 km. Nearest SNCF: Neussargues. Stock: Bort-les-Orgues.

Part of the closed Neussargues–Bort-les-Orgues line. Operates Sundays late April to late September, daily in July and August.

4 diesel railcars.

CF du Haut-Forez   CFHF
www.cheminferhautforez.com

Estivareilles–Craponne-sur-Arzon–Sembadel (C). 36 km. Nearest SNCF: Firminy.
Connects with AGRIVAP at Sembadel (C). Runs Sundays early May to mid October, half the line
Wednesdays and Fridays June and August plus the whole line Wednesdays and Fridays in July
and August

3 diesel railcars.

CF des Landes de Gascogne   CFLG
Sabres–Marquèze (SW). 4 km. Stock: Sabres. Nearest SNCF: Labouheyre.

Operates daily as part of the visit to an interesting open air museum (Écomusée de la Grande
Lande), June to end September. Steam on Sundays.

1 steam, 6 diesel, 1 diesel railcar.

CF de Sainte-Eutrope   CFSE
Parc de Sainte-Eutrope (C). 2.5 km. 600 mm. Nearest SNCF: Orangis Bois l'Épine.

Whilst garden railways are not documented here, this park railway is included as it has a good
collection of stock and is in the Paris area. Operates Sunday afternoons all year plus Saturdays
Easter to 11 November.

7 steam, 9 diesel, 1 diesel railcar.

CFT des Hautes Falaises   CFTHF
http://cfthf.monsite.wanadoo.fr

Les Ifs (NW). Nearest SNCF: Fécamp. Trains pass Les Ifs but do not stop.
Not a tourist railway but basically one person dedicated to saving coaches from the Orient Express
and locomotives. Sadly the person has never found money for operation or restoration so the
collection, including the first Picasso railcar and other interesting items, is rotting away in the
open. Only the steam loco is active. Much of the stock came from the CF de la Forêt de la Londe
at Elbeuf, now closed.

1 steam, 5 diesel, 1 diesel railcar.

CFT du Haut Quercy   CFTHQ
www.trainduhautquercy.info

Martel–St. Denis-près-Martel (SW). 7 km. Nearest SNCF: St. Denis-près-Martel.
Operates with steam on Sundays, diesel Tuesday and Thursday April to October. Steam daily
except Friday and Saturday (when there is diesel) mid July to end August.

2 steam, 4 diesel.

CFT de Pontarlier–Vallorbe (Coni'Fer)   CFTPV
www.coni-fer.org

Les Hôpitaux Neufs–Fontaine Ronde (E). 7.5 km. Nearest SNCF: Pontarlier. Stock: Les Hôpitaux-
Neufs, Pontarlier and Vallorbe.

Also known as Coni'Fer. The first part of the projected reconstruction of the 23 km Pontarlier–
Vallorbe (Switzerland) line. Most of the larger items of stock are stored at Pontarlier or Vallorbe
(SBB depot).

Operates Sundays June to September, extra days in July and daily in August. Steam operation
only occasional.

1 steam, 7 diesels, 1 diesel railcar.

CFT du Rhin   CFTR

http://cftr.evolutive.org

Volgelsheim–Sans Soucis (NE). 9 km. Nearest SNCF: Colmar.
Tourist operation over a freight line serving the Rhine port. Near the beautiful town of Colmar.
Steam operates afternoons on Sundays May to September.

5 steam, 8 diesel.

CFT de la Seudre   CFTS

Saujon (SNCF)–La Tremblade (W). 21 km.

This line is currently not in operation. Some stock has been transferred away.

1 steam, 1 diesel, 1 diesel railcar.

CFT du Sud des Ardennes   CFTSA

http://cftsa.free.fr/

Amagne-Lucquy–Challerange (N). 40.3 km. Nearest SNCF: Amagne-Lucquy. Depot: Attigny.
Formerly known as CFT Amagne-Lucquy-Challerange. Operates Sundays and public holidays
late June–early September.

4 diesel railcars.

CFT du Tarn   CFTT

St. Lieux-lès-Lavaur–Les Martels (SW). 3.5 km. 500 mm gauge. Nearest SNCF: St. Sulpice.

A small railway north-east of Toulouse. Operates Sunday afternoons April to October, Saturdays
to Tuesdays mid-July to end July and daily during August.

5 steam, 25 diesel, 1 electric.

CFT de la Traconne   CFTT

Esternay–Sézanne (C). 15 km. Stock: Esternay. Nearest SNCF: La Ferté-Gaucher.

Tourist operations on freight line. Operates Sunday afternoons May to mid-October, plus mornings
on first Sunday of each month. Possibly not operating in 2008.

2 diesel, 1 diesel railcar.

CFT du Vermandois   CFTV

www.trains-fr.org/cftv

St. Quentin (SNCF)–Origny–Ste.-Benoîte (N). 22.5 km. Depot: St. Quentin.
Operates steam and diesel trains on Sundays and public holidays in summer.

3 steam, 6 diesel, 2 diesel railcars.

CFT de la Vallée de l'Aa   CFTVA

http://cftva.free.fr/

Arques–Lumbres (N). 15 km. Depot: Arques. Nearest SNCF: St. Omer.
Operation over the St. Omer–Lumbres freight line. Close to Calais with several other tourist
attractions nearby, including V2 launch site! CFTVA has Polish 2-10-0 Ty52 6690 but this still
does not run. Operates Sundays May to September plus Saturdays June to August.

1 steam, 1 diesel, 2 diesel railcars.

Chemin de Fer de la Vendée   CFV

www.vendee-vapeur.fr

Mortagne-sur-Sèvre–Les Epesses–Les Herbiers (W). 22 km. Depot: St. Laurent-sur-Sevre.
Museum: Les Epesses. Nearest SNCF: Cholet.
Steam operates Sundays June to September plus Wednesdays and Fridays in July and August.

2 steam, 2 diesel, 1 diesel railcar.

CF du Vivarais   CFV

www.ardeche-train.com

Tournon–Lamastre (SE). 33 km. Metre gauge. Nearest SNCF: Tain l'Hermitage (across river Rhône from Tournon). Depot: Tournon, Lamastre.

Once part of a much larger system. Extremely scenic and now one of the best known French operations. Operates Saturdays and Sundays mid-March to October, daily except Monday in May, June and September and daily July and August. Operation was suspended in April 2008 due to bankruptcy. Expected to run again once money is found.

7 steam, 2 diesel, 4 diesel railcars.

CF de la Vallée de la Canner   CFVC

http://train-de-la-canner-57.over-blog.com

Vigy–Hombourg-Budange (E). 12 km. Stock: Vigy. Nearest SNCF: Hombourg-Budange. Operates on Sundays May to September from Vigy. Steam every other week.

1 steam, 1 diesel, 1 diesel railcar.

CF de la Vallée de l'Eure   CFVE

http://cfve1.free.fr

Pacy-sur-Eure–Breuilpont et Cocherel (N). 16 km. Nearest SNCF: Bueil. Depot: Pacy-sur-Eure. Operates trains on Sundays from June to September. Patchy timetable at other times.

10 diesel, 3 diesel railcar.

CFT de la Vallée de l'Ouche   CFVO

www.lepetittraindebligny.com

Bligny-sur-Ouche–Pont d'Ouche (SE). 5 km. 600 mm gauge. Nearest SNCF: Beaune. Operates with steam Sundays May to September plus diesel daily in July and August.

4 steam, 4 diesel.

CF du Val de Provence   CFVP

www.trainavapeur-valdeprovence.com

Barbantane-Rognonas–Châteaurenard–Noves. Depot: Châteaurenard.

Formerly known as Train Vapeur Méditerranée (TVM), the railway uses part of the Barbantane–Plan d'Orgon line run by RDT13. Steam on Sundays Easter to 1 November plus diesel Wednesdays and Fridays in July and August.

1 steam, 1 diesel.

CF de la Provence   CP

http://cccp.traindespignes.free.fr

Puget-Théniers–Annot (SE). 20 km. Metre gauge. Nearest SNCF: Nice. Depot: Puget-Théniers. Steam trains, the "Train des Pignes" on this part of the Nice–Digne line on Sundays between mid May and mid October. Connections by regular DMU are programmed from Nice.

2 steam.

Centre de la Mine et du Chemin de Fer   CMCF

http://ffmf.nord.free.fr/pagesclubs/cmcf/cmcf.htm

Oignies (N). Nearest SNCF: Libercourt.

A growing museum concentrating on the old coal mines and railways. The larger locos are often stored near Libercourt or in Dourges yard but displayed over the last weekend of August.

1 steam, 5 diesel, 2 electric.

Ecomusée de Haute Alsace   x

www.ecomusee-alsace.fr

Currently, a stored collection of metre gauge stock linked to the open-air museum at Ungersheim (E) which hopes to run trains on the Guebwiller–Bollwiller line.

3 electric railcars.

Ecomusée du Haut Pays   (EHP)

Breil-sur-Roya (S). Nearest SNCF: Breil-sur-Roya.

A small museum devoted to transport in the Nice area and adjacent mountains.

1 steam, 1 diesel, 2 electric, 1 diesel railcar.

Musée du Cheminot   MdC

http://musee.cheminot.free.fr

A small collection of memorabilia at Ambérieu SNCF depot.

1 electric.

Matériel Ferroviaire Patrimoine National   MFPN

http://membres.lycos.fr/sitek8/

An association devoted to preserving 231 K 8 (owned by FACS) and CC 40110 at Paris La Chapelle depot. No regular visits.

Musée de la Mine du Carreau Wendel   MMCW

www.la-mine.fr

Petite Roselle–Puits Simon (E). 8 km. Nearest SNCF: Forbach.

A mining museum with a short line and some stock. Open daily in the afternoon July to mid-October. Train rides only once a month.

2 steam, 20 diesel, 2 electric, 2 diesel railcars.

Musée Provençal des Transports Urbain et Ruraux MPTUR

A small museum at La Barque-Fuveau (SE) with a motley collection of stock including a former PLM shunter. Nearest SNCF station: Gardanne.

1 steam, 12 diesel, 2 trams.

Musée des Transports de Pithiviers   MTP

http://pagesperso-orange.fr/amtp45/

Pithiviers–Bellébat (C). 4 km. 600 mm gauge. Depot: Pithiviers. Nearest SNCF: Malesherbes.

This system was once part of a large sugar beet carrying network. The line is noteworthy for being the first preserved railway in France with operations starting in 1966. Operates with diesel Friday and Saturday afternoons plus steam on Sunday afternoons May to October. In September steam operates Thursday and Sunday afternoons. In October, Sunday afternoons only.

13 steam, 2 diesel, 2 diesel railcars.

Musée des Transports Urbains   MTU

http://www.amtuir.org

The Paris urban transport museum, with a collection of 170 trams, metro cars and other items was ejected from its St. Mandé site in 1998 and was temporarily moved to store in Colombes in 2000/1. Plans to set up the museum there were rejected by the new mayor and the latest plan is to build a new museum in Chelles, east of Paris, possibly on part of Vaires marshalling yard. No date had been set for opening in 2008.

Musée de Transports de la Vallée du Sausseron   MTVS

http://www.trains-fr.org/mtvs/fr/accueil.htm

Valmondois–Butry-sur-Oise. 1 km. 1000 mm. Nearest SNCF: Valmondois.

A short line attached to a transport museum, operating Saturdays and Sundays May to November with steam on the first and third Sundays of each month.

10 steam, 5 diesel, 1 electric railcar, 3 diesel railcars.

Petit Train de la Haute Somme   PTHS

http://appeva.club.fr

Froissy–Cappy–Dompierre. 7 km. 600 mm gauge. Nearest SNCF: Albert. Depot: Froissy.

The remains of a network serving the Front during World War 1. The biggest collection of 600 mm gauge locos in France. Operates Sundays from late April to late September plus Tuesday to Saturday in July and August.

13 steam, 15 diesel.

Pacific Vapeur Club   PVC

An association operating Pacific 231 G 558 from Sotteville (NW). The loco is usually kept in Sotteville SNCF depot but during rebuilding was in the old Buddicom works during 2008

Quercyrail

http://pagesperso-orange.fr/quercyrail/sommaire.htm

Cahors–Cahors–Capdenac (SW). 71 km. Stock: Cahors. Nearest SNCF: Cahors and Capdenac.

Operates charters along valley of river Lot in July and August, Sundays only in September and October. Operation suspended since 2003. The club hopes to operate on just part of this line.

1 diesel, 3 diesel railcars.

Rive Bleue Express   (RBE)

www.lelac.com/rbe

Evian-les-Bains–Le Bouveret (Switzerland). 20 km. Stock: Le Bouveret. Nearest SNCF: Evian

An international line along the southern shore of Lac Léman (lake Geneva). Operation suspended since 2004.

1 diesel.

Tacot des Lacs

http://tacotdeslacs.free.fr

Bourron Port-au-Sable–La Plaine (C). 2.5 km. 600 mm gauge. Nearest SNCF: Nemours.

A bit more than a garden railway. The line operates Sunday afternoons July and August and for reserved groups at other times.

5 steam, 6 diesel.

Trains du Pays Cathare et du Fenouillèdes   TPCF

http://www.tpcf.fr/

Rivesaltes–Axat (S). Nearest SNCF: Rivesaltes. Depot: Caudiès de Fenouillèdes.

A recently-established but fast-growing operation in a superbly scenic area. Runs Sundays April–October, daily July and August, plus extra days May to September.

3 diesels, 4 diesel railcars.

CFT de la Sarthe   TRANSVAP

www.transvap.fr

Connerré-Beillé–Bonnétable (C). 17.8 km. Nearest SNCF: Connerré.

Operates Sundays in July and August.

3 steam, 5 diesel, 3 diesel railcars.

TT de l'Ardèche Méridionale (Viaduc 07)   TTAM
www.viaduc07.fr

Vogüé–St. Jean le Centenier (SE). 14 km. Nearest SNCF: Montélimar.

The remains of the Le Teil–Aubenas line. Runs daily in July and August and Wednesdays and Sundays May to September.

1 diesel; 4 diesel railcars.

TT du Bas Berry   TTBB
http://traintouristiquedubasberry.com/

Luçay-le-Mâle–Ecueillé–Argy (C). Nearest SNCF: Luçay-le-Mâle.

The SABA association was formed to preserve stock from the Blanc-Argent metre gauge and run tourist services on the southern end of the line. Runs Sundays mid June to late September plus Wednesdays in July and August.

1 steam, 6 diesel, 2 diesel railcars.

TT de Blaise et du Der   TTBD
Éclaron-Braucourt–Wassy–Doulevant-le-Château (E). 38 km. Stock: Wassy. Nearest SNCF: St. Dizier.

Tourist operation close to France's largest lake, the Lac du Der-Chantecoq. Railway also operates "short line" freight to St. Dizier. Operates on Sundays at 15.00 from Wassy in July and August, to Éclaron the first and second Sunday of the month, to Doulevant the other days.

4 diesels, 2 diesel railcars.

TT du Cotentin   TTC
http://ttcotentin.monsite.wanadoo.fr

Carteret–Port Bail (W). 10 km. Nearest SNCF: Carentan.

Operates late June to the end of August. The Carentan–Baupte section of this line has been abandoned.

1 diesel, 1 diesel railcar.

TT du Centre Var   TTCV
http://attcv.ifrance.com/

Carnoules Les Platanes–Brignoles (S). 30 km. Nearest SNCF: Carnoules.

An association operating tourist services on the Carnoules–Brignoles line. Runs Sundays April to October plus Wednesdays June to September. Two return trips per day in high summer.

1 diesel locomotive, 3 diesel railcars.

Train Thur Doller Alsace   TTDA
www.train-doller.org

Cernay–Sentheim (E). 14 km. Nearest SNCF: Cernay. Depot: Burnhaupt.

Previously known as the CFT de la Vallée de la Doller. Runs from Cernay St. André, not the SNCF station. Operates Sundays June to September plus Wednesdays in July and August. The line's unique Mallet was used in Brittany during summer 2008.

4 steam, 4 diesel, 5 diesel railcars.

TT Étretat–Pays de Caux   TTEPAC
www.lafrancevuedurail.fr/ttepac

Étretat–Les Loges (W). 6 km. Nearest SNCF: Fécamp. Stock: Les Loges, Étretat.

A minor operation in a very pleasant coastal area. Operates most of year to a very complex timetable. 2 diesel, 2 diesel railcar.

TT Guîtres–Marcenais   TTGM
http://ttgm.guitres.free.fr/

Guîtres–Marcenais (SW). 15 km. Depot: Guîtres. Nearest SNCF: Coutras (5 km).

Operates steam on Sunday afternoons May to October plus diesel Wednesdays mid July to mid August. The line's massive 241 P is to be returned to service.

2 steam, 4 diesel, 2 diesel railcars.

TT des Monts du Lyonnais   TTML

http://cftb.free.fr/

L'Arbresle–Sainte Foy l'Argentière (SE). 20 km. Depot. Sainte Foy. Nearest SNCF: L'Arbresle.

Also known as the CFT de la Brévenne (CFTB) . Steam operation every Sunday late June to late September. Uses a freight branch serving a quarry at Sainte Foy.

1 steam, 5 diesel.

Trains Touristiques à Vapeur en Limousin   TTVL

http://www.trainvapeur.com/

Previously known as Vienne Vézère Vapeur (VVV), the group Chemin de Fer Touristique Limousin Périgord (CFTLP) operates steam over scenic SNCF lines from Limoges (C). Stock is stabled at Puy Imbert, north of Limoges. CFTLP expects to return 140C 38 (Vulcan Foundry, 1919) to service in 2009.

2 steam, 1 diesel.

TT de la Vallée du Loir   TTVL

Thoré–La Rochette–Trôo (C). 18 km. Nearest SNCF: Vendôme.

Operates Saturday and Sunday afternoons in July and August plus Sunday mornings from mid July.

1 diesel railcar.

Train à Vapeur des Cévennes   TVC

http://www.trainavapeur.com/

Anduze–St. Jean du Gard (S). 13.2 km. Depot: Anduze.

Operates steam and diesel trains daily April to early September then daily except Monday to end October. Uses traction from CITEV. Buses run on weekdays from Alès and Nîmes. Close to the famous Pont du Gard.

4 steam, 3 diesel, 1 diesel railcar.

Train à Vapeur de Touraine   TVT

http://tvt37.free.fr/intro.htm

Chinon–Richelieu (C). 20 km. Depot: Richelieu. Nearest SNCF: Chinon.

Operations suspended. Some stock moving elsewhere.

2 steam, 1 diesel 1 diesel railcar.

Voies Ferrées du Velay   VFV

www.asso-vfv.net

Dunières–St. Agrève (SE). 37 km. 1000 mm gauge. Depot: Tence. Nearest SNCF: Firminy.
Part of the old CFD Vivarais system (see also CFV). It is hoped to reintroduce steam traction in the future. Operates in two sections from Tence to Dunières and Tence to St. Agrève on Tuesdays, Thursdays and Sundays in July and August plus Sundays from Dunières to Chambon-sur-Lignon in June and September.

1 steam, 2 diesels, 2 diesel railcars.

ADDITIONAL ABBREVIATIONS

AAATV   Amicale des Amis et Anciens de la Traction Vapeur.
CFV3V   Chemin de Fer à Vapeur des Trois Vallées, Mariembourg, Belgium.
CITEV   Compagnie Internationale des Trains Express à Vapeur.
FACS   Fédération des Amis des Chemins de Fer Secondaires.

APPENDIX I. BUILDERS

The following builder codes are used in this publication:
(All are in France unless stated otherwise).

ACEC	SA Ateliers de Construction Electriques de Charleroi, Belgium. Now Alstom.
Adtranz	ABB/Daimler Benz Transport, Zürich and Berlin.
Alsthom	Société Générale de Constructions Électriques et Mécaniques Alsthom.
Alstom	Alstom, Belfort, Raismes and Aytré, France.
ANF	Ateliers du Nord de la France, Blanc Misseron. Now Bombardier.
Arbel Fauvet Rail	Arbel Fauvet Rail, Lille.
Baldwin	Baldwin Locomotive Works, Philadelphia, Pennsylvania, USA.
BBC	Brown Boveri, Baden, Switzerland.
BDR	Établissements Baudet-Donon-Roussel.
Berliet	Automobiles M. Berliet, Lyon.
Billard	Anciens Établissements Billard & Cie., Tours.
BN	La Brugeoise et Nivelles, Brugge. Now Bombardier.
Bombardier	Bombardier Transportation, Crespin. (Formerly ANF)
Brissonneau & Lotz	SA des Établissements Brissonneau & Lotz, Aytré. Also known as B&L.
Brush	Brush Traction, Loughborogh, UK.
CAFL	Compagnie des Ateliers et Forges de la Loire, St. Chamond. Later Creusot-Loire.
Carde et Cie.	Carde et Compagnie, Bordeaux.
Carel & Fouché	Établissements Carel & Fouché SA, Le Mans.
Caterpillar	Caterpillar Rail Power Systems, Mossville, Illinois, USA.
CEM	Compagnie Electro-Mécanique, Le Havre, Le Bourget & Nancy.
CFD	(Compagnie de) Chemins de Fer Départementaux.
CGC	Compagnie Générale de Constructions Batignolles, Paris, Châtillon & Nantes.
CIMT	Compagnie Industrielle de Matériel de Transport, Marly les Valenciennes. Now Alstom.
Creusot-Loire	Formerly SFAC and CAFL. Now Alstom.
Cummins	Cummins, Columbus, Indiana, USA.
Daimler-Benz	Daimler-Benz, Stuttgart, Germany.
De Dietrich	De Dietrich & Cie., Reichshoffen. Now Alstom.
De Dion	Société des Automobiles De Dion, Puteaux, Paris.
Decauville	Société Nouvelle Decauville-Âiné, Corbeil.
Deutz	Klöckner Humbldt Deutz, Köln, Germany.
Esslingen	Maschinenfabrik Esslingen, Esslingen am Nackar, Germany.
Études	Société d'Études pour l'Electrification des Chemins de Fer.
Fauvet Girel	Établissements Fauvet-Girel, Suresnes, Arras & Lille.
Fives-Lille	Compagnie de Fives-Lille pour Constructions Mécaniques et Entreprises, Fives, Lille.
Franco-Belge	Société Franco-Belge de Matériel de Chemin de Fer, Raismes. Now Alstom.
Francorail-MTE	Consortium of Carel et Fouché, Creusot-Loire, De Dietrich, Jeumont-Schneider and MTE.
Garnéro	
GEC-Alsthom	GEC-Alsthom, Belfort and Aytré, France. Now Alstom.
GM EMD	General Motors EMD, La Grange, Illinois, USA.
Henschel	Henschel Werke, Kassel, Germany.
Holec	Holec-Riddewerk, The Netherlands. Now Alstom.
Jeumont	Société des Forges et Ateliers de Constructions Électriques de Jeumont.
Jung	Jung Lokomotivfabrik, Jungenthal bei Kirchberg, Germany.
KM	Krass Maffei, München, Germany.
LHB	Linke-Hoffmann-Busch, Salzgitter, Germany. Now Alstom.
Lilloise	Société Lilloise de Matériel de Chemins de Fer, Aulnay-sous-Bois.
MaK	Maschinenbau Kiel, Kiel, Germany.
MAN	Maschinenfabrik Augsburg-Nürnberg, Germany.
Moyse	Établissements Gaston Moyse, La Courneuve.
MTE	Le Matériel de Traction Électrique. Formed from SFAC, Jeumont and SW.
MTU	Motoren und Turbinen Union, Friedrichshafen, Germany.
Oerlikon	Société Oerlikon, Switzerland.
Pétolat	Boilot-Pétolat, Dijon.
Poyaud	

Renault	Regie Nationale des Usines Renault, Billancourt.
SACM	Société Alsacienne de Constructions Mécaniques, Mulhouse.
Saurer	Adolf Saurer, Arbon, Switzerland.
Schneider	Société des Forges et Ateliers du Creusot, Usines Schneider, Le Creusot.
Schöma	Christoph Schöttler Maschinenefabrik, Diepholz, Germany
Sécheron	SA des Ateliers de Sécheron, Genève, Switzerland.
SEMT	Société d'Études de Moteurs Thermiques-Pielstick, St. Denis. Now Alstom.
SFAC	As Schneider, renamed in 1949.
Siemens	Siemens AG, Berlin, Nürnberg & Erlangen, Germany.
SLM	Schweizerische Lokomotiv- und Maschinenfabrik, Winterthur, Switzerland.
Socofer	Société de Construction Ferroviaire, Tours.
Soulé	Soulé Fer et Froide, Bagnères de Bigorre. Now CFD.
Sprague-Thomson	Société Parisienne de Matériel Roulant, Paris.
Stadler	Stadler Rail, Bussnang, Switzerland.
Sulzer	Gebrüder Sulzer, Winterthur, Switzerland.
SW	Schneider-Westinghouse.
SWS	Schweizerische Wagons und Aufzügefabrik AG, Schlieren.
TCO	Société Traction CEM-Oerlikon.
Unidiesel	Formerly SACM and SSCM (Poyaud).
Verney	Société des Automobiles et Matériels Verney, Le Mans
Vevey	Ateliers de Constructions Mécaniques SA, Vevey, Switzerland.
Voith	J. M. Voith, Heidenheim, Germany.
Vossloh	Vossloh Locomotives, Kiel, Germany. Formerly MaK.
Weitz	Ateliers de construction Jules Weitz, Lyon.
Whitcomb	Whitcomb Locomotive Company, Rochelle, USA.

APPENDIX II. PASSENGER VEHICLE TYPE CODES

The vehicle type codes used in France are as follows:

B	Bimode driving motor.
TGV	TGV driving motor.
TGVZ	TGV vehicle with one power bogie.
U	Tram-train vehicle.
X	Diesel railcar or multiple unit driving motor.
Z	Electric multiple unit driving motor.
R	indicates a trailer vehicle. (French = remorque).

A	1st Class.
B	2nd Class.
D	Luggage, i.e., vehicle with luggage space and guard's compartment.
r	Catering vehicle.
P	Post, i.e., vehicle with compartment(s) for mail (and guard).
x	indicates a driving trailer.

Examples:

XBD	Second class DMU driving motor with luggage/guard's compartment.
ZRABx	Composite EMU driving trailer.

Note – The continental system does not differentiate between open and compartment stock, but all railcars and multiple unit vehicles are open.

Under "accommodation" are shown the number of 1st and 2nd class seats, the number in brackets indicates fold-down seats, and this is followed by the number of toilets, e.g. 24/49 1T indicates 24 first class seats, 49 second class seats and one toilet.

APPENDIX III. COMMON TERMS IN ENGLISH & FRENCH

English	French
railway	le chemin de fer
train	le train
locomotive	la locomotive
passenger coach	la voiture
freight wagon	le wagon (de marchandises)
sleeping car	la voiture-lits
stock	le materiel
passenger	le voyageur
station	la gare
platform	le quai
ticket	le billet
single	aller simple
return	aller-retour
first class	la première classe
second class	la deuxième classe
to change (trains)	changer
rail	le rail
track	la ligne/la voie
steam	la vapeur
wheel	la roue
class (of vehicles)	la série
marshalling yard	(la gare de) triage
late	en retard
driver	le conducteur
guard, conductor	le chef de train/controleur

APPENDIX IV. SNCF DEPOT, REGION & LIVERY CODES

DEPOT CODES

AC	Achères (Paris)		NC	Nice St. Roch
AV	Avignon		NI	Nîmes
BD	Bordeaux		NV	Nevers
BZ	Béziers		PA	Vitry-Les Ardoines (Paris)
CA	Caen		PC	Châtillon (Paris)
CB	Chambéry		PE	Paris Sud Est
CF	Clermont Ferrand		PJ	Les Joncherolles (Paris)
CY	Chalindrey		PL	Paris La Chapelle
DP	Dijon Perrigny		PN	Noisy-le-Sec (Paris)
EP	Épernay		PQ	Ourcq (Paris)§
HE	Hendaye		PS	Paris St. Lazare (Clichy)
LE	Lens		RS	Rennes
LG	Limoges		SA	Saintes
LI	Lille Champ-de-Mars		SB	Strasbourg
LM	Le Mans		SG	St. Gervais les Bains*
LN	Longueau (Amiens)		SO	Sotteville (Rouen)
LT	Lyon Guillotière †		TL	Toulouse
LV	Lyon Vaise		TP	Tours St. Pierre
LY	Le Landy (Paris)		TR	Trappes (Paris)
MB	Marseille Blancarde		TV	Thionville
MR	Montrouge (Paris)		VE	Vénissieux (Lyon)
MZ	Metz		VF	Villefranche de Conflent*
NB	Nantes Blottereau		VG	Villeneuve St. Georges (Paris)

* metre gauge
† Under construction in 2008.
§ also known as Technicentre Est Européen!

The following abbreviations are used after the depot code:
(D)   Departmental use.
(S)   Stored serviceable.
(U)   Stored unserviceable.

The following depot codes of other railway companies are also used:

AL	Alizay, near Rouen (ECR)		MY	Massy (RATP)
BY	Boissy St. Leger (RATP)		NP	London North Pole (Eurostar)
FF	Brussels Forest (SNCB/NMBS)		RU	Rueil-Malmaison (RATP)

REGION CODES

All multiple units are now purchased by and allocated to specific regions, although there may be pooling arrangements between neighbouring regions. Transfers between regions are relatively rare. Codes used in this book are as follows:

Code	Region	Main centre(s)	Livery
AL	Alsace	Strasbourg, Mulhouse	
AU	Auvergne	Clermont-Ferrand	
AQ	Aquitaine	Bordeaux	
BN	Basse Normandie	Caen	
BO	Bourgogne	Dijon	TER with red and yellow ends.
BR	Bretagne	Rennes	
CA	Champagne-Ardenne	Reims	
CE	Centre	Tours, Orléans	
FC	Franche-Comté	Besançon	
HN	Haute Normandie	Rouen, Le Havre	

IF	Île de France	Paris	
LI	Limousin	Limoges	
LO	Lorraine	Metz, Nancy	TER plus yellow flash.
LR	Languedoc-Roussillon	Montpellier, Nîmes	White, red ends.
MP	Midi-Pyrénées	Toulouse	
NP	Nord-Pas-de-Calais	Lille, Dunkerque, Arras	
PA	Provence-Alpes-Côte d'Azur (PACA)	Marseille, Nice, Avignon	
PC	Poitou-Charentes	Poitiers, La Rochelle	TER plus orange rectangles.
PI	Picardie	Amiens, St. Quentin	
PL	Pays de la Loire	Nantes, Le Mans	Grey, turquoise, pink.
RA	Rhône-Alpes	Lyon, Chambéry	

Most regions have a maintenance depot on their territory but for reasons of productivity, maintenance sometimes takes place in the adjoining region. Examples are Lorraine X 76500 in Strasbourg, Haute Normandie X 76500 in Caen, Languedoc-Roussillon B 81500 in Marseille (these will move to Nîmes once a new depot has been built there), Nord-Pas-de-Calais X 76500 in Longueau.

Corsica (Corse) is treated separately.

SNCF LIVERY CODES

The following codes for liveries are either used in number lists or in class introductory notes:

A TGV livery. Metallic grey with blue window band.

B White with a blue window band and front end. Adopted by the regions Centre, Basse Normandie, Champagne-Ardennes, Pays de la Loire, Midi-Pyrénées, Franche-Comté and Provence-Alpes-Côte d'Azur.

BO Bourgogne region livery. As livery T but with yellow nose at one end and red nose at other plus red and yellow doors.

C Cement grey with orange bands. Standard 1980s/90s electric loco livery.

D Blue and grey with white lining. Standard main-line diesel livery.

E "En Voyages" livery – metallic grey with light blue and purple band showing pictures and the slogan "en voyages". Adopted for main line passenger locos from mid 2000s

F Fret SNCF livery. Two-tone grey with green ends and large "FRET" logo.

G White with green window band and front end. Adopted by the regions Auvergne, Bretagne and Haute Normandie.

H Île de France dark blue with a white lateral block relieved by coloured blobs.

I Île-de-France livery for greater Paris region. White with blue window bands plus red doors and front ends on EMUs. White with blue and red panels on Class BB 8500, BB 17000 and BB 25500 locos.

J Orange with brown lining. Was the standard shunting loco livery.

LR Languedoc-Roussillon region livery. Metallic grey with red front ends and roof plus orange flashes.

M "Massif Central". Blue with a white window band. This was the standard multiple unit/railcar livery in the 1970s/80s.

MO Monaco livery. White with red front end, doors, plus roof and solebar.

N Nonstandard. Refer to text.

P "Multiservices" or "Corail Plus" livery. Metallic grey with red flash on side and front end. Adopted in 1997 as standard livery for both diesel and electric passenger locomotives matching "Corail Plus" refurbished coaches.

R White with red window band. Standard mid-80s DMU livery. Also adopted by the regions Alsace, Aquitaine, Limousin, Rhone-Alpes.

S Class specific livery. Refer to text.

T TER livery. Metallic grey with blue ends and large light grey TER logo on bodyside.

U Unpainted stainless steel.

V Dark green with yellow panels or lines.

W New Île de France white livery with coloured patches.

X Red and cream with dark grey around windows. Classic DMU livery.

Y White with yellow window band. Adopted by the regions Bourgogne, Languedoc-Roussillon, Lorraine, Nord-Pas-de-Calais.

Z Dark blue with red front end and doors. The original livery of all Z2 EMUs.